D0863388

Public Sociologies Reader

Public Sociologies Reader

Edited by
Judith Blau
and
Keri E. Iyall Smith

ROWMAN & LITTLEFIELD PUBLISHERS, INC.
Lanham • Boulder • New York • Toronto • Oxford

ROWMAN & LITTLEFIELD PUBLISHERS, INC.

Published in the United States of America
by Rowman & Littlefield Publishers, Inc.
A wholly owned subsidiary of The Rowman & Littlefield Publishing Group, Inc.
4501 Forbes Boulevard, Suite 200, Lanham, Maryland 20706
www.rowmanlittlefield.com

PO Box 317
Oxford
OX2 9RU, UK

Copyright © 2006 by Rowman & Littlefield Publishers, Inc.

All rights reserved. No part of this publication may be reproduced,
stored in a retrieval system, or transmitted in any form or by any
means, electronic, mechanical, photocopying, recording, or otherwise,
without the prior permission of the publisher.

British Library Cataloguing in Publication Information Available

Library of Congress Cataloging-in-Publication Data

Public sociologies reader / edited by Judith Blau and Keri E. Iyall Smith.
     p. cm.
   Includes bibliographical references and index.
   ISBN-13: 978-0-7425-4586-1 (cloth : alk. paper)
   ISBN-10: 0-7425-4586-5 (cloth : alk. paper)
   ISBN-13: 978-0-7425-4587-8 (pbk. : alk. paper)
   ISBN-10: 0-7425-4587-3 (pbk. : alk. paper)
   1. Sociology—Philosophy.   2. Globalization.   I. Blau, Judith R., 1942–   II. Iyall-
Smith, Keri, 1973–   III. Title.

HM585.P835   2006
303.48′2—dc22   2006006389

Printed in the United States of America

∞ ™ The paper used in this publication meets the minimum requirements of American
National Standard for Information Sciences—Permanence of Paper for Printed Library
Materials, ANSI/NISO Z39.48-1992.

Dedicated to
All Our Students and Teachers—
those inside and outside our classrooms

CENTRAL ARKANSAS LIBRARY SYSTEM
LITTLE ROCK PUBLIC LIBRARY
100 ROCK STREET
LITTLE ROCK, ARKANSAS 72201

Contents

Part II. The Rights of Humans

Part III. Sustainability and Peace

Part IV. Rethinking Liberalism

Acknowledgments

Without the support of others, books could only be imagined projects. We especially want to thank Kevin Lenahan, for research assistance at Stonehill College, and the support of Katie Conboy, Karen Talentino, and Susan Guarino-Ghezzi, also at Stonehill. At the University of North Carolina, Chapel Hill, we are grateful to Vickie Wilson for her gracious and efficient assistance. It is said that it takes a village to rear a child; likewise, it takes a team of topnotch professionals to produce a book. We happily had that team at Rowman & Littlefield: Luann Reed-Siegel, Lynn Weber, Alex Masulis, and Alan McClare. We thank them all.

Preface

Failing to curb the proliferation of weapons, refusing to cooperate with other states to slow global warming, being the world's main backer of neoliberal capitalism, and having launched a unilateral war in the Middle East, the United States has put the planet and its peoples in grave jeopardy. How is it possible not to be completely fatalistic in the face of all this? The answer is that there are powerful contradictions in the world. The same technology that made neoliberal capitalism possible also makes possible people-to-people connections on a scale inconceivable even a decade ago. Around the globe people are increasingly connected with one another. Of course, these connections involve but a fraction of the world's population, but Internet technology and other media provide indirect connections and there is an emerging collective awareness of shared destinies, and deep desires to change current conditions and trajectories.

Writing about these new connections, philosopher Peter Singer observes, "For most of the eons of human existence, people living only short distances apart might as well, for all the difference they made to each other's lives, have been living in separate worlds. Now people living on opposite sides of the world are linked in ways previously unimaginable" (Singer, 2002: 9–10). In Singer's view, there is an emerging understanding that we make up "one world." From a philosopher's perspective, this entails an ethic of responsibility and cooperation. Social scientists—the authors in this volume—embrace this perspective too. Yet we social scientists concretize how consciousness and ethics take shape—as new forms of social glue and social solidarities, activism and advocacy, participatory democracy, political movements, and new pedagogies. We look at what it means to live in one borderless world, analyzing communities, relationships, and social forms within it. The contributors to this volume also connect in another way with contemporary thinking in philosophy and humanities, by clarifying the relevance of a human rights perspective for a social science framework.

NEW SOCIAL FORMS IN THE MAKING

For philosopher Singer, these connections token a new ethic. Sociologists have the tools to analyze the "one world" ethic critically to identify the features and nature of this vast, discontinuous order. But as students of markets, states, society, and communities, social scientists have their radar screens tuned to detect new social forms. We stressed at the very beginning the terrifying prospects for the world's peoples, but here we briefly suggest some of the countervailing forces possible because of these new social forms, accompanied by peoples' awareness of inhabiting one shared world.

New social forms are indeed evolving. Many are "messy" because they are grassroots, ad hoc, experimental—whereas others are relatively organized, something like stacked (local-regional-national-global) networks. Some new forms have evolved from old ones. To illustrate: there are nonprofit banks that grant micro-credit loans to the very poor, to women especially; global networks that link coalitions of nongovernmental organizations (NGOs) working on particular projects in their own nations; pilot programs for community sustainability; e-governance community projects launched in partnership with the UN Educational, Scientific and Cultural Organization (UNESCO); and intervillage alliances to, for example, promote job creation, reduce AIDS transmission, and increase literacy. In 2005 a worldwide conference of nomads was held so they could share information and their experiences with desertification. It takes only a little imagination to understand that nomads will use satellite-tracking devices to monitor weather and changes in vegetation growth!

Such new social forms may help us better understand how communities and societies can manage markets in their own interests, rather than, as is now the case, capitalists having the upper hand. These forms offer the sociologist abundant opportunities for research and study, and public sociologists might see themselves as creative conceptualizers and advocates. Innovators—those who are "growing" new social forms on the ground—are the experts, but social scientists become their advocates when they conceptualize the forms and the processes, and disseminate their findings and interpretations in publications. Because these social forms are completely novel, or novel combinations of old repertories, the learning curve is steep. Social scientists can be helpful as social diagnosticians, offering rigorous methods and theoretical concepts. Arguably, social science knowledge lags behind these new social forms because many of these practices are evolving outside the perimeters of the rich Western nations. Partnerships are invaluable. To illustrate, scientists at MIT have launched an initiative to produce $100 laptops, and with the support of countries and foundations, the aspiration is to put one in the hands of all poor youngsters in the world (MIT Media Lab, 2005). Familiarity with the local context is essential: dialogue with local innovators will enable sociologists to ask and analyze relevant questions.

Perhaps the best analogy in the annals of American sociology of an eagerness to document, conceptualize, and diagnose new social forms is the Chicago School of Sociology. Under the umbrella of "ecology" and unquestionably influenced by philosopher-activist John Dewey and community advocate Jane Addams (who was awarded the 1931 Nobel Peace Prize for her advance of social justice), these Chicago sociologists were extraordinarily innovative and productive. They extensively documented and theorized emerging modern social forms and processes—to name a few, the ghetto, the central business district, the spatial distribution of mental illness, and the effects of capitalist expansion on the neighborhoods of the city. The extraordinary productivity of these early sociologists, in the first decades of the twentieth century, reveals how academics can be energized when they feel they are on the brink of discovering new social forms.

THE GLOBAL CRISES

The urban ecologists documented the early social and economic ills of modernizing urban America. In retrospect, these were but a trifle compared with the challenges facing us today. The exponential growth in trade, financial markets, and capitalist production has hardly reaped the immense benefits to humankind touted by the International Monetary Fund (IMF), the World Bank, and the World Trade Organization (WTO). In its Annual Report, the United Nations Development Programme (2004: 23–24) refers to the egregious errors made by economists in these international economic agencies. Under the general umbrella of "neoliberalism," IMF and WTO policies have led to rampant exploitation of vulnerable labor pools, and the underwriting of financial speculation that has destabilized countries and entire regions, forced governments to trim their welfare and educational programs, and led to trading practices that greatly advantage rich countries over poor ones and large transnationals over small firms.

The United States has spearheaded these policies that rapidly advanced privatization, speculative financial markets, deregulation, and free trade, and is obstinate in the face of worldwide protests. Congress members have been naïve and irresponsible, allowing the rapid increase of economic inequalities, unemployment, and human impoverishment that privatization and free trade policies have brought about. Global capitalism has wreaked destructive havoc on communities and entire societies. Sociologists—public sociologists—have abundant opportunities for documenting in detail how this has happened and what needs to be done to ensure that communities and societies participate in global markets in ways that benefit them. Already the voices of the peoples of Third World communities are beginning to be heard in regional and world-wide networks that link communities, NGOs, and the media. They too are global, and some of them make up "networks of networks." Some of the largest ones are Choike, The Third World Institute, and One World Net. Beginning as indigenous networks in a single small region, they now are coalitional networks that pool knowledge and innovations for intercontinental dissemination. Their NGO constituents are embedded in urban and rural communities, women's collectives, slums, refugee centers, and so on. Some of these NGOs are affiliated with the UN, as civil society partners, and in that way help to shape international policies and launch new pilot projects.

We sociologists have the responsibility, but also unique and amazing opportunities, of advancing public knowledge of these new social forms (e.g., these "networks of networks"). There are other challenges: what, say, are the roots of ethnic conflict and how are women vulnerable to becoming the targets of traffickers in sex workers? We need to rethink labor markets, internationalized through "the race to the bottom," and reconsider migration streams, whose members make up far-flung diaspora. We need new frameworks to understand the strains on public goods resources, along with a better understanding of what constitutes a public good and how it can be protected. And we need to document the extensive harms caused by growing poverty and environmental degradation, and the racialized and feminized dimensions of oppression. The tasks ahead for us are far more complicated than they were for the Chicago sociologists a century ago.

To paraphrase Immanuel Wallerstein (2004: 56–57), doing social science entails the quest for certain knowledge in the face of great uncertainty. Moral neutrality can only be an affectation: "[T]here is no search for truth that does not involve arguments about the good and the beautiful" (57). Over the past decade social scientists have increasingly abandoned their claims to moral neutrality, indebted to the honesty of those who led this shift: scholars who openly advocated racial, gender, and labor justice. Courses on race, gender, feminism, sexuality, poverty, and inequality are now commonplace in sociology departments across the country. The authors in this volume engage issues from a perspective of responsibility and a commitment to justice, which is to say, an ethical perspective. We use values as Weber intended, to guide us to the important research questions. A next challenge is critiquing the United States as others see us, as a state and society, and as the motor of the global economy. Another is globalizing the curriculum. As Peter Singer (2002: 13) states it, "[H]ow well we come through the era of globalization (perhaps whether we come through it at all) will depend on how we respond ethically to the idea that we live in one world."

OVERVIEW OF THE VOLUME

Michael Burawoy's theme of public sociology at the 2004 meetings of the American Sociological Association sparked amazingly open and broad discussions about the social responsibilities of sociologists, about a just society, and about the role of sociologists in exposing oppression and exploitation. There was for many, perhaps the majority, a sense that the floodgates had at long last been opened and that they were liberated to profess a sociology that was relevant, engaged, critical, and publicly responsible, if not in partnership with publics.

In the introductory chapter, Burawoy joins his arguments for public sociology to a defense of a human rights perspective. But he does not stop there: he argues for a thoroughgoing epistemological revolution, recentering the sociological enterprise on the axioms of human rights. Long the topic for humanists and philosophers, a sociological perspective on human rights is distinctive for it focuses attention on persons as having equal dignity and being equally entitled to live lives that are fulfilling. Sociologists can contribute to this perspective because of our interests in humans' material existence—in social relations, communities, work settings, and habitats. Burawoy also argues that public sociology can bring certain understandings to the most heinous violations of human rights, namely, crimes of genocide committed against civilians, precisely because they occur where human populations are weakened by the duress and oppression of states and markets, and where interethnic and civil conflict has totally spun out of control.

Global studies require multidisciplinary, if not unitarized, analyses. This is a theme in many of the chapters, and highlighted by Michael Burawoy (chapter 1), William I. Robinson (chapter 2), Jackie Smith (chapter 4), Walda Katz-Fishman and Jerome Scott (chapter 5), and Havidán Rodríguez and Carla N. Russell (chapter 11). More forcefully, they argue that intellectuals/researchers must not only pool their knowledge among themselves to share with publics, but they must work with publics, as advocates and activists. Knowledge and praxis are intertwined. This conception, as the organic intellectual, has its roots in the works of Frantz Fanon, Antonio Gramsci, Paulo Freire, W. E. B. DuBois, and Jane Addams. Keri Iyall Smith (chapter 9) proposes that just as organic intellectuals in the United States have forged bonds of solidarity with some oppressed groups in America, they have not championed the rights of all, and, in particular, not those of the indigenous peoples. Inclusiveness, solidarity, and the recognition of differences must be complete, embracing all.

Angela Hattery and Earl Smith (chapter 15) take the argument for the organic intellectual in a different direction, as they introduce us to ways of deeply engaging students in thinking about poverty and racism. By raising students' discomfort levels (safely), Hattery and Smith have found new ways of engaging privileged students to help them to begin to understand the ordeals of being black and being poor in the American South. Like Katz-Fishman and Scott, they problematize the gaps between the academy and communities and propose ways of overcoming them. Barbara Risman (chapter 16) identifies the role of teaching in contributing to a justice-focused orientation beyond the academy.

As developed by Robinson in chapter 2, *critical globalization studies* would address local issues in a global context and global issues from local perspectives. Scholars and intellectuals must work alongside and learn from peoples' movements to unmask powerful elites, expose systems of oppression, and critically confront the structures and processes that threaten to implode on human civilization. Jackie Smith (chapter 4) clarifies that, on the ground, in colleges and universities, there is already an indication that democratic and critical studies have taken off, and they draw from a human rights culture that unifies coalitions of students, faculty, and community activists.

Globalization itself engenders social and cultural oppositional dialectics, and as elaborated by Gerard Delanty (chapter 3), an emergent social dynamic that accompanies migration and growing population diversity relates to new, transnational identities, assertions of personhood rights, global solidarities, internationalization of universal rights, and cultural pluralization. Such "cosmopolitan citizenship" is new, possible only because of economic globalization, while creating strands of far-flung connectedness involving persons, groups, and communities. They embed the seeds of solidarities and personal liberation. The far-flung connections in the global economy, by contrast, are dark and oppressive for those who work at the distant end of commodity chains. Economist Robert Pollin (chapter 6) documents the dynamic of "the race to the bottom," and why it has been a successful strategy for transnationals. There are diminishing opportunities in agriculture for workers in poor countries, making the labor pools of these countries especially attractive to manufacturers. Employers do pay pitifully low wages and can get by with substandard working conditions. Sweatshops, to be sure, were ever as much an ugly chapter in the history of industrialization in the West, but now they are spread through many countries that define the contours of the Third World, or the Global South. Yet Robert Pollin also draws on another type of connection by showing that U.S. college student-activists have increased consumer awareness of sweatshop conditions and set in motion a process for monitoring production sites.

Social, economic, and housing rights, as well as peoples' rights to their cultures and identities, women's rights, migrant rights, children's rights, and environmental rights form the backbone of international human rights law. In addition, there is the Rome Treaty that established the International Criminal Court, which has jurisdiction over four offenses: genocide, crimes against humanity, war crimes, and the crime of "aggression." The U.S. government has long taken the position that it is above international law, and it has signed few of the UN Human Rights Treaties, UNESCO Conventions, and International Labour Organization Standards. Nor has the United States signed the Rome Treaty or the Kyoto Protocol to the Framework Convention on Climate Change.

It is axiomatic for Robert Pollin that workers have labor rights, and other authors draw on human rights assumptions as well. Deana Rohlinger and Jill Quadagno (chapter 7) argue that social rights are necessary as "protection against the exigencies of the marketplace." They provide a sobering account of the ascendance and decline of these rights in the United States, and how as welfare state provisions they are protected only by legislation, not constitutionally. Antonio Ugalde and Núria Homedes (chapter 8) place health at the center of a rights agenda, because state responsibilities to protect the health of citizens also entail state responsibilities for provision of adequate housing, safe work conditions, a healthy environment, and a reliable and safe food supply. States in Latin America, however, have a declining capacity to meet their constitutional provisions regarding citizens' health, which Ugalde and Homedes trace to neoliberal capitalism and the "relentless drive for corporate profits, directed by the WTO, the World Bank, and the IMF."

Anthony M. Orum and Arlette Grabczynska (chapter 10) likewise start from the position that all humans have rights, and under a 2003 international treaty, migrants do have formal labor and security rights. (The United States has not ratified this treaty.) They describe how impoverishment in Latin Americans' countries—taking Salvadorians as an example—spurs migration north; once in the United States, migrants have none of the protections formally accorded U.S. citizens.

Cultural and identity rights, and rights to group membership and heritage, are probably the most complex of human rights, because to be genuinely secure, group cultures need to be fully recognized by others as equal and as different. These are the rights of recognition, less easily codified than, say, socioeconomic rights (Fraser and Honneth, 2003). Keri Iyall Smith describes the distinctiveness of indigenous peoples—their strong connections to their lands and habitats—as making up "internal colonies" of states. No doubt the confoundedness of economic inequalities with both racial differences (Hattery and Smith, chapter 15) and gender differences (Barbara Risman, chapter 16) can partly be connected to culture. Many, though not all, African Americans contend there is a distinctive black culture, rooted in faith and family practices, with a rich musical heritage that embodies and expresses a legacy of slavery and oppression. Charles A. Gallagher (chapter 17) looks at the other side of the coin, namely, how white liberalism is also a culture, now taking an exaggerated form of "neoliberalism." This is a culture of "choice" with the self-deception that all have choices and a meritocracy prevails, that society is inclusive, and that whites are themselves fully tolerant of others. Whites are deceiving themselves. Likewise, we can ask, along the lines Barbara Risman pursues in chapter 16, are men deceiving themselves in their professions that women and men are equal? Following feminists, our research questions can be guided by a value of justice; we can cross disciplinary boundaries to better understand social conditions; and we can do this work as activist scholars.

With increasing global connectedness and the rapid expansion of private control of the world's economies, there is growing concern about the preservation of public goods—namely goods in the public domain for all to share (Kaul et al., 2003). A main conception of public goods focuses on the environment and environmental resources, but there is new interest in an expanded definition that includes social goods and benefits, say, as provided by the welfare state, democracy, and international agreements that center on human rights. Peace is the ultimate public good. Is it a chimera? Jerry Pubantz and John Allphin Moore, Jr. (chapter 13) argue that it is not and there is international persistence in developing frameworks and international laws that promote global peace. They also provide a helpful insiders' view and interpretations of recent changes in the United Nations' structure and programs.

In chapter 12, Kenneth Gould frames questions about sustainability in a way that powerfully demonstrates the connections between social justice and environmental justice, between human society and the natural world. He draws from political economy, conceptions from political and social movements, and an understanding of global neoliberalism. Like other contributors to the volume, he insists on radical democratization of decision making and broad sharing of knowledge. To learn from experts on how to manage collective, public goods, Judith Blau and Alberto Moncada (chapter 14) propose that Westerners turn to peoples in Third World countries, where many communities manage their affairs by democratic, participatory self-governance and organize work in self-managed, collective enterprises.

Many of the themes of this volume come together in chapter 11, "Understanding Disasters," by Havidán Rodríguez and Carla N. Russell. Natural disasters have the most devastating effects on poor communities and countries and on the most vulnerable groups within a population—the poor, women, children, the elderly, and racial and ethnic minorities. The calamitous hurricane Katrina, which hit the Gulf Coast of the United States in Fall 2005, provides ample evidence of this. Yet, the authors also urge us to consider vulnerabilities and inequalities in a global context, and they provide readers with their observations of Honduran communities following Hurricane Mitch and Indian communities in the wake of the 2004 tsunami. Natural disasters are not like social and economic processes in that they bring finality in their wake—sudden death, sometimes to many thousands, and abrupt transitions in the lives of many, many more, who face abject misery. Teams of researchers from many disciplines and many countries work together in the aftermath of a natural disaster, and these teams also work alongside survivors and NGOs in participatory projects. In stark ways, these communities and peoples are the casualties of Westerners' greed and irresponsible exploitation of natural resources. It was not uncommon not so long ago for social scientists to speak of "progress." We are now wiser.

PUBLICS AND THE ARTS

There are abundant reasons why public sociologists might consider the arts as playing an important role in community projects, in the classroom, and in their own conceptual work. Whether affirming social solidarities, as Lenin insisted; or expressing individual freedoms, which abstractionist Robert Motherwell stressed; or celebrating the glorious beauty of nature (Corot and Ansel Adams) or of the human form (Michelangelo), artworks provoke us to make synthetic connections involving experiences, ideas, aspirations, and emotions in a way that language cannot. Artworks, as John Dewey (1958 [1934]: 346–49) pointed out, are not arch moralizers as people sometimes are. To convey this we include photographs of wall murals painted by Turbado Marabou. And to illustrate a theme of the volume—that activists can bring about social change—we include photographs of demonstrations by Kenneth Gould that he took at the World Social Forum and in Washington,

D.C. Public poetry might initially appear to be an oxymoron, but poems that raise social awareness and social consciousness are also public art. A few of sociologist-poet Rodney Coates's poems are reproduced, with the hope that this genre makes its way into the toolkits of public sociologists.

REFERENCES

Dewey, John. 1958. [1934] *Art as Experience*. New York: Capricorn Books.

Fraser, Nancy, and Axel Honneth. 2003. *Redistribution or Recognition?* London: Verso.

Jackson, Derrick Z. 2005. "Where Is Ansel Adams When We Need Him?" *Boston.com*. November 5, 2005: www.boston.com/news/globe/editorial_opinion/oped/articles/2005/11/05/where_is_ansel_adams_when_we_need_him/ (accessed November 6, 2005).

Kaul, Inge, Pedro Conceiçao, Katell Le Goulven, and Ronald U. Mendoza. 2003. *Providing Public Goods*. New York: United Nations Development Programme and Oxford University Press.

MIT Media Lab. 2005. One Laptop per Child: http://laptop.media.mit.edu/.

Singer, Peter. 2002. *One World: The Ethics of Globalization*. New Haven, Conn.: Yale University Press.

United Nations Development Programme. 2004. *Human Development Report*. New York: UNDP.

Wallerstein, Immanuel. 2004. *The Uncertainties of Knowledge*. Philadelphia: Temple University Press.

1

Introduction: A Public Sociology for Human Rights

Michael Burawoy

A public sociology that will tackle the public issues of today requires the transformation of sociology as we know it. This is the stirring message of this volume—at the heart of sociology must lie a concern for society as such, the protection of those social relations through which we recognize each other as humans. Thus, the chapters focus on those fundamental human rights that uphold human community, first and foremost, against the colonizing projects of states and markets. In this vision of sociology, as Judith Blau and Alberto Moncada (2005) underline in their book *Human Rights: Beyond the Liberal Vision*, society can no longer be taken for granted. The devastation of society—whether in civil war or in famine, in prison or in ghetto—cannot be consigned to some marginal specialty or to some other discipline. Rather it must be the principle focus of our discipline, casting into relief threats to society's very existence.

What could more exemplify the devastation of society at the hands of market and state than Hurricane Katrina? To be sure this was no tsunami. As I write, two months after the storm, the death toll is at 1,055 but still climbing as more bodies are continually being recovered. Yet in neighboring Cuba it is a national tragedy if a single person dies in a hurricane, even one so fierce as Katrina. And so it should be; hurricanes are predictable in their effects and give ample warning of their arrival. But warnings were ignored by a state bent on war abroad and repression at home, sacrificing levees for arms, and social relief for "homeland" security. When the water flooded out, markets flooded in—corporate America would gorge itself on the disaster, on lucrative con-

1

tracts to rebuild New Orleans for a new privileged class, a New Orleans rebuilt on the backs of cheap imported labor, suspended labor codes, and the expulsion of indigenous poor and blacks. When the state fuels corporate America with outsourcing, suspending labor rights and withdrawing social rights, then "the other America," the underside of urban apartheid, whose livelihood depends upon those hard-won rights, must resort to the most basic human rights as the only rights they have left to defend.

One can indict this individual or that, President Bush or Mayor Nagin; this agency or that, the Federal Emergency Management Agency (FEMA) or the National Guard; this organization or that, the media or the churches; but such a politics of blame misses the bigger picture: the levees of society came crashing down in the storm of a rapacious capitalism—a rapacious capitalism that destroys everything in its path, from wetlands sacrificed to real estate and the leisure industry, to oil extraction from the Gulf, leading to the subsidence of its coastlands, to global warming that intensifies the hurricanes that sweep through the region. To grapple with the destruction of human community we need a new public sociology that brings together state, economy, and society; that draws on different disciplines; and that is not bound by the nation-state. It will be a sociology, as Eric Klinenberg (2002) shows in *Heat Wave*, of everyday immiseration and isolation that stand revealed in human catastrophe.

The race and class wars of the United States are, so far, silent if nonetheless palpable in their effects. Another area for a public sociology of human rights is the not-so-silent civil wars of the post–Cold War period, with their untold human suffering. Ahead of Rwanda, Afghanistan, Bosnia, and Herzegovina, the civil war in Sudan tops the list of the ten deadliest armed conflicts in the world between 1986 and 2000, with nearly 1.3 million people killed (Ron, Ramos, and Rodgers, 2005: 569). This figure does not include the latest round of atrocities in Darfur—an all-too-little understood war in the west of Sudan, which has so far left over four hundred thousand dead and two million displaced. The majority were killed at the hands of the Sudanese state and its marauding Arab militia, known locally as the Janjaweed, the devil on horseback.

It was no accident that the hostilities in Darfur began in February 2003 just as Sudan's twenty-one-year Second Civil War between the so-called Arab north and the so-called African south was coming to an end. The rebel groups in Darfur—the Sudanese Liberation Movement (Army) and the Justice and Equality Movement—wanted to be included in the spoils of the peace agreement that would divide up the Sudanese oil revenues between the elites of north and south. There were festering local antagonisms too with nomadic Arab herders encroaching on the shrinking lands of African farmers. The military cabal running the government in Khartoum sided with the Arab population, colluding with the Janjaweed, on the pretext of quelling the rebel movements. The Sudanese government turned Darfur into a zone of ethnic cleansing, and so it became a maelstrom of international forces as concerned to protect the rich oil deposits of south Sudan as to protect the population of Darfur from murder, rape, and pillage.

The United States has been deeply involved here, as in other epicenters of human devastation. In this case it used social science to justify an opportunistic reversal of policy, which would turn a blind eye to the genocide in Darfur. In the summer of 2004 both houses of Congress unanimously passed resolutions condemning genocide in Darfur. It was left to the State Department to produce compelling evidence for genocide, that is, the deliberate, premeditated attempt to destroy a population in whole or in part. Based on a survey conducted in the refugee camps of Chad, Colin Powell, then secretary of state, did indeed conclude that there had been genocide, perpetrated by the Sudanese government. That was September 2004. Less than a year later in April 2005, with Powell gone, Assistant Secretary of State Robert B. Zoellick refused to repeat or confirm the claim of genocide. This coincided with his mission to Sudan to seek, so it was reported, the cooperation of the Sudanese government in the war on terrorism. The Sudanese government had been host to Osama Bin Laden and a center of Al Qaeda operations in the 1990s, but now was supposedly developing a strong partnership with the CIA.

Along with the renewed ties between the Sudanese government and U.S. intelligence forces came revised figures of the death toll. The State Department claimed that between 60,000 and 160,000 people had died in Darfur since the hostilities began, much lower than the previously cited figures. At this point sociologist John Hagan and his collaborators entered the war of numbers to lay bare the war of atrocities. The State Department's lower figure, Hagan, Rymond-Richmond, and Parker (2005) argue, came from a misleading review of surveys conducted by various international health organizations and the Sudanese Ministry of Health in the summer of 2004. This survey was based only on deaths within the refugee camps, that is, deaths from disease and starvation, since the Sudanese government obstructed surveys of death through violence. The latter were calculated by Hagan et al. from a survey also conducted in 2004 by the Coalition for International Justice, sponsored by the U.S. State Department in support of Powell's earlier testimony concerning the Darfur genocide. It was administered in the refugee camps in Chad where a large sample was interviewed about deaths in the villages from which they had fled. Hagan et al. came up with a total death toll of 390,000—a figure close to other calculations— which, together with the descriptions of hostilities given in the interviews, led them to conclude that this was indeed a case of genocide. This claim based on the larger mortality figures was given some play in the national media, in opinion columns in the *New York Times* and the *Washington Post*. Nonetheless, the U.S. government stuck to its lower figures, but with little attempt at justification.

In a paper he wrote with Heather Schoenfeld and Alberto Palloni, John Hagan (2006) reflects on his frustrated advocacy of public sociology around human rights. First, criminology has been in a state of denial when it comes to crimes against humanity, genocide, and ethnic cleansing. Just as criminology made a great leap forward when Sutherland recognized corporate crimes so now it must also be prepared to take on states. Criminology must step into the field of human rights, but it must do so together with demographers who study mortality from "natural" causes. By accepting the separation of the investigation of public health from violence, the U.S. state has been complicit in covering up the crimes of its intermittent ally, the Sudanese government. The U.S. government, as well as the UN and other major world powers, was unwilling to consistently declare genocide in Darfur not only because they did not wish to offend their collaborator in the war against terrorism or disturb the exploration of the rich oil deposits in southern Sudan, but because they did not want to have to deploy troops in Darfur. Whatever the reason, the United States colluded in a defense of the indefensible. It might be more difficult for governments to hide genocide, Hagan and his colleagues concluded, if social scientists were to develop an integrated approach to human rights that would, for example, connect the analysis of state crimes and public health. This would be just a small piece of the revamping of sociology to meet the urgent need for an effective public sociology of human rights.

HUMAN RIGHTS: WHOSE RIGHTS? WHICH RIGHTS?

Expanding catastrophes, whether genocide, civil war, military occupations, hurricanes, global warming, or earthquakes, call for a public sociology for human rights, built on a professional sociology that refuses to compartmentalize or decontextualize the sources of suffering. In pursuing such a sociology of human rights we must not confound human rights with the rights of states and markets. We see how the U.S. prosecution of the war against terror, in principle an eminently defensible human rights project, entails the sacrifice of populations in the United States, the suppression of genocide in Darfur, and the occupation of Iraq. The public defense of human rights becomes a cover for their violation.

Indeed, human rights are the currency of contemporary international relations, an ideology of domination deployed by the United States, in particular, as a cover for wars and occupations as well as sanctions and hostilities. It has justified atrocities and interventions in Iraq and Afghanistan; it has been the alibi for sanctions against countries such as China and Cuba, although even here profits speak louder than human rights as U.S. sanctions against China have been especially tame for fear of endangering lucrative trade agreements. Human rights have been the ideological advance guard of occupation and recolonization, whether for geopolitical or economic ends. It has been used to divide the world into good and evil: those nations defending human rights and those supporting terrorism.

Even on its own terrain the so-called U.S. Patriot Act has sanctioned the erosion of civil liberties by the Department of Homeland Security in the name of the "greater good," in the name of the war against terrorism. It has denied others the right to examine the U.S. record of human rights, whether in Guantánomo Bay or Abu Ghraib, not to mention the abuse meted out in its own prisons. It has outsourced the torture and interrogation of suspects to third-party states out of sight and beyond U.S. law. It has opposed the development of an international court of law for fear human rights abuses would be turned against the practices of its own soldiers on foreign soils. In the schizophrenic view of the U.S. state, human rights are always abused by others and always upheld by the United States. It has resisted applying human rights to itself, not just in its foreign operations but also on the domestic front, especially when it comes to marginalized populations—labor, racial minorities, immigrants. If human rights discourse has been corrupted by its use as an ideological weapon of a conquering state, can it also be turned against that state, can it provide the basis of a public sociology? The chapters in this book come to a common verdict—an unqualified yes. But how?

The advantage of a human rights framework is its widespread appeal. Who, after all, can be against human rights? If the collective will is present, universalism can eventually be turned against any power that seeks to justify atrocities in its name. But "eventually" too often means after untold human suffering. The disadvantage of human rights is not only the often-slow pace of implementation but also the way they have been tainted by geopolitics. It might be appealing in the United States, where the population is naïve and misinformed about U.S. military adventures abroad, but much less appealing in other countries where the underside of "human rights" interventions is readily apparent. To the subjugated, parading human rights too easily appears as yet another civilizing mission of foreign ("liberating") powers. If it is to gain credibility among oppressed peoples the defenders of human rights must be prepared to turn this ideological weapon against its misuse by colonizing powers and their satrapies. In particular it must be turned against the United States both in its imperial adventures abroad but also on its domestic terrain.

The danger in the use of human rights, therefore, is their abstract character. Bandied around as if they belong to some disembodied but essential human being, they can assume any meaning their purveyors wish. Disconnected and abandoned, the refugees of Darfur have no human rights at all, while predatory states can proclaim they are their authentic voice. Or to enjoin two familiar examples: just like the battered woman who can stand the violence no longer and kills her abuser, so the suicide bomber cannot be separated from the terrorist state that knows no limits to the application of force to deny humans self-determination (Pape, 2005). Rights (or their absence) cannot exist outside the institutions that guarantee (or deny) them, and which they in turn support (or challenge).

A sociology of human rights must take as its first principle the investigation of the institutional context of human rights. In the world of capitalism there are three sets of institutions: the market economy, the liberal state, and civil society. Each has its associated rights. The market economy demands the rights of property, and the freedom to buy and sell, to exchange. The state is concerned with its own coercive stability and, in a liberal democracy, with rights to vote, rule of law, freedom of speech. In contrast, collective organization in society defends human rights of survival whether against the commodification of the market or the violence of the state. If the first two have been the realms of economics and political science, the latter is characteristically the realm of sociology and the allied disciplines of anthropology and human geography. In short, human rights become publicly defensible if they become part of a public sociology.

THREE WAVES OF MARKETIZATION, THREE ERAS OF SOCIOLOGY

The framework that presents society as an endangered species in the face of state and market aggression derives from Karl Polanyi's (1944) *The Great Transformation*—the classic analysis of the devastation wrought by the market. If the state initially sponsored the rise of the market in eighteenth-century England, once established the market generated a momentum of its own, attempting to reduce everything to a creature of itself. There were no limits to commodification, even entities that were never intended to be commodities, what Polanyi calls fictitious commodities. Paramount among these were labor, land, and money. If labor is commodified, bought and sold at will, then it will lose its human form and thus its character as labor, capable of creatively and spontaneously transforming nature. If land—and we could substitute the environment—becomes a commodity, defiled in the interests of profit, then it will no longer serve to nourish the human species. Finally, if money itself is freely bought and sold, businesses themselves will be threatened by the uncertainty of fluctuating exchange rates. When it becomes subject to arbitrary changes in value money can no longer function effectively as a medium of exchange.

In short, markets tend to destroy the very conditions of their own existence and generate a countermovement by society for its self-protection. Here Polanyi focuses on how the commodification of labor in England in the first half of the nineteenth century led to a counterrebellion by society. The rise of labor organizations, cooperatives, and Chartism conspired to impose restrictions on the commodification of labor, imposing minimal conditions on employment such as the length of the working day, constraining the whim of the employer. The landed classes sought to protect agriculture from competition through tariffs as well as erect legal limits on the use of land, while the business classes forged the control of national currencies through the creation of a central bank. Similar defenses against the market came somewhat later in Europe and the United States, defenses that involved political parties and the state in the former and more laissez-faire social self-protection in the latter.

This was the first period of sociology, responding to the rawness of markets with a strong moral and reformist bent. You might call this the period of *utopian sociology*. In England it was represented by the critical thinking of practitioners such as Robert Owen, while in the United States utopianism was rife in the postbellum period. Many of these schemes were rooted in the *rights of labor*, the defense against its commodification, against the tyranny of the unforgiving market in labor. In the era of the Gilded Age sociology took up the cause of the working class, especially when economics, within which sociology had hitherto developed, distanced itself from the critique of capitalism and adopted the professional mantle of neoclassical theory, of marginalism.

The countermovement to the first epoch of market expansion was impelled by the self-organization of society in the nineteenth century, starting out at the local level and finally rising to the level of the state. In Polanyi's scheme the next century saw the renewed expansion of the market at the international level. The movement for free trade was temporary halted by World War I but then redoubled its momentum in the 1920s with the advance of the gold standard. In the 1930s, however, nation-states recoiled against the menacing uncertainty of the global market, leading to extreme reactions—Fascism, Communism (Stalinist collectivization and planning), New Deal and Social Democracy—all aiming at insulation from international markets and at the same time subjugating national markets to state control. In Polanyi's view these new forms of state—destroying society or reconstructing it in the image of the state—owed their origins to the overextension of the market. In some countries—Nazi Germany and Stalin's Soviet Union—this meant the end of sociology, while in other countries, such as the United States, sociology turned toward policy science. Funded by foundations such as Rockefeller or Carnegie, and then by the state itself during the Depression, World War II, and most extensively after the war, academic sociology engaged social issues defined by various clients. This was the era of *policy sociology* concerned with *social rights*. It was the era in which sociology, as we now know it, was established with its distinctive concerns, namely, social inequality, status attainment, stability of liberal democracy, participation in organizations, and the conditions for modernization. State and civil society were viewed as allies in the containment of the excesses of the market economy.

With the experience of the nineteenth and twentieth centuries Polanyi assumed that the lesson of the market had been learned, namely it had to be carefully regulated if it was to serve humanity. Writing *The Great Transformation* in 1944, he imagined a socialist world in which market and state would be subordinated to the self-organization of society. He was overly optimistic. The twentieth century ended just as it began with a renewed commitment to the market—the neoliberal messianism that surpasses, both in ideology and in practice, the previous two rounds of market idolatry. It began with the economic crisis of the 1970s and was consolidated by the collapse of holdouts against market supremacy, the disintegration of the Soviet Union, the market transition guided by the Chinese party state, and the slow erosion of social democracy in Europe. This third wave of marketization, the era of neoliberalism, has a global dimension never before achieved, promoted this time by supranational agencies such as the International Monetary Fund (IMF), World Trade Organization (WTO), and World Bank, as well as by nation-states themselves, often organized into regional consortia.

The countermovement by society has therefore had to grope forward from local and national to a global scale, something never anticipated by Polanyi. Insofar as it speaks for this countermovement, sociology has to keep its distance from states and even supranational regulatory agencies since these are now no longer opposing or containing the market but promoting its expansion. Neoliberalism and militarism become partners in the destruction of community. The collusion takes different forms: in Darfur neoliberalism turns its back on genocide, while in New Orleans the neoliberal state casts militarism in the form of limited social support. Whether distant or proximate the connection of neoliberalism and militarism calls for a countermovement that appeals to multiple publics knitted together across the world, often sustained by nongovernmental organizations (NGOs) and social movements. This is the period of a *public sociology* concerned to protect distinctively *human rights* of local communities—freedom from the depredations of markets and states, freedoms to survive and collectively self-organize.

If labor rights were won on the terrain of the economy and social rights on the terrain of the state, then human rights will be won on the terrain of self-organizing society. This succession of rights is an ascendant movement toward ever greater universality—just as social rights include labor rights, so human rights include social rights as well as labor rights. The universality of rights is the reaction or countermovement to the universality of markets. The chapters in this book speak to a public sociology, defending human rights in the face of threats to society from the third wave of market expansion. Human rights are a last ditch defense against the headlong retreat of labor rights before capital's property rights, and the retreat of social rights before the state's regulatory rights.

THE EROSION OF LABOR AND SOCIAL RIGHTS

The broad parameters of this public sociology are sketched by William Robinson (chapter 2) as critical globalization studies, taking for granted the entities that Polanyi could barely imagine, not so much the supranational political bodies such as the UN, WTO, IMF, and World Bank, but the development of a transnational civil society, made up of NGOs, environmental movements, and traces of international working-class solidarity. Jackie Smith (chapter 4) points to this organic global civil society as a repository of a new set of rights associated with the UN's Universal Declaration of Human Rights, and along with these emancipatory human rights come new forms of postnational citizenship, the basis of what Gerard Delanty (chapter 3) calls a new cosmopolitanism. Here we find rights that attach to human beings irrespective of their national status, the rights of migrants that pertain irrespective of location. As the consciousness of a global citizenry these human rights do indeed become the experiential basis of a public sociology, defending society against neoliberal globalization.

One can catalogue the movements that have captured the public imagination, as Walda Katz-Fishman and Jerome Scott (chapter 5) do, but one must be wary of romanticizing this embryonic global civil society. It does, after all, operate on a terrain dominated by powerful nation-states. As James Ron, Howard Ramos, and Kathleen Rodgers (2005) have shown, even such a reputable and independent organization as Amnesty International adopts an information politics influenced by the power of states, the proclivities of media,

and the amount of military assistance, as well as by actual human rights violations. In Sudan, NGOs, the World Health Organization, and agencies monitoring peace initiatives operate on a difficult military terrain controlled by the
Sudanese state (Hutchinson, 2005). No less important are the influences of
market forces on global civil society—influences that see international NGOs
crowding one another out, scrambling for resources that make them prey to
the interests of large funding agencies (Cooley and Ron, 2002). They become
the lubricant and contraceptive of third-wave marketization. Global civil society is Janus-faced—decisively shaped by and connected to the interests of
nation-states and multilateral agencies even as it is also a terrain for contest-
ing those interests.

Just as serious are the deep and abiding fissures within the transnational
civil society, fissures brought about through the collusion of markets and
states. A global market means the mobility of capital as it seeks out ever
cheaper labor. Robert Pollin (chapter 6) writes of the sweatshop labor in the
Global South where indeed working conditions may be monstrous, but where,
as we are repeatedly told, it is better to be super-exploited than not to be
exploited at all—a condition that is itself the product of capitalism seeking
markets for its surplus products, uprooting populations from access to their
means of existence, turning them into surplus populations, dependent on
sweatshop labor. This is a return to the nineteenth century but with a ven-
geance and a difference—the sweatshops exist side by side with a Global
North, whose richest and poorest consumers benefit from the cheap commodities, the sweatshirts that contain no trace of the sweat, of the expended life
that has gone into them. Pollin calculates that an increase of 1.8 percent in
price is equivalent to a 100 percent increase in wages—that's a public procla-
mation of the way some make gains at the expense of others within that same
putative transnational civil society.

If one strategy of capital is to seek out cheap labor abroad, another strategy
is to import cheap labor. The United States is home to all manner of migrant
workers—legal and illegal—defenseless against the practice of capital. They
work under appalling conditions in the garment trade or they are the day
laborers of the construction industry. Migrant workers can be assumed to be
single and, thus, employers are not responsible for paying a family wage. For
the same reason states also profit, not having to foot the welfare and education bills for absent family members. As Anthony Orum and Arlette Grabczynska (chapter 10) describe, migrant workers are subject to arbitrary
abrogation of their rights; no wonder that they are often the first to form
unions—whatever their legal status. The national social rights response to
second-wave marketization marginalized (im)migrant workers, and segregated them from mainstream labor movements, but with third-wave marketi-

zation they are at the vanguard of organizing campaigns, the prototype of the broadening swath of disenfranchised labor, embedded in networks that stretch across continents.

Indeed, the prominence of migrants may in part explain the assault on the welfare apparatuses of the state. It may be the hidden story behind the attempt to dismantle social security that Deana Rohlinger and Jill Quadagno (chapter 7) describe in their chapter. If the second wave of market expansion brought all manner of welfare provisions to guard against the uncertainties of com-modifying labor, so now in the face of third-wave marketization those protec-tions are being dismantled. This is an account of social rights being subordinated to property rights, how the freedom to choose takes priority over the freedom to live, pretending that we are all putative owners in the ownership society, ignoring the very distinction between owners of property and those who own nothing but their labor power. Like the peasants of the Global South, the laborers in the Global North are torn from their means of livelihood, but that does not mean they have common interests.

Are there, however, issues around which North and South, East and West could unite, human rights that they could commonly defend? There is one way in which everyone's life is threatened, and that is through the degrada-tion of the environment. Hence the broad appeal of the environmental justice movement. Global warming, toxic waste, and pollution do not recognize social or geographical boundaries. We are all affected by the destruction of the environment. Yes, but not equally affected. As Havidán Rodríguez and Carla Russell (chapter 11) show, just as "natural" disasters have their social and economic origins, so they also have uneven social consequences. As they become more numerous or more hazardous, their costs are more unequally distributed. An earthquake in Pakistan has many more casualties than one of equal strength in Los Angeles; a hurricane in Honduras kills many more peo-ple than one in the United States, which in turn suffers a much higher death rate than Cuba. Within a single country the distribution of suffering mirrors the social structure. As we know only too well, blacks, the poor, and the elderly bore the greatest costs of Hurricane Katrina.

For Kenneth Gould (chapter 12) the costs of the ecological system cannot be separated from the social order. The need for an ecologically sound system becomes all the more urgent as it becomes politically infeasible precisely because privileged races, classes, and nations can more effectively protect themselves from the fallout of environmental degradation. The idea of tech-nology as panacea misses the social and political context of invention and implementation. Gould argues that we must democratize economic decisions, making powerful economic actors and states accountable to public concerns.

Pushing the risks of environmental degradation upwards in the class hierarchy may be the only way to rescue the ecosystem from destruction.

Is this totally beyond the realm of possibility? Simone Pulver's (2004) analysis of the pressure that energy NGOs brought to bear on the major oil corporations of the world is encouraging—pressure exercised in a global public sphere constituted to address climate regulation. The very success in getting European oil companies to acknowledge the problem led to a split with U.S. corporations, which, however, had the perverse consequence of disabling the very environmental groups that had led the struggle. Once again we must be wary of any triumphalism, of detaching the global public sphere from supranational agencies, nation-states, and powerful economic actors that still decisively shape its terrain and wreak havoc with deliberative processes.

THE DEFENSE OF HUMAN RIGHTS

Karl Polanyi thought the devastation of community wrought by the commodification of labor in nineteenth-century England spontaneously brought about society's self-protection. Nothing could be further from the truth. From Edward Thompson to modern social movement theory we have learnt that organization cannot be taken for granted. Secret societies, cooperatives, and diverse forms of trade unions arose to defend labor rights only through extended class struggle, and their survival was always uncertain. In the twentieth century social rights were no less a function of intense struggles on the terrain of national politics. Although enshrined in the law and guaranteed by the state, they too have suffered reversal, and not just in the United States. Equally, there is nothing natural, inevitable, or eternal about the twenty-first-century struggle for human rights; there is no law of spontaneous counterhegemonic globalization. So what institutions might defend human rights? And will those institutions manage to restore labor rights and social rights as well as advance human rights?

Time and again the chapters in this volume refer to the United Nations and its 1948 Universal Declaration of Human Rights. What role is there for such a supranational body in guaranteeing the security of human populations? Jerry Pubantz and John Allphin Moore, Jr. (chapter 13) pin their hopes on the United Nations as increasingly responsive to a global civil society built on the foundation of an ever widening circle of NGOs. Its involvement in setting up war crime tribunals and peacekeeping forces, and establishing a global rule of law as well as fostering nation-building endeavors all augur well, so they argue, for the United Nations to create a democratic public sphere—a forum for the discussion, definition, and intervention in major world crises to defend human rights. This is the optimistic scenario in which global civil society, connected by a thousand threads to the UN, can contain or even prevent unilateral interventions by states and internal civil wars. But how much autonomy does the UN possess? Is it no more than a mopping-up operation that enters only after civil wars or predatory leaders have destroyed societies, and even then is its intervention strictly limited by local warlords or by members of the Security Council, the United States in particular?

Thus, Antonio Ugalde and Núria Homedes (chapter 8) are much less sanguine about the possibilities of supranational agencies protecting the welfare of the Global South. They see the World Bank, WTO, and World Health Organization as less concerned to develop effective health facilities and more interested in promoting the profits of the pharmaceutical industry, peddling their useless and expensive brands rather than generic drugs. International agencies surreptitiously conspire to privatize national health care, with the result that both access and subsidies become ever more skewed toward the rich. The World Bank, for example, quietly insinuates itself into health ministries, restructuring health provisions and circumventing any public discussion. There are emergent countermovements such as People's Health Movement and the Bangkok Charter on Health, and the success of one or two states, such as Brazil, in repelling the plundering of pharmaceuticals. Still, the overwhelming power lies with the proponents of commodified health care, disadvantaging not only the poor people of the Global South, but also the forty million poor Americans without health insurance.

A critical public sociology for today therefore will have to connect these disparate communities, facing pincer moves of state and markets. Its goal must be to develop a common language through which we can recognize common experiences at different ends of the world order. A public sociology will have to recognize the global character of public issues. It will succeed in this project only by capturing the imagination of publics with visions of alternatives. It is not a matter, however, of dreaming up alternatives and speculating on their possibility, but of focusing on real utopias, rooted in concrete movements and organizations. The Baptist Movement that challenged the Mexican state and the North American Free Trade Agreement constructed a real utopia out of the defense of the rights of indigenous communities. Keri Iyall Smith (chapter 9) extends such an appeal to the rights of indigenous communities across the world. Judith Blau and Alberto Moncada (chapter 14) extend the idea of collective self-organization to discover commonalities that stretch across the Global North and Global South. Local communities have inherent tendencies to form themselves into self-governing collectives when threatened by invasions of markets or states. The bases for such collectives vary from depleting shared natural resources to collectives of fate cast together by accident such as the barrios of the world's largest cities; to communities of deliberate self-government such as Montage; and, finally, to the organization weapons, the terrorist cells that proliferate in the face of terrorist states. These are the concrete fantasies, the currency of public sociology, which can galvanize a collective will, mobilizing publics toward full-fledged alternative principles of organization.

PUBLIC SOCIOLOGY BEGINS AT HOME: FEMINISM, RACISM, AND TEACHING

Public sociology must begin back in the university. Its very possibility depends on the recognition of publics, something all too new for sociology. Going back to Durkheim or to Weber we find sociologists suspicious of publics. Durkheim and a long tradition that followed him saw social movements not as the voice of a public but as a sign of social pathology, while Weber spoke of an inarticulate mass given to irrational sentiments, easily manipulated by leaders. It was the idea of a mass society—not a society of publics—that propelled post–World War II sociology in the United States, justifying on the one side a retreat to professional sociology and on the other side an "applied" or policy sociology designed to regulate politics and consumerism. Even C. Wright Mills, a most vocal critic of sociology as market research, embraced mass society as an inescapable reality. He saw critical intellectuals as the only meaningful and progressive force in society. It was only the civil rights movement, and the women's movement in particular, that gave to sociology the idea of articulate publics that could rationally fight for their interests outside the realm of conventional politics. Social movement theory, critical race theory, and feminism brought about a revolution in sociology, making possible a sociology of publics and thus a public sociology.

Barbara Risman (chapter 16) is a forthright advocate of feminism as public sociology. The short history of feminism demonstrates that the pursuit of social justice is quite compatible with an expanding and vigorous research program around gender inequality. By their own careers feminists have shown they can sustain a public profile or at least contribute to public debate at the same time as being active scholars. Most importantly they have shed disciplinary chauvinism by bridging disciplines in pursuit of women's rights but also by joining forces with other extra-academic projects in the defense of human rights. One thinks, for example, of the successful feminist struggles to bring domestic violence to public attention, and how "sexual harassment," "wife battery," and "the battered woman's syndrome" have not only entered public but also legal discourse. If only advances similar to those made by feminists against patriarchal violence could be made in the understanding of state violence, thus, for example, suicide bombers could be viewed not as pathologically demonic individuals but desperate responses to colonizing states.

Yet, there is also a downside to the feminist struggles for the expansion of the rights of women. Legal framings of domestic violence have led to the administration of women's needs, neutralizing their continuing political effectiveness, and sometimes even turning against women. The danger is that we now live in a postfeminist world, which regards male oppression as a thing of the past. So, in this regard, there is nothing more to achieve, even though the glass ceiling still exists and women are still paid, on average, considerably less than men. The same is true in the field of race relations, where the civil rights movement has supposedly ended institutional racism. This is a trap as Charles Gallagher (chapter 17) argues. We now have a color-blind racism, the racism that continues despite legal rights, the racism that gives rise to staggering rates of African American incarceration, the racism so apparent in the abandonment of the African American victims of Hurricane Katrina. Gallagher asks how we can sustain a dialogue about the rights of racial minorities in a world of publics that no longer wants to listen.

There is one thing we can do, and that is think of teaching as public sociology. Just as feminism, critical race theory, and social movement theory revolutionized how we understand and engage with subordinated and marginalized groups, so we are in the midst of a revolution in the teaching of sociology. Students are no longer seen as passive, empty vessels into which we pour our pearls of sociological wisdom, but as active citizens, capable of absorbing a rich lived experience, participants in public debates they carry beyond the classroom. Angela Hattery and Earl Smith (chapter 15) show us just what teaching can be by discussing their own strategies to bring new experiences to their students, getting them to enact remote and unfamiliar worlds. They do this through imaginative assignments that require students to participate in unfamiliar worlds, forcing them to recreate the world of welfare. Or, in another example, they take students on an expedition through the South, rediscovering the civil rights movement through interviewing participants in local communities. This is labor-intensive teaching, but it builds organic connections to marginalized communities and long-lasting experiences, deeply etched in the student's sociological habitus. It is not a matter of teaching public sociology but teaching *as* public sociology, the promotion of dialogues between teacher and taught, among the students themselves, and thence between students and other publics. Teaching is the medium in which we all swim and through which we all can become public sociologists.

More than that, we can also ask the reverse question, whether teaching in this dialogical mode is a model for public sociology. Can teaching be the metaphor for the way we relate to publics more broadly as it was for Paulo Freire? If so, we have to steer a course between two dangers, between, on the one side, the Charybdis of vanguardism, preaching, or worse, dictating to those we engage and, on the other side, the Scylla of faddishness, pandering to the lowest common denominator, to spontaneous prejudices. As its goal an organic public sociology tries to achieve a symmetrical, two-way conversation between publics and sociologists. As in teaching proper so in public sociology: the danger is one in which the imbalance of power can threaten the educative function. The teacher with her captive audience and an array of sanctions at her command all too easily imposes herself upon the students. Still even within these constraints it is possible to conduct fruitful dialogue, as Angela Hattery and Earl Smith demonstrate, by strategies that empower the lived experience of the student.

More usually, in the world beyond the protected sphere of the academy, the public sociologist finds herself competing for the attention of publics with television, film, and newspapers that have more immediate access and have no qualms about distorting communication. Public sociology of the more traditional as well as the organic type, that is, public sociology in which the sociologist is vehicle for generating dialogue within and among publics as well as public sociology in which the sociologist is the interlocutor, must learn to exploit these media for their own messages. In this area, too, we have still much to learn about how best to communicate sociological narratives that are alien to the common sense, narratives that see social forces where participants only see individual motivations, narratives that focus on social structure and institutions that both trap and enable individual self-realization.

REENVISIONING SOCIOLOGY

Public sociology may start at home but we cannot stay there—not in today's world. Living in the third wave of market expansion presents a specific set of challenges and opportunities. In the first wave the destructive power of markets was countered by local communities that hung on to labor rights enshrined in custom and practice rather than in a system of law. As the second wave of marketization eroded labor rights, it generated a countermovement. This time it was states that would regulate commodification, restoring labor rights but also promoting welfare or what I call social rights.

Today, we face a very different situation. Nation-states no longer contain markets, instead they unleash them through deregulation of industry, privatization of public services, and the reversal of both labor rights and social rights. Once again society has to spring to its own defense, drawing on its own resources. This time the scope of societal self-protection is not confined to the local or national but extends to the global. Accordingly, the language of its defense has to be universal—the language of human rights, of self-determination that includes both labor and social rights. The era of human rights opens up the era of public sociology, that is a sociology that first engages with publics and only secondly with states.

As we saw in the case of Darfur, where we began, this involves understanding the local in terms of state and global forces. Sociology of the second wave of marketization took the nation-state as its unit of analysis, which continues to be an abiding framework for theorizing. We have to absorb it, however, into a global context, which means not only seeing things through an international perspective but also in terms of transnational connections, supranational agencies, and postnational consciousness—all three being terms of a human rights framework. It is not only a matter of increasing the scale of the sociological investigation, it is also a matter of reconfiguring the internal relations among subfields—criminology must join hands with public health, environmental studies must insinuate themselves into the study of social inequality, and so forth. Finally, sociology will have to join forces with other disciplines as it tackles environmental catastrophes, civil wars, famines, militarization, and so forth. It will have to forge alliances with human geographers and cultural anthropologists, with dissident groups in political science and economics, in other words, with those who recognize society as a value worth preserving.

I am not, however, proposing a single social science. Far from it. We have to maintain the integrity of sociology's critical standpoint, namely civil society, in the face of challenges from economists and political scientists who are largely responsible for ideologies justifying the collusion of market tyranny and state despotism, and thus, the abrogation of labor rights and social rights. If we don't follow the methods and models of conventional economics and political science, we have still much to learn from them, in particular the way their power derives from constituting a distinct object of investigation. The success of the economists in the policy world, but also in the public world, lies in their creation of a distinct object, the market economy, about which they have a monopoly of knowledge—a monopoly of knowledge that then furthers the autonomy of the economy with its untrammeled rights of property and free exchange. A successful public sociology will depend upon and encourage sociology to constitute its own object—society—and the project would be to subjugate state and markets to societal self-organization and the defense of human rights, including the initiation or restoration of labor rights and social rights.

ACKNOWLEDGMENTS

Thanks very much to Jim Ron and John Hagan for reading a draft of this introduction and helping me through the murky realm of human rights.

REFERENCES

Blau, Judith, and Alberto Moncada. 2005. *Human Rights: Beyond the Liberal Vision.* Lanham, Md.: Rowman & Littlefield.

Cooley, Alexander, and James Ron. 2002. "The NGO Scramble: Organizational Insecurity and the Political Economy of Transnational Action." *International Security* 27(1): 5–39.

Hagan, John, Wenona Rymond-Richmond, and Patricia Parker. 2005. "The Criminology of Genocide: The Death and Rape of Darfur." *Criminology* 43(3): 525–61.

Hagan, John, Heather Schoenfeld, and Alberto Palloni. 2006. "The Science of Human Rights, War Crimes and Humanitarian Emergencies." *Annual Review of Sociology* (forthcoming).

Hutchinson, Sharon. 2005. "Perverse Outcomes: International Monitoring and the Perpetuation of Violence in Sudan." Unpublished Manuscript.

Klinenberg, Eric. 2002. *Heat Wave: A Social Autopsy of Disaster in Chicago.* Chicago: University of Chicago Press.

Pape, Robert. 2005. *Dying to Win: The Strategic Logic of Suicide Terrorism.* New York: Random House.

Polanyi, Karl. 1944. *The Great Transformation.* New York: Farrar and Rinehart.

Pulver, Simone. 2004. *Power in the Public Sphere: The Battles between Oil Companies and Environmental Groups in the UN Climate Change Negotiations, 1991–2003.* PhD Dissertation, University of California, Berkeley.

Ron, James, Howard Ramos, and Kathleen Rodgers. 2005. "Transnational Information Politics: NGO Human Rights Reporting, 1986–2000." *International Studies Quarterly* 49: 557–87.

1

THE LOCAL AND THE GLOBAL

2

Critical Globalization Studies

William I. Robinson

If academics and intellectuals are to play a meaningful part in addressing the urgent issues that humanity faces in the twenty-first century—those of war and peace, social justice, democracy, cultural diversity, and ecological sustainability—it is incumbent upon us to gain an analytical understanding of globalization as the underlying structural dynamic that drives social, political, economic, and cultural processes around the world. My colleague Richard Appelbaum and I recently put out a call for a *critical globalization studies* (henceforth, CGS):

> We believe that the dual objective of understanding globalization and engaging in global social activism can best be expressed in the idea of a *critical globalization studies*. We believe that as scholars it is incumbent upon us to explore the relevance of academic research to the burning political issues and social struggles of our epoch, to the many conflicts, hardships, and hopes bound up with globalization. More directly stated, we are not indifferent observers studying globalization as a sort of detached academic exercise. Rather, we are passionately concerned with the adverse impact of globalization on billions of people as well as our increasingly stressed planetary ecology. Moreover, we believe that it is our obligation as scholars to place an understanding of the multifaceted processes of globalization in the service of those individuals and organizations that are dedicated to fighting its harsh edges. We are not anti-globalists, but we are staunchly opposed to the highly predatory forms that globalization has assumed throughout history, and particularly during the past quarter century. (Appelbaum and Robinson, 2005: xiii)

In the present chapter I want to reiterate—and expand on—this call for a CGS. But I am concerned here as well with a related question: What is the role and responsibility of intellectual labor in global society? In what ways do we—or ought we to—participate in the public life of the new global society taking shape?

I believe that all intellectual labor is organic, in the sense that studying the world is itself a social act, committed by agents with a definite relationship to the social order. The role of intellectuals in society is, of course, a very old and recurrent theme. To talk of public sociologies today is to underscore both the social role and responsibility of intellectuals and academics. Scholars are indeed public intellectuals, whether or not we identify ourselves as such. By teaching, publishing, and participating in the administration of our universities and other social institutions, we engage in forms of social communication that influence the development of public consciousness, public understanding of social processes and political life, appraisals of the purpose and potential of social action, and imageries of alternative futures.

But there is more to the intellectual enterprise than this. Intellectual production is always a collective process. By collective I do not just mean collaborative projects among scholars or ongoing research programs. I want to foreground here the social and the historical character of intellectual labor. All those who engage in intellectual labor or make knowledge claims are *organic* intellectuals in the sense that all such labor is social labor, its practitioners are social actors, and the products of its labor are not neutral or disinterested. We must ask ourselves, what is the relationship between our intellectual work and power? What is the relationship between our research into globalization, and power in global society? To what ends and whose interests does our intellectual production serve? In short, as academics and researchers examining globalization, we must ask ourselves, whose mandarins are we?

We are living in troubling times. The system of global capitalism that now engulfs the entire planet is in crisis. There is consensus among scientists that we are on the precipice of ecological holocaust, including the mass extinction of species; the impending collapse of agriculture in major producing areas; the meltdown of polar ice caps; global warming; and the contamination of the oceans, the food stock, water supply, and air. Social inequalities have spiraled out of control and the gap between the global rich and the global poor has never been as acute as it is in the early twenty-first century. While absolute levels of poverty and misery expand around the world under a new global social apartheid, the richest 20 percent of humanity received in 2000 more than 85 percent of the world's wealth, while the remaining 80 percent had to make do with less than 15 percent, according to the United Nation's oft-cited annual Human Development Report (UNDP, 2001). Driven by the imperatives of overaccumulation and transnational social control, global elites have increasingly turned to authoritarianism, militarization, and war to sustain the system. Many political economists concur that a global economic collapse is possible, even probable.

In times such as these intellectuals must choose between legitimating the prevailing social order and providing technical solutions to the problems that arise in its maintenance, or exposing contradictions in order to reveal how they may be resolved by transcending the existing order. How do we address the crisis of global capitalism, clearly a crisis of civilizational proportions? While I cannot provide the answer, my contention here is that solutions require a *critical* analytical and theoretical understanding of global society, which is the first task of a CGS.

GLOBAL CAPITALISM

The task of a CGS is certainly daunting, given such a vast and complex theoretical object as emergent global society, and the character of the current situation as transitionary and not accomplished. Globalization in my analysis is a qualitatively new stage in the history of world capitalism (Robinson, 2004). If earlier stages brought us colonial conquest, a world economy, an international division of labor, the partition of the world into North and South, and rising material prosperity amidst pauperization, this new era is bringing us into a singular global civilization, in which humanity is bound together as never before, yet divided into the haves and the have-nots across national and regional borders in a way unprecedented in human history. This new transnational order dates back to the world economic crisis of the 1970s and took shape in the 1980s and 1990s. It is marked, in my analysis, by a number of fundamental shifts in the capitalist system. These shifts include, first, the *rise of truly transnational capital* and the integration of every country into a new global production and financial system. The era of the primitive accumulation of capital is coming to an end as commodification penetrates every nook and cranny of the globe and invades public and community spheres previously outside its reach. In this process millions have been wrenched from the means of production, proletarianized, and thrown into a (gendered and racialized) global labor market that transnational capital has been able to shape.

Second is the appearance of a new *transnational capitalist class* (TCC), a class group grounded in new global markets and circuits of accumulation, rather than national markets and circuits. In every country of the world, a portion of the national elite has become integrated into this new transnationally oriented elite. Global class formation has also involved the rise of a new global working class—a labor force for the new global production system—

yet stratified less along national than along social lines in a transnational environment. Third is the rise of a *transnational state* (TNS), a loose but increasingly coherent network comprised of supranational political and economic institutions, and of national state apparatuses that have been penetrated and transformed by the TCC and allied transnationally oriented bureaucratic and other strata. Once captured by such forces, national states tend to become components of a larger TNS that serves the interests of global over national or local accumulation processes. The TNS has played a key role in imposing the neoliberal model on the Global South. It has advanced the interests of transnational capitalists and their allies over nationally oriented groups among the elite, not to mention over workers and the poor. National states become wracked by internal conflicts that reflect the contradictions of the larger global system.

Fourth is the appearance of *novel relations of inequality* in global society. As capitalism globalizes, the twenty-first century is witness to new forms of poverty and wealth, and new configurations of power and domination. Global capitalism has generated new social dependencies around the world. Billions of people have been brought squarely into the system, whereas before they may have been at the margins or entirely outside of it. The system is very much a life-and-death matter for billions of people who, willing or otherwise, have developed a stake in its maintenance. Indeed, global capitalism is hegemonic not just because its ideology has become dominant but *also*, and perhaps primarily, because it has the ability to provide material rewards and to impose sanctions.

Globalization is anything but a neutral process. It has produced winners and losers, and therefore has its defenders and opponents. There is a new configuration of global power that becomes manifest in each nation and whose tentacles reach all the way down to the community level. Each individual, each nation, and each region is being drawn into transnational processes that have undermined the earlier autonomies and provincialisms. This makes it entirely impossible to address local issues removed from global context. At the same time, resistance has been spreading throughout global society. There are burgeoning social movements of workers and the poor, transnational feminism, indigenous struggles, demands for human rights and democratization, and so on.

Where do scholars and academics fit in all of this? Where *ought* they fit in? Universities are centers for the production and reproduction of knowledge and culture. As do all social institutions, they internalize the power relations of the larger society to which they belong. Over the past decades, and in tandem with the spread of capitalist globalization, we have witnessed relentless pressures worldwide to commodify higher education, the increasing privatization of universities and their penetration by transnational corporate capital. If the university is to pull back from such a course it must fulfill a larger social function in the interests of broad publics and from the vantage point of a social logic that is inevitably at odds with the corporate logic of global capitalism.

EXERCISING A "PREFERENTIAL OPTION" FOR THE SUBORDINATE MAJORITY OF GLOBAL SOCIETY

In the 1960s and 1970s in Latin America and elsewhere, lay people and grassroots clerics from the Catholic Church questioned the precepts of the prevailing dogma and turned to constructing a church of the poor under the banner of liberation theology. These leaders of the popular church had begun working in social and self-help projects in the countryside and among impoverished urban neighborhoods. They soon realized, however, that a narrow self-improvement outlook was insufficient in the face of glaring injustices and entrenched power structures. Liberation theology called for Christians to exercise a "preferential option for the poor" in their social and evangelical work.

What the popular church recognized in the 1960s and 1970s for the Catholic Church—namely, that it is part of a larger society, reflects the divisions, struggles, and power relations of that society, and that members of the church are not neutral in the face of the battles that rage in society—holds true for the university. I want to call for scholars and intellectuals in the twenty-first century to exercise a preferential option for subordinate majorities of emergent global society.

What does it mean to exercise a preferential option for the majority in global society? In my view, what is required in global society, seen from the needs and aspirations of the poor majority of humanity, for whom global capitalism is nothing short of alienation, savagery, and dehumanization, are organic intellectuals capable of theorizing the changes that have taken place in the system of capitalism, in this epoch of globalization, and of providing to popular majorities these theoretical insights as inputs for their real-world struggles to develop alternative social relationships and an alternative social logic—the logic of majorities—to those of the market and of transnational capital. In other words, a critical globalization studies has to be capable of inspiring emancipatory action, of bringing together multiple publics in developing programs that integrate theory and practice.

This does not mean that practicing a CGS is reduced to running out and joining mass movements. It is, to be sure, a good idea to do so, although academics must be careful not to impose their "knowledge power" on these movements. Great scholars throughout the ages, those that have truly had an impact on history, have also been social activists and political agents. But the key thing here is to bring our intellectual labor—our theorizing and systematic research—to bear on the crisis of humanity. This involves *critical thinking*. The distinction between critical and noncritical ways of thinking is what Max Horkheimer (1972) first called "traditional" versus "critical" thinking, and what Robert Cox (1995) more recently has referred to as "problem solving" versus "critical" thinking. The critical tradition in the social sciences, not to be confused with the related but distinct *critical theory* as first developed by the Frankfurt School in Western Marxist thought, refers in the broadest sense to those approaches that take a critical view of the prevailing status quo and explicitly seek to replace the predominant power structures and social hierarchies with what are seen as more just and equitable social arrangements. Critical thinking therefore cannot take place without linking theory to practice, without a theoretically informed practice. Praxis is at the core of a CGS.

Does such a CGS imply that scholarship and the academic profession become comprised by "politicizing" them in this way? There is no value-free research, and there are no apolitical intellectuals. (This is not to say that our research should not adhere to the social science rules of logic and empirical verification; indeed it *must* be lest it is reduced to propaganda.) We know from the philosophy and the sociology of knowledge that knowledge is never neutral or divorced from the historic context of its production, including from competing social interests (see, inter alia, Therborn, 1985; Fray, 1987; Chalmers, 2000; Sartre 1974; Robinson, 1996). Intellectual production always parallels, and can be functionally associated with, movement and change in society. There is no such thing as an intellectual or an academic divorced from social aims that drive research, not in the hard sciences, and much less in the social sciences and humanities. The mainstream scholar may "well believe in an independent, 'suprasocial,' detached knowledge as in the social importance of his expertise," observes Horkheimer. "The dualism of thought and being, understanding and perception is second nature to the scientist. . . . [Such mainstream scholars] believe they are acting according to personal determinations, whereas in fact even in their most complicated calculations they but exemplify the working of an incalculable social mechanism" (1972: 196–97).

Many "mainstream" academics, shielded by the assumptions of positivist epistemologies, would no doubt take issue with this characterization of intellectual labor as, by definition, a social act by organic social agents. There are those who would posit a free-floating academic, a neutral generator of knowledge and ideas. But few would disagree that scholars and intellectuals are knowledge producers and that "knowledge is power." Hence it is incumbent on us to ask, *Power for whom? Power exercised by whom? Power to what ends?* The theoretical and research trajectories of social scientists, policy makers, and others within the academic division of labor are influenced by their social position as shaped by class, as well as by gender, race, and culture. But many academics are linked to the state, to other social institutions, and to dominant groups in a myriad of ways, from corporate and state funding of research, to the status, prestige, job security, and social approval that come from integration into the hegemonic order, in contrast, as Ollman shows, to the well-known sanctions one risks in committing to a counterhegemonic project (1976: 119–32).

Academics who believe they can remain aloof in the face of the conflicts that are swirling about us and the ever-higher stakes involved are engaged in a self-deception that is itself a political act. The claim to nonpolitical intellectual labor, value neutrality, and so forth is part of the very mystification of knowledge production and the ideological legitimation by intellectual agents of the dominant social order. Such intellectuals, to quote Sartre following Gramsci, are "specialists in research and servitors of hegemony" (1974: 238). The prevailing global order has its share of intellectual defenders, academics, pundits, and ideologues. These "functionaries of the superstructure" (Sartre, 1974: 238) serve to mystify the real inner workings of the emerging order and the social interests embedded therein. They become central cogs in the system of global capitalism, performing not only legitimating functions but also developing practical and particularist knowledge intended to provide technical solutions in response to the problems and contradictions of the system. In short, whether intended or not, they exercise a "preferential option" for a minority of the privileged and the powerful in global capitalist society.

The mood in academia, especially in the United States, generally trails behind and reflects that of the political and social climate. At times of rising popular and mass struggles, when counterhegemonic forces are coalescing, the academy can become radicalized. At times of conservative retrenchment the academy retreats, and those playing a major role in intellectual legitimation of the state of affairs (and the affairs of the state) move more on the offensive and academic repression can set in. If the 1960s and 1970s saw a radicalization of the university in the United States and elsewhere, then the 1980s and 1990s saw a conservative counteroffensive. In the 1980s and onwards we have witnessed, in tandem with the onslaught of neoliberalism and capitalist globalization, the privatization of higher education (and increasingly of secondary education), the rise of neoliberal private universities, the defunding of the public academy, the unprecedented penetration—

often takeover—of universities by transnational corporate capital, and the ever greater commodification of education.

SEVERAL INTERWOVEN TENETS OF A CRITICAL GLOBALIZATION STUDIES

Reflexivity and History

Critical theory, in the view of one well-known nineteenth-century social thinker, is *"the self-clarification of the struggles and wishes of the age"* (Marx, as cited in Fraser, 1987: 31). A CGS must be concerned with reflexivity and with history, such that it does not take for granted the prevailing power structures, but rather problematizes and historicizes existing arrangements and established institutions. A critical studies can *only* mean that we do *not* accept the world as we find it as being in any sense natural. Hence the first step in any CGS is to *problematize* the social reality that we study and in which we exist, to acknowledge that the society in which we live is only one possible form of society and that as collective agents we make and remake the world even if, as Marx famously admonished, under conditions not of our own choosing. If we acknowledge the historical specificity of existing social arrangements, then we cannot engage in a critical studies without identifying and foregrounding the nature of the particular historical society in which we live, which for us is *global capitalist* society.

Once we ask, what is the beginning—and how may we imagine the end—of the existing order of things, then the next question a critical studies must ask is, *What are the collective agents at work? What are the real and potential human agencies involved in social change? What is their relationship to the prevailing order and to one another?* Among the myriad of multilayered social forces in struggle, in analytical abstraction and simplified terms, there are those that seek to reorganize and reconstruct on new bases these arrangements, that is to say, struggles for social emancipation, and there are those that seek to defend or sustain these arrangements. We want to acknowledge struggles from below and struggles from above and focus our analytical attention on the interplay between them.

A Global Perspective

A CGS must take a global perspective, in that social arrangements in the twenty-first century can only be understood in the context of global-level structures and processes, that is to say, in the context of globalization. This is the "think globally" part of the oft-cited aphorism "think globally, act locally." The perceived problematics of the local and of the nation-state must be located within a broader web of interconnected histories that in the current era are converging in new ways. Any critical studies in the twenty-first century *must be,* of necessity, also a globalization studies.

But global-level thinking is a necessary but not sufficient condition for a critical understanding of the world. Transnational corporate and political elites certainly have a global perspective. Global thinking is not necessarily critical and is just as necessary for the maintenance of global capitalism as critical global-level thinking is for emancipatory change. If we can conceptualize a CGS then we should be able to conceive of a "noncritical globalization studies." If a CGS is one that acknowledges the historical specificity of existing social arrangements, then a "noncritical globalization studies" is one that takes the existing world as it is. Such a noncritical globalization studies is thriving in the twenty-first-century academy. It is a studies that denies that the world we live in—twenty-first-century global society—is but one particular historical form, one that has a beginning and an end, as do all historical forms and institutions.

The Subversive Nature of a CGS

In the tradition of critical studies, a CGS is subversive insofar as it explicitly seeks to replace predominant power structures and social hierarchies with what are seen as more just and equitable social arrangements. A CGS involves exposing the ideological content of theories and knowledge claims often put forward as social scientific discourse, the vested interests before the façade of neutral scholarship, and how powerful institutions really work. This means challenging the dominant mythologies of our age, such as that ecologically sound development is possible under capitalism, that "democracy" exists where tiny minorities control wealth and power, or that we are moving toward an "ownership society" when in fact we live in a usurped society in which the lot of the majority is one of increasing dispossession. In this sense, a CGS is a counterhegemonic practice that seeks to rebuild public discourse by "speaking truth to power."

It involves making visible and unmasking power relations in our institutions and professional associations, in our locales, and in the larger— ultimately global—society. While the substantive agenda of a CGS must be open, the underlying enterprise involves applying our training and experience to elucidating the real inner workings of the social order and the contradictions therein. This must include putting forward a cogent and systematic critique of global capitalism that exposes injustices, makes invisible problems visible, and reveals pressure points in the system. Rendering visible what

Paul Farmer (2003) terms the "pathologies of power" means "bearing witness," but more than that it means showing how suffering is a consequence of the structural violence that is *immanent* to the prevailing system and that links together apparently disconnected aspects of that system. We should recall, in this regard, Sartre's admonition, in his "A Plea for Intellectuals," that "the exploited classes do not need an *ideology* so much as the practical truth of society; they need knowledge of the world in order to change it" (1974). As regards a CGS, we would do well to follow Susan George's advice to study not so much the oppressed as the powerful:

> Those that genuinely want to help the movement should study the rich and powerful, not the poor and powerless. Although wealth and power are in a better position to hide their activities and are therefore more difficult to study, any knowledge about them will be valuable to the movement. The poor and powerless already know what is wrong with their lives and those who want to help them should analyze the forces that keep them poor and powerless. Better a sociology of the Pentagon or the Houston country club than of single mothers or L.A. gangs (2005: 8).

In the end, a CGS involves questioning everything, deconstructing everything, interrogating every claim to knowledge, yet it also means reconstructing what we have deconstructed and contributing to the construction of an alternative future.

Engagement with Everyday Concerns

To engage in a CGS means to maintain contact with everyday concerns, a connection with social forces from below, in its theoretical and empirical research concerns. Such engagement with everyday concerns is the "act locally" of the oft-cited aphorism. People experience global capitalism in their localities and everyday lives. For a CGS, the local–global link means identifying how global processes have penetrated and restructured localities in new ways, organically linking local realities to global processes. Burawoy et al. have shown in their diverse locally situated studies what they call a "global ethnography," how "ethnography's concern with concrete, lived experience can sharpen the abstractions of globalization theories into more precise and meaningful conceptual tools" (2000: xiv).

It is at this local, experienced level of global capitalism that intellectuals engage in active participation in everyday life, acting as agents or organizers, or in Gramsci's words, as "permanent persuaders" in the construction of hegemonic social orders (1971: 9–10). The intellectual in this case contributes to the active construction of hegemony by particular social forces that construct and maintain a social order on an ongoing basis. But such intellectual labor can also entail a connection with opposing initiatives, with forces from below and their attempts to forge a counterhegemony by drawing out the connections, through theoretical reflection, that link the distinct lived realities, everyday spontaneous and organized forms of struggle. By propagating certain ideas, intellectuals play an essential mediating function in the struggle for hegemony, Gramsci reminds us, by acting as "deputies" or instruments of hegemony, or by performing a valuable supporting role to subordinate groups engaged in promoting social change (5–23; 52–55).

CGS as Praxis

As should be clear from all the above, a CGS is a *praxis*. (Indeed, the broader point that I am unable to elaborate on here is that all intellectual labor is praxis and for that reason organic. The question is, a theory-practice by whom, for whom, and to what end?) A CGS is grounded in the linkage of theory to practice, insofar as we cannot really know the world without participating in efforts to change it, which is the same as to say that it is only when we engage in collective efforts to change the world that we truly come to know the world. At the pedagogical level, the praxis of a CGS is a pedagogy of the oppressed, a process of conscientization, understood as learning to perceive social, political, and economic contradictions, and to take action against the oppressive elements of reality. A CGS must not only link intellectual production and knowledge claims to emancipatory projects. It must also enjoin discursive with material struggles, lest the latter become reduced to irrelevant word games.

To reiterate, the *praxis* of a CGS implies bringing the intellectual labor of social scientists—our theoretical work and systematic research—to bear on the crisis of humanity. Universities, think tanks, and NGOs must be bastions of critique of the twenty-first-century global order, incubators for critical thinking, and reservoirs for debate, alternative ideas, and counterhegemonies. A CGS must be capable of contributing in this way to the development of programs that integrate theory with practice and the local with the global, of *inspiring emancipatory action*. A CGS is not satisfied with "the art of the possible"; its labor aims to help us move beyond the limits of the possible.

EPISTEMOLOGICAL "GROUND RULES" OF A CGS

There are certain "epistemological ground rules" for "doing a CGS," including a transdisciplinary, holistic, and dialectical approach that focuses on systemic connections that underlie the various aspects of the social—in this case, global—reality it studies. A CGS should be an open space, broad enough to house a diversity of approaches and epistemologies, from Marxist to radical variants of institutional, Weberian, feminist, poststructural, and other traditions in critical thought, and should as well emphasize including questions of contingency, culture, and subjectivity. But, to reiterate, what distinguishes (or *must* distinguish) a CGS from a noncritical globalization studies is reflexivity, a critical global perspective, the subversive nature of its thought in relation to the status quo, and a praxis as theoretically informed practice.

A CGS is, by definition, interdisciplinary—or more accurately, transdisciplinary. It is holistic in conception and epistemology, which is not to say, as a matter of course, that particular studies necessarily take the "whole" as the object of inquiry. As Palan has noted, "the broadly critical tradition in the social sciences is naturally attracted to holistic interpretations of social relations. . . . The assumption being that there are totalizing processes driven by a predominant logic which we call capitalism, and that such totalizing processes manifest themselves in all aspects of social life" (2000: 16). The critical tradition maintains therefore that there is no point in studying each facet of social life as an independent system of relationships—for the simple reason that they are not independent but interdependent, as internally related elements of a more encompassing totality. Consequently, the critical tradition does not accept the analytical legitimacy of formal academic divisions.

This does not mean that there is any single "right" way to engage in a critical globalization studies. I would insist, nonetheless, that it is not possible to understand global society in the absence of a political economy analysis. Political economy historically has concentrated on the analytical as well as prescriptive questions of how order and change come about. The history of the breakup in the nineteenth and twentieth centuries of political economy into artificial and compartmentalized "disciplines" is well known (Blackburn, 1972; Wallerstein, 2001; Therborn, 1985). We need to recapture the critical essence of political economy, which takes as its basis the production and reproduction of our material existence, and on that basis seeks to ask how change can be brought about, by whom, and for whom.

Yet it is equally true that the manifold dimensions of the social totality cannot be reduced to epiphenomena of the material bases of global society. Such an approach would not be dialectical—that is, holistic—but mechanical and misleading. The opposition of political economy to cultural analysis, for instance, is a false dualism that obscures rather than elucidates the complex reality of global society, insofar as our material existence as humans is always, of necessity, only possible through the construction of a symbolic order and systems of meaning that are themselves the products of historically situated social forces and have an ongoing recursive effect on material reality. Indeed, as Raymond Williams, among others, has constantly reminded us, culture is itself a material force.

A CGS therefore requires dialectical thought at the level of epistemology, as a way of knowing. In epistemological terms, dialectics means a dialogue seeking truth through exploration of contradictions and through identifying the *internal* relations that bind together diverse and multifaceted dimensions of social reality into an open totality. In the dialectical approach the different dimensions of our social reality do not have an "independent" status insofar as each aspect of reality is constituted by, and is constitutive of, a larger whole of which it is an internal element. An *internal relation* is one in which each part is constituted in its relation to the other, so that one cannot exist without the other and only has meaning when seen within the relation, whereas an *external relation* is one in which each part has an existence independent of its relation to the other (Ollman, 1976). Viewing things as externally related to each other inevitably leads to dualist constructs and false dichotomies (e.g., political economy versus culture, the local/national and the global). The distinct levels of social structure—in this case, global social structure—cannot be understood independent of each other, but neither are these levels reducible to any one category. They are internally related, meaning that they can only be understood in their relation to each other and to the larger social whole.

Critical thought, in this regard, means applying a dialectical as opposed to a formal logic, one that focuses not on things in themselves but on the interrelations among them. A dialectical logic involves identifying how distinct dimensions of social reality may be *analytically distinct* (such as the three most salient axes of social inequality—race, class, and gender) yet are *mutually constitutive* of each other as internal elements of a more encompassing process. Our task is to uncover internal linkages among distinct sets of historical relationships and their grounding in an underlying (that is, more primary) historic process, which in my view are material relations of production and reproduction and the historical ordering principle those relations put forth. This is to argue that historical processes of production and reproduction are *causal* processes. To take the case of race and class, it is not that racialization processes occurring around the world in the twenty-first century can be explained in terms of class but that class itself became racialized in the formative years of the world capitalist system because of the particular history of that system. I will not draw out the point further here. Suffice it to note that ultimately we are concerned here with the dialectical relationship between consciousness and being.

Twenty-first-century global society is characterized by a far greater complexity and much faster change and interaction than at any time in human history. It is only possible to grasp both the complexity of these structures and processes, and the dynamics of change, through a dialectical approach. For Ollman, the dialectic method involves six successive moments. The *ontological moment* has to do with the infinite number of mutually dependent processes that make up the totality, or structured whole, of social life. The *epistemological moment* deals with how to organize thinking in order to understand such a world, abstracting out the main patterns of change and interaction. The *moment of inquiry* appropriates the patterns of these internal relationships in order to further the project of investigation. The *moment of intellectual reconstruction* or *self-clarification* puts together the results of such an investigation for oneself. The *moment of exposition* entails describing to a particular audience the dialectical grasp of the facts by taking into account how others think. Finally, the *moment of praxis* uses the clarification of the facts of social life to act consciously in and on the world, changing it while simultaneously deepening one's understanding of it (Ollman, 1998: 342). Applied to the matter before us, we could say that, through social engagement, active theorizing, and political work, a critical globalization studies becomes *self-knowledge of global society*.

CONCLUSION

With the apparent triumph of global capitalism in the 1990s, following the collapse of the old Soviet bloc, the defeat of Third World nationalist and revolutionary projects, and the withdrawal of the Left into postmodern identity politics and other forms of accommodation with the prevailing social order, many intellectuals who previously identified with resistance movements and emancipatory projects seemed to cede a certain *defeatism* before global capitalism. Such defeatism has no place in a CGS. The decline of the Left and socialist movements worldwide, a result, among other factors, of the chronic gap between theory and practice, thought and action, led to a degeneration of intellectual criticism as well. An embrace of the "End of History" thesis (Fukuyama, 1992) is the end not of history but of critical thought.

The current epoch is a time of rapidly growing global social polarization between a shrinking majority of haves and an expanding minority of have-nots. It is a time of escalating political and military conflict as contending social forces face each other in innumerable yet interwoven struggles around the world. The global capitalist system faced by the turn of the century a structural crisis of overaccumulation and also an expanding crisis of legitimacy in the face of the "irresistible" rise of a global justice movement (Notes from Nowhere, 2003). There was certainly no wanting of mass mobilization and political protagonism from below before which a CGS could contribute much.

ACKNOWLEDGMENTS

I would like to thank Jackie Smith, John Foran, Richard Appelbaum, and Keri Iyall Smith for comments and suggestions on earlier versions of this chapter.

REFERENCES

Appelbaum, Richard P., and William I. Robinson (eds.). 2005. *Critical Globalization Studies*. New York: Routledge.

Blackburn, Robin (ed.) 1972. *Ideology in Social Science: Readings in Critical Social Theory*. Suffolk, UK: Fontana/Collins.

Burawoy, Michael, Joseph A. Blum, Sheba George, Zsuzsa Gille, Teresa Gowan, Lynne Haney, Maren Klawiter, Steven H. Lopez, Sean O Riain, and Millie Thayer. 2000. *Global Ethnography: Forces, Connections, and Imaginations in a Postmodern World*. Berkeley: University of California Press.

Chalmers, Alan, F. 2000. *What Is This Thing Called Science?* 3rd ed. Indianapolis: Hackett Publishing Co.

Cox, Robert W. 1995. "Critical Political Economy." In *International Political Economy: Understanding Global Disorder*, ed. Bjorne Hettne, 31–45. London: Zed.

Farmer, Paul. 2003. *Pathologies of Power: Health, Human Rights, and the New War on the Poor*. Berkeley: University of California Press.

Fraser, Nancy. 1987. "What's Critical about Critical Theory? The Case of Habermas and Gender." In *Feminism as Critique: On the Politics of Gender*, ed. Seyla Benhabib and Drucilla Cornell, 31–56. Minneapolis: University of Minnesota Press.

Fray, Brian. 1987. *Critical Social Science*. Cambridge: Polity Press.

Fukuyama, Francis. 1992. *The End of History and the Last Man*. London: Penguin.

George, Susan. 2005. "If You Want to Be Relevant: Advice to the Academic from a Scholar-Activist." In *Critical Globalization Studies*, ed. Richard P. Appelbaum and William I. Robinson, 3–10. New York: Routledge.

Gramsci, Antonio. 1971. *Selections from the Prison Notebooks*. New York: International Publishers.

Horkheimer, Max. 1972. "Traditional and Critical Theory." In *Critical Theory: Selected Essays*, trans. Matthew J. O'Connell, 188–243. Toronto: Herder and Herder.

Notes from Nowhere. 2003. *We Are Everywhere: The Irresistible Rise of Global Anticapitalism*. London: Verso.

Ollman, Bertell. 1998. "Why Dialectics? Why Now?" *Science and Society* 62(3): 339–57.

———. 1976. *Alienation*. 2nd ed. Cambridge: Cambridge University Press.

Palan, Ronen. 2000. "New Trends in Global Political Economy." In *Global Political Economy: Contemporary Theories*, ed. Ronen Palan, 1–18. London: Routledge.

Robinson, William I. 2004. *A Theory of Global Capitalism: Production, Class, and State in a Transnational World*. Baltimore, Md.: Johns Hopkins University Press.

———. 1996. *Promoting Polyarchy: Globalization, U.S. Intervention, and Hegemony*. Cambridge: Cambridge University Press.

Sartre, Jean-Paul. 1974. "A Plea for Intellectuals." In *Between Existentialism and Marxism*. London: New Left Books.

Therborn, Goran. 1985. *Science, Class & Society: On the Formation of Sociology & Historical Materialism*. London: Routledge.

United Nations Development Program. 2001. *Human Development Report*. New York: United Nations/Oxford University Press.

Wallerstein, Immanuel. 2001. *Unthinking Social Science: The Limits of 19th Century Paradigms*. Philadelphia: Temple University Press.

3

Cosmopolitan Citizenship

Gerard Delanty

One of the most notable features of the current day is a shift from people-hood to personhood. Throughout the world in recent times governments are forced to recognize the integrity of the person, not as an abstract individual as in liberal political theory but as an embodied being shaped by social strug-gles. Personhood challenges the hitherto dominant notion of peoplehood that has been a feature of the era in which the modern national state determined the nature of political community. Peoplehood has mostly been defined in terms of nationhood, for the national community has been for the greater part the community of the national state. Current developments, which can be linked to the local–global nexus, suggest a rescaling of peoplehood along with political community more generally in the direction of personhood. This has been reflected in the growing importance of international law, the rights of minorities, global solidarities and global justice, and cultural rights of vari-ous kinds. What is invoked by the turn to personhood is a conception of polit-ical community that avoids both communitarianism and individualism and which can be termed *cosmopolitan*. Cosmopolitanism indicates a transforma-tive conception of belonging whereby the citizen is neither a passive entity nor a pre-political being. In this chapter, then, an alternative notion of politi-cal community to nationhood will be discussed around the confluence of citi-zenship and cosmopolitanism in terms of local–global links. This is a view of cosmopolitanism that includes the poor—who in a sense are the universal class—as opposed to a transnational class or multiethnic social group, often taken to be the carriers of cosmopolitanism.

The first section outlines the growing tension between nationality and citizenship under the conditions of globalization. This leads into a definition of citizenship, and in the third section some of the main developments relating to the transformation of citizenship will be discussed. The thesis of the erosion of nationality will be developed in the fourth section around the cosmopolitan alternative. This leads to a discussion in the next section of the idea of cosmopolitan citizenship as a conception of citizenship appropriate to the current situation where globalization rather than the national state is the main context for citizenship. The aim of the chapter is to link citizenship with cosmopolitanism as opposed to nationality and to establish a stronger link with democracy. Cosmopolitanism, it is argued, is essential to public sociology, giving it a perspective that goes beyond the limits of national perspectives and at the same time suggests a tension with globality. Neither reducible to the national nor the global, cosmopolitanism refers to the autonomy of the social field in which social struggles shape the new face of citizenship.

THE EROSION OF NATIONALITY

It is possible to speak of an erosion of nationality today. The nation-state has been challenged within and from outside by developments that oscillate around the encounter of the local with the global. In particular, the relentless drive of globalizers and neoliberalism has challenged the national state. The modern age was based on the state project, and modern society was largely shaped by nation and class since the modern nation-state was developed alongside industrial society. Today global capitalism and global markets are playing much the same role that industrial capitalism played in the formative phase in the making of the modern nation-state. The nation-state was highly successful in shaping political community and, in particular, in organizing citizenship into a formal framework, which was part of the wider process of democracy. Through the institution of citizenship the state was connected with civil society and anchored in private lives. Along with changes in the nature of statehood and the movement toward a global civil society, this connection has changed today.

The state is no longer a nation-state, that is, a state defined by its relation to a nation. To follow Max Weber's definition, states are centers of the monopoly of violence over a given territory, and while they continue to define nationality they do not entirely define citizenship. Before commenting on this further it can be noted that states now exist in a globally connected world dominated by global markets. The world economy that came into existence in the sixteenth century and in which hegemonic national economies were predominant, has now finally given way to a global economy in which transnational firms have emerged to fill the place of the nation-state. Instead of struggling to gain power over states, most states are now struggling to control global capitalism (see Strange, 1996). But this does not mean the end of the state, but its transformation (see Sorensen, 2004). One important change in the nature of statehood is the rise of what has been called the regulatory state. By this is meant a shift in the primary role of the state from a provider (of social goods) to the role of a regulator, a shift that has been particularly apparent in the emergence of so-called third-way politics in Europe. Arising out of this is a sharing of sovereignty and an increase in the transnationalization of the state, a development that is most notably illustrated by the European Union, which can be seen as a regulatory state. The result is an unavoidable erosion of independent sovereignty. The state has not disappeared but has been transformed by global geopolitics and polycentric networks; it has become multilayered and multicentric; and government has given way to governance, that is, a mode of political rule in which power is exercised by multiple actors. Political power emanates from numerous sites; it cannot be explained by reference to any one particular center such as a dominant elite. States, individuals, and civil society groups are connected in multiple ways that have major implications for political community in terms of democracy—especially in its local forms—and the organization of citizenship. Nationality has ceased to be the institutional glue that binds the citizen to the state. One way of putting this is to say that with the erosion of nationality, the substantive dimensions of citizenship emerge to enhance the overall democratization of society.

But a note of caution must be made. Although we can speak of the erosion of nationality and a resulting release of citizenship, the result can be an increase in nationalism. The global challenge to the nation-state in many cases has pitted the nation against the state, releasing potent new kinds of nationalism. Much of radical right-wing nationalism in Europe today can be explained as the revolt of the nation against both the state and the transnational European state, both of which are often perceived to be agents of globalization. Globalization is many faceted, but it certainly has led to new expressions of statehood that have been on the whole detrimental to the established national community: in other words, nation and state have become seriously bifurcated. This dislocation of nation and state has often led to a revival of nationalism as a backlash against the transnationalization of the state. Although this has been particularly pronounced in Europe as a result of Europeanization, it also emerges in the transition to market economies in the former communist countries and is also an aspect of new religious nationalisms.

So with the rise of nationalism, on the one side, and on the other the grow-

ing power of global capitalism, the role of citizenship is particularly important. Its importance consists in the fact that it is reducible neither to
nationhood nor statehood.

WHAT IS CITIZENSHIP?

Citizenship can be understood to mean participation in political community,
and it is an essential aspect of democracy, which entails three dimensions:
representation (i.e., majority decision making through parliamentary democracy), constitutionalism (setting limits to what majorities can do), and citizenship, or public participation in civil society. Without citizenship democracy
would be minimal and lacking a public dimension. Citizenship thus gives to
democracy a substantive dimension, linking it to individuals and to civil society. However, citizenship is itself both substantive and formal and although
the substantive role has been important on the whole, until the last few decades citizenship has been largely formal. In the famous definition of citizenship by T. H. Marshall, it is a formal status based on rights, which defines the
relation of the individual to the state. This could be said to characterize liberal
citizenship, the kind of citizenship fostered by the modern liberal democracy,
but of course includes, as in Marshall's account, social rights. The modern
liberal democracy was also a nation-state, and as a result citizenship became
indistinguishable from the bundle of rights associated with nationality. What
we are witnessing today in our global age is, with the emergence of new kinds
of citizenship, the growing importance of the substantive dimension and the
dislocation of nationality and citizenship (see Delanty, 2001; Isin, 2002).

In formal terms, citizenship can be understood in terms of rights and
duties. The classic rights of citizenship are political rights (the right to vote
and stand for election), civic rights (which generally concern individual liberties), and social rights (rights to public goods, such as education and health
care, and generally social protection from the free market). These rights are
underpinned by duties, such as the duties of taxation, jury service, mandatory
education, and in some cases conscription. In substantive terms, citizenship
is expressed in active public participation, such as voluntary action—the vir-
tuous citizen—and in collective identities, as in, for example, national identity and loyalty to the state and nation. While there is no reason why
citizenship and democracy more generally have to be confined to the bounds
of the nation-state, the reality is that citizenship developed alongside the
nation-state: citizenship became indistinguishable from nationality and is
often equated with the passport, which came into existence with the modern

nation-state and the need to control large-scale and potentially mobile populations. So with the liberal nation-state, citizenship became defined in terms of the rights and duties of citizens to the state, which also defined the polity more generally as well as civil society. This meant that citizenship was based on exclusion and was the means by which the state distinguished between members and nonmembers of the polity.

It is also the case that citizenship has been fairly apolitical in the sense that it has been largely a passive condition by which the individual was the recipient of rights bestowed by the benevolent surveillance state and for which the citizen had to perform duties. The historical experience has been that citizenship preceded mass democracy—seventeenth-century England is such an example—and there are many examples of citizenship having no connection with democracy, as in communist countries, which had institutionalized social citizenship. There are also cases of political citizenship existing without social citizenship. An example of a substantive kind of citizenship that has been connected with democratization is the republican heritage of citizen participation, which allegedly is the basis of social capital. However, this tradition, which has been influential in the United States, has often been criticized for being based on a highly exclusionary model of civil society rooted in localism and small-scale rural communities. It has been argued that this civic republican conception of citizenship is nostalgic for a kind of political community that is no longer pertinent for large-scale multiethnic societies.

Neither the republican nor the classic liberal conception of citizenship is appropriate to the present day. As a result of the transformation of the state, the globalization of markets and communication, the rise of a global civil society, and new configurations of global and local connections, the assumptions of these conceptions of citizenship can be called into question. Radical pluralists have criticized these conceptions of citizenship for being apolitical and exclusionary. Despite their differences, both kinds of citizenship saw only a limited connection with democratization and shared a belief in the homogenous nature of the political community as a relatively bounded and territorial national community. We can now consider the main aspects of the transformation of citizenship.

THE TRANSFORMATION OF CITIZENSHIP

It is important to see that despite the equation of citizenship with nationality there is no necessary link. This means new opportunities for citizenship, but it also means that some of the rights of citizenship as a condition underpinned by the nation-state dissolve. One of the features of the present day is the rise of new kinds of citizenship that go beyond the classic rights and duties associated with the nation-state, on the one side, and, on the other, the increasing recognition that the nation-state is unable to provide a framework for all aspects of citizenship. The current situation can be described as an uncoupling of nationality and citizenship. This is reflected in a number of developments such as the blurring of the difference between national rights and international human rights, the rise of cultural rights, the challenge of technological citizenship, and the emergence of a global political community (see Stevenson, 2002).

With regard to international human rights, the observation can be made that the traditional separation of national and international law is no longer valid. It is now more difficult for states to equate nationality and citizenship since many rights can be claimed on the basis of human rights. In short, membership rights are not exclusively defined in terms of a community of decent or of birth but of residence. Rights now extend unavoidably across borders (see Jacobson, 1996).

Cultural rights concern at least three areas. In place of the individual as the bearer of rights, it concerns group-based rights, largely for minorities. In several countries, most notably Canada, Australia, and New Zealand, rights for native or precolonial peoples have been central to the politics of citizenship. Such demands for special collective rights have introduced a distinction between the rights of migrant groups and the rights of aboriginal groups, with the latter having different claims from groups who settled as a result of migration (see Kymlicka, 1995). Cultural rights concern some of the core issues in identity politics, in particular issues relating to women and to group-specific demands. The upshot of this is that citizenship can no longer be seen in purely formal terms as a formal equality between individuals, but must reflect group-specific concerns. It is now generally recognized that such concessions do not undermine the individual person as the bearer of rights but are an essential dimension of democracy that is enabled rather than hampered by cultural rights, which can be seen in terms of a politics of recognition based on pluralism (Cowan, Dembour, and Wilson, 2001). In short, citizenship has entered the domain of culture at a time when culture is being more and more seen in pluralist terms. Citizenship thus comes to reflect the pluralism of contemporary culture and the fact that there is no single national culture but contested sites of belonging (see Guttman, 2003).

Cultural pluralism has also impacted citizenship in the area of lifestyle, with an important expression of rights, now including consumer rights. In a world in which most people, as least in the developed Western world, are primarily consumers rather than producers, cultural citizenship is particularly important and includes rights related to mobility. As a result of the tremendous transformation in temporality and space that has been a feature of the present day with global travel and informational capitalism, citizenship extends beyond the territorial limits of a given state and is a global condition. The global nature of consumption is also a reason to see the cultural face of citizenship in global terms.

In addition to cultural citizenship there are also additional rights relating to new technologies and environmental concerns. It is possible to speak of technological citizenship and environmental citizenship with respect to rights that pertain to concerns that did not exist in the era of the modern nation-state. The characteristic feature of these rights is that they are not easily reduced to nationality and cannot be guaranteed by the nation-state. A further illustration of this is the growing salience of corporate citizenship, that is, the expectation that global firms have a responsibility to society.

These examples illustrate the rise of what can be called a cosmopolitan concept of citizenship, which in the new literature on citizenship varies from being a modification of the traditional understanding of citizenship in liberal political theory to an emphasis on global citizenship and postnational kinds of membership. The erosion of nationality is an undeniable feature of the present day. This situation does not result in the obsolescence of citizenship but rather in new expressions. The characteristic feature of the new face of citizenship could be described as cosmopolitanism. This will now be discussed and in the subsequent section related specifically to citizenship.

THE COSMOPOLITAN ALTERNATIVE

The argument advanced here is that there is an alternative to nationalism and to patriotism as a basis of political community. This entails establishing citizenship on a foundation separate from nationality. The cosmopolitan alternative advocated in this chapter is partly an expression of globalization, but it is not reducible to globalization: it is an expression of the local–global nexus.

Cosmopolitanism suggests a certain tension with globalization and at the same time has a resonance in one particular dimension of globalization, namely global civil society (see Kaldor, 2003; Keane, 2003). This is often referred to as "cosmopolitanism from below" and is based on globally organized forms of solidarity (see Kurasawa, 2004). Global civil society exists in a space beyond the state and the global market and has been important in influencing global politics in the direction of multilateralism and global solidarity; it has been important too in leading to the formation of a global normative culture, that is, a communicative frame of reference with which global politics is increasingly having to define itself. One of the characteristic features of global civil society is that it does not have one space but many; it is polycentric and not based on any single principle of organization other than the fact that it is globally organized through loosely structured horizontal coalitions and networks of activists. Globalization has created a complex web of conflicts, dislocations, and fluid political forms. However, this condition is not to be equated with a new global order, rather it is a case of the rise of global civil society. A global political order represented by the United Nations certainly exists and is largely based on nation-states. In contrast, global civil society exists in the new spaces that are beyond the state and the intergovernmental domain and are independent of global capitalism.

This global civil society has an undeniable reality in a plethora of new sites of cosmopolitanism as reflected in, for example, international nongovernmental organizations (INGOs) and various grassroots organizations as well as in various social movements, including globally organized anticapitalist protests and global civil society movements such as the World Social Forum and anti-sweatshop movements. A dimension of global civil society that is significant for citizenship is the public sphere. Until recently this was generally seen in terms of a national model of public discourse, but with the growing significance of global civil society, along with various kinds of transnational processes, it has taken a pronounced cosmopolitan form. Global public discourse has become central to national political communication and is the context in which citizens debate national and local political issues such as environment, health, and safety. The expansion of the global public sphere and its insertion into all national and local public spheres gives a basis to cosmopolitanism, which could be seen as the political philosophy of global civil society. A key dimension of this is the cosmopolitanism of the political struggles of the poor. The Internet has made a huge difference for empowering isolated groups.

What is cosmopolitanism? Cosmopolitanism concerns processes of self-transformation in which new cultural forms take shape and where new spaces of discourse open up, leading to a transformation in the social world. It has a critical role to play in opening up discursive spaces of world openness and thus in resisting both globalization and nationalism. The main tradition in modern cosmopolitan thought, which derives from Immanuel Kant, sought to extend republican political philosophy into a wider and essentially legal framework beyond the relatively limited modern republic. With this came the vision of a world political community extending beyond the community into which one is born or lives (see Cohen, 1996). Today we normally see cosmopolitanism in post-universalistic terms (see Breckenridge et al., 2002). There are many cosmopolitan movements that cannot be subsumed under an overarching notion of modernity (Cheah and Robbins, 1998). This kind of cosmopolitanism is different from the Enlightenment's model of cosmopolitanism, which was often Eurocentric and individualistic, based as it was on a notion of the citizen of the world; rather, it is one that is represented by movements from the periphery and whose carriers are diasporic groups, most significantly the global poor.

It may be suggested too, following Habermas, that the pluralization of cosmopolitanism can be furthermore linked to modernity as a dialogic process (Habermas, 1996, 1998). A post-universal cosmopolitanism is critical and dialogic, seeing as its goal alternative readings of modernity and the recognition of plurality rather than the creation of a universal order, such as a cosmopolis. This is a view that enables us to see how people were cosmopolitan in the past and how different cosmopolitanisms existed before and despite Westernization.

Cosmopolitanism is not to be equated with postmodernism or the simple fact of multiplicity or pluralism. Cosmopolitanism does not require hyphenated or hybrid identities, as is often thought; it is a disposition characterized by a reflexive relation to one's identity and a refusal to accept the given situation in which one finds oneself. The reflexive relation is different from a hyphenated one as such, signaling instead a critical and transformative self-understanding. There is an undeniable confrontation with the culture of the other in contemporary society, which has wider political ramifications and resonances in contemporary thought. Cosmopolitanism suggests then a concern with global justice and global solidarity. Despite their differences, the message in recent cosmopolitan philosophies is the challenge of living in a world of diversity and a belief in the fundamental virtue of embracing the values of the other.

One of the most influential expressions of a cosmopolitan conception of political community is Jürgen Habermas's theory of constitutional patriotism. This vision of the nation claims that the only kind of identification possible today is identification with the principles of the constitution. The basis of Habermas's argument is that political identity does not have to be based on a cultural identity. Culture is particular, while political identity offers in principle the possibility of a limited universalism. Originally advocated in the context of post–World War II German debates on the viability of national identity, it is relevant to all postnational societies. It is pertinent insofar as it avoids the problems of a narrow collective identity for large-scale and diverse societies. Moreover, the multicultural reality of contemporary society makes it impossible for a collective identity to be based on a particularistic conception of peoplehood. This position goes beyond the presuppositions of liberalism and republicanism in that it suggests a transformation of identities as opposed to an accommodation of them. A view of postnational political community might be conceived as articulated through discursively mediated identities and critical dialogue. In this view, one can simultaneously be a member of different political and cultural communities.

This does not mean that the category of the nation is no longer relevant to political community. Globalization does not present an alternative to the idea of a national community for several reasons. Globalization has brought about not so much the end of national forms of political community but their transformation. One of the most important expressions of this transformation of national identities is cosmopolitanism. The crucial point is that much of cosmopolitan transformation has emanated from the transformation within national identity under the conditions of globalization. To reiterate a point made earlier, cosmopolitanism arises out of local and global links; it is not simply the rule of the global over the local. *Cosmopolitan* refers to the end of the "closed society" of the nation-state, but it does not spell the end of the nation. Various cosmopolitan theorists thus speak of a "rooted cosmopolitanism" to refer to what is a really existing cosmopolitanism in the world today, which corresponds to multiple attachments and forms of belonging (see Appiah, 2005). The nation-state is itself a demonstration of the cosmopolitan principle that people can imagine a political community beyond the context of their immediate world. So it is possible to see contemporary cosmopolitanism as an extension of the cosmopolitanism of the national community to an acknowledgment of a wider political community beyond the national community.

THE IDEA OF COSMOPOLITAN CITIZENSHIP

It is now possible to speak of political community beyond the nation-state in a real sense. The notion of cosmopolitanism discussed in the foregoing provides a new political context for citizenship. There is now sufficient evidence to suggest that cosmopolitan citizenship exists as a reality in itself. Therefore the arguments made by both liberals and republican communitarians that community is beyond the nation-state can only be thin and therefore meaningless. This position, advocated for instance by Michael Walzer, which claims that only the nation-state can offer thin forms of identity and belonging and that citizens cannot identify with anything like a world community or with people beyond their immediate worlds, can be challenged on several grounds.

The argument that there is no community of any substance beyond the nation-state can be challenged by pointing to strong forms, such as those discussed above. There are many examples of global civil society exercising strong forms of identity. It is possible to speak of global solidarity in a meaningful sense and indeed in a sense that goes beyond national forms of solidarity (see Calhoun, 2003). Concern about global issues such as global poverty and the environment are two of the main examples of thin values that have tangible substance. In addition there are numerous globally organized networks of activists based on a concern for global justice that cannot be dismissed as marginal. Global solidarity is having an impact on capitalism in terms of issues such as fair trade, anti-sweatshop production, and a movement in the direction of corporate citizenship. It is present too in humanitarianism and a concern with human rights. Issues around global solidarity were central to the G7 Summit in Edinburgh in July 2005. The richest countries are unable to resist the power of global civil society and the kinds of cosmopolitan solidarity that it can mobilize.

A second argument is that the nation-state is not exclusively based on thick forms of identity. The anticosmopolitan position takes for granted a view of the nation-state as rooted in substantive kinds of citizenship that do not extend beyond its borders. The reality is that the nation-state is not the entity it is in liberal and republican thought. It is considerably more contested, and underlying its surface appearance of homogeneity is a plurality of cultures and diverse forms of loyalty. The point is that the distinction between "thick" and "thin" forms of loyalty disguises the reality of multiple identities and ones that extend beyond the national community.

Thirdly, the anticosmopolitan position, especially in its republican-communitarian form, assumes that the nation-state does not include cosmopolitanism. Liberals are less hostile to cosmopolitanism, but those liberals who argue that cosmopolitanism can be reconciled to liberalism generally see this as a concession and relevant only to a limited range of rights. In general, both liberals and communitarians place cosmopolitanism on the outside of the nation-state when in fact it can be argued that cosmopolitanism has been integral to the nation-state itself and that therefore the distinction between national and cosmopolitan community is a false one. As is suggested by the well-known notion of the "imagined community," the nation-state presupposes the very capacity of citizens to imagine a world beyond their immediate context. There is no reason why this cannot extend beyond the nation-state. Although not in itself an example of global solidarity, there is much evidence that shows that significant numbers of Europeans identify with Europe as a transnational entity and, more importantly, there are increasing numbers of Europeans who claim to identify both with their home countries and with Europe (see Herrmann, Risse, and Brewer, 2004).

In view of these considerations the liberal and republican repudiation of cosmopolitanism can be questioned. Cosmopolitanism is not a straightforward product of globalization but arises out of the encounter of the global with the local or national. In this sense, then, it exists in relations of tension and in transformative dynamics; it is not a given condition or goal to be reached. In other words, cosmopolitanism exists within all societies and can be seen as a transformative process (see Beck, 2005).

It is in reconciling the universalistic rights of the individual with the need to protect minorities that the cosmopolitan citizenship is most evident. In this context cosmopolitan citizenship is to be understood in terms of a cultural shift in collective identities to include the recognition of others. Cosmopolitan citizenship is marked by a decreased importance of territory, in particular as measured by the place of one's birth in the definition of citizenship rights. In addition, cosmopolitan citizenship entails a lesser salience on an underlying collective identity, for a cosmopolitan political community does not have to rest on an underlying cultural community. Cultural rights are thus possible in the space that has been created by multiple and overlapping identities. As Seyla Benhabib has argued, "Cosmopolitanism, the concern for the world as if it were one's *polis*, is furthered by such multiple, overlapping allegiances which are sustained across communities of language, ethnicity, religion, and nationality" (Benhabib, 2002: 174–75). Such developments have arisen as a result of cultural pluralization arising from migration, ethnic multiculturalism, cultural diversity of all kinds, and the growing demands for the recognition of different life choices.

The result of this is that nationality has been eroded and citizenship has moved into the political space opened up by global civil society and by the internal transformation of the nation-state. *Cosmopolitanism* is the appropriate term to describe these developments since it includes within it the local and the global. The local is especially important in cosmopolitan citizenship since it is on this level that some of the most important political struggles take place and it is the site of the voice of the global poor. We thus speak of cosmopolitan citizenship as opposed to global citizenship to capture this sense of the local–global dimension.

Taking some of the main components of citizenship—rights, duties, participation, and identity—the cosmopolitan turn is evident in a shift away from nationality and from a territorially bounded citizenship. This is most evident in the domain of rights, which, as a result of the growing incorporation of international law into national law, are no longer confined to rights acquired by birth. Increasingly states have to recognize the rights of others—migrants, political asylum seekers, indigenous groups—and in many cases have to grant special rights. The duties of citizenship are also no longer confined to the duty to serve the state but extend to cosmopolitan responsibilities beyond the state and even to future generations. The dimension of participation now covers a wider sphere than national civil society and extends into global civil society, which can be seen as encroaching upon national civil society. Finally, as an identity the loyalties of citizenship are not confined to loyalty to the nation-state but take cosmopolitan forms, as in multicultural identities and loyalties shaped by concerns with global justice.

CONCLUSION

In view of arguments made in this chapter the limits of patriotism should be apparent. The nation-state is both too big and too small for citizenship. It is too big in that much of the actual practice of citizenship takes place on the local level rather than on the national level. National parliaments are generally felt by citizens to be remote and unconnected with local issues. On the other side, the nation-state is too small in that it is often felt to be inadequate when it comes to dealing with global challenges. However, it would be wrong to say that the state is no longer relevant and that all political problems can be addressed on the local or the global levels. The state is still vital to democracy, and the failure of the state results in the collapse of civil society, as the examples of Rwanda, Bosnia, and Kosovo illustrate. The argument advanced in this chapter is that citizenship operates on all levels, the local/national and the global, and for this reason it is meaningful to speak in terms of cosmopolitan citizenship. But it is also more than an expression of multileveled governance.

Returning to a point made at the outset, the move toward cosmopolitan citizenship can be characterized in terms of a shift from a notion of citizenship determined by peoplehood to one based on personhood. The collective struggles and global solidarities that characterize much of the political landscape of democratic politics around issues of global solidarity and social justice are all based on the individual person rather than the collectivity. Cosmopolitanism is also pertinent to the new cultural expressions of citizenship around issues of the environment, consumption, technology, and corporate responsibility.

The cosmopolitan turn in citizenship represents an important subject for public sociology; it draws attention to the existence of social relations that are not primarily shaped by the nation-state. One of the main contributions such a sociology can make is to examine the impact of global developments on the lives of individuals. Citizenship is a highly pertinent category to address such issues. It has been the aim of this chapter to outline some of the ways citizenship has undergone major transformation in recent times as a result of changed local–global links. The present situation as far as citizenship is concerned is very different from the contained world T. H. Marshall described in 1950: citizenship has ceased to be an instrument of social control and has become a site of social struggles and political contestation.

REFERENCES

Appiah, Kenneth. 2005. *The Ethics of Identity*. Princeton, N.J.: Princeton University Press.

Beck, Ulrich. 2005. *The Cosmopolitan Vision*. Cambridge: Polity Press.

Benhabib, Seyla. 2002. *The Claims of Culture: Equality and Diversity in the Global Era*. Princeton, N.J.: Princeton University Press.

Breckenridge, Carol A., et al. (eds.). 2002. *Cosmopolitanism*. Durham, N.C.: Duke University Press.

Calhoun, Craig. 2003. "'Belonging' in the Cosmopolitan Imaginary." *Ethnicities* 3(4): 531–53.

Cheah, Pheng, and Bruce Robbins (eds.). 1998. *Cosmopolitics: Thinking and Feeling Beyond the Nation*. Minneapolis: Minnesota University Press.

Cohen, Joshua (ed.). 1996. *For Love of Country: Debating the Limits of Patriotism*. Chicago: University of Chicago Press.

Cowan, Jane K., Marie-Bénédicte Dembour, and Richard A. Wilson (eds.). 2001. *Culture and Rights: Anthropological Perspective*. Cambridge: Cambridge University Press.

Delanty, Gerard. 2001. *Challenging Knowledge*. Buckingham, UK: Open University Press.

Guttman, Amy. 2003. *Identity in Democracy*. Princeton, N.J.: Princeton University Press.

Habermas, Jürgen. 1998. *The Inclusion of the Other: Studies in Political Theory*. Cambridge, Mass.: MIT Press.

———. 1996. *Between Facts and Norms: Contributions to a Discourse Theory of Law and Democracy*. Cambridge: Polity Press.

Herrmann, Richard, Thomas Risse, and Marilynn Brewer (eds.). 2004. *Transnational Identities: Becoming European in the EU*. Lanham, Md.: Rowman & Littlefield.

Isin, Egin. 2002. *Being Political: Genealogies of Citizenship*. Minneapolis: University of Minnesota Press.

Jacobson, David. 1996. *Rights across Borders: Immigration and the Decline of Citizenship*. Baltimore, Md.: Johns Hopkins University Press.

Kaldor, Mary. 2003. *Global Civil Society: An Answer to War*. Cambridge: Polity Press.

Keane, John. 2003. *Global Civil Society: Old Images, New Visions*. Cambridge: Polity Press.

Kurasawa, Fukuyi. 2004. "Cosmopolitanism from Below: Alternative Globalization and the Creation of a Solidarity without Bounds." *European Journal of Sociology* XLV(2): 233–55.

Kymlicka, Will. 1995. *Multicultural Citizenship*. Oxford: Oxford University Press.

Sorensen, Georg. 2004. *The Transformation of the State*. London: Palgrave.

Stevenson, Nick. 2002. *Cultural Citizenship: Cosmopolitan Questions*. Buckingham, UK: Open University Press.

Strange, Susan. 1996. *The Retreat of the State. The Diffusion of Power in the World Economy*. Cambridge: Cambridge University Press.

4

The Struggle for Global Society in a World System

Jackie Smith

Former American Sociological Association president Michael Burawoy argued that sociologists have a responsibility to help "represent humanity's interest in containing the unbridled tyranny of market and state." In an increasingly integrated world economic system, this is especially important, since the globalization of capital has generated unprecedented concentrations of wealth alongside persistent inequalities within and among states. We need sociological theory that integrates our understandings of global structures with concrete ideas to guide efforts for social change. This chapter argues that sociologists and other social scientists can more effectively redress rising global inequalities if they become actively engaged in asking questions about how, given the material conditions society faces, we might help *empower* global civil society as an agent for change in the world system. This requires steps to both cultivate a global society characterized by a human rights culture and to enhance the skills and capacities people and communities have for engaging in politics at local, national, and international levels. This will require that we actively confront and work to dismantle the structures that exclude more and more people from economic and social life while cultivating new spaces for democratic participation in today's world system (this idea builds upon Bello's [2003] notion of "deregulation").

As capitalism strengthens its global reach, this increases the need for international institutions with real deliberative and enforcement capacities if civil society is to thrive. It cannot thrive in the current system described earlier by William Robinson, where the United Nations is subordinated to the transna-

tional state—namely, the global economic institutions, rich country governments, and capitalist forces that shape these. Sociologists have particular
skills to contribute to these efforts. They are trained to understand connections between social and economic structures and individual biographies.
They know how culture and institutions operate to shape the thinking and
actions of large groups. They also have access to a wealth of research on how
organizations work and on the interaction of structure and agency over time.
They are researchers and teachers. These are all important tools for the construction of the sort of active, global human rights culture that is essential to
democracy at local, national, and global levels. In this chapter I consider
some possibilities for improving connections between the work of sociologists and the needs of the social movements for global justice.

It is clear that we need more concerted efforts to resist the institutions and
political arrangements that help sustain current inequalities. And as my conversations with scholars from around the world show, these struggles are
increasingly taking place on our own campuses. At the most recent World
Social Forum, participants in workshops aimed at launching a new International Network of Scholar Activists identified three major areas where
scholar-activists were particularly active, and these insights should help others consider how their local activities might link to a broader, global web
of struggle. First, scholar-activists have been involved in resisting neoliberal
economic policies on campuses. They have done so by, for instance, fighting
cuts in public funding for education, supporting living wage campaigns for
campus workers, and defending access to public spaces on campus. While
many of these issues can seem very local, our analysis of global economic
processes as well as the fact that we see such similarities on campuses around
this country and internationally shows that the sources of our problems are
global. Second, they were resisting the enclosure of the knowledge commons
by using direct action tactics and by promoting open source methodologies
to encourage information sharing. They also are working to raise awareness
of how global trade agreements affect access to information around the
world. Third, they were working to support civil society through their teaching, research, and community activities. Below I outline a framework for
thinking about how each of these tasks fits within the broader struggle for
global justice.

FRAMING THE STRUGGLE

In my research on transnational global justice activism I have found it helpful
to conceptualize this struggle as one between two "rival transnational net-

works" (see Maney, 2001). On one side we have the transnational capitalist class and its various national and transnational agents (including what Robinson calls the transnational state) working together with varying degrees of unity to promote a global order that favors the profit-seeking interests of capital. On the other side is what we might call the democratic globalization network, which seeks to promote a vision of global integration that emphasizes the expanding realization of human rights over all other aims. Democratic globalization proponents (and most sociologists) would argue that, while economic growth might indeed contribute to improved human rights practices (as neoliberals claim), it does not do so automatically, and it will not do so in the absence of truly democratic government. More importantly, neoliberal policies are not necessarily the best route to economic growth, and in some cases have been counterproductive. Thus, policy makers must consciously emphasize human rights objectives over others if they wish to improve the human condition. This democratic globalization network consists of a much more diverse array of individuals, organizations, and government officials and agencies that work to promote alternatives to global capitalism in various ways. Actors in the network will vary tremendously in how much attention and energy they devote to social change goals. Like the capitalist network, this network will vary over time and place in how unified and coherent it is. A strong challenge to global capitalism, however, requires a much more unified and cohesive network of democratic globalization proponents.

The network concept helps us capture both the fluid nature of contemporary transnational organizing and the variation in the kinds of actors that are involved in attempts to promote one rival vision or another. It also sensitizes us to how actions by opponents affect the possibilities for movements and vice versa. We might sharpen our discussions of global capitalism and of resistance to it by considering how network processes operate to affect power relations and institutional practices. For instance, work by Sklair (2001) and Robinson (2004) on the transnational capitalist class provides insights into how the global neoliberal network exerts influence as well as where its vulnerabilities lie. We should seek to build upon this work to identify strategic opportunities to exploit divisions within this network and challenge global networking among capitalists and politicians. Similarly, we might use network theories to expand our insights into how strong collaborative ties can be built across very diverse social groups. It is to this latter question that I address the remainder of the chapter.

The network concept captures a wide range of actors and actions that are oriented toward a particular social change objective. An important contribution of the network idea is that rather than treating social movements as phenomena that are distinct from "normal" politics, it places what we

traditionally define as "protest politics" along a continuum of political participation that ranges from the least risky and costly (e.g., engaging in political
conversations, voting) to the most (staging violent revolution). Those of us
who have been involved in them know that social movements are collections
of individuals and organizations engaged in various forms of collective action
to promote social change. While scholarly writing generally emphasizes mass
demonstrations and other "unconventional" forms of political action, in practice many movements involve political action that ranges from voting to lobbying to civil disobedience. Networks help link those groups most closely
connected to government and policy networks with those engaged in "outsider" strategies to educate and mobilize a broad base and to press for more
radical changes. Such connections enable movements to use a division of
labor (often an unconscious one) to take advantage of institutional openings
while cultivating and responding to needs of local constituencies.

The rival networks framework helps sensitize analysts to the centrality of
alliance building to social change efforts. Because—by definition—social
movements are relatively weak, to have much political impact, they must
mobilize allies from other sectors of society. In fact, the mobilization of powerful networks of actors is probably equally if not more crucial in any framing
struggle as the mobilization of ideas, as messages are more likely to find
receptive ears among those with whom we have some familiarity and trust.
Also, the nature of the modern state means that allies can often be found
in government bureaucracies, among the many people whose work involves
actually solving some technical problem or relating to a very particular con-
stituency (McCarthy and Wolfson, 1992). Movements can bring information
and analyses to practical problems that government agents must address, and
they can also help generate a popular base for an agency or official, offering
officials a justification for agency budgets as well as a layer of protection
from bureaucratic infighting. This is true both within countries as well as in
global institutions (Keck and Sikkink, 1998; Smith, Pagnucco, and Chatfield,
1997). Successful movements are those that can cultivate allies within government agencies, the mass media, churches, and other groups in society,
including colleges and universities. When movement allies are found in
places where they can influence the views of elites or the operations of the
policy process, as well as the views of the wider public, this helps advance
social change goals (Lipsky, 1968).

Networks that link people and groups with movement ideas, moreover, can
neutralize the impact of rival networks. For instance, by reaching out to
schools and churches, anti-sweatshop campaigners can help a wider range of
consumers become more wary of corporate marketing strategies that make
misleading claims about a company's labor practices. Fair trade and

community-supported agriculture activists, for their part, plant the seeds of suspicion that capitalism might not be the only logical economic system by demonstrating how economic practices might be reorganized. And "guerilla gardeners," "critical mass"/"reclaim the streets" activists, and other "culture jammers" encourage people to question widely held assumptions and practices and their negative social impacts.

Maney's research (2001) shows that successful challenges are those where social change advocates manage to effectively *mobilize resources* for their cause, take advantage of *favorable political opportunities*, and create *positive relational dynamics* within the network. While movements themselves cannot completely control the relative balance of resources and opportunities available to their particular network, thinking about the struggle in this way helps them map out the possibilities for both expanding their own advantages while also minimizing advantages of rivals.

Sociologists and other social scientists can contribute to the struggle for a more equitable and just global order by working to help this "democratic globalization network" mobilize resources—including participants, ideas, and access to information. They can also play key roles to help identify favorable political opportunities and strategies for taking advantage of these. Finally, they also may be particularly crucial as brokers that can foster positive relational dynamics in the network while expanding its boundaries. In a recent symposium in *Social Problems*, Michael Burawoy and a group of prominent public sociologists at Boston College summarized various ways they have engaged in this kind of bridge building and boundary expansion (albeit mostly at local and national levels), and their experiences and observations should serve as a useful guide to future work in this area (Burawoy et al., 2004).

The network idea, in short, can help bring our thinking and writing about social movements into the mainstream of social life. If we are to identify ways of changing the world into one that is more equitable, sustainable, and peaceful, we must find ways to reach people in their everyday routines. Network structures are capable of expanding and permeating boundaries, and even individual scholar-activists may feel confused or inhibited from actively engaging in social change work if they feel they must join a particular organization or engage in civil disobedience. If we think of how the particular kind of work we do might contribute to broader network dynamics, we can find new and possibly innovative ways to contribute to social movements. Moreover, as social analysts, we can help social movement actors better understand both the broader social network structures in which they are embedded and the various possibilities these offer for advancing social change agendas.

MOBILIZING NETWORK RESOURCES

As many conservative think tanks and pundits have pointed out, universities are settings where critical thinking about global processes is nurtured. Universities have been shaped in important ways by social movements, and indeed the emergence of programs devoted to cross-disciplinary studies such as gender studies, peace studies, black studies, and even global or development studies emerged at least in part from the critiques of social relations articulated by social movements of the 1960s (Rochon, 1998). Universities are in many ways crucial spaces that help nurture the development of what Rochon calls "critical communities." Critical communities are supportive social settings and networks in which critical ideas about the state of social affairs and ideas about alternatives can evolve and spread. They serve as incubators for social critiques and prescriptions for change, helping create ideological resources and networks that support broader social movements. We should not be surprised, then, that conservative politicians and activists have sought to curb academic freedom and chill political discourse on campuses in the United States as well as to limit public funding for higher education.

While the political climate in the United States in recent years has limited some of the more overt political engagement on campuses, scholars can and must continue to work to reclaim the universities as free spaces whose openness to political inquiry and debate are defended as essential elements of a democratic society as well as a productive economy. Understanding our role in shaping critical communities in the places where we work is essential to helping foster new generations of people capable of analyzing political situations and generating creative responses to complex social problems. The role of critical communities may be particularly important within a global context, since these communities help "[create] a map of the social and political world. Movement mobilization occurs when large numbers of people are able to locate themselves on that map" (Rochon, 1998: 161). The remoteness of global institutions, coupled with highly inadequate education and media reporting on these institutions (especially in the United States), mean that more work must be done to create spaces where people can learn about the global political system and their place in it.

Public intellectuals can also contribute resources to the democratic globalization network through their own research, writing, and speaking on questions relevant to struggles against global inequalities. Our intellectual contributions can help expand the reach of the network to new groups. While many of us have plenty of incentives to focus on the research and writing, perhaps fewer of us consider disseminating the results of our research through popular writing or public speaking. Even fewer consider public speaking engagements that are truly public, rather than to audiences of other academics. High schools, retirement communities, and community groups of all kinds are often eager to bring people together to learn about contemporary issues. While it does take some effort to figure out how to organize these kinds of events and to speak in a way that engages these audiences, this can be rewarding in many ways.

Scholars can also contribute to the resources of the network by helping expand free and public access to information. This might simply involve working more consciously to help our students learn about events, problems, and viewpoints left out of mainstream media discourse. I was surprised to learn that my students believed they could be arrested just for attending a global justice march in New York City (even as student "observers"). Upon reflection, though, I realized that their understanding is shaped by mainstream media coverage of these events that focuses on violent confrontations with police and mass arrests. Few in their social networks are likely to point out contradictions between these images and Americans' legal rights to free speech and assembly. The classroom is a space where people should learn about the rights and responsibilities of citizens, and where they should learn about important debates of the day. Too often we think of our role as preparing students to join the workforce. But our more important role is to prepare them to be active and engaged citizens. This is in fact the principal goal of many liberal arts programs/institutions, although this mission has been overshadowed in many cases by an emphasis on training students for a globally competitive labor market. When it is appropriate to our courses, we should present critical and impartial information about protest movements of the day and their relevance to broader political processes and debates.

Another way scholars can help expand movements' access to resources is to resist the growing commodification of knowledge. As I mentioned above, scholar-activists engaged in discussions at recent World and Regional Social Forums emphasized the importance of and techniques for supporting a global "knowledge commons" that would protect the rights of all peoples to information. This concept rests on the observation that in an information society, we must maintain free access to information or we will very quickly exacerbate existing inequalities. There is growing support for a "copy-left" movement to create an alternative to traditional copyright processes while also advancing direct action to undermine corporate attempts to enclose, or privatize, the knowledge commons. While we may feel little impact from this at our North American universities, our international counterparts report serious handicaps they face in their research and teaching because of limited access to copyrighted information. The newly emerging International Network of Scholar Activists (www.inosa.org) is working to coordinate and expand international efforts to democratize access to the information resources that are essential to survival in today's economy. (If you're intrigued by the possibilities of electronic communication technologies and find "hacktivism" appealing, you'll be particularly inspired by this creative group.) Sociologists are urged to join this effort as they also work to make their own published work freely available under fair use policies promoted by copy-left.

POLITICAL OPPORTUNITIES

Scholars can contribute to the efforts of the democratic globalization network to understand and assess the complex political context in which it operates. In an increasingly integrated global political economy, policy is affected not only by national-level processes, but by an increasingly complex array of transnational ones. Public intellectuals can help demystify global politics by explaining the links between national and global-level politics and by offering analyses of how to advance particular campaigns within this multilevel polity. Many organizers are quite capable of analyzing local and national political contexts, but they have more difficulty seeing how their struggle might be advanced by making connections to transnational politics. They also are likely to be overwhelmed by the range of issues and organizations working beyond their local communities. Indeed, in a survey of participants in a transnational environmental group, I found that one of the main barriers to local groups' participation in global campaigns was their difficulty in relating local issues to global processes. Public intellectuals can help people develop the skills they need to make such connections.

Looking back, we might ask whether the struggle for racial equality in the United States would have gone further than it did if it was framed as a human rights rather than a civil rights struggle. Many early civil rights activists embraced the Universal Declaration of Human Rights as an organizing tool. But as a recent Ford Foundation report details, Cold War politics led these efforts to be cast as subversive and even treasonous, with lasting consequences. The report goes on to observe that "this brand of cold war politics sought not only to discourage U.S. activists from invoking human rights in their domestic work, but also to distort the very meaning of human rights for Americans by eliminating its economic and social dimensions" (Ford Foundation, 2004: 8). Similarly, one wonders whether the U.S. women's movement efforts to defend women's right to reproductive choice could have been more effective if they were oriented toward establishing and defending such rights on a global rather than national scale, such as at UN conferences on women's rights. While the U.S. government has refused to recognize women's reproductive health as a human rights issue, its interest in promoting an image of itself as a human rights leader makes it vulnerable to pressure in this regard. And while mainstream women's groups have not mobilized their base around this, conservative groups have secured U.S. aid policies that deny reproductive health assistance (including access to condoms) for countless women around the world. Moreover, a global standard would reduce the chances that recognition of reproductive rights could be denied by state and national courts. These illustrations suggest the wide-ranging implications of the strategic choices of movements about the level of government at which to engage a struggle. We need more systematic analyses of the opportunities and pitfalls of engaging transnational processes as well as of limiting conflict to national contexts.

Public intellectuals can contribute their training in political and institutional analysis to helping make a case for movements to "go global," but they also should be willing to stick around to help hammer out the details of what that actually means on the ground. Knowing the rules of the game does not make one certain of how best to advance a particular policy initiative, but movements can benefit from having skilled, attentive, and especially trusted political advisors throughout the course of campaigns (see Kleidman, 2004). Moreover, given the strong opposition to many claims for equity, we need clever strategic thinking that can only emerge from engaged scholarship. Being active in groups working to promote policy changes can help analysts to understand how policy processes play out "on the ground," while enabling them to gain insights into the strategic possibilities of movements.

POSITIVE RELATIONAL DYNAMICS

The rival networks model sensitizes analysts and activists to the centrality of network-building efforts to the course of struggle. Often social movement activists focus their energies outward, thinking about how best to reach their targets. Less thought is given to how to cultivate the social bonds of trust and solidarity that can help activists work together for the long haul. But as history tells us, without conscious efforts to foster positive relations among actual and potential allies, network participants can turn their struggles inward rather than outward, toward the collective struggle. Networks require conscious efforts to manage or coordinate the activities of widely varying network members with highly unequal capacities and political access. This task is likely to be far easier for the more ideologically unified and more centralized neoliberal network than it is for the very heterogeneous and less ideologically cohesive democratic globalization network. But the current surge in transnational global justice activism enhances possibilities for strengthening the ties among a very diverse collection of actors promoting different, if complementary, visions of a global order.

Democratic globalization proponents are faced with the added challenge of mobilizing adherents who are—whether by choice or by fate—at least materially dependent upon if not committed to the capitalist mode of production that is promoted by the rival neoliberal network (see chapter 2, by Robinson). To win new allies, the network must demonstrate how people's long-term interests are best met with a fundamentally different approach to politics and economics even where one's short-term survival requires a paycheck. Ideally, movements can and should develop their own labor markets that enable people to work outside of capitalist modes of production and exchange. Public intellectuals can help legitimize and spread awareness of these alternatives. As the limitations of capitalism become increasingly evident in environmental degradation and rising inequalities, it may become easier to convey this message.

Public intellectuals can play important roles in helping to link diverse networks of people who might be sympathetic with the aims of creating an alternative to globalized capitalism. The professional activities in which these individuals are involved are more likely to give them access to information and experiences that extend beyond their local community origins. Students and scholars tend to leave their local communities in search of knowledge and experiences, and this nurtures a spirit of inquiry that makes them open to new and different experiences and ideas. We are trained to empathize with people from very different cultural, political, and experiential contexts. This, coupled with analytical training, helps us articulate broadly shared visions for social change and allows us to understand the differences and commonalities across different local cultures and sectoral groupings. I don't want to suggest that formal training is a necessary criterion for defining intellectual leadership in social movements; some leaders develop these skills without such training. But certainly the tools required for scientific inquiry can be helpful in the process of integrating and assimilating diverse ideas and experiences into a coherent collective vision (Baud and Rutten, 2005).

Scholars also may have privileged access to national and international officials, enabling them to serve as liaisons between government officials and movements. Even in the United States, characterized by a strong anti-intellectual tradition and a particularly hostile Bush regime, local officials and members of more technically oriented agencies often seek allies from the ranks of intellectuals to help them do their jobs. And we might learn from our international counterparts how to expand our inroads in government agencies or at least to cultivate a more open and inquisitive cultural climate.

Thus, we are particularly well positioned to serve as *brokers* between different groups, making us potentially important players in processes of coalition building that are central to any social movement, particularly transnational ones (see, e.g., Rutten and Baud, 2005; Tarrow, 2005). For instance, in their review of research on social movement leadership, Morris and Staggenborg (2004) note that high levels of education are common among movement leadership. They conclude from their overview that "teams of diverse leaders anchored in authoritative organizational structures that are conducive to open and critical debate and challenging deliberations are more likely to succeed because of the creativity and innovation such leaders generate as they execute leadership activities" (190).

Creating positive network dynamics requires leadership. And analyses of the role of popular intellectuals show that they tend to be leaders in the movements within which they work (see, e.g., contributions in Baud and Rutten, 2005). Again, this is not to say that it is only formally trained intellectuals who serve in such roles, but that the experience and training of intellectuals makes them well suited to fill this particular need within movements. Specifically, analyses of how leaders helped foster positive dynamics among diverse movement participants identified their role as translators, educators, innovators, and conflict managers (see, e.g., case studies in Baud and Rutten, 2005; Bandy and Smith, 2005). Organizations such as Project South and Global Exchange are just two examples of spaces where people with professional academic training are actively working to build popular knowledge and skills while also shaping broader movement campaigns. And scholars with backgrounds in conflict resolution and facilitation are vital resources for many movement groups.

Effective leaders helped translate between different constituencies, sometimes literally but often figuratively. Translation involves helping diverse groups better understand and appreciate the perspectives and needs of other network members, fostering empathy and a commitment to unity despite diversity. To do this, the translator must gain the trust of all relevant groups, something that generally requires that s/he demonstrate a commitment to the cause by showing up consistently and contributing to the collective effort in various ways.

Effective leaders are also good educators. They help participants of differing abilities understand complex political realities and the various circumstances and perspectives of diverse movement allies. Ideally they develop skills at training activists with less formal education to be "intellectuals" (Rutten and Baud, 2005) who will go on to lead and contribute to the expansion of the network. They are also innovators, generating and disseminating new ideas and analyses of the problems the movement faces and their possible solutions.

Finally, good leaders are able to bring together the abilities to translate, educate, and innovate to act as conflict managers. Conflict managers must be able to anticipate lines of (inevitable) division among different groups and help head off destructive forms of conflict escalation. Sensitivity to the often very subtle manifestations of power inequities is a particularly important trait for leaders in the democratic globalization movement. They know when to bring groups together for dialogue, and they know when steps at de-escalation are needed. They can prepare groups in advance to avoid destructive conflict dynamics, and they can bring a broad perspective that might offer new insights into resolving differences without compromising vital interests of any group (on conflict resolution within transnational coalitions see Snyder, 2003; Starhawk, 2002: part 2; Wood, 2005; Cullen, 2005).

Beyond these tasks, public intellectuals can contribute to the democratic globalization struggle by working to foster more broadly the cultural values and identities that contribute to positive network dynamics. Essentially these values are ones that should be at the core of all democracies, namely tolerance of diversity, respect, equality, and a commitment to compromise and to nonviolent conflict resolution. Donatella della Porta and her colleagues have observed this sort of culture emerging from settings of global justice activism. Their research at regional and local social forums has revealed among movement participants a sense of "flexible identities" and "multiple belongings" (della Porta, 2005). In the United States and elsewhere, political parties, mass media, and other formal institutions of democracy have largely failed in their duty to help socialize citizens into the values and practices that are essential to healthy democratic societies, contributing to declining political participation in these countries. The failure to inculcate values of tolerance and respect within nominally democratic polities makes more likely the rise of nationalism and other separatist causes seeking to advance the interests of particular ethnic or cultural groups to the exclusion of the interests and well-being of others (UNDP, 2004). The social forums might serve as models for expanding spaces for learning and practicing participatory democracy. And public intellectuals can help disseminate this model as well as help communicate about the linkages between local and global, between interdependence and democracy, and between politics and economics.

By working more self-consciously to help people appreciate how global interdependence creates multiple layers of social responsibility and belonging, public intellectuals can help nurture more inclusive and democratic cultural practices. Encouraging people to adopt "flexible identities" reduces the appeal of politicians who would mobilize people around nationalistic and other exclusive identity groupings. Creating a sense of "multiple belongings" can foster commitment to a global community that actually accentuates people's appreciation for the unique features of their and other local and national communities. Such appreciation can help people find new ways to link the struggles of diverse groups, and it can also help them see possibilities for working in ways that complement others in the network.

NURTURING A GLOBAL SOCIETY WITHIN THE WORLD SYSTEM

If our analysis of the contemporary global situation leads us to conclude that there is an urgent need for major social transformation, then how can we as individuals and as sociologists be part of a broader process of change? The framework outlined above advocates a focus on strengthening the transnational network of actors working to promote alternatives to economic/corporate-led globalization (see, e.g., Waterman and Timms, 2004). We might view such work as helping to build a global society within the world system. I summarize some more general ideas about contributions sociologists might make to this larger project.

First, a global society, as opposed to a world system, emphasizes common values, identities, and institutions that connect people across more traditional national boundaries. *World system*, on the other hand, refers to a global capitalist project that has for centuries glorified the individual and treated the world as a giant, if not endless, source of raw materials and markets. Rather than community and solidarity, the world system is guided by principles of profit maximization and competition. Reorienting the world system means confronting the incompatibilities between a sustainable global society and world system. It requires engaging people in thoughtful dialogue about what their preferred world might look like, and how we might get there. It means helping people to imagine themselves as part of a community that transcends their national context. Indeed, if we all must share one finite planet, it is imperative that we learn to think more collectively about how to manage it wisely.

Sociologists have many opportunities to help students and community members expand their notions of community, and we should encourage those we work with to think in global terms, to see themselves as global citizens. If nation-states are only "imagined communities," (Anderson, 1991) then certainly we can expand the boundaries to consider a global imagined (i.e., human) community that might correspond better with the ecological and social realities we face. This identity work is being done in transnational social movements, and as sociologists we can surely contribute to this important intellectual task of fostering notions of a "global we" either directly, through participation in movements, or indirectly through our teaching and research.

As teachers we can structure a variety of opportunities for students to consider themselves as part of a global context. Whether we ask students to consider their role in global commodity chains, expose them to foreign cultures and ideas, or invite them to submit proposals to their own campus "social forum," we help them appreciate how they are part of an interdependent and complementary global community. We also can challenge them to be more proactive, critical, creative, and engaged global and national citizens. Encouraging curiosity about the world while helping provide basic road maps or frameworks that can help students make sense of it can help nurture global citizens and move us toward the type of global community we might imagine.

As researchers, we can expand our own perspectives by rethinking some of our research questions to ask if we would be framing them in similar ways if we were sitting in another part of the world. We might make connections to scholars from other parts of the world so that we can learn more about the similarities and differences in our respective work and life environments. We might join groups that bring us into contact with international scholars for either professional reasons or for the purpose of advocating for political change. These exchanges can only make us better sociologists, as they sensitize us to some of our own blind spots.

Another contribution sociologists and other social scientists can make is by offering analyses of how our political institutions (national and international) might generate more humane and just outcomes. Research in sociology has told us much about the dysfunctions of institutions and about the possibilities for organizational change. What does it tell us about how national and international institutions might be reshaped so that they are more responsive, democratic, and/or effective? More prescription-oriented analyses are needed, especially those that bring sociological insights to our knowledge of global institutions.

A particular concern of mine is that global institutions appear to be closing rather than opening spaces for participation from civil society. This comes at a time when civil society's vitality and creativity is most needed to overcome U.S. unilateralism as well as to help the global community confront pressing problems. One must also worry about what will happen as citizens mobilized around calls for global justice are told that they cannot be part of the decisions being made in Geneva or New York. Where will their energy and momentum go? We need to encourage more creative thinking and dialogue about what sort of institutional arrangements would facilitate more democratic input and accountability at the global level. Without it, we will watch as global institutions have more power over more issues while having less and less legitimacy in the eyes of an increasingly attentive global public.

Finally, this book emphasizes human rights as essential to the work of public sociology. And in parts of this chapter I have referred to the idea of a human rights culture, which many would see as a logical foundation for global society. Indeed, the Universal Declaration of Human Rights is a globally recognized set of ideals that people everywhere have come to embrace (even if their governments have not). United Nations officials and even member governments refer to the Universal Declaration to bolster the appearance of democratic legitimacy within the global system. Without people mobilized to make claims for the rights laid out in the Universal Declaration, the words themselves are meaningless, and our system remains illegitimate.

A human rights culture is also vital to efforts to curb mass violence and terrorism. We now have a wealth of studies of truth commissions designed to help societies experiencing mass violence and genocide heal. Virtually all of these truth commissions incorporate some civil society component, and fostering broad understandings of and appreciation for human rights principles (i.e., building a human rights culture) is an important part of what civil society contributes to these efforts (Borer, forthcoming). If an engaged civil society and human rights culture are important to helping violence-torn societies heal, they are also essential to preventing mass violence in the first place. And if our aim in studying society is to learn what makes societies most healthy and productive for their members, we might take these two lessons to heart and actively promote ideas for enhancing democracy in the UN and other international, as well as local and national, bodies.

CONCLUSION

In short, what I'd like to leave readers with is the idea that intellectual workers have important contributions to make to efforts to promote greater equity and justice in our world. The first set of tasks contributes to people's understandings of global interdependencies and the operations of global political and economic institutions. Our analytical skills and informational resources can help those working for social change better navigate the complex environment in which they must operate. We can contribute to efforts to develop political strategies that are appropriate for our multilevel global polity. The second set of tasks focuses on helping groups develop lasting coalitions. Coalition work is essentially democracy work, as the values that help sustain voluntary alliances are the same ones that help bind diverse groups within a common democratic polity. Teachers, scholars, and political activists should work to be more self-conscious about their role in helping nurture democratic values, skills, and practices. Any work that contributes to a global human rights culture is a step in the direction of a more equitable and just global system.

Organizers with the People's Movement for Human Rights Education claim that "democracy is a human rights delivery system." (See www.pdh-re.org. The PDHRE website is an excellent resource for details and analyses of major international human rights agreements, organized according to topic.) Indeed, those concerned with advancing human rights over the long term must work to insure that people have the opportunity and capacity to claim and defend their own rights. This is true both within particular countries as well as globally. Given this perspective, we should worry about the question of how human rights will fare within a global political order that is seriously lacking in democratic participation and accountability. Efforts to reform global institutions so that they reflect greater interstate democracy as well as greater popular participation and accountability are the only way to achieve a more just and less violent world. This conclusion resonates with Mary Robinson's message to the 2004 meeting of the American Sociological Association. She urged sociologists to educate ourselves and our students about the Universal Declaration of Human Rights and about UN programs such as the Millennium Development Goals, both of which—to be realized—require popular pressure to hold governments to their international commitments. Whether our research and teaching is local or global, we can certainly find ways to integrate ideas about the connections between these. How well we do this will determine whether a global society might eventually overtake the world system.

ACKNOWLEDGMENTS

I am grateful to Neil McLaughlin for his contributions to my thinking on public sociology, to Judith Blau for the opportunity to write on this topic, and to Diane Barthel-Bouchier for her encouragement. Support for travel related to this research was provided by the Office of the Vice President of Research and the Dean of Arts and Sciences at the State University of New York at Stony Brook.

REFERENCES

Anderson, Benedict. 1991. *Imagined Communities: Reflections on the Origin and Spread of Nationalism*. London: Verso.

Bandy, Joe, and Jackie Smith. 2005. "Factors Affecting Conflict and Cooperation in Transnational Movement Networks." In *Coalitions across Borders: Transnational Protest in a Neoliberal Era*, ed. J. Bandy and J. Smith, 231–51. Lanham, Md.: Rowman & Littlefield.

Baud, Michiel, and Rosanne Rutten (eds.). 2005. *Popular Intellectuals and Social Movements: Framing Protest in Asia, Africa, and Latin America*. New York: Cambridge University Press.

Bello, Walden. 2003. *Deglobalization: New Ideas for Running the World Economy*. London: Zed Books.

Borer, Tristan Anne (ed.). Forthcoming. *Telling the Truth: Truth Telling and Peace Building in Post-Conflict Societies*. Notre Dame, Ind.: University of Notre Dame Press.

Burawoy, Michael, William Gamson, Charlotte Ryan, Stephen Phol, Diane Vaughan, Charles Derber, and Juliet Schor. 2004. "Public Sociologies: A Symposium from Boston College." *Social Problems* 51:103–30.

Cullen, Pauline. 2005. "Obstacles to Transnational Cooperation in the European Social Policy Platform." In *Coalitions across Borders: Transnational Protest in a Neoliberal Era*, ed. J. Bandy and J. Smith, 71–94. Lanham, Md.: Rowman & Littlefield.

della Porta, Donatella. 2005. "Making the Polis: Social Forums and Democracy in the Global Justice Movement." *Mobilization* 10: 73–94.

Ford Foundation. 2004. "Close to Home: Case Studies of Human Rights Work in the United States." At www.fordfound.org (accessed January 18, 2005).

Keck, Margaret, and Kathryn Sikkink. 1998. *Activists beyond Borders*. Ithaca, N.Y.: Cornell University Press.

Kleidman, Robert. 2004. "Community Organization as Engaged Scholarship." *ASA Footnotes* (May/June issue). At www.asanet.org/footnotes/mayjun04/fn10.html (accessed July 7, 2005).

Lipsky, Michael. 1968. "Protest as a Political Resource." *American Political Science Review* 62: 1144–58.

Maney, Gregory M. 2001. "Rival Transnational Networks and Indigenous Rights: The San Blas Kuna in Panama and the Yanomami in Brazil." *Research in Social Movements, Conflicts and Change* 23: 103–44.

McCarthy, John D., and Mark Wolfson. 1992. "Consensus Movements, Conflict Movements, and the Cooptation of Civic and State Infrastructures." In *Frontiers in Social Movement Theory*, ed. A. Morris and C. M. Mueller, 273–300. New Haven, Conn.: Yale University Press.

Morris, Aldon D., and Suzanne Staggenborg. 2004. "Leadership in Social Movements." In *The Blackwell Companion to Social Movements*, ed. D. A. Snow, S. A. Soule, and H. Kriesi, 171–96. Oxford: Blackwell.

Robinson, William. 2004. *A Theory of Global Capitalism*. Baltimore, Md.: Johns Hopkins University Press.

Rochon, Thomas. 1998. *Culture Moves: Ideas, Activism, and Changing Values*. Princeton, N.J.: Princeton University Press.

Rutten, Rosanne, and Michael Baud. 2005. "Concluding Remarks: Framing Protest in Asia, Africa, and Latin America." In *Popular Intellectuals and Social Movements: Framing Protest in Asia, Africa, and Latin America*, ed. M. Baud and R. Rutten, 197–217. New York: Cambridge University Press.

Sklair, Leslie. 2001. *The Transnational Capitalist Class*. Cambridge: Blackwell.

Smith, Jackie, Ron Pagnucco, and Charles Chatfield. 1997. "Transnational Social Movements and Global Politics: A Theoretical Framework." In *Transnational Social Movements and Global Politics: Solidarity beyond the State*, ed. J. Smith, C. Chatfield, and R. Pagnucco, 59–80. Syracuse, N.Y.: Syracuse University Press.

Snyder, Anna. 2003. *Setting the Agenda for Global Peace: Conflict and Consensus Building*. Burlington, Vt.: Ashgate.

Starhawk. 2002. *Webs of Power: Notes from the Global Uprising*. Gabriola Island, BC: New Society Publishers.

Tarrow, Sidney. 2005. *The New Transnational Activism: Movements, States, and International Institutions*. New York: Cambridge University Press.

UNDP. 2004. *Human Development Report 2004*. New York: Oxford.

Waterman, Peter, and Jill Timms. 2004. "Trade Union Internationalism and a Global Civil Society in the Making." In *Global Civil Society 2004/5*, 175–202. London: Sage.

Wood, Leslie. 2005. "Bridging the Chasms: The Case of People's Global Action." In *Coalitions across Borders: Negotiating Difference and Unity in Transnational Coalitions against Neoliberalism*, ed. J. Bandy and J. Smith, 95-119. Lanham, Md.: Rowman & Littlefield.

5

A Movement Rising: Consciousness, Vision, and Strategy from the Bottom Up

Walda Katz-Fishman and Jerome Scott

> Philosophers have only interpreted the world, in various ways; the point how-
> ever is to change it.
>
> —Karl Marx

As we write this piece, Atlanta has been selected as the site for the first ever U.S. Social Forum (USSF) in the summer of 2007. Project South is the anchor Atlanta-based organization for a local coalition of over twenty-five organizations that make up the host committee (www.projectsouth.org and www.us-socialforum.org). The mantra of the social forum process—*"another world is possible"*—becomes, in this context, *"another United States is possible"* and yes, *"another U.S. South is possible!"*

This is the story of the rising grassroots movement for justice, equality, and popular democracy of the last two decades through the lens of our participation in it and analysis of it. We locate ourselves and our communities, organizations, and struggles within the objective realities of social history—the electronic revolution, the transformation of work, and destruction in every aspect of social life; a powerful global capitalism and its repressive and deadly neoliberal policies; and a violent U.S. empire spreading war, militarism, and abusive prison systems at home and abroad.

Project South: Institute for the Elimination of Poverty & Genocide was born out of the struggles in the 1980s during the opening rounds of the neoliberal attack on our communities. We were part of the defense of voting rights in the west Alabama Black Belt in 1986; helped organize and educate the Up & Out of Poverty Now! Campaign in the Southeast from 1989 to 1991; and joined the indigenous resistance to over five hundred years of genocide in 1992. We developed along with the growing struggles of the 1990s and 2000s—the passage of the North American Free Trade Agreement (NAFTA) and the Zapatista uprising in 1994, welfare "reform" in 1996, and the World Social Forum process in 2001. From our beginning we represented both low-income and people of color grassroots activist and scholar- and student-activist communities. We brought these communities together on the basis of equality to do the educational work necessary to build a movement for social and economic justice. Today Project South is a southern-based movement-building organization that works with communities pushed forward by the struggle to strengthen leadership and provide popular political and economic education for personal and social transformation. We build relationships with organizations and networks in the United States and the Global South to inform our local work and to engage in bottom-up movement building.

From our perspective of the movement-building process—the overlapping stages of consciousness, vision, and strategy (CVS)—we analyze the subjective side of the developing movement: the realities of growing consciousness about the systemic root causes of our problems and crises; the creation of a bold vision of our local communities and the global society and planet we are fighting for; and the deepening bottom-up movement of peoples fighting for their freedom, their dignity, their humanity, and mother earth herself. Our movement is locally grounded in the soil of the U.S. South and in grassroots, labor, indigenous, people of color, immigrant, women, youth, and sexually diverse communities and organizations across the United States. Our movement is nationally networked and is globally connected, and intends to grow ever clearer, stronger, broader, and deeper to be an equal partner with our sisters and brothers in struggle in the Global South and world over.

Today's movement is challenged with finishing the unfinished program of earlier movements in the United States over the last five plus centuries of global capitalism in one form or another. These earlier struggles reformed various aspects of capitalist economic structures, the state, and ideology; but the capitalist system remained intact. They failed to fundamentally transform capitalist relations and structures and their unending forms of exploitation, oppression, poverty, misery, war, and human and ecological destruction. The power to decide whether hard-fought reforms remained or were eliminated, the power over life and death itself, was left in the hands of the rich, the superrich, the global corporations, and their functionaries whose interests are in opposition to the needs and interests of the majority of humanity. This is the strategic focus of today's rising movement.

A WORD ABOUT PUBLIC SOCIOLOGY
FROM THE BOTTOM UP

You may very well ask what this has to do with public sociology. And we say "everything." There are two main paths to public sociology—the path from the social struggle to the academy and the path from the academy to the larger social struggle. Social location and how unified theory and practice are in a coherent and continuous dialectical and transformative process are decisive factors. The bottom-up path comes from social struggle and the need and desire to understand root systemic causes of the human degradation and destruction experienced by the women, men, and youth of exploited and oppressed peoples, classes, and communities; to articulate a vision of what a world of equality, justice, peace, and popular democracy would look like; and to develop a strategy to guide the process of systemic change. The other—more top-down—path comes from the academy and the canons of sociology—professional, critical, policy, clinical, etc.—in search of relevance and audiences.

For many of us Karl Marx was the first bottom-up "public sociologist." In the twentieth century many more have used historical materialism/Marxism as a revolutionary theory and practice, and they have been located primarily in political struggles and building socialist states outside the academy. Examples of political leaders who have done this intellectual and practical work include V. I. Lenin in Russia, Mao Zedong in China, Ho Chi Minh in Vietnam, and Ernesto "Che" Guevara and Fidel Castro in Cuba. Others include Goyathlay "Geronimo," Harriet Tubman, John Brown, Ida Wells-Barnett, Jane Addams, W. E. B. DuBois, Emma Goldman, Ella Baker, Paulo Freire, Myles Horton, Kwame Nkrumah, Frantz Fanon, Cesar Chavez, Malcolm X, Martin Luther King, Jr., Walter Rodney, Audre Lorde, Elizabeth Martinez, Leonard Peltier, and Winona LaDuke—to name a few. There have also been powerful organizations, networks, and collectives such as the Industrial Workers of the World—"Wobblies" (IWW)—Congress of Industrial Organizations (CIO), Student Nonviolent Coordinating Committee (SNCC), Black Panther Party, League of Revolutionary Black Workers, American Indian Movement, Combahee River Collective, Up & Out of Poverty Now! Campaign, Economic Human Rights Campaign, and Zapatistas that have combined theory and practice from the bottom up.

The bottom-up path brings activists, organizations, and movements to social analysis and social theory out of their social practice and as a necessity for social transformation. The analytical and methodological tools of social analysis are not the "private property" of academics and the academy. Rather, theory and practice are two aspects of a powerful, dialectical unity coming out of and continuously tested in the social struggle to end all forms of exploitation and oppression. Neither can exist without the other. (In chapter 4, Jackie Smith speaks to what this process looks like from the scholar/academic point of view.)

We believe that the location of a bottom-up public sociology organically within social movements for fundamental change is essential in this moment. Scholar- and student-activists who come to movements through the academy must eventually cross the divide between campus and community and all the power and privilege of the "top down," and locate themselves within community-based movement-building spaces. At the same time, scholar- and student-activists who are connected to social struggle are a bridge from the community to the classroom through curriculum transformation, reframing our teaching and learning spaces and putting movement building at the center. (See Project South's website, www.projectsouth.org, for a popular education curriculum centered around movement building for classroom and community.) Bottom-up public sociology means that whoever we are, we immerse ourselves and our analysis in a social practice that embraces organizations in many fronts of struggle linked in a coherent movement that calls for fundamental and qualitative social change, and is central to our historic struggle for human liberation in the most inclusive sense.

POPULAR EDUCATION TOOLS FOR ANALYSIS AND TO GUIDE POLITICAL PRACTICE

As organic public sociologists in the trenches we have participated in the bottom-up intellectual and political work of the emerging movement of the late twentieth and early twenty-first centuries. This work of understanding the world for the purpose of transforming it has always been our perspective. What this meant concretely was developing popular education curricula—tools and methods for analysis, practice, and social struggle—that we could use in community organizing and movement building as well as in campus and classroom spaces.

To analyze where the movement-building process was and to guide our political work, we developed the social history time line and the consciousness, vision, and strategy (CVS) model of movement building. While Marxism/historical materialism as theory and science guided our political practice and the work of Project South, we knew we had to develop popular education tools to make this analysis more accessible to the grassroots and low-income organizations we were working with as well as to our students and colleagues who were open to a movement-building lens. The first popular education tool we developed was the social history time line, and it remains at the center of our popular education and movement-building work. Social history helps us see the process of social change—that is, where we have come from, how our past shapes our present, and what lessons we need to take from our past and present to move into the future. The social history time line also lifts up three key structures and processes that profoundly impact our lives—economics, power and politics, and popular struggles and movements.

As a popular education and consciousness-raising method, people begin by telling their stories and sharing their lived experiences. These realities are located on the social history time line that includes three interacting dimensions: economic history—money, markets, technology, and economic elite interests and realities; popular movement history—the bottom-up struggles and demands of exploited and oppressed classes, peoples, and genders; and government policy history—the power relations and policies resulting from these conflicting interests and forces. People in struggle today are able to see their daily realities within this big-picture context of structures and systems and to derive lessons learned for today's struggles from the victories and losses of earlier movements as well as from the long-term thinking and planning of the ruling class. (For the most recent social history time line and a longer discussion on how to use the time line as an educational and political strategy tool, see *Today's Globalization*, 2nd edition, Project South 2005.)

Combined with the social history time line we developed, again rooted in theory, the CVS model—consciousness, vision, and strategy stages—of movement-building and popular education tools to help us to understand and talk about movement building in our daily work. The CVS model presents movement building as an ongoing process that has definite, but overlapping, stages of development that we can identify through analyzing people's actions and their thinking about the problems they are confronting, the proposed solutions to their problems, and their plan to get there. It highlights the continuities of classism, racism, sexism, and the oppression of indigenous peoples. It shows, in a concrete way, how people have been exploited by corporate owners, employers, and landlords; how city, state, and federal officials have passed laws that favor these elite interests and are repressive toward those at the bottom; and why people must resist and create a vision and strategy for the bottom-up struggle.

In the consciousness stage people experience more and more problems and crises in their lives because of the objective conditions of global capitalism and join organizations to fight back, to hold on to what they have, or to make short-term gains. Eventually in this stage people and organizations must look to connections among problems and systemic root causes. In the vision stage, people and their organizational leadership understand systemic root causes and begin to envision the world we are fighting for—that is, what our communities will look like when we have resolved our problems and have fundamentally transformed societies worldwide. The final stage, the strategy stage (including tactics, of course), is a movement-wide coordinated plan for organizing and educating the long-haul struggle to make the vision a reality. (For the theoretical foundations of the CVS model see Marx and Engels [1998] and Lenin [1978]; and for a longer discussion about how we use the CVS model and tools in Project South see *The Midnite School: Creating a Vision for Our Movement*, Project South 2004.)

Based on our participation in the social struggle, we found movement building to be in the consciousness stage in the 1990s and first years of the twenty-first century. So the primary work we had to do was consciousness raising—deepening people's understanding of the root causes of the problems affecting our communities locally, nationally, and globally, their systemic and historical nature; and developing the leadership to think about solutions, short term, but especially long term. In July 2004 Project South held the Midnite School, our first popular education gathering to explore "vision" and to strengthen the emerging leadership, both individual and collective, that would guide the movement to the vision stage and be able to bring into the movement in an organized way the thousands of new people and organizations being pushed forward by the struggle. Since then some movement leaders have been requesting and we have been creating and using more vision tools in our popular education work (Project South, 2004). In 2005 more and more organizations and their leadership in local–global justice and equality struggles were at the beginning of the vision stage, though many individuals and organizations were still in the consciousness stage. Our task is through continuous analysis, practice, and education to be part of moving the movement-building process forward.

RAISING CONSCIOUSNESS: UNDERSTANDING THE NEW MOMENT

The late 1970s and 1980s represented a new moment in our social history—technologically, economically, politically, and socially and in terms of people's everyday lives. The electronic revolution with automation, robots, instant communication, ever faster transport, and labor-replacing technology was taking hold. The welfare state reforms of the New Deal, civil rights movement, and War on Poverty were being replaced with the so-called war on drugs and the mushrooming prison-industrial complex. Poverty was growing while wealth was ever greater and more concentrated; white supremacy, the oppression and exploitation of women and youth, and homophobia were on the rise. The ever tighter integration of global capitalism, neoliberal policies at home and abroad, and U.S. empire and war adversely impacted the lives of working and poor people on every continent. Clearly there were no more reforms left within the global capitalist system, including here in the United States.

What did this did mean for our bottom-up struggle in the short term and, more importantly, for the long haul? How did we understand these new realities? The thorough globalization of capital and global corporations, of neoliberalism and militarism, set in motion the objective conditions for our global bottom-up movement for justice and equality. But it took us some time to get the big picture. These twenty or so years remained in the consciousness stage of the movement-building process.

For us the first concrete indication that the reform era was over and the era of intensifying repression was on the rise was in 1986. Our story begins that year in the west Alabama Black Belt. It was that year that the U.S. government attack on the very fundamental political right of so-called democracies—the vote—began. We saw this attack become pervasive in the 2000 and 2004 presidential elections. But we return to west Alabama in 1986.

The FBI had launched the largest investigation of alleged vote fraud by historic civil rights activists who had authored the 1965 Voting Rights Act. We joined activists from across the South and the country in the "I'll vote on campaign" to defend voting rights that had been won only twenty-one years earlier. Central to the movement-building process was the educating of a new generation of movement leaders about the strategic role of the South in U.S. history—as a site of heroic resistance and victory in the face of enormous exploitation and repression—and about why reforms were being rolled back and increasingly repressive policies were being put in their place. Project South was born out of this struggle and took up the task of political and economic education for strengthening leadership for building today's movement.

We were part of organizing and educating ourselves and those most adversely affected by the slashing of the social safety net and the passage of neoliberal policies who were stepping up in their own defense and taking leadership in new bottom-up grassroots organizations and struggles. The Up & Out of Poverty Now! Campaign, led by the victims of poverty, was formed in Philadelphia in 1989 by the National Welfare Rights Union, the National Union of the Homeless, and the national Anti-Hunger Coalition. We returned to Atlanta and committed to organizing the Up & Out of Poverty Now! Campaign in the Southeast, and especially in Georgia. Over the next few years we helped organize two Up & Out of Poverty Now! Southern Summits and *Street Heat* magazine. Activists in the Kensington neighborhood of

Philadelphia organized the Kensington Welfare Rights Union. The Poor People's Economic Human Rights Campaign grew out of these organizing campaigns and the relationships and networking connected to them.

In 1992 we were part of the struggles of indigenous and African peoples in resistance to over five hundred years of genocide, exploitation, oppression, and ecocide. The 1994 passage of NAFTA and the Zapatista uprising in Chiapas, Mexico, was another critical moment in our growing struggles. NAFTA was a key neoliberal policy in the economic integration of North America (Canada, United States, and Mexico) and the race to the bottom that profoundly affected job loss, economic and environmental deterioration, and immigration to the United States—especially the South—from Mexico and elsewhere. Finally, in 1996, Clinton's welfare "reform" eliminated "welfare as we knew it"—while structural poverty, underemployment, and unemployment continued their upward trend. This, combined with a booming prison-industrial complex, was a real marker for the breaking of the social contract that had been in place since the New Deal. It brought home to the American people the harsh economic and political realities that peoples across the world often suffered at the hands of U.S. empire and global capital. This set the material basis for a new kind of solidarity and for the emerging local–global movement for social and economic justice that is reflected in the World Social Forum process beginning in 2001 (Katz-Fishman and Scott, 2004, 2005a; Mertes, 2004).

An important piece of political work we did was political and economic education for leadership development and building the capacity of the social and economic justice movement that was beginning to form—with many fronts of struggle and new groups as well as older groups networking, dialoguing, and joining forces. The movement was local and national, with a strong southern base, and took on a global character with the Zapatista rebellion in Chiapas in response to NAFTA.

Our thinking was "outside the box." We understood that the technological revolution—electronics, computers, robots, etc.—was replacing labor and causing many problems for working people within capitalism since jobs and wages are essential to survival. At the same time it created an abundance of goods and services and made possible an end to scarcity—and thus to poverty, inequality, and all the related social and political ills—once capitalism and private productive property were also transformed to a cooperative and shared economy. Our challenge was to bring this analysis to the consciousness and vision stages in the movement-building process.

For many global justice activists, the 1999 "battle in Seattle" against the World Trade Organization—the latest in the list of terrible neoliberal policies—was a turning point. But indigenous and people of color activists asked "where were the people of color?" They reminded the emerging movement and many white and middle-class activists that they had been resisting global capitalism for over five hundred years. The coming together of grassroots, low-income, and people of color–led organizations to help build the rising local–global justice and equality movement was happening with increasing intentionality and frequency.

In the first years of the new century we saw powerful resistance to intense internal repression and war as well as to the intensifying economic crisis in people's lives in the post-9/11 years. We worked with many organizations across the country, and beginning in 2002 we participated internationally with the Convergence of Movements of Peoples of the Americas (COMPA), the Grassroots Global Justice Alliance (GGJ), and the World Social Forum (WSF) process.

The Zapatistas organized the First Intercontinental Encuentro— "encounter"—for Humanity and against Neoliberalism in Chiapas, Mexico, in 1996. This encounter, which brought together three thousand participants from forty-three countries, was the inspiration for the first World Social Forum in Porto Alegre, Brazil, in January 2001 (Committee of Indigenous Solidarity, 2005). The WSF was a popular—civil society—gathering of the world's worker, peasant, youth, women, and oppressed peoples struggles in response to the World Economic Forum in Davos, Switzerland—a gathering of the global economic and political elites. The first WSF attracted twenty thousand people from 117 countries. The next two WSFs were also in Porto Alegre. By 2002 the WSF International Council realized it had to take the WSF to other developing world regions to further globalize the bottom-up movement. Though initially declining to host the WSF, India agreed after playing a key role in the very successful Asian Social Forum; and in 2004 the WSF was in Mumbai—formerly Bombay (Mertes, 2004). In January 2005 over one hundred and fifty thousand people from 135 countries representing social struggles and movements across the globe converged in Porto Alegre, Brazil, to challenge global capitalism, its neoliberal policies, and U.S. empire and war.

Within the WSF process an early U.S. grassroots movement emerged at Porto Alegre in 2001 that would later become the GGJ Alliance. They looked around and saw that the U.S. social and economic justice movement was not represented by those most adversely affected by the ravages of globalization and neoliberal policies, but by big nongovernmental organizations (NGOs), foundations, think tanks, and academics—mostly white and middle class. The GGJ took up the task of bringing to the WSF process the faces and voices of worker, youth, people of color, indigenous, and low-income-led organizations—of the "developing world" within the belly of the beast. In 2003 in

Porto Alegre, in 2004 in Mumbai, and again in 2005 in Porto Alegre, the GGJ brought one hundred grassroots leaders from the United States.

April 2005 marked a critical moment in building the bottom-up movement for justice, equality, and peace in the United States that is locally grounded, national in scope, and connected to global spaces. It was the formalization of Grassroots Global Justice (GGJ) as an alliance of U.S. base-building groups integrally linked to the WSF process, global movement building, and the first ever U.S. Social Forum. The GGJ held its founding gathering from April 29 to May 1, 2005, in San Antonio, Texas. Forty-five community, worker, and youth organizations participated in this historic gathering. A few, such as United Electrical, Radio, and Machine Workers of America (UE) have a long tradition of bottom-up struggle. Many others were founded in the 1980s, 1990s, and the first years of the twenty-first century. We organized in response to the new realities of global capitalism, neoliberalism, and the transition in state policies from reform and concessions to rollback and attacks. But we connected today's struggles to the history of colonialism and imperialism on U.S. soil and in the lands some of us came from.

We met for two and a half intense days of analysis, visioning, action, and organization building. The GGJ affirmed its commitment to the social forum process and agreed to continue to play a key role in the process it began in April 2004 to make the USSF a reality in 2007. The GGJ also committed to organizing a delegation of its members to participate in the WSF in January 2006. This was a polycentric WSF with social forums in three world regions—Caracas, Venezuela; Karachi, Pakistan; and Mali. Before leaving our founding gathering thirty-one organizations joined; and by August 2005 the GGJ Alliance was thirty-seven strong (Grassroots Global Justice Alliance, 2005a, 2005b).

Many of us in the GGJ and in our own organizations appreciate the incredible promise that the social forum process holds for building the global justice movement in the United States. We also know there are real issues we must address if we are to make it work. From its early inception as the first Encuentro (encounter) in Chiapas, Mexico, in 1996 to its present form as the upcoming sixth WSF, the social forum process has become increasingly "professionalized." But, at the same time, the rapid deterioration in the economic and social conditions of the lives of the majority of the world's peoples and the intensifying militarism and political and cultural repression are also strengthening the anticapitalist forces around the world and in the United States. And many of us are part of the WSF process.

It has often been noted that the U.S. movement lags behind the movement in other world regions. We believe this reflects the fact that the movement in other world regions is more theoretically grounded, has a practice that includes open conversations about socialism and communism, and more often than in the United States includes participants who are members of radical and revolutionary political organizations—not just 501(c)(3)s (nonprofit organizations licensed by the government). To move our movement forward, we will have to be more intentional about uniting theory with practice, building our bottom-up movement in openly political and anticapitalist as well as 501(c)(3) organizations.

The challenge to our rising U.S. movement remains articulating the deep systemic interconnectedness of capitalism, imperialism, racism, and patriarchal oppression and visioning "outside the box" the world we are fighting for. This work is yet to be done. We believe that political and economic education that is popular as well as theoretical is essential in making these connections and moving us from the consciousness to the vision and strategy stages of our struggles and movement. A key piece of the vision and strategy stages is to politically organize our movement to reorganize society—locally, nationally, and globally—in our interests, that is, in the interests of those classes, nations, peoples, and genders most exploited and oppressed by the current system. Our vision is a world evolving from the continuous struggle of liberated people. We will create cooperative, globally interconnected communities in which the resources of the earth are shared by all the people of the earth to satisfy human needs. Our societies will value the power of diversity and difference and strive for the time when all humanity is free to develop to its fullest potential (Scott, Katz-Fishman, and Brewer, 2005).

THINK FORWARD, NOT BACKWARD: THERE ARE NO GOOD OLD DAYS

A public sociology from the bottom up holds great potential to be a bridge between scholar- and student-activist spaces—teaching, research, and community learning spaces—and movement-building spaces where the larger movement is growing and giving shape to the local–global struggle for justice, equality, and human emancipation. Whether this potential becomes a reality in the opening decades of the twenty-first century is the question we must answer. How our generation of public sociologists and student- and scholar-activists answers this key question is related to how we answer several other questions.

Will we come to the table as equals with those most adversely affected by the exploitation and multiple oppressions of global capitalism and U.S. empire building? Will we celebrate our difference and diversity? Will we use the popular communication and popular education necessary for building a broad and deep popular movement? Will we reframe our classroom space and curricula to put movement building at the center? Will we develop the consciousness, the bold vision, and the long-term strategy needed to win? Will we stay connected for the long haul and become one with today's bottom-up movement? Will we "walk the talk"—uniting theory and practice in the dialectics of our historic struggle for human life and human rights, human spirit and human liberation, and for the very survival of our planet?

We have the elements to build our movement and transform our world. The technological and productive capacity exists—because of electronics—to resolve age-old problems of scarcity, inequality, and poverty in its many forms. In this moment vision is key. Humankind can create a cooperative, just, and equal society. Our long history of popular struggles has taught us valuable lessons for today's struggles. A rising bottom-up grassroots global justice movement is taking root in organizations and communities across the United States. A global process grounded in nations and world regions is growing to connect our struggles and movement for justice and equality through the WSF process. The next step is to grow our bottom-up global justice movement in the United States stronger so we can be worthy of joining our sisters and brothers in the Global South. We have a USSF planned for summer 2007 in Atlanta in the historic battleground of the U.S. South. Go to www.ussocialforum.org for details.

REFERENCES

Brewer, Rose. 2005. "Response to Michael Burawoy's Commentary: The Critical Turn to Public Sociology." *Critical Sociology* 31: 353–59.

Burawoy, Michael. 2005. "The Critical Turn to Public Sociology." *Critical Sociology* 31: 313–26.

Bush, Rod. 1999. *We Are Not What We Seem: Black Nationalism and Class Struggle in the American Century.* New York: New York University Press.

Committee of Indigenous Solidarity. 2005. *Chronology of the Zapatista Uprising 1994–2005.* E-mail communication cis-dcz@riseup.net.

Freire, Paulo. 1995 [1970]. *Pedagogy of the Oppressed.* New York: Continuum.

———. 1994. *Pedagogy of Hope: Reliving Pedagogy of the Oppressed.* New York: Continuum.

Georgakas, Dan, and Marvin Surkin. 1998. *Detroit: I Do Mind Dying, A Study in Urban Revolution, updated edition.* Cambridge, Mass.: South End Press.

Grassroots Global Justice Alliance. 2005a. *Founding Meeting Report.* E-mail communication joann@ggjalliance.org; www.ggjalliance.org.

———. 2005b. *GGJ Monthly Report.* E-mail communication: joann@ggjalliance.org; www.ggjalliance.org.

Hennessy, Rosemary, and Chrys Ingraham (eds.). 1997. *Materialist Feminism: A Reader in Class, Difference, and Women's Lives*. New York: Routledge.

hooks, bell. 1994. *Teaching to Transgress: Education as the Practice of Freedom*. New York: Routledge.

Horton, Myles (with Judith Kohl & Herbert Kohl). 1990. *The Long Haul: An Autobiography*. New York: Doubleday.

Katz-Fishman, Walda, and Jerome Scott. 2005a. "Global Capitalism, Class Struggle, and Social Transformation." In *Globalization and Change: The Transformation of Global Capitalism*, ed. Berch Berberoglu, 123–40. Lanham, Md.: Lexington Books.

———. 2005b. "Comments on Burawoy: A View from the Bottom-up." *Critical Sociology* 31: 371–74.

———. 2004. "A Movement Rising." In *An Invitation to Public Sociology*, 53–55. Washington, D.C.: American Sociological Association.

Kelley, Robin. 2002. *Freedom Dreams: The Black Radical Imagination*. Boston: Beacon Press.

Lenin, V. I. 1978 [1961]. *What Is to Be Done? Burning Questions of Our Movement*. New York: International Publishers.

Marx, Karl, and Frederick Engels. 1998 [1848]. *The Communist Manifesto*. New York: Verso.

———. 1986. *Selected Works*. New York: International Publishers.

Mertes, Tom (ed.). 2004. *A Movement of Movements: Is Another World Really Possible?* New York: Verso.

Peery, Nelson. 2002. *The Future Is Up to Us: A Revolutionary Talking Politics with the American People*. Chicago: Speakers for a New America.

Project South. 2005. *Today's Globalization, 2nd edition*. Atlanta: Project South.

———. 2004. *The Midnite School: Creating a Vision for Our Movement—Report Back from Project South Gathering 2004*. Atlanta: Project South.

———. www.projectsouth.org (popular education curriculum, programs).

Ransby, Barbara. 2003. *Ella Baker and the Black Freedom Movement: A Radical Democratic Vision*. Chapel Hill: University of North Carolina Press.

Rodney, Walter. 1981. *How Europe Underdeveloped Africa*. Washington, D.C.: Howard University Press.

Roy, Arundhati. 2004. *An Ordinary Person's Guide to Empire*. Cambridge, Mass.: South End Press.

Scott, Jerome, Walda Katz-Fishman, and Rose Brewer. 2005. "Global Movement on the Rise: World Social Forum 2005—Brazil." *As the South Goes. . .* 13(1): 10–11.

In Pursuit of Justice

Photographs by Kenneth Gould
and Wall Mural by Turbado Marabou

Global change—WSF.
(Photo by Kenneth Gould)

IMF/WB protest banner.
(Photo by Kenneth Gould)

NAACP in Washington, D.C.

(Photo by Kenneth Gould)

Jubilee South fights H₂O privatization—WSF.

(Photo by Kenneth Gould)

Dismantling the TNC discussion—WSF.

(Photo by Kenneth Gould)

Their generation.
(Photo by Kenneth Gould)

Morning meeting, Robert Taylor Homes, Chicago, 1992 (now demolished).
(Photo by Deshawn Moore)

Turbado Marabou, Association House, Chicago, 1993.

(Photo by Deshawn Moore)

Turbado Marabou, mural, Living off the Waters of Creation, *Chicago, 1993.*
(Photo by Turbado Marabou)

Turbado Marabou, detail, Living off the Waters of Creation, *1993.*

(Photo by Turbado Marabou)

Turbado Marabou, mural, Breaking Barriers, *1993.*

(Photo by Turbado Marabou)

Turbado Marabou, detail, Breaking Barriers, *1993.*

(Photo by Turbado Marabou)

Poetical Reflections of Social Reality

Rodney Coates

Segue, from social observations to poetical observations on social existence; poetry may well be the oldest vehicle by which people have critiqued their society. Thus from the caves of Ghana to the walls of Rome, from the Shrines in Palestine to the Halls of Congress—poetry poignantly discusses, interrogates, and helps us clarify not only what is, but what can be. I offer you the public poetry of rodneyc.

The Public Poet

Standing on the edge of a tomorrow that may not come,
Wondering in the fields of dreams that could really be,
Stranded in a world where vision is limited, and hope is rare,
Wanting to reach the child that lies within each of our souls.

Worshiping at the altar of Love and Forgiveness,
Singing on the shores of Beauty and Contentment
Wordsmith fashioning for all to see
Speaking of the good that lies within our destiny.

Seeking the rainbow within the storm
Weeping the tears that others would weep
Sentinel watching over our troubled sighs
Waiting for the dawn to come.

Writing of heaven, living in hell.
Singing of wonder, crying of pain.
Willingly giving while being denied
Spring of our desires, the public poet.

To Cry for Peace

Flags drape these windows as coffins, united we seek refuge—stand up for right or is it might, lids covering innocent blood shed in the name of innocence while the guilty plan for more insanity.

Another life, another lie, another dream spent, lost while approval for murder sings a chorus of unity, as we dig graves for our brothers/sisters across the way, across the sea across the great divide that unites us in this mission of revenge.

Unfurl the flag, write the eulogies, sing the songs for the youth who die too old to know that another just war is being waged for their souls but such justice sings a pale song in the wilderness of our collective graves.

Walking nightmares, tales told to empty spaces, billions found to maim, destroy, and kill, but nothing for the hungry, poor, and diseased. Damn, it seems that we continually find new ways to screw up the dream, as another plan gets reamed, against the seams of another flag unfurling for justice—understand this it is also patriotic to cry for peace.

Message from the Ghetto Gurl

Chocolate fantasy, intellectual rhapsody
Sweet comedy played within this concrete
maze.

East Boogie born South of the torn.
Grew up fast, hard and against the whacks.

Funky times misbegotten rhymes
Sordid Schemes perverse Strategies
Tired Excuses for forgotten Dreams
and tired promises.

Sistaah truth warrior sleuth Breakin rules clockin fools
Nickle Johns and Ten-cent whores

Catch this drift watch this rift Work this lift as you
bum rush the door.

All you player haters and young skirt chasers
dis-miss by the score.

Message from the Ghetto Gurl

She **don't** give a damn bout your world.

The Hounds of Hell

So we try to find our way amidst the chaos and decay.
From the belly of the beast the hounds of war have been unleashed.

Blood and mangled bodies melted into concrete and steel
by an inferno, hell walkith among us.

This is a time for patriots and heroes to stand up **and** scream down the insanity the
pain, the emptiness the void someone must plead for peace.

Empty ambulances give way to funeral barges where the dead will see no more. Silent
screams of horror blot out the songs of Angels. As children wait in vain for the
mommy and daddy that won't come home again.

Whosoever digith the pit shall fall in it. Whosoever unleashes the hound of war will
be bit by it.

So unfurl the blood tattered flags and let them fly at half-mast and as the cast of
characters line up at last let us remember that peace is what we all crave for.

War is the ultimate act of the incompetent. Violence is the song sung by those caught
up in victim insecurity trying to prove their manhood by seeing who can cause the
most blood to spill, producing babies today who cry and say tomorrow they will drink
of the blood that was spilled this day.

So let's repaint the human landscape red from the dead that go before us to our collective destruction. This is the time for patriots, saints, and heroes to stand in the gap
and demand that this insanity must end, we can stand no more war.

Those that have eyes let them see, those with ears let them hear, do not turn away
from the carnage that is before you someone must witness their death. **S**omeone must
scream to the future no more, no more, no more.

If there was ever a time to pray, then now is that time. Steel, flesh, concrete, blood, bones, glass, mangled twisted mashed, smashed, crumbled, compacted, dashed against my window pain as the hound of hell has been unleashed.

Jezebel and Sapphire: Revisited and Reclaimed

Sisters, refusing to conform, raped, abused then scorned.
Today we revisit the crime, unveil the sublime
And listen to your voices through the pages of time.

Ridiculed, confused, despised for being too different.
Tried, and condemned for being too beautiful,
Ignoble fates decreed for you were too blunt
or just too damn stubborn, reduced, sullied, and disgraced as
misogynist buried you in a lonely grave.

Today's would be pimps, commercial temps, and
Intel wannabes, caught up in the myth fail to see
The beauty—60-second dreams, 30-minute conversations
(do you really love me) 90-day wonders, and 1-year
party-thons (has anyone seen my thongs)—
Poverty prostitutes, intellectual wimps, seduced by the
Time this rhyme has died against the plane of your mind.
He said, she said, they said—it was cool to be a fool, but then
They found her moment when he could not see the reality of their
Silence.

Sisters, of our discarded past, lost against the backdrop of our pain,
Raped, scorned and still looking to be free.
Despised for your beauty, condemned for your sass,
Ridiculed for your bluntness and for daring to be—you.
Today, we honor and reclaim your virtue long lost on the back stairs of
A racist mind.

Operation Putrid Smell

Truth—the first causality of war falters on the slopes of conscience as we strive to silence the outcries of injustice.

Hope—the first loss in the crisis of despair sinks against the pale of righteous indignation by those who merely claim to worship God.

Faith—the embodiment of our collective struggle hides within the music made loud by those who only seek revenge, hate, and mayhem.

Stench—Bush's burning in the house that would be White Contracts written in the
blood of children let's rebuild upon the legacies of past insanities as our souls recoil
from this war we dub Operation Putrid Smell.

The little things

Micro-aggressive arrogance dressed in the garbs of sincerity.
Minimalist policies masquerading as grand visions, schemes aimed to debunk the
    truth,
destabilize the reality of another's pain.
Whimsical diatribes confined to the recesses of forgetfulness while
wanton distraction rules the day.

Blissful folly trapped in the half-filled glass where the dimwitted drink
their fill drunk with self-glorification and denial of all others.
Sordid tales played against the backdrop of insanity where all reality is clouded
with the frantic passion of deceit and profit at any cost.

Little slights, fragments of gossip, a twist of the truth, a little deception
a bit of anger masked as sincerity, and the stage is set for the little things
that gradually erode, minimally destroy, silently detract from the essential dignity we
all need—it truly is the little things.

Found—weapons of mass destruction

    There, in the dark spaces
Between   faces   deep in the recesses of minds
Gone   blank from too long dealing with too little.

Against   backdrops of complacency
Fumbling through   corridors lined with minuscule
Concerns, bordering upon contempt for those who would
Dare be born into despair.

Wanting   to be   heard, silenced by those too busy to hear
Tearing away at the recesses of our hearts laden with a guilt that
Refuses to be   as   they   wonder, wander, and lose
Sight of why they exist at   all.

There, under the stair,   under the glare, under the maze where
We hide those   we   refuse   to   see.

Hear their cries, steely black eyes against the fragile face on top of the swollen bodies
Bloated with air, pockets empty, packets of skin just hanging on to a life that refuses
to be ignored.

Found—famine, ignorance, pestilence, poverty, arrogance, indifference, nihilism,
war—the weapons of mass destruction.

"The Ghetto"—A Film Review

Coming to a theater Near you!

Live and in living colors starring the boyz from hood
The sisters in the street. Mothers on welfare and
The fathers desperately seeking another jail sentence, high, or just a minute's peace.

Look at them coming to a theater near you
Don't have to go there. Just wait!
We will bring it to you. Digitalized.

All of the feelings, without being close
You don't have to fear come in watch them
as they live their lives so desperately
The Ghetto! Coming to a theater
Near you . . . This summer.

Guaranteed to make you cry, moan, angry, and smile, thankful it isn't you,
this will make you happy, hell you might even buy a button (we sell them on your
    way out) "save the little ghetto children" to be worn proudly right next to
your "save the spotted pigeon."

Come on, come to see The Ghetto come watch them fulfill all
Get off with your fantasies. . . . doing all the things you thought they'd do
Just for you. In 3D too! come, come, come to a theater Near to you.
Come, come, come Check Out the Ghetto in a theater near you.
Come check out the crack heads Climbing the walls, beating up their
Mothers just for a ball. come watch it on your video . . . no need to explore the real
    thing. We can do it better, finer, cheaper, And all the proceeds will go to prevent
    them from leaving "The Ghetto."

The Ghetto.
Staring Shaq the Quack, The Proud but tragic hero
Destined to die . . . The Brothers 4 standing on the

Corner singing Porgy and Bess To that old time Do Wat, Do Wat,
Sha bang, bang. Jus waiting, jus waiting.

"Who cares if it has no relevance to reality,
Oops, wrong script,"

Have your most intimate fantasies fulfilled your nightmare fulfilled . . .

Warning this film has absolutely nothing to do with reality . . . But it does represent
. . . it is rated stupidity XXX.

The voyage: Hello today

Pensively, the morning mist caressed the walls of my soul
as I contemplated the day that was to be.

Yesterday's anxiousness, frustrated dreams of a today
that seemed never to come, has finally ended.

Paths, furtively pursued only to end in circles
caught up in a rhapsody of questions that refused answers,
lay behind in the tortured refuse of a not so distant memory.

Desires—born of grief and sorrow, loneliness and abandonment—
now take refuge in a newfound forgetfulness
that lurks on the shadows of what never should have been.

Dawn—bright and poignant, mysterious and wondrous—
gently ushers in new hopes, new vision and new dreams
of a day where all can be in fields patiently plowed.

Morning of my today, sweet rhapsodies of the days to come,
no longer hidden among the shadows of yesterday,
now unfolds and comes into view.

Chains finally broken, soaring above the rainbows
where all secrets are revealed and all are released to be, to see, to actively pursue
their all . . . hello today . . . thanks for coming into my life.

The revolution will not be digitalized

Voices beyond the pale way past the point of reason and being
Ignored, isolated from the loop still doped sitting on the stoop
never part of the game never invited to the party

Voices in the middle of nowhere screaming insanely into the well
But you don't hear them do you?

Too busy, too busy, too busy . . . the revolution will not be digitalized
It will not appear on virtual reality you won't see it on the net
You won't even be able to get to that the revolution will not be digitalized

II

It will rise up out of those broken promises exaggerated commitments misbegotten friendships feigned family can you get to this can you understand where I'm coming from can't you see that the revolution will not be digitalized it will not appear on your virtual screen the reality of that reality will be real.

III

while you pontificate and ruminate while you demarcate and obfuscate while you dictate and elucidate understand this change is on the horizon! but you will be caught with your pants down once again and after the fact you will attempt to reify, and deconstruct that once again resurrecting yourself by saying how you were always part of the plan what can I tell you

the revolution will not be digitalized it will not be stored in a database it will not be processed by a newsgroup it will not be up for discussion on a chat board it will not be at your local market found in the five and dime in between some idiots last exploits it will not be on the cover of Time pictures will not appear in Look, Jet won't have it yet, you see it will not be digitalized

you won't find it on HBO, Showtime or TNN, you won't find it at the Sheridan as the super sheik revolutionaries of the day . . . come and greet themselves . . . genuflecting to their own egotistical wonders, the greatness of their excess, the buoyancy of their anal rectitude.

IV

you won't find it at a conference called by the radically bodacious inspired giants of mediocrity it will not be publicized, it will not be digitalized, it will just be . . . you know the revolution the hungry and the homeless will rise up, tired of waiting for our leadership, tired of being pimped by the prostitutes of distractions and obfuscation. They will determine and dictate the policy of their own future While we sit back and speculate or otherwise examine our navels Or was that an anal disorder that we first chose to discover.

And write about . . . um I don't know navel gazing and anal retentiveness.
But past all that . . . the revolution still won't be digitalized

Concerned people talking about this and that . . . why and when,
They and them . . . will once again get caught short
Once again wonder why, once again exclaim with a cry. . .
Damn! The revolution wasn't digitalized!

II

THE RIGHTS OF HUMANS

6

Neoliberal Globalization and the Question of Sweatshop Labor in Developing Countries

Robert Pollin

Globalization and *neoliberalism* are two of the leading economic buzzwords of our time. But what do these terms mean? The answer is not obvious. The major technical innovations in communications and transportation technologies over the past generation have, of course, dramatically reduced the costs of maintaining effective economic links on a global scale. Moreover, the collapse of the Soviet system eliminated this challenge to capitalist hegemony, even though the governments professing Communism had long since abandoned any serious claim to a democratic, egalitarian alternative to free market capitalism. The result, in any case, was that huge areas of the world economy were now open to capitalism to a degree unprecedented in generations.

Neoliberalism is a contemporary variant of classical liberalism, holding that opening national economies to free trade and multinational capital investments, deregulating labor and financial markets, sharply cutting back government spending, eliminating government deficits and inflation will, in combination, produce a social order that is more fair and efficient than any feasible alternative. Neoliberalism has been the guiding ideological and policy framework within which capitalism has spread in the contemporary epoch.

Corresponding with the ascendancy of neoliberal globalization has been the emergence of several crucial new patterns in global economic activity. One of the most important of these new patterns has been the rise in manufacturing productive capacity in less-developed economies. This development could not have occurred without the advances of our time in communications and transportation technology. But equally, we cannot understand this development without placing it in the context of neoliberal economic policies.

These developments—globalization, neoliberalism, and the rise of manufacturing productive capacity in developing countries—all come together in one of the most hotly debated economic questions of our time, at least in the United States. This is the rapid spread of sweatshop labor conditions throughout the developing world. Among other things, the rise of sweatshop labor conditions in developing countries has spawned a widespread and vibrant, and in many respects, highly successful political movement in opposition to sweatshop conditions.

In this chapter, I examine five central issues regarding the global spread of sweatshop labor and the rise of the anti-sweatshop movement. The first is to situate the rise of the anti-sweatshop movement within the broader historical context of rising manufacturing capacity in less-developed countries. I then pose this simple question: Are sweatshops really so bad? Many analysts contend that they are the best option available for the world's poor. If this weren't so, then workers simply wouldn't allow themselves to be hired into such employment conditions. In opposition to this view, I argue that people accept sweatshop jobs not because they are a favorable option by any absolute scale, but because they don't have viable fallback positions. Or to put it somewhat less technically, people accept sweatshop jobs because they like to eat. The reason they don't have a viable fallback position—that is, the reason they don't see alternative routes to gaining their daily bread—is due to how neoliberal globalization has transformed conditions for both agricultural and manufacturing workers in developing countries. I then consider whether neoliberal globalization has foreclosed any serious alternative to sweatshop conditions for workers in developing countries. I try to show that viable alternatives to sweatshop working conditions can be advanced even within the current historical and political conditions through the simple device of raising retail prices modestly to cover the incremental costs of providing decent employment conditions for production-level workers. I conclude by considering whether it is really feasible to expect that raising retail prices would not simply generate additional revenue for retailers, but would actually get passed back through the production chain to workers at the point of production. In answering this question in the affirmative, I reach an overall conclusion that viable alternatives to sweatshop working conditions in developing countries have already been advanced to a significant, if still early, extent through pressures created by the anti-sweatshop movement.

NEOLIBERALISM AND THE RISE OF SWEATSHOP
LABOR IN DEVELOPING COUNTRIES

The reports that first attracted widespread media attention in the United States were about the production of Nike athletic shoes, beginning with a 1992 story in *Harper's* that described workers in Indonesia assembling nearly fourteen pairs of Nike shoes every day and earning fourteen cents per hour, less than the Indonesian government's standard for "minimum physical need" for a full-time worker. The next heavily reported revelations concerned the clothing line endorsed by TV personality Kathie Lee Gifford, whose popular appeal rested heavily on her wholesome image. In April 1996, Charles Kernaghan of the New York–based National Labor Committee told a U.S. congressional committee that Gifford's clothes were made by Honduran girls earning thirty-one cents per hour laboring in sweatshops. (The rise of anti-sweatshop activism in the United States is chronicled in Shaw, 1999.)

Similar reports continued. For example, an October 2, 2000, *BusinessWeek* story titled "A Life of Fines and Beatings" described conditions in Chinese factories that make products for Wal-Mart, among other Western companies. One handbag-producing firm profiled in the story employed nine hundred workers. It charged them $15 a month for food and lodging in a crowded dormitory, which the article describes as a "crushing sum" given that a newly hired worker would clear $22 in his or her first month. The company also forced new workers to relinquish their personal identity cards, so "workers risked arrest if they ventured out of their immediate neighborhood."

These news reports detailing conditions in individual production sites are also consistent with more extensive and systematic studies sponsored by, among others, the International Labour Organization of the United Nations, and various U.S. university groups. Considering the apparel and footwear industries alone, such reports found extremely low pay, dangerous and unhealthy working conditions, and restrictions on workers' basic rights—that is, all features that we commonly associate with the term *sweatshop*—to be common in the developing world. (This literature is summarized briefly in Pollin, Burns, and Heintz, 2004.)

But certainly an abundance of poorly paid jobs and bad working conditions are hardly novel phenomena in less-developed countries. Indeed, these are among the main features that define a country as being "less developed." Is there really anything new about the sweatshop labor conditions that have been widely publicized in recent years? Or is it simply a matter of the media in rich countries suddenly paying more attention to a long-standing and pervasive situation?

In fact, the current high level of attention to global sweatshop conditions does reflect more than just a rise in awareness. The underlying reality behind the rise in sweatshops is the extremely rapid increase over the past twenty-five years in less-developed countries producing manufactured products for export markets. We can see this pattern in figure 6.1, showing the share of manufacturing exports as a percentage of total exports for the less-developed countries. As the figure shows, manufacturing exports amounted to 17.7 percent of total exports for less-developed countries as recently as 1980. By 1998, the figure had risen to 71.6 percent. The most rapid growth in exports among these countries has been in Asia—especially China, South Korea, Taiwan, Thailand, Malaysia, Indonesia, and India. But Latin American and African countries have also experienced significant increases in their export markets.

Of course, not all manufactured exports from less-developed countries are produced under sweatshop conditions. But the strategy of many business owners in less-developed countries—just as in the advanced countries—is to

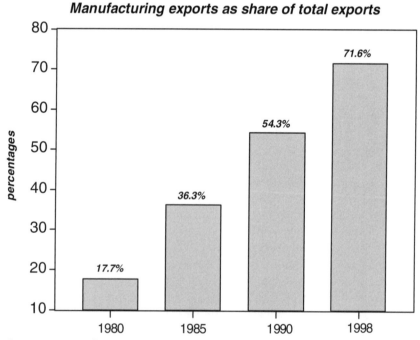

Figure 6.1.   Manufacturing exports in developing countries.

Source: World Bank, *World Development Indicators, 2001* CD-ROM

gain a competitive advantage through squeezing workers, and thereby driving down labor costs as far as possible. In many countries, business firms are able to proceed unchecked with such "race to the bottom" employment practices because of a lack of reasonable laws governing minimum wages, working conditions, and the basic rights of workers. Perhaps even more frequently, reasonable labor standards do exist on paper in less-developed countries but are not enforced in practice. These are the conditions that have fostered the rapid spread of sweatshops throughout the developing world.

ARE SWEATSHOPS REALLY SO BAD?

But recognizing the existence of sweatshops is one thing: is it reasonable to also assume that sweatshops are a problem for less-developed countries? In fact, many well-known economists and other commentators consider the spread of sweatshops in these regions as a highly favorable development. This view is expressed straightforwardly in a September, 24, 2000, *New York Times Magazine* article titled "Two Cheers for Sweatshops," by *Times* columnists Nicholas Kristof and Sheryl WuDunn, focusing on conditions in Asia. Kristof and WuDunn write:

> Fourteen years ago, we moved to Asia and began reporting there. Like most Westerners, we arrived in the region outraged at sweatshops. In time, though, we came to accept the view supported by most Asians: that the campaign against sweatshops risks harming the very people it is intended to help. For beneath their grime, sweatshops are a clear sign of the industrial revolution that is beginning to reshape Asia.
>
> This is not to praise sweatshops. Some managers are brutal in the way they house workers in firetraps, expose children to dangerous chemicals, deny bathroom breaks, demand sexual favors, force people to work double shifts or dismiss anyone who tries to organize a union. Agitation for improved safety conditions can be helpful, just as it was in 19th-century Europe. But . . . the simplest way to help the poorest Asians would be to buy more from sweatshops, not less.

Jeffrey Sachs, a leading economist at Columbia University, expresses this same perspective even more emphatically when he says that the problem is "not that there are too many sweatshops, but that there are too few." Also endorsing this view, the Princeton economist and *New York Times* columnist Paul Krugman explains that "the result [of sweatshop employment] has been to move hundreds of millions of people from abject poverty to something still awful but nonetheless significantly better," and thus, that "the growth of sweatshop employment is tremendous good news for the world's poor."

However else one might react to such perspectives, they do bring attention to a simple, but extremely important fact about sweatshops: the single most important reason that sweatshops exist is that people accept these jobs. True, once workers are hired into sweatshop firms, they are often forced to stay on the job through harsh forms of compulsion, as the *BusinessWeek* story quoted above makes clear. Still, for the most part, workers could escape sweatshop conditions simply by refusing to show up at work. The fact that they do show up means that sweatshop employment represents an option for hundreds of millions of workers in developing countries that is superior to their next best alternative. Presumably, this is the sense in which Kristof and WuDunn offer "two cheers" for sweatshops, Professor Sachs calls for more sweatshops, and Professor Krugman praises them as "tremendous good news" for the world's poor. (The quotations from Sachs and Krugman are cited in an excellent essay by Miller, 2003.)

But is it actually true that there is no alternative to creating ever more sweatshops if developing countries are to reduce poverty and succeed economically? In fact, this perspective is seriously misguided, because it ignores some crucial facts about the way that conditions have changed dramatically under neoliberal globalization.

SURPLUS WORKERS IN
LESS-DEVELOPED COUNTRIES

At least since World War II, rural workers in developing countries have been migrating out of agricultural employment. This migration has freed up more workers to contribute toward the production of nonagricultural goods and services, which, in turn, has generally contributed positively to economic growth in developing countries. But this migration out of agriculture also created a new problem: the supply of workers moving out of agriculture was exceeding the demand for these workers in other forms of employment. This pattern led to the formation of a massive pool of "surplus" workers—people who were forced to scramble for a living any way they could. A high proportion of them migrated into the queue for jobs in the manufacturing sectors in developing countries with virtually nothing as an alternative fallback position. These are the conditions under which poor working people might well regard a sweatshop factory job as a better option than any immediately practical alternative. (These issues are developed more fully, with citations, in Pollin, forthcoming.)

This pattern has worsened under neoliberal globalization, resulting from the interaction of several factors. First, the reduction or elimination of tariffs on agricultural products has enabled cheap imported grains and other agricultural products to capture a growing share of the developing countries' markets. This has made it increasingly difficult for small-scale farmers in developing countries to survive in agriculture, which, in turn, has accelerated the migration into the nonagricultural labor market. Neoliberal policies have also brought reductions, if not outright elimination, of agricultural subsidies to smallholders.

As conditions have thus worsened for small-scale agricultural producers, their opportunities for finding jobs in manufacturing have also been limited by several factors also associated with neoliberal policies. The first has been the overall decline in economic growth and average incomes in most developing countries in the neoliberal era. As income growth fell, so did the expansion of domestic markets, and thus also the expansion of jobs producing goods for domestic consumers.

But what about the sharp rise in manufacturing exports by developing countries? In fact, even this development has not generally translated into a comparable rise in jobs producing goods for export markets (with some important exceptions, notably China again, but also Malaysia and Chile). Many of the countries that are now manufacturing exporters—in particular the large Latin American economies, Mexico, Argentina, and Brazil—did already have large-scale manufacturing sectors in operation, though these earlier-vintage manufacturing sectors, under the import substitution model, concentrated on producing for their domestic markets. The liberalization of trade policies has therefore produced improvements in their exporting capacity, but, concurrently, a corresponding increase in the penetration of their own domestic markets by foreign imports. Moreover, firms in the relatively new export manufacturing countries have been forced to appropriate higher productivity production methods in order to compete in the global market. This has made their operations more efficient but has also entailed reducing the number of workers they employ.

Workers in developing countries thus face a double squeeze: diminishing opportunities to continue earning a living in agriculture, but nothing close to a compensating growth of job opportunities outside of agriculture. These are the circumstances that have pushed more working people in developing countries into a desperate situation where they must accept a sweatshop job to continue to live. But this situation can hardly be construed as "tremendous good news for the world's poor," as Paul Krugman put it. They are simply the raw facts of life for hundreds of millions of people under global neoliberalism.

SWEATSHOP JOBS VS. NO JOBS:
NO ALTERNATIVES?

In fact, there is evidence in considering the pattern of manufacturing production in less-developed countries that offers grounds for optimism about alleviating sweatshop conditions. The argument that sweatshops are "tremendous good news for the world's poor" is based on a simple premise: if working conditions in developing countries were to become more desirable—that is, if wages were to rise, workplaces to become cleaner and safer, and workers were able to exercise basic rights—then labor costs in these countries would become excessive. The firms producing in developing countries would then be out-competed on global markets, and job opportunities for the poor would dry up, despite the best intentions of anti-sweatshop activists. But this simple premise is contradicted by the actual patterns between wage and employment growth in the apparel industries of developing countries. Table 6.1 offers evidence that speaks to this question.

More specifically, table 6.1 gives data on the relationship between real wage and employment growth in the apparel industries for twenty-two developing countries between 1988 and 1997 (these twenty-two developing countries were the only ones for which adequate data were available). I have grouped the countries into four categories, those in which:

1. employment and real wage growth *rose* together
2. employment and real wage growth *fell* together
3. employment *fell* while real wage growth *rose*
4. employment *rose* while real wage growth *fell*.

As we can see from the table, the countries in which employment and real wages rose together, shown in panel A, is the largest category—both in terms of the total of eight countries included in this category, and in terms of the 1.2 million workers employed in these countries as of 1997. These figures clearly contradict the notion, at least in the apparel industry, that developing countries must maintain labor costs as low as possible in order for job opportunities to grow. It is true that wages rose only modestly in most of the eight countries listed, but the fact that they are rising at all demonstrates that factors other than maintaining sweatshop working conditions are contributing to the growth of jobs. Some of these other factors are the productivity levels in the apparel plants, the quality of the local transportation and communications infrastructure, and the effectiveness of the marketing channels through which the newly manufactured clothing items reach retail markets.

Panel B includes three countries—Kenya, Guatemala, and Barbados—in

Table 6.1   Relationship between Employment and Real Wage Growth in Developing Countries' Apparel Industries

A) Countries in Which Employment and Real Wages *Rose* Together

(listed according to total employment levels in 1997)

	Total apparel employment in 1997	*Employment growth average annual rate 1988–1997 (percentages)*	*Real wage growth average annual rate 1988–1997 (percentages)*
1) Indonesia	393,300	+17.4	+1.3
2) India	270,000	+29.9	+0.7
3) Philippines	161,300	+4.8	+1.2
4) Morocco	116,900	+10.3	+2.3
5) Colombia	66,700	+3.7	+1.2
6) Malaysia	60,500	+4.4	+3.8
7) Costa Rica	32,900	+4.1	+2.9
8) Chile	13,800	+1.6	+6.5
TOTAL EMPLOYMENT FOR ALL COUNTRIES	1,215,400		

B) Countries in Which Employment and Real Wages *Fell* Together

	Total apparel employment in 1997	*Employment growth average annual rate 1988–1997 (percentages)*	*Real wage growth average annual rate 1988–1997 (percentages)*
1) Kenya	7,300	−1.2	−1.9
2) Guatemala	1,900	−2.1	−10.3
3) Barbados	1,300	−3.1	−6.1
TOTAL EMPLOYMENT FOR ALL COUNTRIES	10,500		

(continues)

which apparel workers' wages fell over 1988–1997, but employment nevertheless declined as well. This is a small grouping of countries, which also employs a small number of workers. But it is still useful to observe examples in which pushing wages down did not succeed in stimulating job growth.

Panel C shows the countries in which wages rose while employment declined. But these cases need to be interpreted carefully. South Korea, for example, experienced the fastest real wage growth of the twenty-two countries in the sample, at an average annual rate of 8.3 percent, while the number

Table 6.1   Continued

C) Countries in Which Employment *Fell* While Real Wages *Rose*

	Total apparel employment in 1997	Employment growth average annual rate 1988–1997 (percentages)	Real wage growth average annual rate 1988–1997 (percentages)
1) South Korea	151,500	− 5.7	+ 8.3
2) South Africa	126,300	− 0.5	+ 2.1
3) Mauritius	66,400	− 1.3	+ 7.0
4) Mexico	24,500	− 2.1	+ 1.8
5) Puerto Rico	20,100	− 3.6	+ 0.3
6) Singapore	8,100	− 11.5	+ 4.8
7) Panama	4,300	− 0.7	+ 1.8
TOTAL EMPLOYMENT FOR ALL COUNTRIES	401,200		

D) Countries in Which Employment *Rose* While Real Wages *Fell*

	Total apparel employment in 1997	Employment growth average annual rate 1988–1997 (percentages)	Real wage growth average annual rate 1988–1997 (percentages)
1) Uruguay	11,300	+ 0.2	− 6.3
2) Jordan	4,900	+ 8.7	− 3.3
3) Ecuador	3,900	+ 1.5	− 10.2
4) Bolivia	2,200	+ 18.5	− 1.9
TOTAL EMPLOYMENT FOR ALL COUNTRIES	22,300		

Source: World Bank, *World Development Indicators, 2001* CD-ROM

of jobs in the apparel industry was declining at 5.7 percent annual rate. Two developments explain this pattern: rising productivity among apparel producers and growing strength by the country's labor movement, which pushed successfully for higher wages while operating in a democratic environment for the first time. Jobs in which both wages and productivity are rising rapidly should be considered a positive development. But it does still create a challenge at the same time: that job opportunities be created elsewhere in the Korean economy, to prevent unemployment from rising.

The countries in panel D conform most closely in their experiences to the claims of sweatshop enthusiasts: they experienced employment growth while wages declined. But this grouping consisted of only four countries, employing 22,300 workers.

The overall point is that there is no single formula that will deliver a successful manufacturing sector in developing countries. Maintaining sweatshop working conditions and other "race to the bottom" business practices may indeed be successful in driving down costs and thereby enhancing competitiveness. But the evidence presented here also shows that there are other ways to establish a growing manufacturing sector in developing countries and pushing labor costs down will, in itself, guarantee nothing.

There is another important consideration at play here: the fact that consumers in the United States and other wealthy countries express strong preferences to not purchase products made under sweatshop conditions, the entreaties of sweatshop enthusiasts notwithstanding. Consider the results of a 1999 survey of U.S. consumers sponsored by the National Bureau of Economic Research. This poll found that, on average, consumers were willing to pay 28 percent more on a $10 item and 15 percent more on a $100 item to ensure that the products they bought were made under "good working conditions" (the poll results are in Elliot and Freeman, 2003).

These polling results are especially striking, given the findings from a study I conducted with Justine Burns and James Heintz (2004). We estimated how much retail prices in the United States would have to rise in order to fully finance a 100 percent wage increase for apparel production workers in Mexico. Our study examined the case for Mexico only because, among developing countries, it provides the most comprehensive government statistics on production costs in its apparel industry. We recognized that a one-time 100 percent wage increase for Mexican workers—a doubling of existing wage rates—was well beyond what was likely to result even in a political environment dominated by a broadly shared commitment to eliminating sweatshops. But for the purposes of the exercise, it was important that we not err by underestimating how much labor costs might have to rise to eliminate sweatshops. The result we obtained was that retail prices in the U.S. clothing market would have to rise by only *1.8 percent to fully cover this 100 percent wage increase.* Consider, for example, the case for a $100 sport jacket. To finance a 100 percent wage increase for Mexican workers producing this jacket, the retail price of the jacket would have to rise by $1.80, to $101.80. At the same time, the National Bureau of Economic Research poll finds that U.S. consumers would be willing to pay $115 for this jacket if they could be assured that it had not been made under sweatshop conditions.

WOULD THE EXTRA REVENUES
REALLY GET PASSED BACK?

Of course, by itself, this simple exercise does not demonstrate that sweatshop labor conditions could be readily wiped out through modest increases in consumer prices. The world is obviously more complex than our exercise allows. Take just one additional layer of complexity. If the jacket's retail price really did rise from $100 to $101.80 in the U.S. market because U.S. consumers want their clothes manufactured under non-sweatshop conditions, how would the consumers actually know whether that extra $1.80 that they spent on the jacket is actually getting channeled back to the production-level workers in Mexico, as opposed to getting pocketed by the owners of their local JCPenney outlet? There is no airtight answer to this or several other similar questions.

WILL REVENUES ACTUALLY GET PASSED BACK?

The links between the production and the retail marketing of garments are complex, often occurring among business entities operating in different parts of the world. Nevertheless, if workable methods for monitoring production sites can be established, it is correspondingly realistic to expect that price increases at the level of retail could be consistently passed through to production-level workers.

The garment industry operates through three core links: the contractors, responsible for production; the manufacturers, responsible for design and distribution; and the retailers. Note, again, that the "manufacturers," such as Polo, Ralph Lauren, or Nike, create and maintain labels, but they generally are not directly involved in the actual production of clothing and footwear.

In the contemporary U.S. garment industry, retailers operate with substantial market power, especially relative to manufacturers and contractors rather than with consumers. This is primarily because of the high degree of concentration in the retail industry, with the "lean retailing" revolution, beginning in the late 1970s, only having increased the extent of concentration. For example, as reported by Abernathy and colleagues, between 1977 and 1992, the percentage of total sales through general merchandising outlets accounted for by the fifty largest general merchandising firms rose by 14.5 percentage points, from 77.3 to 91.8 percent. The four largest general merchandising firms—Sears, Wal-Mart, KMart, and JCPenney—themselves accounted for 47.3 percent of sales in 1992 (1999: 75–76). By 1999, the share of total sales of the four largest chains—with Wal-Mart the largest and Target moving just ahead of JCPenney as fourth largest—rose still further, accounting for 73.2 percent of total general merchandising sales, that is, an increase of nearly twenty-five percentage points above the 1992 level (see *Fortune Magazine* April 17, 2000, F-64).

While the major U.S. retailers clearly possess substantial market power, the oligopolistic structure of the industry does not preclude strong price competition within this industry. None of the major retailers can expect to raise prices significantly without experiencing consumer defections. This competitive environment could limit the ability of any given retailer to raise prices. But even recognizing this, it is also true that the competitive success of the major retailers depends less on specific pricing strategies than on other factors, including quality of service, advertising, responsiveness to consumer demands, adoption of information technologies, and managing supply chains. These issues are discussed at some length in Abernathy et al. (1999: 39–54).

Another aspect of the competition among retailers needs to be especially emphasized here, which is their distribution arrangements, which allow them to carry merchandise of the most popular manufacturers. This provides the popular name-brand labels with a significant degree of market power as well, which they fight to maintain and strengthen through massive expenditures on image-enhancing advertising.

All of this would suggest that price markups could be sustainable at the retail level. However, it still would not necessarily follow that the additional revenues generated by these markups would get passed back to production-level workers, rather than absorbed at either the retail or manufacturing levels. This is especially so, given that business owners would of course prefer that they, rather than production workers, receive the extra revenues generated by higher retail prices.

Nevertheless, establishing a framework for revenue pass-backs from retail to production workers can still be viable. Two factors appear crucial here: that retailers and manufacturers do exert market power over contractors and that much of the success of business at these levels is determined by creating positive brand images. If the retailers and manufacturers conclude—no doubt with reluctance—that their marketing efforts are damaged by negative associations between themselves and sweatshop labor conditions, they have the market power to impose a system of regulation on their contractors. This is the process that is now occurring with the U.S. college logo apparel market in setting up so-called codes of conduct, and financing the operations of agencies that monitor compliance with these codes. The arrangements that evolve in this could be generalized to other retailers and manufacturers. In short, the rising concentration of retailing power, combined with the importance of positive brand images to the retailers, creates an increasingly favorable environment for establishing codes of conduct that reach back to the level of apparel production. The importance for manufacturers of effective methods of monitoring was expressed by Doug Cahn, director of Reebok's Human Rights Program, as follows: "Paying money up front [for monitoring] helps protect against criticisms of your brand image . . . because the brand image stands for something that can't be [allowed to] erode" (quoted in Burnett and Mahon, 2001: 71).

Perhaps the most challenging issue here is whether contractors would adhere to such codes of conduct in practice, regardless of whether they have accepted them in writing. For the college logo apparel market alone, somewhere between roughly three thousand and six thousand production sites operate throughout the world. It is not practical to expect that monitoring agencies could maintain contact with all of these sites on a regular enough basis to assure compliance with the codes at all, or even most, of them. What this implies is that production sites will need to be monitored largely by the on-site workers themselves; that is, monitoring agencies need to develop effective procedures to hear the voices of the on-site workers. Such an approach to monitoring is in the process of being implemented by the Workers Rights Consortium, the monitoring entity that emerged in 2000 out of the anti-sweatshop protest movements. The success of this monitoring methodology is likely to be crucial to the success of the entire anti-sweatshop monitoring enterprise. Burnett and Mahon emphasize the importance of open methods to the success of establishing credible monitoring techniques. They conclude, "Credible arrangements for the monitoring of overseas labor standards will have to be more intrusive, unpredictable, and expensive for the firms being monitored. With spot verification by nonmonitors being so important to consumer trust, openness to this verification becomes a key foundation for ex-ante credibility" (2001: 67).

Of course, many more layers of complexity present themselves in a broader consideration of employment problems in developing countries in our era of neoliberal globalization. Perhaps the most vexing question remains that a job in a sweatshop is almost always a superior alternative to no job whatsoever. Given this simple fact, opponents of sweatshop working conditions in developing countries will need to increasingly embrace within their analytic and political frames of reference the broader issues of unemployment, underemployment, and informal employment in the developing world. At the same time, grappling with this broader set of employment issues has been, and will continue to be, substantially illuminated by the insistent questions and answers advanced by the anti-sweatshop movement.

ACKNOWLEDGMENTS

This paper is adapted from chapter 5 of Pollin (2003) and Pollin, Burns, and Heintz (2004).

REFERENCES

Abernathy, F. H., J. T. Dunlop, J. H. Hammond, and D. Weil. 1999. *A Stitch in Time: Lean Retailing and the Transformation of Manufacturing—Lessons from the Apparel and Textile Industries*. Oxford: Oxford University Press.

Burnett, E., and J. Mahon, Jr. 2001. "Monitoring Compliance with International Labor Standards." *Challenge*, March–April: 51–72.

Elliot, Kimberly, and Richard B. Freeman. 2003. *Can Labor Standards Improve under Globalization?* Washington, D.C.: Institute for International Economics.

Miller, John. 2003. "Why Economists Are Wrong about Sweatshops and the Antisweatshop Movement." *Challenge*, January–February: 93–122.

Pollin, Robert. 2006, forthcoming. "Globalization and the Transition to Egalitarian Development." In *Human Development in the Era of Globalization*, ed. James K. Boyce, Stephen Cullenberg, Prasanta Pattanaik, and Robert Pollin. Northampton, Mass.: Edward Elgar.

———. 2003. *Contours of Descent: U.S. Economic Fractures and the Landscape of Global Austerity*. London: Verso.

———, Justine Burns, and James Heintz. 2004. "Global Apparel Production and Sweatshop Labor: Can Raising Retail Prices Finance Living Wages." *Cambridge Journal of Economics*: 153–71.

Shaw, Randy. 1999. *Reclaiming America: Nike, Clean Air, and the New National Activism*. Berkeley: University of California Press.

7

Framing the Social Security Debate

Deana Rohlinger and Jill Quadagno

Democracy is a complex concept that involves three main types of rights: civil rights, which is the right to work without compulsion; political rights, which is the right to vote and to participate in the political process; and social rights, which is the right to protection against the exigencies of the capitalist marketplace. Social rights are designed to protect an individual's standard of living from the volatility of "pure market forces" (Marshall, 1964: 82). They take the form of national welfare programs for work-related injuries, unemployment, illness, widowhood, and the loss of work capacity in old age.

In most countries these programs were first enacted at the end of World War II and were largely completed by the early 1970s, the so-called golden age of welfare states. Although they varied in scope and coverage, all were organized around a doctrine of social insurance with its emphasis on income security across the life course, its recognition of shared risks, and its promise of an earned right to benefits (Esping-Andersen, 1999). The era of welfare state expansion came to a halt in the early 1970s when an international oil crisis battered the world economy. However, even after the oil crisis abated, unemployment and economic stagnation persisted. What appeared initially to be a temporary aberration became a permanent economic transformation as the working population aged, the structure of employment opportunities and the skills necessary to succeed in the workplace changed, budget deficits persisted, and the economy became more globalized (Quadagno and Street, 2005).

A vast majority of democratic countries dealt with these concerns by restructuring their welfare benefits through a combination of tax increases, benefit adjustments, and work incentives but rarely by changing the basic character of social insurance. For the most part, social programs were still concerned with income protection against shared life course risks coupled with efforts to keep people in the labor market. In the United States, by contrast, the future of social insurance has become a contested issue. While progressives seek to protect the core structure of Social Security and Medicare, the two main American social insurance programs, conservatives have sought to replace social insurance with market fundamentalism—the notion that society should be subordinated to self-regulating markets (Somers and Block, 2005). The attack on the welfare state has been directed especially at Social Security, the largest and seemingly most invincible welfare program.

In the new politics of old age policy, the political struggle over the future of Social Security has been masked behind inflammatory rhetoric about generational equity, runaway entitlement spending, and investment opportunities for younger generations. What has made Social Security vulnerable to these attacks is the distinctly American interpretation of the social insurance principle. Unlike European countries where social insurance was understood to be a collective effort to ensure the basic economic security of all workers, in the United States Social Security was framed in more individualistic terms from its inception in 1935. Workers believed that their payroll taxes were contributions to a trust fund and that they had separate accounts in their own names, which, like a private insurance annuity, would provide a monthly benefit at retirement. In reality, Social Security, like all public pensions, operates as a pay-as-you-go system with current benefits being financed by current payroll taxes. The lack of public understanding of how Social Security really operates, which initially sustained the program, became a weapon against it as critics charged that the trust fund was going bankrupt and that the government would be unable to meet its obligations to future generations (Beland, 2005).

In this chapter, we examine the various ways Social Security has been framed over time both by progressives who believe it is the key welfare state program and by conservatives seeking to dismantle it. Framing refers to the process of constructing and defining events for public consumption. A frame is a central organizing idea that tells an audience what is at issue, outlines the boundaries of a debate, and defines the range of solutions to a given problem (Benford and Snow, 2000). Politicians, interest groups, think tanks, and mass media all present frames to define a situation and articulate a solution to the problem. Ultimately, one of these frames dominates political discourse and sets the course for public policy.

As conservatives have sought to reshape the way the public thinks about Social Security, progressives have been put in the position of defending the status quo. Thus, an examination of conservative arguments and the progressive response to them provides a lens through which we can analyze the assumptions and values underlying policy debates and existing social programs. In each instance, individuals and groups with opposing points of view try to steer political debates in ways that will allow them to meet their own policy goals. Our discussion draws on articles, newsletters, news releases, conference material, and advertisements from conservative and progressive organizations as well as governmental reports and public statements.

FRAMING OLD AGE SECURITY

Social Protection

The stock market crash in 1929 that led to a deep depression destroyed the faith of many Americans in laissez-faire economics. As the unemployed and the elderly took to the streets demanding relief from economic uncertainty, President Franklin D. Roosevelt championed a New Deal that would provide income security across the life course, including "the right to adequate protection from the economic fears of old age, sickness, accident and unemployment" (Campaign address on the "Economic Bill of Rights" October 28, 1944). As Roosevelt proclaimed in his message to Congress on January 17, 1935:

> Fear and worry based on unknown danger contribute to social unrest and economic demoralization. If, as our Constitution tells us, our Federal Government was established among other things, "to promote the general welfare," it is our plain duty to provide for that security upon which welfare depends.

At the core of this "social protection" framework was the idea that the government was responsible for protecting workers from an unpredictable marketplace and its potentially devastating social and economic consequences. The concept of social protection provided the principle underlying the Social Security Act of 1935, the first national welfare benefits for the unemployed, single mothers and their children, and the elderly. Because the elderly were viewed as particularly vulnerable to the volatility of the marketplace, they won two benefits. The first, Old Age Assistance, a joint federal/state program of welfare for the aged poor, was intended to relieve the immediate problem of unemployment and poverty. The second, Social Security, a social insurance program for retired workers aged sixty-five and older in industry and manufacturing, was designed to address the long-term issue of income security in retirement. As originally set up, workers and employers would each contribute 1 percent on the first $3,000 of a worker's earnings.

These contributions would be preserved in a trust fund that would fund the worker's retirement at age sixty-five. Over the next two decades Social Security was expanded to include dependents of retired workers (1939), other groups of non-covered workers (1952), and the disabled (1956). In 1956 women were allowed to retire at age sixty-two with a reduced benefit, and that right was extended to men in 1961.

Despite the increasing scope of Social Security benefits, poverty rates for people over the age of sixty-five hovered around 30 percent in the mid-1960s. Poverty among the elderly persisted because the value of Social Security benefits failed to keep pace with inflation and because high health care costs could easily decimate savings. In response to these concerns and a decade-long effort by the AFL-CIO, in 1965 Congress created Medicare, a new social insurance program that provided health care coverage for Social Security beneficiaries sixty-five and older. Then between 1968 and 1972, Social Security benefits were increased substantially and automatic cost-of-living increases were granted in 1972. By the mid-1980s poverty rates among the elderly had tumbled to around 12 percent.

The social protection frame not only provided the underlying rationale for increasingly generous Social Security benefits and Medicare, it also fundamentally altered how Americans viewed the role of the state. It highlighted that the well-being of the economy and society were inextricably linked, and that, as a result, federal programs were necessary to ensure the basic economic security of those most vulnerable to market volatility. What made the social protection frame different in the United States from that in other Western democracies was that it did not conceptualize social insurance as a collective effort based on the concepts of community and solidarity. Instead it largely presented social insurance programs as a social contract between the individual and the state. According to the terms of the contract, the individual was obligated to work whenever possible and the state was obligated to provide basic financial security only when an individual was incapable of working. Thus, the seeds of contention in future debates were planted in the original framing of the program.

Generational Equity

The challenge to Social Security initially came from the corporate community, which responded to the benefit hikes and payroll tax increases of the early 1970s by attempting to reframe Social Security as a problem of "generational equity." The central theme of the generational equity frame was that the elderly were consuming an unfair share of national resources and adversely affecting the future economic security of younger generations. In this framework the young and old were pitted against each other in a battle over a shrinking economy, and the young were losing the war to politically savvy and extraordinarily greedy seniors.

The first salvo came from the chairman of the Federal Reserve Bank of New York, who described Social Security as a "huge Ponzi scheme" that extracted a heavy burden on already overtaxed workers (quoted in Peterson, 1982: 50). The result would be a war between generations. Bendix Corporation chairman William Agee agreed, "Young and old will be pitted against one another in a fearful battle over the remains of a shrinking economy" (Quoted in Ehrbar, 1982: 36).

The generational equity frame gained credence in 1984 when a respected demographer, Samuel Preston, published an article in a leading scholarly journal decrying the rise in child poverty. Preston noted that public expenditures on children had been declining even as expenditures on older people rose. He attributed this shift to the political clout of senior lobbying organizations, which demanded benefits for the elderly, and to the lack of any organized lobbying on behalf of children. Preston's article was trumpeted by conservative think tanks and the organization Americans for Generational Equity (AGE), whose funding came from Social Security's prime competitors, banks, insurance companies, defense contractors, and health care corporations (Quadagno, 1989). These groups expanded and sensationalized his argument, charging that the older generation would exhaust the Social Security trust fund and force younger workers to fend for themselves when they reached retirement age.

The generational equity frame is based on the assumption that there is a trade-off between spending on the elderly and spending on children. Yet the evidence shows that no such trade-off exists. Pampel (1994) analyzed international trends in eighteen Western nations and found that high spending for the elderly was *not* associated with low spending for children. To the contrary, nations with high levels of spending on the elderly also spent more on children. Despite the lack of evidence for a generational trade-off in spending, by the late 1980s the generational equity theme had become a staple in political debates in the United States. Mass media consistently presented Social Security as a drain on scarce resources and depicted seniors as placing their desires above the needs of their children and grandchildren (Cook et al., 1994: 97). When Congress voted against a 1988 bill to provide home health care to the disabled, a measure that would have substantially benefited older people, an article in the *New York Times* (June 23, 1988, 1A) declared that "the vote reflected a consensus that the elderly and their supporters were being greedy" and that the defeat indicated "growing resentment of increasing federal benefits for the elderly."

The generational equity frame also succeeded in making Social Security a subject of political debate. Until the 1970s Social Security had been considered the third rail of American politics: politicians that dared propose cutting benefits risked an abrupt ending to their careers. The generational equity frame, however, cast the program in a new light and suggested that, like abortion and the environment, Social Security was simply another political issue where powerful interest groups worked behind the scenes to advance their policy interests. In this case, it was the elderly who financed organizations like the AARP (American Association of Retired Persons) that worked to maintain the financial comfort of seniors at the expense of children.

Although conservatives promoted the generational equity frame to undermine public support for Social Security, this concept failed to gain ascendance in the political sphere for several reasons. First was that most people did not see the elderly as a greedy or menacing group but rather as contributing members of their own families. Second was that senior organizations like the AARP mobilized an opposition movement to respond to these attacks. Third, some modest changes incorporated into the 1983 amendments to the Social Security Act, which raised the payroll tax and taxed the benefits of upper-income beneficiaries, solved a short-term deficit in the trust fund (Palmer, 2005). The amendments also addressed the long-term solvency problem by raising the age of eligibility for full benefits from sixty-five to sixty-seven but phased in gradually beginning in 2000 so there would be no immediate political costs.

In the 1990s, conservatives devised a new frame, incorporating a critique of Social Security into a broader "entitlement crisis." The entitlement crisis combined the frame of generational equity with dire predictions about the deficit, the erosion of family income, and the future of the economy.

The Entitlement Crisis

Formally, what distinguishes entitlements from other government programs is that they are governed by formulas set in law. Unlike discretionary spending programs, they are not subject to annual appropriations by Congress. Although there are hundreds of entitlement programs, the two largest are Social Security and Medicare. The concept of an "entitlement crisis" first became a public policy issue in 1993 when President Bill Clinton created the Bipartisan Commission on Entitlement and Tax Reform to recommend long-term budget saving measures. The commission descended into partisan bickering and failed to agree on a set of recommendations, but its interim report identified two distinct messages that together formed an "entitlement crisis."

The first message was that entitlements were consuming a disproportionate share of the federal budget, crowding out spending for other social needs and causing the federal deficit to skyrocket (Bipartisan Commission on Entitlement and Tax Reform, 1994). As business publications picked up the theme, a budget concern was translated into moral outrage against middle- and upper-middle class seniors, who could clearly fend for themselves during their retirement years. As a *Fortune* magazine article declared:

Want to pin a face on America's persistent deficit and savings crisis? Forget those hoary clichés—the welfare queen, lazy bureaucrat, greedy businessman, weapons-crazed general or rich Third World potentate living off U.S. aid. Reach instead for a photograph of your mom and dad. That's because the main engine driving federal spending ever upward is the explosive growth in entitlement programs that churn out benefits aimed mostly at older middle- and upper-middle Americans (Dowd, 1994).

The second message in the Entitlement Commission report reasserted the generational equity theme. This iteration of the generational equity frame gave the "entitlement crisis" a sense of immediacy, by coupling it with dire predictions about deficit spending. The commission noted that current spending trends would not be sustainable once baby boomers, at seventy-seven million strong, reached retirement age. By 2030 Social Security and Medicare would consume all federal revenues, leaving nothing for tomorrow's retirees without exorbitant deficit spending. Deficit spending, in turn, would harm the American economy and ultimately erode the income of young workers.

The notion of runaway entitlement spending greatly exaggerated actual trends. Although entitlement spending did rise from 22.7 percent of the federal budget in 1965 to 47.3 percent by 1993, the cause was simply the start-up costs associated with Medicare. In the ten-year period from 1983 to 1993, entitlement spending increased by just 2 percent of all federal expenditures. Moreover, no immediate surge in entitlement spending was expected. As the director of the Congressional Budget Office, Robert Reischauer, testified before the Entitlement Commission, "Entitlement spending is not expected to surge before the retirement of the baby boom generation some 25 years from now, so a precipitous policy response is not required now" (cited in Quadagno, 1996: 103).

It was not a logical analysis of budgetary trends that undermined the concept of the entitlement crisis, however, but rather a shift from a budget deficit in 1992 to a surplus by 1996. If the budget deficit could disappear so quickly, even though no changes of significance had been made in Social Security or Medicare, then it was difficult for critics to hold entitlement spending responsible for the budget deficit in the first place. However, rhetoric about generational equity and dire predictions about the future of the economy did not disappear but rather were transformed into a new frame that incorporated these themes into a broader call for an "ownership society."

The Ownership Society

In the late 1990s, conservatives proposed solving the imminent Social Security "crisis" with privatization. Under privatization workers would be allowed to divert a portion of their share of payroll taxes into private accounts, which would be invested in the stock market. What differs from previous efforts to dismantle Social Security is that pro-market privatization proposals have been wrapped in the popular universal framework of the American Dream. In the 1930s, Roosevelt argued that if the American Dream was to be within reach of the average worker, the state needed to provide a basic level of financial protection against market volatility. As he signed the Social Security Act into law, Roosevelt noted, "The law will flatten out the peaks and valleys of deflation and of inflation. It is, in short, a law that will take care of human needs and at the same time provide the United States an economic structure of vastly greater soundness" (www.ssa.gov). Roosevelt's message was clear: social insurance programs would protect individuals, families, and communities from the financial devastation that can result from market volatility and ensure that individuals could resume their pursuit of the American Dream.

In endorsing privatization President George W. Bush posed an alternative interpretation. Allowing workers to invest a portion of their payroll taxes in private retirement accounts "gives people the security of ownership" and the opportunity to "build wealth, which they can use for their own retirement and pass on to their children" (Moynihan and Parsons, 2001). The "ownership society," as described by Bush, ignores the peaks and valleys inherent to markets and instead suggests that the American Dream can only be achieved through laissez-faire economics. Privatization would not only save Social Security from bankruptcy, it would also limit the need for large benefit cuts in the future (Herd, 2005) and allow workers to accumulate personal wealth. The key point is that this approach embraces market fundamentalism by subordinating social rights to economic rights.

Two themes are central to the ownership society frame. The first theme concerns the role of government. Conservatives argue that Americans have become dependent on government paternalism, that is, a government that provides for their individual needs without rights or responsibilities. Social Security has made American workers dependent on the government for their retirement income, which, in turn, has led to inadequate individual savings and huge payroll taxes. As Daniel Mitchell, a fellow at the conservative think tank the Heritage Foundation argues, Social Security "[encourages] workers not to save for their own retirements but to rely on a program that was designed as a safety net, not as a sole source of income for retirees" (February 2, 2005). Privatization is central to an ownership society, because it would help sever government dependency and give individuals an incentive to save for their futures and those of their families.

The second, and related, theme concerns individual rights. Government paternalism narrows individual liberties. This supposedly has been the case with Social Security because individuals do not have a legal right to a specific benefit. Rather, Congress can change or reduce benefits at any time without consulting workers. Privatization would thus protect individual rights by wresting the money out of the hands of government. As Michael Tanner, the director of the Project of Social Security Choice at the libertarian think tank the Cato Institute, explains: "[Privatization] would reduce Americans' reliance on government and give individuals greater ownership of wealth, as well as responsibility for and control over their own lives. It would be a profound and significant increase in individual liberty" (February 17, 2004).

Clearly, there are profound differences between Roosevelt and Bush in how each envisions the path to the American Dream, and these divergent visions have implications for the existence of social insurance programs. Roosevelt conceptualized the state as the protector of the people. In his view, the well-being of the economy and society were inextricably linked. As such, it was the state's duty to provide individuals a basic layer of protection against volatile markets. It was society's responsibility to shoulder some market risks and shield retired workers from the exigencies of the capitalist marketplace because it would create a common good. This perspective provided the underlying foundation, rationale, and public support for Social Security. Bush's ownership society, in contrast, undermines this foundation by offering a different conceptualization of the role of state. In his view, the state's only obligation is to set and enforce the rules of the marketplace. Individuals have a personal responsibility to use their talent and effort to succeed in the marketplace and secure their own retirement. The ownership society frame thus shifts the risks of the marketplace away from society and places the burden squarely on the shoulders of the individual.

The ownership society frame currently dominates political and public discourse because it stokes fears about the shortcomings of the Social Security program. In a country founded on rights and responsibilities, these themes have a great deal of cultural resonance and the power to mobilize the masses against a named injustice (Benford and Snow, 2000). The ownership society frame taps into this discourse by implying that government programs undermine individual economic rights and hinder the pursuit of the American

Dream. This sense of injustice is heightened by misleading claims that Social Security faces an imminent crisis.

The impeding retirement of the baby boomers does mean that Social Security will require some adjustments to fully pay all promised benefits, but second careers and incentives already in place to defer retirement means that future workers will be less likely to retire in their early or midsixties. The trend toward later retirement is already apparent, as the downward drift in age at retirement that began in 1962 has halted. If the trend toward later retirement continues, the "crisis" may be pushed into the distant future, not occurring until 2050 or even later. Moreover, this strain will be temporary as the economics, demographics, and occupational mix of the country continues to change. Thus, while it is necessary to make some reforms to Social Security, the system is not in any immediate danger.

Will private account funds invested in the stock market pay workers a higher rate of return than Social Security? This is a questionable assumption, because predictions about rates of return often exclude discussions of the administrative costs of private accounts or of the risk of a stock market plunge. Because of stock market fluctuations, some retirees may earn a higher rate of return than what they would receive from Social Security, but others may earn considerably less. Individuals who retire during "bull" market years would likely have sufficient resources to cover basic needs, while those who retire during "bear" market years may struggle to stay above the poverty level. Indeed, the retirement of the baby boomers may contribute to market volatility as people draw down their savings and shift from riskier investments to less risky holdings as they age.

Another problem with privatization is that the cost of transitioning the current program to private retirement accounts will be very high and require huge increases in federal borrowing. Nearly all privatization proposals promise current retirees and workers approaching retirement age that their Social Security benefits will not be touched. Yet privatization will significantly reduce trust fund revenues. To meet promises to current and near-retirees, the government would have to borrow an estimated 4.9 trillion dollars over the next twenty years, and young workers would have to carry this debt. Ultimately, the strain of this debt on a weakened Social Security system would require deep benefit cuts.

Following the terrorist attacks of 9/11, the stock market declined precipitously, and opposition to privatization grew as people began to understand the potential consequences more fully (Beland, 2005). In response, President Bush shifted gears and called instead for "progressive indexing," a plan being sold as a way to ensure the redistribution of wealth by cutting Social Security benefits for high-income beneficiaries while protecting the benefits of lower-income beneficiaries. Critics note, however, that Social Security already redistributes wealth from more affluent to less affluent people. Lower-income workers receive a higher "replacement rate," that is, Social Security pays them a higher percentage of their preretirement income than what higher-income workers receive. Progressive indexing would convert Social Security from a social insurance benefit into a means-tested welfare program, a shift that would undermine its political support among the middle class.

Although privatization has generated intense public debate, it is not the only potential solution for ensuring the solvency of Social Security. Other options include funding a portion of benefits from general revenues rather than from payroll taxes, raising the cap on payroll taxes or eliminating it entirely, or adjusting the way Social Security benefits are calculated for higher-income beneficiaries. As the debate over Social Security reform gains momentum, it remains unclear what frames and policy solutions will ultimately dominate public debate. What is clear is that privatization of Social Security is part of a broader policy blueprint for restoring market fundamentalism.

CONCLUSION

There has been a revolution in the public debate over the largest entitlement program, Social Security, during the last thirty years. Once considered the "third rail" of American politics, touch it and you die politically, proposals to privatize Social Security are now commonplace. This paradigm shift from recognition of shared risks and a commitment to social insurance to a focus on individual responsibility and ownership was not accidental. It was the result of a concerted effort to transform the parameters of public debate and to reframe the options considered to be acceptable solutions to the long-term financing problems of Social Security. Struggles over policies do not only involve concrete options for change but also meaning and interpretation. The outcome of these struggles organizes the political terrain and places limits on the options that are under consideration.

Although the various frameworks used to construct a politics of old age policy appear to be about budgetary issues, age groups, and generations, what is at the core of these debates is a fundamental disagreement over the relationship between the state and society. Conservatives believe that the state should create an environment that allows individuals and society as a whole to prosper but that operates within a legal framework that limits state power and protects individual rights. In other words, the state should only provide services that due to their scope and society-wide impact cannot otherwise be achieved (such as environmental protection, trade regulation, and national defense). The marketplace, in their view, should be largely self-regulating. The only role the state should play in the market is to set and enforce the rules of the game. This means that the state should not be involved in redistributing wealth or providing retirement income but simply should provide an environment that makes the accumulation of wealth possible. Underlying this ideology is the belief that, ultimately, an individual's ability to achieve the American Dream is solely contingent upon his/her talents and efforts in the marketplace. It is, then, the responsibility of workers to appropriately plan for retirement and take precautions that will protect them from the exigencies of the market. Given this understanding of the state, it is easy to see why conservatives seek to dismantle the current Social Security system. Privatization, in their view, will give poor and wealthy workers alike ownership of their wealth and an opportunity to make investment decisions about their own futures.

Like conservatives, progressives believe that the state should provide a framework in which individuals can develop their own lives and contribute to society. Where they differ from conservatives is in their view of regulation and the relationship between the economy and society. Progressives argue that regulation of the marketplace is necessary to ameliorate poverty and discrimination, ensure the integrity and safety of the public, and protect society from potentially devastating exigencies of market fluctuation or collapse. Because the economy and society are inextricably linked, it is the responsibility of the state to provide basic protections to the most vulnerable in society in order to guarantee quality of life for all. Progressives also are concerned with systemic inequality and oppose privatization because they believe that markets reproduce, rather than ameliorate, inequality. Markets by definition facilitate the exchange of goods, and these economic exchanges are blind to ethics, morality, and social obligation. A universal Social Security program recognizes that individuals do not have equal opportunity in the labor market. High-income workers have advantages such as wealth and education that are transmitted from generation to generation. The current Social Security program recognizes these inequities and redistributes wealth from the rich to the poor when they are the most vulnerable. Further, privatization asks the most vulnerable workers, such as low-income workers, to assume the risks of the marketplace. Markets are volatile, and while high-income workers who likely have a range of other assets might find market volatility an inconvenience, low-income workers could be financially devastated by market fluctuations. Thus, privatization would actively reproduce inequality across society.

As the first wave of the baby boomers reaches retirement age, it is important to have a public discussion about the long-term solvency of the Social Security trust fund. However, the solvency problem cannot be understood solely in socioeconomic terms. Rather it is also important to understand the discursive frameworks that have been used to defend and attack the Social Security program and to assess the validity of the assumptions and arguments that underpin these debates. Moreover, it is important to remember that the framework that we as a society adopt affects public policy and thus the social rights of workers. A conservative framework subordinates social rights to the marketplace and makes individual workers responsible for their economic well-being, even in circumstances that may be beyond their control (workplace injuries, death, unemployment, and market fluctuations). A progressive framework emphasizes solutions that balance economics and societal well-being while recognizing the importance of collective goods.

ACKNOWLEDGMENTS

We thank Sarrah Conn for her research assistance on this project and Keri Iyall Smith and Daniel Beland for their comments on an earlier draft.

REFERENCES

"Aid to Elderly Divides Young, Old and Politicians." 1988. *New York Times*, June 23, 1A.

Beland, Daniel. 2005. *Social Security*. Lawrence: University Press of Kansas.

Benford, Robert, and David Snow. 2000. "Framing Processes and Social Movements: An Overview and Assessment." *Annual Review of Sociology* 26: 611–39.

Bipartisan Commission on Entitlement and Tax Reform. 1994. Interim Report to the President. Washington, D.C.: Superintendent of Documents.

Cato Institute. 2005. "The Real Issues of Social Security Reform." *New York Times*, June 13, 3A.

Cook, Faye, Victor Marshall, Joanne Gard Marshall, and Julie Kaufman. 1994. "The Salience of Generational Equity in Canada and the United States." In *Economic Security and Intergenerational Justice*, ed. Theodore Marmor, Timothy Smeeding, and Vernon Greene, 91–132. Washington, D.C.: Urban Institute Press.

Dowd, Ann. 1994. "Needed: A New War on the Deficit." *Fortune*, November 14, 191.

Ehrbar, E. F. 1982. "Heading for the Wrong Solution." *Fortune*, December 13, 35–38.

Esping-Anderson, Gosta. 1999. *Social Foundations of Postindustrial Economies*. London: Oxford University Press.

Herd, Pamela. 2005. "Universalism without the Targeting: Privatizing the Old Age Welfare State." *The Gerontologist* 45(3): 292–98.

Longman, Philip. 1982. "Taking America to the Cleaners." *Washington Monthly*, November, 24.

Marshall, T. H. 1964. *Class Citizenship and Social Development.* Chicago: University of Chicago Press.

Mitchell, Daniel. 2005. "Rising Benefits Threaten Social Security." The Heritage Foundation (Feb. 5, 2005) www.heritage.org (accessed February 14, 2005).

Moynihan, Daniel, and Richard Parsons. 2001. "Strengthening Social Security and Creating Personal Wealth for All Americans." President's Commission to Strengthen Social Security, Washington, D.C.

Palmer, John. 2005. "Entitlement Programs for the Aged: The Long-Term Fiscal Context." *Research on Aging.* In press.

Pampel, Fred. 1994. "Population Aging, Class Context and Age Inequality in Public Spending." *American Journal of Sociology* 100: 53–95.

Peterson, Peter G. 1982. "The Salvation of Social Security." *The New York Review*, Dec. 16, 50–55.

Powell, Lawrence, Kenneth Branco, and John Williamson. 1996. *The Senior Rights Movement.* New York: Twayne.

Preston, Samuel. 1984. "Children and the Elderly: Divergent Paths for America's Dependents." *Demography* 21(4):435–57.

Quadagno, Jill. 1996. "Social Security and the Myth of the Entitlement Crisis." *The Gerontologist* 36: 391–99.

———. 1989. "Generational Equity and the Politics of the Welfare State." *Politics and Society* 17(3): 353–76.

———, and Debra Street. 2005. "Ideology and Public Policy: Antistatism in American Welfare State Transformation." *Journal of Policy History* 17(1): 57–75.

Somers, Margaret, and Fred Block. 2005. "From Poverty to Perversity: Ideas, Markets and Institutions over 200 Years of Welfare Debate." *American Sociological Review* 70(April): 260–87.

8

Latin America: Capital Accumulation, Health, and the Role of International Organizations

Antonio Ugalde and Núria Homedes

The right to health was first recognized in the 1948 Universal Declaration of Human Rights, which proclaimed that all humans have the right to a standard of living adequate for the health and well-being of himself (sic) and his family including . . . medical care and . . . the right to security in the event of . . . sickness, disability.

—UN 1948

Properly understood, the Universal Declaration of Human Rights implies that first and foremost the state has the responsibility to ensure that the social and economic organizations of a society are not a threat to the well-being of its citizens. Health is an essential component of well-being, and, consequently, the state needs to promote the achievement of the highest level of health for the population. For example, the state needs to minimize the presence of environmental hazards (i.e., contaminants, air pollution); guarantee access to affordable housing, healthy nutrition, potable water, and waste disposal systems; promote healthy occupational environments; and facilitate the adoption of healthy behaviors. To achieve these objectives, the state has to establish a regulatory system that protects citizens against the potential abuses of industries and corporations. Thus, to ensure access to healthy food, the state has to regulate the means of food production (i.e., use of fertilizers, poultry and cattle feeds), food processing, food labeling, marketing, and distribution; and in so doing it has to comply with international regulations and trade agreements. This list of health determinants is not exhaustive but is useful to understand that the right to health implies actions in most sectors of

137

society. In addition, when citizens experience an illness or injury they are entitled to receive services to restore health or, when the condition is irreversible, to slow down the deterioration process and reduce suffering.

Most Latin American constitutions guarantee the right to health. Governments have interpreted the right to health restrictively and have prioritized access to health care. In this region, as in others, the range of health services offered depends greatly on each country's economic, human, and technological resources. A variety of health systems have been devised and all of them are imperfect; but some are better than others. With exceptions, poor and middle-income countries have had more difficulties than affluent nations in satisfying the basic health needs of their populations.

Governments in the region have failed to fulfill their constitutional mandates, and people are dying or suffering irreversible damage from lack of access to potable water and waste disposal systems, detrimental environmental conditions, preventable infectious diseases, poor housing, and insufficient access to health services and treatments. The prevalence of these problems is not due to lack of resources. If we exclude Haiti, all other countries in the region have sufficient resources to provide comprehensive and universal primary and hospital care, and have the expertise and technical knowledge to implement preventive and promotional programs.

The weaknesses and inefficiencies of the health systems were well documented by governments and international organizations from the 1970s through the 1990s. Health sector assessments attributed the failure to the governments' inability to regulate special interest groups; the tendency to allocate resources to expensive hospital and urban-based interventions; the neglect of health promotion and disease prevention activities; and to widespread corruption.

The development model followed in Latin America favored economic growth at the expense of improving the quality of life. Industrialization and agricultural development were pursued without regard to the environmental degradation, air and water pollution, and to their impact upon health. Many observers have recognized that the reforms promoted by international organizations that were supposed to assist the countries to resolve these problems have not resolved them. Some critics go further and claim that they have increased them. The World Trade Organization (WTO) is limiting the ability of governments to pass legislation to improve health. The WTO Agreement on the Application of Sanitary and Phytosanitary identifies the type of seeds, fertilizers, and pesticides that peasants in any given country are allowed to use, and governments cannot ban products that they consider hazardous. The Trade-Related Intellectual Property Rights Agreement (TRIPS) creates barriers for the poor to access medicines, and clearly benefits the transnational pharmaceutical corporations (TPC). The Agreement on Technical Barriers to Trade affects the labeling of products, including tobacco, spirits, and pharmaceuticals, making it difficult for governments to regulate the use and marketing of these products. The General Agreement on Trade and Services obligates governments to open the doors to private health insurance and care delivery networks; the result is a fragmentation of the health systems and the weakening of social security schemes.

Empirical studies and projections of the environmental impacts of trade liberalization show severe ecological damage. The World Health Organization (WHO) estimates that almost 25 percent of disease and injury worldwide is connected to environmental problems caused by industries that have shifted production to countries with weak environmental and safety regulations. In addition, in the event of international disputes, the WTO tribunal favors industries and economic development over public health. Of five hundred trade-related disputes, the only one resolved in favor of public health was a French ban on Canadian asbestos (September 2000). On the other hand, the WTO ruled against the government ban on imported tobacco in Thailand; against the European Union ban to sell meats from cattle treated with artificial hormones; and against the United States' tougher standards on gasoline to reduce emissions, limits on pesticide residues in food, and requirement to pasteurize milk products.

In this chapter, we discuss the role of international institutions in Latin America. For reasons of space we will limit our discussion to the World Bank (WB)—the largest health lender and globally most influential health policy adviser—the WTO, and bilateral aid agencies, all of which have had an important impact on health in the region. For the same reason we will only examine the consequences of the interventions of these institutions on reshaping the health care systems, leaving aside the analysis of the impact on other determinants of health. After a short discussion of the development of international institutions and agencies, we will present two case studies (pharmaceutical policies and health reforms) to illustrate how these development institutions have failed in helping governments to fulfill the constitutional mandate of the right to health for Latin American citizens.

THE INSTITUTIONAL FOUNDATIONS OF NEOLIBERALISM

The aftermath of World War II saw the creation of a number of global institutions to provide world economic and political stability and assist in the rehabilitation of Europe. The United Nations, the IMF, the World Bank Group, regional development banks, bilateral agencies, and private assistance organizations came into existence in the decades of the 1940s and 1950s.

Europe's fast and successful reconstruction had two consequences: it forced agencies that had been created to work in Europe to seek new clients. For example, USAID and CARE, originally created to assist Europe, began to work in Third World countries and led development experts and many economists to erroneously believe that the technical assistance and capital provided by international institutions and agencies would allow the poor in Third World countries to overcome their poverty.

Concomitantly to the reconstruction of Europe, the world witnessed the end of the colonial era, and the United States' experience in Latin America demonstrated that it was possible to exploit the poor in Third World countries without maintaining formal political dominance. Transnational capitalism sized the opportunity, began the transformation of the postcolonial into the new neocolonial era, and discovered that the institutions and agencies that had a mandate to help Third World countries to develop and reduce poverty could be effectively used to accelerate capital accumulation.

Neocolonialism and the strengthening of transnational capitalism developed hand in hand during the second part of the twentieth century. One of the essential differences between colonialism and neocolonialism is that the latter is not interested in the control of a country but in facilitating capital accumulation for the benefit of the capitalist class. Transnational corporations (TCs), the instruments used after colonialism by the capitalist class, by their very nature do not have alliances with any country. They operate at the global level and shift their centers of production to locations where they maximize capital accumulation, either by lower wages, tax incentives, weak environmental and safety laws, adequate infrastructure, or the availability of professional expertise. As a result, certain production functions may be carried out in developed nations and others in less affluent countries.

The second half of the twentieth century has witnessed, through mergers and buyouts, the creation of giant TCs that amassed formidable power. The consolidation continues, and it is hard to predict when it will end. Most TCs are headquartered in the West/industrial nations but the location is not particularly important, and we see that a growing number of TCs have headquarters in middle-income countries (for example, Mexico and Brazil) and in poor nations (for example, India and China). As we will discuss later, in some special circumstances national governments may tend to defend "their corporations," but TCs change the location of their headquarters when they can benefit from the change, and there is little that national governments can do about it. The important point is that more and more economic decisions are global, and are made by a shrinking number of executives who do not think in national terms. What we are witnessing is a transformation in which national boundaries are blurring and the capitalist class does not need the colonial world order to dominate; they use the TCs that—when in need—lobby governments to advance their interests.

This analysis does not deny the significance of nationalism in international and economic relations today. Reasons of space do not allow us to delve with the required detail into the complex coexistence of transnational and national forces. When politically expedient, politicians of all ideological persuasions utilize the nationalist card. In the early years of the twenty-first century, nations have shown that nationalism is used to protect "transnational" corporations; but these interventions cause tensions within transnational capitalism. Thus, the intervention of the French government in favor of Danone, Aventis, and other corporations was criticized by CEOs of other "French" TCs. The Italian government continues to protect its banking institutions from takeover by "foreign" transnational banks in spite of criticisms by other TCs. The United States government is more subtle and invokes the principle of national security when "foreign" TCs attempt to purchase United States corporations such as airlines or oil companies, and omits any reference to the complaints of other "United States" TCs. The tension between the two tendencies—nationalism and transnationalism—will probably continue for many years to come. On the other hand, members of the transnational capitalist class share a culture; those members, for example from India or Mexico, feel more "at home" with other members of the same class from other countries than in the company of slum dwellers from Bombay or peasants from Chiapas, respectively.

The transnational-national tensions have not precluded institutions such as the IMF, WB, regional banks, and bilateral aid agencies from contributing to the accumulation of transnational capital instead of helping to eradicate poverty. They do so by supporting policies that benefit TCs. To the extent that TCs do not have to answer to national parliaments, they work with minimum transparency, and their enormous economic power enables them to be global promoters of the most pure neoliberal ideology. Transnational capitalism has successfully selected the new tools that facilitate capital accumulation. It is at the meetings of the G-7 (now G-8) that the leaders of the most powerful "democratic" nations agree on the key policies that the boards of directors of the IMF and WB will implement.

The Organization for Economic Cooperation and Development (OECD), which represents thirty nations (most European countries, the three members of the North American Free Trade Agreement—NAFTA—and Japan), provides analytical and policy support to the IMF and the WB; or, better said, the decisions made by these institutions are influenced by the same interests and tend to reinforce each other. The policies approved by regional development banks, bilateral agencies such as USAID, the UK Department for International Cooperation, the European Union cooperation programs, and other "donors" such as private foundations are by and large in tune with those of the IMF and the WB. There are some exceptions, but the amount of capital handled by deviant agencies is by comparison insignificant.

More recently created organizations such as the WTO have been organized to promote the interests of transnational capital. Conflicts that have surfaced regarding free trade negotiations between nations are in reality fraction conflicts, that is, conflicts among the transnational capitalist class. When conflicts are not resolved within the WTO, the capitalist class has utilized governments to sign bilateral trade agreements in spite of the strong opposition by the transnational working class.

Popular movements have a clear understanding of the use of international institutions by transnational capitalism. In July of 2005, the Second International People's Health Assembly that brought together thirteen hundred delegates from eighty countries under the motto "Health is a human right, not a commodity" highlighted how global forces are impacting individuals everywhere and declared: "The relentless drive for corporate profits, directed by the WTO, the WB and the IMF, has resulted in the privatization of health care at the expense of public health. People's rights to clean air, potable water and sanitation, safe housing, adequate land and food—in short the conditions that determine people's health—have all been sacrificed as impediments to the 'freedom to profit.'"

In a global economy, it is very difficult to follow policies that are not acceptable to the transnational capitalist class. When UN agencies such as the World Health Organization (WHO), the United Nations Development Programme (UNDP), and the United Nations Educational, Scientific, and Cultural Organization (UNESCO) have implemented or attempted to implement programs that might negatively impact the accumulation of capital, the programs have frequently been derailed. UN decision makers have to anticipate and take into account the reaction of transnational capital to their policies, and that leads to the watering down of policies and programs that could be beneficial to the majority of the population.

Armada, Muntaner, and Navarro (2001) have documented in great detail the decision convergence of the WHO, the WB, and TCs. The People's Health Movement (PHM), an international civil society network of health professionals, academics, and nongovernmental organizations (NGOs), expressed dismay and disappointment with the WHO's adoption in August 2005 of the Bangkok Charter for Health Promotion. In the words of the PHM the charter fails "to highlight the current regime of global economic governance as a primary cause of increased . . . poor health." Equally significant was "the absence of any reference to the negative health impacts of neo-liberal public policy, or the exploitation of natural and human resources by the corporate sector and the wealthy global minority or to the rapidly increasing concentration of wealth. . . . While the Bangkok Charter echoes previous declarations that health is a human right, it has not grasped the opportunity to call for human and health rights to take precedence over the provisions of economic policy and trade and financial agreements" (People's Health Movement, 2005b).

By the end of the twentieth century the gap between the dominant class and the poor had expanded in many developed and developing nations. After more than forty years of development activities, in 1992 the UNDP presented a graphic in the shape of a champagne glass; it had a wide opening at the top (signifying that 20 percent of the world population kept 83 percent of the global wealth), an opening that quickly narrowed down to form a stylish long and narrow stem to indicate that the rest received a very small percentage, and the poorest 20 percent survived with only 1.4 percent. Using the Gini index, the UNDP quantified the change in global wealth inequalities between 1960 and 1990: the index increased from .69 and .87; to put it differently, in 1960 the wealthiest quintile had an income thirty times that of the lowest quintile; by 1990 it was fifty-nine times more. In 2002 the situation had worsened, and the richest 5 percent of the world population received 114 times the income of the poorest 5 percent; and the richest 1 percent received as much as the poorest 57 percent. In a 2005 report on poverty, the UN presents the continuous increment of inequality in the world (UN, 2005). After hundreds of billions of dollars in developmental aid, the international organizations created to improve global political and economic stability and help the poor had been very successful in creating a more unequal global society, and in accelerating the accumulation of capital.

THE IMPACT OF INTERNATIONAL DEVELOPMENT INSTITUTIONS ON HEALTH

In the previous section it is suggested that institutions that were created to reduce poverty have instead facilitated the accumulation of transnational capital. Our analysis of Latin America provides insights on the impact of development institutions on the health sector. We will present two case studies (access to medicines and health reforms) to explain in some detail how the WB and other international institutions have subverted their mandate of eradicating poverty and have mandated policies benefiting the TCs at the expense of the large majority of Latin Americans.

Health, Medicines, and TCs

Researchers have found that poor patients go to health centers mainly to obtain medicines, and centers that do not offer medications have low utilization rates. The logic of the patients' behavior is easy to understand. What patients search for is not so much a diagnosis but a cure, and, if they cannot obtain free or affordable medicines, they believe that the time, effort, and often money spent going to the health center has been wasted. Consequently, interventions to improve the efficiency of health systems require the adoption of appropriate pharmaceutical policies.

In Latin America about 72 percent of pharmaceutical expenditures are out-of-pocket; the poor spend a disproportionate percentage of their income on medications (the lowest income decile spends up to twice as much as the highest). The money spent in medicines is taken away from other basic necessities such as food, water, clothing, housing, and transportation. In short, the right to health implies access to affordable medication, but in some countries in Latin America as many as 50 percent of the population may not have access to needed medication. Studies have shown that the free distribution of needed medicines has a highly distributive impact; for example, in Argentina, a national program that provides free access to thirty-six basic medicines improved equity in household drug expenditures by 60 percent.

That access to medicines should be considered a human right is gaining momentum. For example, during the Fifty-Seventh Session of the Commission on Human Rights the United Nations High Commissioner for Human Rights (2001) approved a resolution stating that in the event of pandemics, such as HIV/AIDS, access to medicines is a basic human right. In our view, this declaration is too restrictive and the right to lifesaving, suffering-reducing, and health-restoring medications should not depend on the origin or characteristics of the illness.

It is estimated that in 2003 drug expenditures in Latin America were about US$19 billion. This amount may not be sufficient, but it is well known that much of this money is wasted and that available pharmaceuticals are often poorly used. For example, physicians prescribe millions of antibiotics and psychotherapeutic agents unnecessarily; poverty forces patients to purchase incomplete treatments, a practice that can be wasteful and very often is iatrogenetic; those who cannot afford the fees and co-payments for professional services recur to self-medication and may purchase the wrong medicine; the preference for brand-name drugs over generic or copies is very costly and their prescription unnecessary; and hundreds of thousands of persons waste scarce pharmaceutical resources in lifestyle drugs, including a fast-growing number of young Latin Americans who do not suffer sexual dysfunction and are misguided by clever marketing techniques, and use Viagra, Cialis, or Levitra.

Many studies and reports have documented the poor's lack of access to needed medication and the health consequences of the inappropriate use of pharmaceuticals. The resolution of these problems should have been at the forefront of the development agencies' agenda. Unfortunately, this has not been the case. The WB in its 1993 World Development Report (WDR) presented the policies that should guide the improvement of health systems (World Bank, 1993). The agenda was based on the WB's neoliberal ideology and included policies aimed at expanding the role of the private sector and limiting public-sector expenditures to the provision of a very small package of basic services for the poor.

In the short section on pharmaceuticals most of the recommendations contradict the WB's neoliberal principles. This inconsistency was caused probably by the scarcity of in-house expertise in pharmaceuticals and the reliance on outside consultants, who had a different ideological perspective. In the acknowledgment for the drug discussions the WDR cites well-recognized scholars, and it would have been embarrassing to change their recommendations or as an alternative to omit the section on pharmaceuticals in a volume dedicated to health. The WDR states that pharmaceutical policies are "the most promising area (in the health sector) for efficiency gains in the short run" (WB, 1993: 159). To this aim, it recommends the use of the essential drug lists that the WHO first developed in 1977 and periodically updates. The 2005 version of the essential drug list includes 310 drugs that, according to the experts, excluding the so-called rare and orphan diseases, can resolve all pharmaceutical needs. With a few exceptions, the drugs included in the list are off-patent. According to the WDR the list should guide the registration of drugs. In Latin America, this recommendation was very much needed. Its markets contain thousands of unnecessary drugs that only serve to increase costs. Mexico has seven thousand drugs in nine thousand presentations; Honduras, fifteen thousand; the Dominican Republic, fourteen thousand; Nicaragua and Peru, over eleven thousand; Ecuador, Colombia, and Bolivia, over eight thousand; and most other countries, over five thousand.

The report also recommends the utilization of generic drugs and the use of cost-effectiveness criteria to choose among all available drugs within the same therapeutic group. This is also a welcome recommendation because it is well known that the use of generics can produce drastic price reductions. In Mexico and Brazil generic drugs were 30 to 40 percent cheaper than brand-name drugs, respectively. In the latter country, the yearly cost of antiretroviral treatment per person was reduced from US$4,860 in 1997 to US$1,000 in 2003 by using generics and threatening the multinational industry with issuing compulsory licenses, that is, breaking the patents. Within months of the approval of the generic prescription law in Argentina, prices of the most commonly prescribed pharmaceuticals decreased by 8 percent and some by 45 percent.

The WDR highlights the benefits of centralized, competitive, and transparent purchasing practices, benefits that are well documented, and the use of nonprofit distributors such as the United Nations Children's Fund (UNICEF) and the International Dispensary Association. In Guatemala, centralized drug procurement for the entire public sector, including the armed forces, resulted in savings of 65 percent and 23 percent for the Ministry of Health and the Social Security Institute, respectively.

A fourth recommendation is to strengthen the drug regulatory authority so that it is better equipped to ensure that all drugs on the market are good quality, safe, and effective. This advice was and remains appropriate since there are numerous reports on pharmaceutical companies that do not comply with International Good Manufacturing Practices, and pharmacies that sell prescription-only drugs over-the-counter and are staffed by clerks with little or no pharmaceutical training. In addition, there are an increasing number of counterfeit and unregistered drugs being found in the Latin American markets. The industry frequently bypasses laws and ethical codes regarding the promotion of medicines, manipulates prices, and engages in unlawful practices to delay the commercialization of generic versions of their brand-name drugs.

The 1993 report also recommends interventions to improve the adequate use of medicines and proposes behavioral changes for patients, prescribers, dispensers, and the industry. The actions suggested include educating consumers to reduce self-medication and requests for injections, which are highly regarded by consumers but carry a high risk of infections and transmission of diseases such as hepatitis and HIV. For physicians and pharmacists the WB recommends continuous pharmacological education and the use of formularies. The recommendations are well justified by the extensive social science and medical literature that has documented the shortcomings of current prescribing and dispensing practices and the detrimental behavior of patients who demand medications, oftentimes regardless of need, and fail to adhere to prescribed regimens.

If the WB in its most important policy document made the above recommendations, we could have expected that subsequent loans to Latin America would have been used to promote these recommendations to assist countries to achieve the intended changes. This was not the case. We have reviewed all WB health-sector loans to Latin America between 1991 and 2002 that included a pharmaceutical component (Homedes et al., 2005). We found that the vast majority of the funds were allocated to the purchase of medicines. Most of the funds of thirty-one of the thirty-seven loans were for drug procurement; seven included managerial improvements such as the development of data systems and increasing the efficiency of the procurement, distribution, and storage systems; six dedicated some funds to improving drug quality control; and two required the organization of revolving drug funds (a strategy to sell medicines to the poor).

The incongruence between the WB's recommendations and the interventions financed by its loans led us to explore the possible reasons for the WB's lip service to the policies outlined in its landmark health policy report. We concluded that perhaps one of the reasons is that if countries in Latin America and other regions implemented the WB-recommended policies the financial consequences for the TPCs could be very negative. The use of essential drug lists to control registration and procurement would have devastated the TPCs; for example, all lifestyle drugs would be left out of the market, drastically reducing the profits of TPCs. The use of unneeded drugs promoted by aggressive and frequently unethical advertisements would also decrease profits significantly. As discussed, the use of generic drugs reduces the financial benefits of the TPCs. For example, Pfizer would lose US$2.5 billion per year (or 19 percent of its total sales) just from not being able to sell Lipitor, its cholesterol-reducing drug, since there are cheaper generic statins in the market.

Did the WB err by including pharmaceutical recommendations in the 1993 report? We think that the staggering amount of money spent globally on pharmaceuticals (about US$500 billion in 2003) could not be ignored in a comprehensive health report, especially when the pharmaceutical sector was considered the most promising area for efficiency gains. It can be suggested that the failure to finance the pharmaceutical initiatives resulted from opposition from the TPCs. This hypothesis is supported by the presence of a pharmaceutical industry representative at WB headquarters. The WB chooses the person from the three-name slate presented by the industry. This person has an office and ample access to health strategy discussions, and de facto functions as a lobbyist for the industry. In 2002 the representative was from Pfizer, the largest pharmaceutical corporation in market capitalization in the world (US$284 billion in April 2004), and the incumbent is from Novartis, the fourth largest (US$118 billion in April 2004).

The silence of the WB during the 2002 WTO meeting's debate on TRIPS and the discussion that followed is indicative of the WB's lack of concern for the right to health. According to the TRIPS agreement, the patent extends the period of market-exclusivity (monopoly) of the new drug to twenty years. The agreement also defines when compulsory licenses (or permits to break the patent monopoly) can be issued and parallel importing (importing cheaper drugs protected by patents from other countries) permitted. As indicated before, many social movements and progressive NGOs such as Doctors without Borders have opposed the role of the WTO in promoting free trade without taking into account basic human rights such as access to food, health services, and medicines.

For radical neoliberals that currently control the United States government, the TRIPS agreement included too many concessions, and they succeeded in postponing the signing of the agreement until 2003. During this time, the WB avoided any critical comments regarding the negative health consequences of the free trade and the WTO rules and did not object to the U.S. government's position. Similarly, the WB has maintained silence regarding free trade agreements between the United States and Third World countries that under pressures from the pharmaceutical TCs include clauses even more restrictive than those established by TRIPS. The bilateral agreements, known as TRIPS +, extend the monopoly of patents to twenty-five years and make parallel importing and compulsory licenses more difficult. Taking into account that the WB in its 1993 Health Report consistently repeated that monopolies were one of the main obstacles to efficiencies in the health sector, its silence regarding TRIPS and TRIPS + can only be interpreted as a revelation of its true alliances and interests. Many Latin American countries, including Chile, Colombia, the Dominican Republic, Central American countries, Ecuador, and Peru (and countries in other regions), have signed or are in the process of signing bilateral/regional trade agreements with the United States that include TRIPS + provisions. By now it is almost a truism to say that the WB does not recognize the right to needed medicines. In case of doubt it is useful to remember that in the 1990s the WB did not favor the provision of antiretrovirals to HIV/AIDS patients in the Third World because of their cost. We now know that the astronomical prices charged for antiretrovirals by the TPCs were unrelated to their production costs. The US$10,000 charged yearly per treatment per person by TPCs has been brought down to slightly more than US$300 by Indian manufacturers of generic drugs. What kept scores of patients from receiving life-saving treatment was the greed of TPCs.

The WB also opposed the Brazilian HIV/AIDS program of free distribution of antiretrovirals (Galvão, 2005). This program is considered exemplary by the WHO and all leading NGOs. The Brazilian government, using a combination of strategies such as the public production of drugs, the use of generics, and aggressive bargaining with transnational pharmaceutical companies, has developed an affordable program that has halved AIDS-related mortality rates, reduced hospital admissions by 80 percent, saved since 1997 over US$2 billion from avoided hospital admissions, and curtailed the incidence of tuberculosis and other opportunistic infections. The savings are more than sufficient to cover the purchases of the antiretrovirals, a fact that questions the competence of the WB economists and raises more fundamental issues about the impact of ideologies on professional judgments. Myopic policies, based exclusively on capital accumulation at the expense of promoting equity and the well-being of the majority, explain the WB's indifference to the right to medicines and the missed opportunities to reduce mortality and human suffering among the poor.

Health Reforms and Profits

Toward the end of the 1970s most Latin American economies entered into a recession that had a severe impact on the poor. Unemployment and salary reductions escalated; for example, in Mexico between 1980 and 1989, the income of the working class was reduced by more than half. Many of the newly unemployed lost their social security benefits, including health coverage; and due to currency devaluations, the price of medicines skyrocketed (many drugs are manufactured in Latin America, but all active principles are imported). The IMF and the WB took advantage of the crisis and imposed "the Washington Consensus" as a condition for new lending to refinance the large accumulated national debt. Among other things, the consensus required the devaluation of currencies and the reduction of public social expenditures. The reduction of funding brought the already underfunded and crisis-riddled health services to a standstill. According to the United Nations Economic Center for Latin America (CEPAL, 1994), the two international organizations were in part responsible for the collapse of the Latin American public health systems.

The damage inflicted on Latin American public health services by the IMF and the WB did not stop there. The two institutions required governments to carry out reforms based on their neoliberal ideology. Two principles guided the reforms: the belief that the private sector is more efficient and less corrupt than the public sector, a principle that was invoked to promote the privatization of health care, and the conviction that competition produces goods of higher quality than monopolies; based on this principle, private health insurance and health care networks were asked to compete among themselves and with social security schemes. As a step toward privatization, the WB encourages and supports the managerial and fiscal autonomy of public hospitals. In the mind of the neoliberal reformers the principle of solidarity should be replaced by market competition. In addition, to reduce the fiscal burden of the national government and free national funds to pay the public debt, neoliberal reforms include the decentralization of public health services to the provincial and local governments, which in turn are required to cofinance the services.

The consequences of reforming Latin America health systems along the lines promoted by the IMF and the WB have been disastrous (Homedes and Ugalde, 2005). Some countries ended up with truncated reforms; others were able to implement only a partial decentralization; and only Chile and Colombia closely followed the neoliberal recommendations. Prior to the neoliberal reform, Chile had a National Health System (NHS), and all Chileans had the right to health care. The NHS was the result of years of political effort by center-left governments. A few years after the 1973 coup that put Pinochet in power, the military government began the implementation of neoliberal reforms. Privatization opened the doors to transnational health insurance companies. Currently, the private sector offers a wide choice of programs to those able to pay: eighty-eight hundred health plans! The poor have little choice but to join the public health insurance and are burdened by increasing co-payments.

Studies have documented that the transnational health insurance companies benefit from cross-subsidies from public health insurance and find legal loopholes to lower expenditures; for example, although it is now illegal, insurance companies continue to drop beneficiaries when they fall sick with costly diseases. In Chile, the quality of private care is not higher than that provided by the public sector; there is evidence that for complex and high technology care, those covered by private health plans use the public health services, even though this practice is illegal. On the other hand, the affiliation of more affluent persons—who tend to be healthier and more educated—to the private sector reduces the availability of funds to the public insurance scheme and has a negative impact on the care of those who cannot afford private premiums.

The decentralization of primary care to the municipalities has not reduced health inequalities; despite benefiting from two solidarity funds, poor municipalities cannot offer the same quality and range of services as those offered by more affluent ones. In 1996 municipalities in the top income decile spent nine thousand pesos per capita more than those in the lowest decile (US$1 = 407 pesos), and in 2003 the Ministry of Health declared that the Chilean health system was "extremely inequitable."

Colombia, where health authorities were aware and tried to avoid the pitfalls of the Chilean reform, presents a more devastating picture. Public hospitals were given autonomy, and from the time the reform was launched in 1993 to the present, the number of closures and bankruptcies has not abated. The

Colombian reform is based on the expansion of health insurance. The government subsidizes the premiums of the lowest income deciles. In theory, all the insured, regardless of their income, could select their health service provider, but in practice private insurance companies are not providing services to as many subsidized beneficiaries as anticipated, and many poor have to resort to public service networks. The government and the WB consider it a tremendous equity achievement that all poor have the right to health insurance, but independent studies show that in 1999 only 61 percent of the population was "covered," while before the reform 75 percent had access to some type of care; in Colombia insurance coverage and access are not synonymous. The figures show that health inequities have increased. In Bogotá between 1993 and 1997, out-of-pocket health expenditures for households in the highest income quintile decreased from 50,043 to 30,674 pesos, while they increased for those in the lowest income quintile from 17,881 pesos to 24,658 pesos (in 1997, US$1 = 1,064 pesos).

WB economists were once more very wrong when they thought that neoliberal reforms could result in significant savings for governments. To make the new system viable, the Colombian government significantly increased allocations to the health sector. The promised efficiencies did not materialize, in part due to large increases in administrative and personnel costs, and because the private sector is not necessarily more efficient than the public one. For example, in 1994, personnel costs represented 50 percent of all hospital operational expenditures; three years later the percentage had grown to 70; and between 1996 and 1998, the operational costs of the health system increased by 24 percent in real terms, while production grew only by 4 percent.

Unfortunately, the higher public expenditures did not result in better quality of care; in fact, the opposite might have occurred. There is evidence that the implementation of basic public health interventions deteriorated: immunization coverage dropped, the prevalence of vector-transmitted diseases increased, and tuberculosis control weakened. Moreover, 66 percent of the medical specialists who were surveyed asserted that disease prevention and health promotion activities had not improved, and 62 percent affirmed that the quality of medical care had deteriorated. Nurses expressed similar opinions and indicated that the market approach to health care had increased their stress levels and job dissatisfaction; forced them to seek multiple employments due to a deterioration of payments; and was keeping them away from the patients because they had to perform new bureaucratic tasks for which they had not been trained. The nurses thought that patients had reasons to perceive them as uncaring and detached because they did not have time to spend with them.

In Mexico and El Salvador the labor unions halted the WB attempts to privatize heath services provided by social security institutes. In the Dominican Republic, a group of prestigious physicians borrowed reform funds to build a luxury high-technology private health complex that only the wealthy could afford.

The process used by the WB to impose the reforms deserves comment. Typically, the WB organizes a reform unit within the ministries of health, and the nationals employed by this unit receive a salary disproportionately higher than the rest of the professionals at the ministry. These overpaid employees, with the assistance of foreign consultants paid by the WB, prepare the blueprints of the neoliberal reform. The reform units work in secrecy. The reforms to be implemented are not shared with members of parliaments, with the staff of the ministries, with other health professionals, with labor unions, or with the public in general. In the case of Mexico, the press discovered the existence of a US$700 million WB loan to carry out the privatization of the Mexican Institute of Social Security (IMSS). Congress leaders were not aware of the loan or of the extent of the reform. Once the news about the loan broke out, the unions mobilized quickly and the privatization of IMSS was derailed.

The failure of decentralization in Latin America has been documented in practically all countries of the region (Ugalde and Homedes, 2002). USAID continues to finance and provide technical support to the decentralization efforts without taking into account that successful implementation requires a number of requisites that do not exist in many countries. For example, countries need to have a relatively equitable geographical wealth distribution; if this is not the case, after decentralization the quality of care may deteriorate significantly. Local leaders need to have some basic education and political maturity; otherwise, local decisions could be detrimental to the health of the citizens and wasteful. In some small municipalities mayors are functional illiterates. Local politicians are inclined to build hospitals even if the municipalities do not have enough citizens to maintain acceptable occupational rates and it is impossible to attract specialists, or impose user fees for primary care to obtain funds for hospitals as was the case in some municipalities in Peru.

The decision to decentralize a health system is a political one that has to be based on the historical, cultural, and political context of each country and cannot be imposed by outsiders with questionable motivations. The unfortunate result of the latter practice is that the decentralization that has taken place in Latin America has not resolved the problems that existed before, in some cases has aggravated them, and in the process governments have spent a considerable amount of resources. According to official figures, the first failed attempt (1983–1988) to decentralize Mexican public health services cost US$452 million, and it should be added that only fourteen of the thirty-one states participated in the program. A few years later, Mexico began again to decentralize, a process that continued until 2004, when new policies unofficially ended the experiment. The second attempt is costing an additional US$35 million in yearly salaries.

After more than twenty-five years of promoting and financing decentralization everywhere in the world, some economists at the WB have began to recognize that decentralization may not be a policy that should be recommended to all countries. For example, in a study about poverty in Mexico led by WB economists, and financed and published by the WB (WB, 2004), the authors acknowledge that decentralization in Mexico may have contributed to the increase of inequalities and to lowering the states' efficient use of the federal health resources allocated to the poor. Yet, officially, the WB has not renounced the policy of decentralization.

CONCLUSION

Other authors looking at the role of international institutions in other regions of the world have documented the undesirable consequences of neoliberal health reforms and the effect of TCs and international institutions on the health of the poor (Fort, Mercer, and Gish, 2004; People's Health Movement, 2005a). Based on the research carried out in other parts of the world and our own in Latin America, we can conclude that with the end of colonialism after World War II, the capitalist class did not waste any time finding new ways of capital accumulation. The international institutions that at the time were created to assist poor countries to develop and reduce global poverty were redirected to help TCs that became the chosen instruments of capital accumulation.

With the passing of time, neoliberal ideology has increasingly been embedded in the ideology of international institutions. It can be said that there is a "culture" of neoliberalism that permeates their staff and leadership. Concomitantly, through mergers and buyouts, TCs have grown in size and in power, and it can be affirmed that at present there is a symbiotic interaction between the TCs and international institutions. Their combined financial resources are of such magnitude that they do not have any problems in co-opting prestigious universities and consultant firms and using them to propagate and implement their programs.

Regardless of their frequent overt manifestations to the contrary, the goal of the international institutions is not poverty eradication. If it were, their efforts have been a dismal failure, and following their own neoliberal principles they should be closed down. While globally extreme poverty has been reduced in some parts of the world, in others it has increased, and where it has been reduced, mostly in China, the IMF, WTO, WB, and USAID were not engaged. Our analysis of pharmaceuticals and medical care suggests that the decisions of the international institutions have helped TPCs and transnational insurance corporations in capital accumulation.

The role of the UN and its specialized agencies is somewhat ambivalent. Most of these agencies have not developed a culture of neoliberalism. On the other hand, their resources often come from international institutions, TCs, and governments that strongly support capital accumulation. At times, the UN specialized agencies object to specific policies of international institutions; other times they are co-opted or silenced by the international institutions, the power of TCs, or threats by neoliberal governments.

What is increasingly vital to improve the health of the population and make the right-to-health principle a reality is the work of social movements. As reported earlier in several examples, social movements have been critical of the role played by TCs and international institutions in the health field. By nature social movements are independent, and their lack of resources is compensated by the number of participants and the dedication of many. At the outset of the twenty-first century, the most promising alternative to transnational capitalism is the work of social movements, at times working in coalitions, or in alliances with UN agencies, and other times jointly with organizations that work on behalf of the transnational working class.

REFERENCES

Armada, Franciso, Carles Muntaner, and Vicente Navarro. 2001. "Health and Social Security Reforms in Latin America: The Convergence of the World Health Organization, the World Bank, and Transnational Corporations." *International Journal of Health Services* 31: 729–68.

CEPAL. 1994. *Salud, Equidad y Transformación Productiva en América Latina y el Caribe*. Serie Documentos Reproducidos, no. 41. Washington, D.C.: Pan-American Health Organization.

Fort, Meredith, Mary Anne Mercer, and Oscar Gish. 2004. *Sickness and Wealth. The Corporate Assault on Global Health*. Cambridge, Mass.: Southend Press.

Galvão, Jane. 2005. "Brazil and Access to HIV/AIDS Drugs: A Question of Human Rights and Public Health." *American Journal of Public Health* 95: 1110–16.

Homedes, Núria, Antonio Ugalde, and Joan Rovira Forns. 2005. "The World Bank, Pharmaceutical Policies, and Health Reforms in Latin America." *International Journal of Health Services* 35: 691–717.

———, and Antonio Ugalde. 2005. "Why Neo-liberal Health Reforms Have Failed in Latin America." *Health Policy* 71: 83–96.

People's Health Assembly. 2005. "Health Is a Human Right, Not a Commodity." Cuenca (Ecuador): Second International People's Health Assembly.

People's Health Movement. 2005a. "WHO's Bangkok Charter a Big Disappointment." Bangkok: People's Health Movement; Press Release, August 18.

———. 2005b. *Global Health Action 2005–2006.* London: Zed Books.

Ugalde, Antonio, and Núria Homedes. 2002 "Descentralización del sector salud en América Latina." *Gazeta Sanitaria* 16: 18–29.

United Nations. 1948. Universal Declaration of Human Rights. General Assembly Resolution 217 (A) (III). New York: United Nations.

United Nations Economic and Social Affairs Department. 2005. *The Inequality Predicament.* Report on the World Social Situation. New York: United Nations.

United Nations High Commissioner for Human Rights. 2001. *Access to Medications in the Context of Pandemics Such as HIV/AIDS.* Commission on Human Rights Resolution 2001 2001/33. Geneva: United Nations High Commissioner for Human Rights.

World Bank. 2004. *Poverty in Mexico. An Assessment of Conditions, Trends, and Government Strategies.* Washington, D.C.: The World Bank.

———. 1993. *World Development Report.* Oxford: Oxford University Press.

9

Indigenous in Itself to Indigenous for Itself

Keri E. Iyall Smith

Miners once used canaries to verify that the air was safe to breathe while they worked deep in the earth. If methane gas was present in the mine, the canary died, indicating to the miner that the conditions were unsafe. American Indians are widely regarded as the miner's canary in American society. One of the first authors to make this comparison was Felix S. Cohen. Thus, when American Indians suffer, this is a warning that the culture, identity, and well-being of all Americans are in danger. This thesis might apply globally as well: when indigenous peoples are endangered, all global cultures and livelihoods are at risk. If indigenous peoples are the canary in our global mine, it will only become more essential to analyze the relationships that are unique to indigenous groups to better understand the conditions of all global citizens.

This chapter begins with a definition of *indigenous* and an explanation of the relational concept, which is useful in further understanding indigenousness. Then I identify the points of contestation in indigenousness—challenges to theoretical and empirical applications of the term. A section analyzing rights sought by indigenous peoples begins with a discussion of the indigenous public: the body in civil society that is advocating most aggressively for freedoms and protections for indigenous people and nations. I then discuss the rights these publics are seeking, with illustrative empirical examples. Finally, I examine the contribution of sociology, highlighting the usefulness of the discipline's strengths. I apply the relational concept to illustrate interactions between indigenous peoples and academia, highlighting the role of public sociology in a decolonized and indigenized academy.

157

INDIGENOUS

Indigenous is not a race, an ethnicity, or a religion: indigenous peoples occupy a political position, in relation to states. Indigenous people are living descendants of the precontact (generally contact by Europeans) aboriginal inhabitants (United Nations Working Group on Indigenous Populations, 1994; Anaya, 1996), who were living in tradition-based autonomous communities (Guibernau, 1999). Indigenous nations are culturally distinct (Anaya, 1996; Guibernau, 1999) and often live as internal colonies, "engulfed by settler societies born of the forces of empire and conquest" (Anaya, 1996: 3; United Nations Working Group on Indigenous Populations, 1994). In the present day, indigenous nations have incorporated elements of the outside society, while remaining rooted in local traditions (United Nations Working Group on Indigenous Populations, 1994). Indigenous peoples are "*indigenous* because their ancestral roots are imbedded in the lands in which they live, or would like to live" (Anaya, 1996: 3; see also Clifford, 1997 [1994]). Indigenous communities should not be confused with minority groups, because their status is not dependent upon the number of people in the community (Trask, 1999). Instead, they occupy a distinct position in relation to the state, often referred to as quasi-sovereign. Additional freedoms, within the state apparatus, are often granted to indigenous groups because of their historical and contemporary ties to the land.

Under the saltwater thesis, *indigenous* is defined by a transoceanic relationship. The colonial power exercises control over a distant, external indigenous group. As it is defined here, indigenous includes European ethnic groups (such as the Basques, Irish, or Welsh) in addition to New World indigenous nations (such as the Native Hawaiians, Tamils, or First Nations of Canada). Limiting the application of *indigenous* to the conventions of the saltwater thesis can oversimplify the term, which is general enough to apply beyond the saltwater limitation. This definition of indigenous calls for a broader application of rights due to indigenous peoples than already exist within the international governing system: for example, mechanisms for the attainment of sovereignty. Instead of watering down its meaning, asserting the breadth of *indigenous* brings out the more technical expression of the term.

The Relational Concept

To more fully consider indigenousness, the relational concept examines the historical and political realities that indigenous groups face. There are three key ways that indigenous is a relational concept: Indigenous to Newcomers, Internal Colonies to the Settler State, and Indigenous to "In Formation" (see figure 9.1). In the first system, indigenous and newcomers have reciprocal relations, even if the newcomers are dominant. For example, at the same time that the United States was beginning to harvest the natural resources on the Hawaiian Islands and establish sugar plantations, the U.S. government formally recognized the sovereignty of the Hawaiian Kingdom. As the economic exploitation deepened, the United States was still forced to admit the political independence of the Hawaiian Islands. In the second system, internal colonies and the settler state have a less egalitarian relationship, which is illustrated by a dotted arrow running from internal colonies to the settler state and a solid arrow running in the opposite direction. For example, during the time window occupied by system two, the United States' federal government was establishing federal Indian law, with landmark decisions made by the Supreme Court. This law applies to Indian tribes, which were supposedly sovereign nations. Thus, the government was able to set legal precedent, and tribes could do little, beyond lawsuits, to respond to the institutionalization of Federal Indian Law.

In the final system, the indigenous and "in formation" are again opposing each other in an unequal relationship, but this time there is a solid arrow running from indigenous to "in formation" and a dotted arrow running in the reverse direction. A current example is in the press: the Inuit are drafting a petition against the United States, asserting that its high rate of energy use is contributing to global warming. The melting of arctic ice, the Inuit argue in the petition, is threatening their lifeways and violating their human rights. Upon completion, this petition will be filed with the Organization of American States. This example illustrates how indigenous peoples have the ability to effect change in the United States and globally. The Inuit's right to be cold

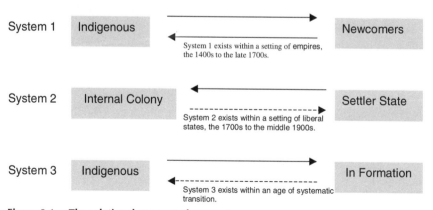

Figure 9.1.   The relational concept: three systems.

has the potential to impact global energy use and perhaps shape the emerging global governance and economic systems. United Nations doctrine promising the protection of culture, the environment, and human rights will make it difficult to ignore the Inuit's petition.

All of the systems exist within a setting of the capitalist world economy (as described by world systems analysis), which is now in an age of transition. Each system exists in an era dominated by one type of political body: for the first system this is the empire; for the second system it is the liberal state; and for the third system it is the liberal empire. When system one becomes politicized it shifts to a relationship as described in system two. When system two becomes globalized it shifts to a relationship as described in system three.

Contesting *Indigenous*

Indigenous is a social and historical construct. As such, it is necessary to discuss some of the ways to problematize this term. Three items stem from the terminology used in the definition: precontact inhabitants, culturally distinct, and tradition based. Three other items are rooted in the empirical application of a definition of *indigenousness*: considering the technical definition versus the normative definition, reliance upon contested histories or imagined communities for data, and the uniformity or diversity of a community. Each source of contestation will be examined in detail below.

While an essential part of defining *indigenous*, the requirement that a group (or individual) be living descendants of precontact inhabitants can be problematic. Establishing this link of familial relations can be complicated. Before contact and even in the early years of colonialism, records of familial ties existed in oral histories. Information that is not documented in writing is often discounted or disregarded. The word of mouth histories are subject to error, as are other sources of documentation of familial relations, and thus oral histories ought to be given equal weight as evidence in contested cases. In the United States, censuses of American Indians were taken at various time points.

These data are unreliable because of the communication gap that may have hindered counting, and it was not uncommon for people to hide their families from the government agents. Racism on the part of officials also limits the information available in some circumstances. Due to the many potential sources of error, it is difficult to offer irrefutable evidence of familial ties to precontact inhabitants. Supporting or denying a group or individual the status of "indigenous," based upon the evidence that an individual or group is a descendant of a precontact inhabitant, is a challenge in the best circumstance. Universal standards are needed, to at least ensure some degree of fairness. Indigenous groups and their claims are often discounted. This has been particularly problematic in the liberal state, which exerts claims for equality and assimilation while resisting population diversity.

Similarly, the element of a distinct culture is a part of what it means to be indigenous and must be included in the definition. Localities remain distinct, sometimes in only subtle ways. Many indigenous groups continue to maintain a distinct community: perhaps by protecting stories or an artisan's technique. They have local knowledge that allows them to survive cyclones ("Solomon Survivors Tell Their Story," 2003) in the Solomon Islands, survive tsunamis in Indonesia, and predict the weather in Australia ("Experts Look to Australia's Aborigines for Weather Help," 2003). Even after contact with outsiders, the indigenous communities are distinct. This might be less evident when the people wear Levi's jeans as opposed to clothing woven of cedar bark. More digging may be necessary to find evidence that supports the assertion that the indigenous culture is distinct, but this does not mean that there is no distinction.

The requirement that an indigenous group be tradition-based is another element of the definition that is problematic. Culture and identity are not static. They change over time, as a result of influences from within as well as outside of the communities. Establishing what it means to be tradition-based in a globalizing society is an empirical problem. This question was asked recently in the Pacific Northwest, where the Makah tribe conducted a whale hunt using both indigenous and modern technologies. The Makah argued that the use of modern conveniences did not render the hunt nontraditional: ceremonial elements of the whale hunt did follow tradition. Questions of authenticity arise as indigenous groups are modernizing. Researchers must carefully consider what it means to be "tradition-based" with whatever data they can gather. The fluid nature of collective identity must be considered to ensure that indigenous nations are tradition based, while not excluding groups that modernize at varying rates.

In talking about indigenousness, there is discord between the meaning of the term in theory and in normative behavior. For example, it is possible for an American Indian tribe to exist, but to have no political rights as a tribe because the norms established within the federal acknowledgment process exclude the tribe from achieving recognition. Many indigenous communities find themselves outside the boundaries of the normative system, either federal or international. This leaves them in a vulnerable circumstance, often experiencing unequal distribution due to their ascribed identity as indigenous, without the protections that are awarded to groups that fall within the normative boundaries of indigenousness.

The reliance upon contested histories and imagined communities (for example language, songs, and stories) for data is problematic when attempting to assess the indigenousness of groups. Establishing whether a group is "indigenous" or not sometimes requires that we rely upon stories, songs, or oral histories. This often matters because more than one group claims ancestral ties to the land or seeks access, hunting, or fishing rights. At other times a group is trying to achieve formal recognition (e.g., federal acknowledgment in the American context). The real world is messy, and it is not simple to determine which community is indigenous to a given territory. Cultural boundaries are blurry. It is not always possible to establish one side as having a greater right to indigenousness. The firm establishment of a group as being indigenous can be impossible in some circumstances, due to a lack of reliability in the data that are required to make an assessment.

Although it might be implied that indigenous groups are uniform, they are not. Within a single community, the people might be diverse due to intermarriage, may vary in the extent they uphold traditions, and may vary in their relations with outsiders. Many tribes in the Northwest have had vitriolic disputes over casino-building projects. Often one side is promoting gaming for its potential as an economic resource and another side is fearful of the risk of tribal members becoming addicted to gambling. While indigenous peoples are one type of group, there is great diversity within the population of indigenous peoples, or within tribes, bands, or nations. Indigenous tribal groupings are not the only groups with a diverse membership. For example, there are differences among feminists, civil rights groups, and political parties. An indigenous group is not completely uniform or homogeneous. Their diversity does not render them unable to act as a collective, and it does not erode their collective identity.

The Indigenous Public

The freedoms of indigenous peoples are at risk. Globalization threatens fragile local cultures, as capital and cultural products flow more freely around the world. Indigenous groups are often highly dependent on environmental resources that are imperiled by global forces. Yet, globalization also creates opportunity for easier and more immediate communication. One result of this is a global movement, indigenism: an "international movement that aspires to promote and protect the rights of the world's 'first peoples'" (Niezen, 2003: 4). A pan-indigenous identity is taking shape in the global context (Wilmer, 1997 [1993]). The pan-indigenous identity refers to the emerging identity shared by all indigenous peoples around the globe. This identity includes all indigenous peoples and is the product of the many indigenous groups coming together. The pan-indigenous identity is also known as *indigenism*, a term coined by Niezen (2003). As a transnational movement, its membership spans the globe. Assimilative education, the loss of subsistence, and state abrogation of treaties drive the formation of a common global indigenous identity (Niezen, 2003).

The pan-indigenous public is both a single public and a diverse one. This paragraph describes some of the intragroup differences. Some groups are internal colonies—nations without a state—and others are diasporized populations; others are a majority group. Overcoming oppression is one of the central goals. Some indigenous groups live with descendants of the colonizers and missionaries; in other cases the colonial agents left. State boundaries may contain multiple indigenous groups or the boundaries may divide indigenous communities (e.g., Basques). Colonial context varied: states practiced direct or indirect rule. Thus, even the experience of colonialism is not uniform. Instead groups experience colonialism, postcolonialism, and sometimes internal colonialism distinctly. In the contemporary context, indigenous peoples of North America experience entrenched discrimination. Indigenous peoples in many Latin American countries are protected by law. In Africa and Asia, indigenous peoples face challenges to politicizing their status as indigenous because the state is liberated from its colonizer (Niezen, 2003).

SEEKING RIGHTS AND PROTECTIONS

Within these multiple contexts, indigenous peoples work independently and as a pan-indigenous movement to seek rights and freedoms from the state and international governing bodies. Among the rights sought are the right to engage in cultural practices, language protections, preservation of indigenous dietary choices, access to and protection of sacred sites, environmental protections, preservation of medicinal plants and their habitats, the right to traditional healing methods, access to homeland, the right to practice religion, freedom to participate in alternative political and social systems, and preservation of a relationship with the land. The key projects of indigenism are affirming local claims of difference, using the language and symbols of states in claims of self-determination, and embracing the universal concept of human rights to protect and develop identity (Niezen, 2003). These rights may be protected under state constitutions in some cases, and in other cases there are international treaties and doctrine that protect and preserve the indigenous public. Protections of the rights of indigenous peoples are not all on a platter for the taking: many must be sought or asserted.

Indigenous forms of resistance are distinguished from ethnicity-based resistance, due to the unique political status of indigenous peoples. Indigenous movements cannot be categorized as new or old social movements. Instead, they embody antisystemic movements in an age of transition. For example, the Native Hawaiian movement, which consists of multiple movement organizations, contains all of the four strategic considerations: open debate about the transition and outcome, short-term defensive action, establishment of middle-range goals, and the development of substantive meaning of long-term goals (Wallerstein, 2002).

For indigenous groups seeking rights and freedoms, the best solution may not be to adhere to an historical document or agreement (Kymlicka, 1995; Trask, 1999). This would mean adherence to an agreement that may have been signed under duress or with a lack of understanding. Given competing histories, it may not be possible to fully understand the circumstances surrounding the initial agreement. Many of the agreements are out of date, "patently unfair," or signed under duress or in ignorance. Indigenous groups' needs exist outside of the boundaries of what the state can provide, and as such they must seek rights from another entity. Also, seeking rights from states reaffirms state powers, particularly over the indigenous people.

Indigenous nations need another source of rights, freedoms, and protections beyond the states that they exist within as internal colonies. Sometimes rights are granted by human rights treaties, which allow for the maintenance of cultural integrity (Corntassel and Primeau, 1995). The United Nations is interested in protecting indigenous peoples, forming a working group and drafting a Declaration of Indigenous Rights designed to "advance the intermediate indigenous goal of holding states accountable to international standards of respect and protection for indigenous peoples, lands, resources, and cultures" (Lam, 1992: 607–8). International human rights doctrine can be a protector of freedoms and rights. Indigenous nations are pushing international human rights beyond the limits of state-centered structures. Now agents—instead of objects—of human rights, indigenous nations are defining and attaining access to human rights (Anaya, 1996).

Human rights can be a means of attaining the rights to self-determination, self-government, the maintenance and development of culture, and the right to hold land collectively. Indigenous nations can seek human rights as a means to protect freedom and agency: "the great advantage of individual human rights is that they allow, even encourage, persons occupying dishonored categories to join together to collectively pressure for recognition of their human rights" (Howard, 1995: 160). Indigenous nations exist outside the realm of many states' governing bodies. As additional policies are adopted, for example the United Nations Declaration on the Rights of Indigenous Peoples and the UNICEF Declaration on Cultural Diversity, the definition of human rights is expanding.

The International Labour Organization (ILO) has been concerned with indigenous and tribal peoples, adopting conventions in 1957 and 1989. Many pieces of human rights doctrine (e.g., International Labour Organization Convention Number 169 1989; United Nations Draft Declaration on the Rights of Indigenous Peoples 1994; and Proposed American Declaration of the Rights of Indigenous Peoples 1997) explicitly state that indigenous peoples and nations are entitled to human rights protections and freedoms. In 2000 a Permanent Forum on Indigenous Issues (UNPFII) was formed by the United Nations. This panel consists of eight indigenous experts, chosen by the indigenous communities, and eight experts elected by the Economic and Social Council. The forum was created on the recommendation of the Commission on Human Rights and will report to the Economic and Social Council. The UNPFII urges the inclusion of indigenous peoples in the creation and implementation of poverty reduction policies, supports the writing of policy to improve indigenous lives, encourages bilingual instruction and the teaching of indigenous culture and traditional knowledge, seeks to protect the environment, promotes human rights and the welfare of women and children, and applies the Millennium Development Goals in indigenous communities. In addition to the Permanent Forum, UNESCO is working to promote the economic and social development of indigenous peoples via doctrine and its programs. Some examples of UNESCO programming include: promoting functional literacy among the indigenous, recognizing local knowledge, seeking unintrusive ways of integrating technologies in indigenous communities, documenting cultural resources, and promoting ILO policy. Indigenous peoples around the globe will gain freedoms as they are able to attain greater rights of self-government, self-determination, and possibly the return of aboriginal homelands.

The worldview of indigenous nations incorporates cosmology and spirituality into political and economic life and promotes a collective reference point instead of using the individual as the basis for rights (Maiguashca, 1994). The cultural distinctness of indigenous nations appeals to the international community and can be mobilized as a resource. Ceremonies, stories, and art are all assets that are unique to indigenous communities. Using culture as a resource that can be mobilized might call attention to the indigenous groups seeking human rights protections. In this case, indigenous identity is a "good" that can be employed to assist in the expanded definition and enforcement of human rights. We are now entering the Second International

Decade of the World's Indigenous People, which is the perfect opportunity for indigenous peoples to influence global conceptions of human rights.

INDIGENOUS PEOPLES AND ACADEMIA

Research will be needed as human rights claims grow in indigenous populations. Agencies will want to understand the current experience of indigenous peoples, and they will need assistance in understanding how to improve conditions. Working groups, such as the United Nations Working Group on Indigenous Populations, the International Work Group for Indigenous Affairs, and the Center for World Indigenous Studies, will work to analyze indigenousness. To better understand the context in which these researchers will be working, I use the relational concept to describe the relationship between indigenous peoples and academia (see fig. 9.2).

As in the initial relational concept described above, the political and economic contexts are as follows: the empire dominates in system one, the liberal state in system two, and the liberal empire in system three. All of the systems exist within a capitalist world economy. The empire is driven by exploration and exploitation of lands and peoples. When system one becomes politicized, the colonial powers politicize studies and analysis of indigenousness. Liberal states develop in some former colonies and others begin to consolidate leadership, via direct or indirect rule. The liberal state engages in assimilation of indigenous peoples in system two. Many indigenous peoples are still living as colonial subjects at this time, subject to assimilation in those settings as well. Co-optation of indigenous knowledge continues to benefit the colonial structure—in both internal and external colonies. The schooling of indigenous youth in colonial education systems usurps the best minds of the indigenous community and slows the transmission of indigenous knowledge systems to the next generation. When system two becomes globalized it shifts to the relationship as described in system three. The forces of globalization, which contribute to the development of a liberal empire, create space for the emancipation of indigenous peoples in system three. Instead of further eroding the agency and power of indigenous peoples, as in systems one and two, in system three of the relational concept indigenous peoples are empowered. A global pan-indigenous identity emerges, identified as indigenism. Modern communications systems and technologies enable indigenous peoples around the globe to share their struggles to maintain traditional culture and knowledge-ways.

In system one, academics are traveling the world, studying flora and fauna along with the inhabitants of foreign lands. Explorers and others are mapping

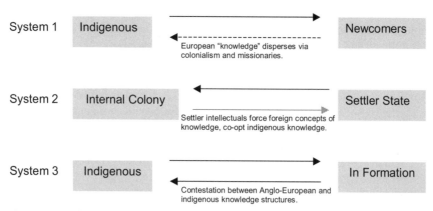

Figure 9.2. The relational concept: in the academy.

the globe. They are conquering lands, and documenting this territory—mapping it and taking censuses of the peoples who live there. Missionaries are creating written alphabets in indigenous languages and translating the Bible into the local language. At this phase, there is some dialogue between the indigenous and the newcomers—as they trade and exchange, seek to translate and communicate, and teach each other about living under the rigorous conditions.

In system two, the indigenous are now living as internal colonies—in their homelands. They are now studied by the settler state's academics—and are subject to this foreign definition of knowledge. Anthropologists are identifying and studying the "exotic other." Historians are appropriating indigenous knowledge and subjecting their histories to Anglo academic standards (where legitimacy is derived primarily from written records). Historic and ceremonial objects are stolen from communities and housed in museums—sometimes poisoned with arsenic and other materials thought to preserve the objects. Blood quantum is conceived in the United States—by legislation, yet this is not an indigenous concept of identity, but a foreign way of defining "who belongs" or in and out group membership. Anthropologists and historians benefit from culture brokers: indigenous peoples who are willing to tell stories and histories to strangers (sometimes stories and histories that tribal members might not agree ought to be told to outsiders). These academics document the stories of the indigenous and build their careers by communicating these stories to an academic audience. Also, children are taken away from communities for their education and sent to boarding schools run by religious missions. The goal of the boarding school is to assimilate the Indian to European language, history, life, and religion.

In system three, indigenous academics are seeking to decolonize indigenous scholarship and studies (Mihesuah and Wilson, 2004; Smith, 1999;
Thornton, 1998; Thornton and Snipp, 1998). A decolonized Native American
Studies, including history, anthropology, and other cross-disciplinary
research, will emerge. This decolonized study of Native Americans (and
other indigenous peoples) will document the past using indigenous voices in
accordance with indigenous tradition and knowledge systems and reinforce
the sovereignty of tribes and indigenous peoples. The UNPFII is also active
in seeking to decolonize the study of indigenous peoples, as evidenced by
two recent workshops: "Workshop on Data Collection and Disaggregation"
(2004) and "Methodologies Regarding Free Prior and Informed Consent and
Indigenous Peoples" (2005). These workshops considered gathering data to
better understand the indigenous experience and the impact of policy, and to
critically analyze the (mis)application of free, prior, and informed consent in
indigenous communities. As this decolonized study develops, it may also, to
some extent, indigenize the academy (Mihesuah and Wilson, 2004). Sociology will be an important contributor in this decolonizing scholarship, as it
recognizes the *existence* of indigenous peoples. It is not only a study of the
past, the artifacts, or the traditions. Sociology specializes in the study of community and group behavior. This can be applied to living and historical communities. The sociological study of indigenous communities, small and large,
historical and contemporary, will inform indigenous studies and American
Indian studies. Sociologists ask distinct questions about relationships that are
unique to groups—the roles of women and men, the family structure, political
structure, and community relations. Answers to these questions will enrich
understandings of indigenous peoples across academic disciplines. The study
of indigenous peoples will also inform sociological study, as this enables the
discipline to apply emerging theoretical concepts in other contexts, cultures,
and historical eras.

Sociology's Contribution

Historically, there is little work in the study of indigenous peoples in the field
of sociology. Yet, the tide on sociological research that studies indigenous
peoples may be shifting. Eva Garroutte (2003) looks at American Indian
identity, and literatures on social movements include the American Indian
Movement (i.e., Cornell, 1988). Other studies of indigenous peoples are
demographic (e.g. Sandefur, Rindfuss, and Cohen, 1996), or consider social
problems in indigenous populations (crime, alcohol abuse, drugs). World systems theorists also study indigenous people (e.g., Dunaway, 2003; Fenelon,
1997; Hall and Fenelon, 2004). At the annual American Sociological Associ-

ation meetings, paper sessions dedicated to the study of indigenous peoples are telling of future research in this subject area and its role in the discipline.

Sociology's potential contribution to the study of indigenous peoples is great. The discipline's expertise in the analysis of relationships that are unique to groups will help it study the interactions between indigenism and other groups. It will also be best equipped to analyze the different groups that exist within this pan-indigenous collective. Sociological theory's strengths— framing puzzles, empirical grounding, and application of theoretical constructs—will be assets to the further study of indigenous peoples and the global context of this public. Public sociology's unique contribution to sociological analysis is its reflexive relationship between publics and academia (Burawoy et al., 2004). Public sociology must grapple with this new element of the global civil society. Sociology is well suited to study this emerging element of civil society: "sociology's distinctive object is civil society and its value is the resilience and autonomy of the social" (Burawoy, 2004: 1615). Public sociology's rooting in dialogue with the community will be essential to understanding indigenousness more fully, and it will affirm the agency of indigenous peoples.

Organic public sociology would be more difficult to successfully engage in, given the context. Traditional public sociology might enable researchers to gain integrity and eventually access. Once traditional public sociology or professional sociology gains legitimacy in the community, organic public sociology will likely be more welcome. Public sociology is particularly useful as a way of doing sociology in indigenous communities. The dialogic element creates space and establishes the legitimacy of local knowledge, demonstrating respect and relevance of the indigenous community and its lifeways.

Indigenous nations are entering the global cultural, political, and economic marketplace. The contribution from sociologists to the literature analyzing indigenous peoples will offer new ideas for debate and analytical research. The perspective of a sociologist is distinct in that it focuses on interactions between individuals and groups and examines rules for living together. Sociologists must consider these communities in greater depth, analyzing how their actions may impact the rights and obligations of all members of the international community.

CONCLUSION

Indigenous peoples are increasingly visible around the world due to globalization, modernization, and indigenism. The indigenous experience is gaining attention in international nongovernment organizations and in international governing organizations. Policies are being enacted to protect indigenous peoples and their cultures. Organizations such as UNESCO are working to revitalize and maintain cultures. The United Nations is working to expand indigenous political rights, especially in regards to political sovereignty.

To fully benefit from the international goodwill and the desire of governing organizations to recognize and protect indigenous peoples and lifeways, indigenism must be critically analyzed. Sociology is well suited to engage in this analysis, and Burawoy and his coauthors (2004) encourage the emergence of a global sociology with local, national, and transnational dialogues, rooted in an emergent transnational civil society. Analysis of indigenous communities and their actions is essential in our globalizing society: it may impact the rights, freedoms, and obligations of all members of the international community. This analysis might, in particular, allow us to discover ways to protect oppressed or endangered peoples and cultures. The pan-Indian and pan-indigenous communities have been once bitten by academia, and are therefore twice shy of future contact with academics, as the relational concept illustrates. Yet, public sociology must persist in seeking entry.

ACKNOWLEDGMENT

My thanks to Stephanie Teixeira for her assistance with the figures.

REFERENCES

Anaya, S. James. 1996. *Indigenous Peoples in International Law*. New York: Oxford University Press.

BBC News. 2003. "Solomon Survivors Tell Their Story." BBC News, January 4, (http://news.bbc.co.uk/1/hi/world/asia-pacific/2626743.stm) (accessed January 6, 2003).

Burawoy, Michael. 2004. "Public Sociologies: Contradictions, Dilemmas, and Possibilities." *Social Forces* 82: 1603–18.

———, William Gamson, Charlotte Ryan, Stephen Pfohl, Diane Vaughan, Charles Derber, and Juliet Schor. 2004. "Public Sociologies: A Symposium from Boston College." *Social Problems* 51: 103–30.

Clifford, James. 1997 [1994]. "Diasporas." In *The Ethnicity Reader: Nationalism, Multiculturalism, and Migration*, ed. Montserrat Guibernau and John Rex, 283–90. Cambridge: Polity Press.

Cornell, Stephen E. 1988. *The Return of the Native: American Indian Political Resurgence*. New York: Oxford University Press.

Corntassel, Jeff J., and Tomas Hopkins Primeau. 1995. "Indigenous 'Sovereignty' and

International Law: Revised Strategies for Pursuing 'Self-Determination.'" *Human Rights Quarterly* 17: 343–65.

Dunaway, Wilma A. 2003. "Ethnic Conflict in the Modern World-System: The Dialectics of Counter-Hegemonic Resistance in an Age of Transition." *Journal of World-Systems Research* IX(1): 3–34.

Fenelon, James V. 1997. "From Peripheral to Internal Colonialism: Socio-Political Change of the Lakota on Standing Rock." *Journal of World-Systems Research* 3(2): 259–320.

Garroutte, Eva Marie. 2003. *Real Indians: Identity and Survival of Native America*. Berkeley: University of California Press.

Guibernau, Montserrat. 1999. *Nations Without States: Political Communities in a Global Age*. Cambridge: Polity Press.

Hall, Stuart. 1997. "The Local and the Global: Globalization and Ethnicity." In *Culture, Globalization and the World-System*, ed. Anthony D. King, 19–39. Minneapolis: University of Minnesota Press.

Hall, Thomas D., and James V. Fenelon. 2004. "The Futures of Indigenous Peoples: 9-11 and the Trajectory of Indigenous Survival and Resistance." *Journal of World-Systems Research* X(1): 153–197.

Howard, Rhoda E. 1995. *Human Rights and the Search for Community*. Boulder, Colo.: Westview.

Kymlicka, Will. 1995. *Multicultural Citizenship*. Oxford: Oxford University Press.

Lam, Maivan Clech. 1992. "Making Room for Peoples at the United Nations: Thoughts Provoked by Indigenous Claims to Self-Determination." *Cornell International Law Journal* 23: 603–22.

Maiguashca, Bice. 1994. "The Transnational Indigenous Movement in a Changing World Order." In *Global Transformation: Challenges to the State System*, ed. Yoshikazo Sakamoto, 356–82. Tokyo: United Nations University Press.

Mihesuah, Devon Abbott, and Angela Cavender Wilson. 2004. "Introduction." In *Indigenizing the Academy: Transforming Scholarship and Empowering Communities*, ed. Devon Abbott Mihesuah and Angela Cavender Wilson, 1–15. Lincoln: University of Nebraska Press.

Niezen, Ronald. 2003. *The Origins of Indigenism: Human Rights and the Politics of Identity*. Berkeley: University of California Press.

Popper, Karl. 1959. *The Logic of Scientific Discovery*. London: Hutchinson.

Reuters (unsigned article). 2005. "Inuit to File Anti-US Climate Petition." Common Dreams NewsCenter, June 15, www.commondreams.org/headlines05/0615-05 (accessed June 16, 2005).

Reuters (unsigned article). 2003. "Experts look to Australia's Aborigines for Weather Help." CNN.com, March 19 (http://www.cnn.com/2003/TECH/science/03/18/offbeat.weather.aborigines.reut/) (accessed March 24, 2003).

Sandefur, Gary D., Ronald R. Rindfuss, and Barney Cohen (eds.). 1996. *Changing Numbers, Changing Needs: American Indian Demography and Public Health*. Washington, D.C.: National Academy Press.

Smith, Linda Tuhiwai. 1999. *Decolonizing Methodologies: Research and Indigenous Peoples*. London: Zed Books, Ltd.

Thornton, Russell. 1998. "Introduction and Overview." In *Studying Native America: Problems and Prospects*, ed. Russell Thornton, 3–14. Madison: The University of Wisconsin Press.

————, and Matthew Snipp. 1998. "A Final Note." In *Studying Native America: Problems and Prospects*, ed. Russell Thornton, 416–21. Madison: The University of Wisconsin Press.

Trask, Haunani-Kay. 1999. *From a Native Daughter: Colonialism and Sovereignty in Hawai'i*. Honolulu: University of Hawaii Press.

Turner, Jonathan. 1998. *The Structure of Sociological Theory*. 6th ed. Belmont, Calif.: Wadsworth.

United Nations. Economic and Social Council. Permanent Forum on Indigenous Issues. 2004. Report of the Workshop on Data Collection and Disaggregation: http://daccess dds.un.org/doc/UNDOC/GEN/N04/236/91/PDF/N0423691.pdf?OpenElement (accessed August 21, 2005).

————. Permanent Forum on Indigenous Issues. 2005. Report of the International Workshop on Methodologies Regarding Free, Prior and Informed Consent and Indigenous Peoples: http://daccessdds.un.org/doc/UNDOC/GEN/N05/243/26/PDF/N0524326 .pdf?OpenElement (accessed August 21, 2005).

————. Working Group on Indigenous Populations. 1994. *UN Draft Declaration on the Rights of Indigenous Peoples*. As printed in *Indigenous Peoples in International Law* by S. James Anaya. 1996. Oxford: Oxford University Press.

Wallerstein, Immanuel. 2002. "New Revolts against the System." *New Left Review* 18 (Nov/Dec): 29–39.

Wilmer, Franke. 1997 [1993]. "First Nations in the USA." In *The Ethnicity Reader: Nationalism, Multiculturalism, and Migration*, ed. Montserrat Guibernau and John Rex, 186–201. Cambridge: Polity Press.

Wilson, Angela Cavender. 2004. "Reclaiming our Humanity: Decolonization and the Recovery of Indigenous Knowledge." In *Indigenizing the Academy: Transforming Scholarship and Empowering Communities*, ed. Devon Abbott Mihesuah and Angela Cavender Wilson, 69–87. Lincoln: University of Nebraska Press.

10

Migrants, Rights, and States

Anthony M. Orum and Arlette Grabczynska

All politics is local.

—Tip O'Neill

Over the course of the past three decades, the world has changed considerably. The economy of global capitalism has been the driving force for these changes. Armed with new technologies and other innovations, the economy has managed to break down otherwise substantial boundaries between nations, and promoted a greater degree of economic integration and planning that would have previously been thought impossible. As Thomas Friedman (2000) proclaims, this situation produces both winners and losers. The winners are corporations and countries that manage to make the transition to the new forms of technology and economic strategies with ease. The losers are those that fail to do so.

Among the most vulnerable of the losers are migrants, people who leave their home countries and move to new countries, often in search of better lives and jobs. Some migrants are more capable than others: they possess special skills and education that provide them with a decided advantage in the country to which they migrate. But many migrants, if not most, are at a decided disadvantage. They lack both ready skills and education, leaving them vulnerable to the vagaries of a rapidly changing economic climate.

The situation of migrants has prompted a growing concern in many quarters. Nations, of course, are concerned because of the rapidly growing size of their numbers, a change that promotes the fortune of some countries, especially rich ones, at the expense of others, especially poor ones. There are also international organizations, like the United Nations, as well as nongovernmental organizations that are deeply troubled by the situation that migrants face. Indeed, the United Nations has gone so far as to propose a set of standard basic rights for migrant workers, and it has strongly promoted those rights over the past couple of decades. These rights are now in the form of a treaty that went into effect in 2003.

The two of us are advocates—strong advocates—for the cause and betterment of the condition of migrants in the world. We abhor the abuses that migrants routinely suffer, often simply because they are so vulnerable and thus open to the whims of governments that are only concerned about the world of realpolitik. We also are aware that the cause of migrants can only be advanced through a careful attention to their situation, to the ways that governments act, to the operations of the courts and, finally, to the politics of everyday life. Indeed, in this chapter the reader will find a continuing thread and tension between the ways in which migrants are treated by governments and the ways in which their lives actually unfold, day-to-day, job-to-job, country-to-country. Ultimately, as advocates for migrants we urge not only that governments be reformed in ways to improve the lives of migrants, but that each and every one of us support those local efforts, in our towns and backyards, to acknowledge the dignity of migrants and, in consequence, to help expand the range of their rights and freedoms.

Toward this end, we shall touch on a number of important issues concerning the topics of migration, citizenship, and states. In particular, we want first to consider the dimensions of the new migration, and what the prospects are for its growth in the coming years. Second, we want to consider the important role of nations both in promoting and in controlling migrant populations. In this regard, we shall focus some attention on how nations handle the matter of citizenship for new migrants and variations among them in terms of the rules of citizenship. This is an extraordinarily important but also rapidly changing political terrain. Third, we want to consider the growing number of voices that call for a broad set of human rights, for migrants but also for people generally. Here we shall just briefly note the efforts in the United States as well as in other countries, and also draw attention to the singular work of such organizations as Amnesty International. Fourth, we shall consider cases that concern migrants and examine how the courts (specifically the United States Supreme Court) handle cases involving both noncitizen residents of the country and immigrants who lack legal status. These cases can be instructive in assessing the prospects that the rights of migrants can be both acknowledged and become institutionalized.

Finally, we shall try to show how the concepts and imagination of sociologists can be used to better understand as well as to advance the cause of migrants. Instead of simply viewing migrants as pawns in the hands of an all-powerful state, we believe that it is equally important to view them also as agents who, coupled with important allies, can exercise choice over their own destinies. But the circumstances and conditions under which they do so are by no means obvious. Thus we will consider some of the ways in which migrants can mobilize power to advance their own interests and purposes. Here we shall provide a few recent illustrations to reveal the leverage and power that migrants possess.

DIMENSIONS OF THE NEW MIGRATION

Migration, the temporary or permanent movement of masses of people from one place to another, has been an ever present feature of the world throughout human existence. Groups of people have shifted from one site to another, often doing so in search of food, or new means of survival. Economic motivation has often been the central factor promoting such movement. Lacking work opportunities in their own homelands, people decide to look elsewhere for such opportunities and, under the right conditions, they will move, many times in massive numbers. For example, at the end of the nineteenth and beginning of the twentieth centuries, millions of Europeans moved to the United States, prompted partly by the poverty they faced at home, but also by the rapidly expanding economy in the United States, an economy that helped to lift their fortunes in dramatic ways. Political conditions can make a difference as well. The revolutions that broke out across Europe during 1848 also resulted in the movement of tens of thousands of people to the United States.

Since the end of World War II, the rate of migration across the world has increased considerably (Castles and Miller, 1998: chapter 4). The usual economic and political reasons help to explain the changing dimensions of this migration, but there are other reasons as well. Wars and violence within some nations have created large groups of refugees in such countries as Vietnam or Cambodia, people who, hoping to escape violence and possible death in their homelands, seek refuge in other, more hospitable lands.

At the same time, growing inequalities between nations have compelled ever larger numbers of migrants to move from poorer countries, such as those in Eastern Europe or in Latin America, to richer ones, such as the United States or the countries of Western Europe. Moreover, the ease with which people can now move across national boundaries has grown considerably. In earlier times, even in the twentieth century, the boundaries between states were hard and served both to exclude foreigners and to contain natives. But now, with an expanding global economy, one that is becoming structured and integrated across national boundaries, the boundaries themselves are beginning, in the words of Xiangming Chen (2005), to bend, if not to break. The effect has been to generate ever larger numbers of people who change locations, from one country to another—and who often make roundtrip journeys, between one country and another—on regular intervals during the course of a single year.

Consider a few numbers that illustrate the magnitude of these movements. It is estimated that as of 2000 about 3 percent of the world's population were migrants, or roughly 175 million people (International Organization for Migration, 2005: chapter 23). Of this number, the large majority were concentrated in Western Europe and the United States: on the order of about 10 to 13 percent of the population of these countries consists of migrants. These numbers only cover documented, or legal, migrants. In the United States, estimates suggest that, beyond the thirty million foreign-born residents who live there, another seven to eight million undocumented migrants also are in residence.

Thus, when we consider the cause of migrants and of taking steps to enhance the quality of their lives, we are talking about almost two hundred million people, a figure that, according to most estimates, will only continue to increase over time (International Organization for Migration, 2005).

STATES AND MIGRATION

States, those territorially bounded sovereign entities that have played such a large part in the history of the twentieth century, play an equally important role in the lives of migrants. (We shall refer hereafter to nations, or nation-states, as states. This is a somewhat technical point in the literature on sociology and political science that deals with such phenomena. States represent, in effect, nations as actors, as organizations that continuously work to exercise their sovereignty both over their territory and their citizens.) States can act to control both who enters and who leaves their domain. Most importantly, as the sociologist Rogers Brubaker so effectively argued (1992), states are also membership associations: they determine who is a citizen and who is not. (Also see Gerard Delanty's chapter in this volume.) And because of this they can exercise a great deal of control over the lives of individuals, grant them benefits, if they choose to do so, but also deny them rights if those individuals do not qualify, under the rules of a specific state, to attain citizenship.

The impact of state authority over matters of migration is thus considerable. A particular state can deny entrance to individuals, or more precisely, a class of individuals, if it chooses to do so. Moreover, states can also decide which residents are entitled to citizenship, and thus full protection under its sovereignty, and which are not. Not all states, however, use the same rules. Indeed, there has been considerable variation among states in the use of particular criteria. For instance, until recently citizenship in Germany was based upon the rule of *jus sanguinis*: this meant that a person was considered a full citizen of Germany if she were related by blood to individuals who were German citizens themselves. Thus, even if someone did not live on German soil, but was in fact the descendant of someone who was German by birth, that person was also considered a citizen of Germany. The effect of such a rule was both expansive and restrictive. It meant that there were German citizens who were scattered across the globe and could, at any time, return and enjoy their full rights in Germany; yet it also meant that other people, many who had resided and worked in Germany for years as part of a broad program of GastArbeiter, or guest workers, were, despite their lengthy residence, not entitled to German citizenship, and thus deprived of the ability to exercise their full rights. This effect was particularly harmful to the hundreds of thousands of Turks who had come to Germany in the 1950s and 1960s as part of the guest worker program.

Other states had different sets of rules, however. The United States, for example, operated on the basis of *jus soli*: a rule by which anyone who is born on United States territory becomes a citizen automatically, even if her parents are not themselves citizens. This rule, in fact, applies to the children of many migrants, even those that are undocumented, or illegal. Thus, for certain groups of migrants in the United States, such as those from Mexico, the nuclear family consists of parents who are not citizens and children who are. Therefore, the children enjoy a much greater degree of freedom and opportunity than their parents. In general, the United States has been among those states, including Australia and Canada, which have been very open and inviting on the matter of migration, and thus it has historically made it much easier for migrants to become citizens here than other countries, like Germany.

The complex rules for membership, or citizenship, among different countries are deeply rooted in the history of these countries. The tightly restrictive rules for citizenship in Germany, Brubaker points out, are bound up with the idea that Germans, as citizens, are not merely regarded as members of a political entity, the state, but are also regarded as members of an exclusive club, the nation, and thus deeply tied to the historical roots and contours of Germany (Brubaker, 1992: chapter 6). The United States, by contrast, from its earliest moments a nation created by migrants, has encouraged considerable diversity and divorced the idea of statehood from nationhood. The effect has been to build a state composed of people from a variety of nations, or what some observers refer to as an immigrant nation (e.g., Joppke, 1999).

These very important structural differences have acted, in effect, as historical filters, determining not only who, but how many people enter and become full-fledged members of a particular state. Yet, in recent years, with the growing numbers of migrants worldwide, the ability of states to act both to include and exclude particular people from an enjoyment of specific rights has diminished considerably. Indeed, a country like Germany has enacted laws in recent years that would permit the large number of guest workers from Turkey to more easily qualify for citizenship. And in the European Union, that political entity whose origins go back to the post–World War II period, the member states now grant both free movement and specific rights to any person who is a citizen of another member state. This rule has been established to ease the mobility of people back and forth across national boundaries, a movement that permits them to work in one country but retain their home base in another.

Today, almost all observers agree on two important facts about states and migration: (1) states differ among themselves because of the nature of the rules they employ to control migration—and granting membership status, thus entitling some to enjoy certain rights of membership—and (2) the magnitude of migration, itself, is forcing the very rules of the game to be changed. Still there are very sharp disagreements about the extent to which states retain their central player status in the lives of migrants. One popular argument maintains that a new form of citizenship has emerged recently, one that has been identified as postnational citizenship. This view, originating in the writings of sociologist Yasemin Soysal (1994), argues that changes found especially in the European Union regarding the expansion of rights for migrants to welfare benefits, family reunion opportunities, and voting presage a new era in world history. This is an era, she insists, in which a new kind of transnationalism is at work, one in which many different organizations and agencies are promoting a broad sense of human rights, based upon the notion of personhood, not nationhood. Her evidence is based, in part, on the broad social rights that migrants from outside the European Union have enjoyed in its member states.

Soysal's argument, while very intriguing, also has produced a number of critics. Most of them argue that states still differ sharply in the rules of membership and therefore in the rights that migrants may enjoy in them. The agenda for a broad campaign and implementation on behalf of human rights, and personhood, they insist, is a laudable goal. But when it comes down to the facts of the matter—and especially to the adjudication of legal disputes—national boundaries, and hence national definitions of rights, still matter greatly. There is a small but powerful group of legal decisions that seem to prove this particular point (as we show below). Even more to the point, a number of scholars argue that the considerable disparity in power among different players on the world scene ultimately undermines a broad program for the human rights of migrants (e.g., Likosky, 2002). The most telling illustration, of course, is that while the United Nations has promoted a program of treaties for human rights, the largest and most powerful state, namely, the United States, has failed to ratify most of those treaties.

Yet, while the differences in power among the nations of the world remain considerable today, with obvious consequences for the implementation of a broad program of human rights, there is nevertheless a growing chorus of nongovernmental organizations and other associations that have taken up the battle cry on behalf of migrant rights. Next, we explore some of these voices.

PROMOTING MIGRANT RIGHTS AROUND THE WORLD

The human rights agenda has spread across the world over the course of the last two decades. At the forefront for the promotion of this agenda have been the United Nations and its affiliates, the UN Educational, Scientific, and Cultural Organization (UNESCO) and the International Labour Organization (ILO). The UN is vigilant about the rights of all people, based upon the general notion that everyone, regardless of their gender, race, ethnicity, or religion, is entitled to a certain basic core of human rights. Such rights include the right to a decent living, the right to respect, and the right to family unification. The UN has been especially forceful in drawing attention to those groups of people who are most vulnerable in the world—children, women, and migrants. Migrants, the UN recognizes, are especially vulnerable because they are people in search of a livelihood, people who are often desperately poor and thus in need of just the basic elements of food and shelter in order to survive.

In 1990 the UN approved the establishment of a convention that would meet regularly to discuss, monitor, and call for improvements in the ways that migrants were treated by different nations. Yet it was not until 2003 that this proposal was actually ratified by a sufficient number of nations—twenty—to actually be realized. This convention established a set of guidelines for the rights of migrant workers and their families. Those guidelines include the promotion of efforts to urge that nations be especially protective of the rights of migrants; that they act to limit racism and discriminatory behavior; and that they promote respect for diversity and multicultural interaction within their boundaries. The secretary-general of the United Nations, Kofi Annan, was a strong supporter of the effort to promote greater attention to the rights of migrant workers. He noted that it was important to have "stronger efforts by the United Nations to increase awareness of the rights of international migrants and the importance of effective integration of international migrants into the host society" (www.ipsnews.net/migration/stories/migpopulation-.shtml).

Yet at the same time, he also noted that of the 191 member nations of the UN, only twenty-five actually supported the 2003 UN convention, at least initially, and, most significantly, none of the major migrant-receiving nations, such as the United States or the countries of Western Europe, endorsed the migrant rights proposals.

There are a host of other organizations and associations across the world that endorse and work hard to promote a broad rights agenda for migrants. They include a number of labor organizations, such as the ILO, along with organizations, such as Migrant Rights International, which are devoted exclusively to monitoring and promoting measures that will improve conditions for migrants who live in different states. Plus there are a host of smaller nongovernmental organizations that endorse and support the same platform. Such organizations range across a broad spectrum of size and policy. The American Civil Liberties Union, for example, has a specific branch, the Immigrants' Rights Project Staff, which is devoted to protecting and defending the rights of migrants. But there are also groups like the Jewish Council on Urban Affairs in Chicago, and the Migrant Trade Union in South Korea that take up a similar call to action.

The success of such efforts depends upon the ability of these organizations to convince both the larger public as well as more powerful nations to take steps to advance and protect the rights of migrants and their families. The strategies pursued by such organizations are limited, but they draw upon the repertoire of strategies used by previous social movements (e.g., Tilly, 1995). For example, one such step was taken shortly after the UN convention went into effect in 2003. In the United States, groups of people organized an Immigrant Workers Freedom Ride that fall. The Freedom Ride, designed along the lines of the famous Freedom Rides in the South during the black civil rights movement, wended its way across the United States, beginning in cities like Seattle and concluding in New York City. As the buses made their way from city to city, they were greeted by small groups of supporters. Participants managed to get their message out to the local media as well. "Long delays, unnecessary restrictions and opaque procedures impose undue hardship on countless immigrant families" was the claim of a document prepared and distributed as part of the Ride (www.nwasianweekly.com/editorial/ride.htm).

And when the riders reached Milwaukee, Wisconsin, the Reverend James Lawson, a companion of Martin Luther King, Jr. during the civil rights Freedom Rides, spoke at a local church, telling members of his audience that "there is no human being in the sight of God who is illegal. No human being is undocumented" (www.nwasianweekly.com/editorial/ride.htm).

Today there is little question that there are many groups and organizations across the world that strongly support the effort to provide migrants basic human rights. But whether such organizations can prove to be effective against the often organized resistance of the most powerful states remains to be seen. Yasemin Soysal's notion of a postnationalist set of rights is certainly a worthy moral goal, and it finds material evidence in the range of groups that support the idea of migrant rights around the world. However, it is one thing to theorize such an idea, and it is quite another to win its acceptance and implementation. We turn now to consider the courts and the ways in which they have treated migrants over the years. Apart from the halls of government itself, this is the one major arena in which the rights of migrants, if they exist, will be both acknowledged and advanced. How have the courts ruled?

MIGRANT COURT CASES AND THEIR ADJUDICATION

While there has been a strong movement to enhance and enforce human rights around the world, and various human rights treaties have been agreed to and implemented by countries, the fact remains that most human rights abuses are dealt with not on an international front but in the nation in which they occur. As Christian Joppke (2002) argues, liberal states have established human rights protections within their domestic law and thus they limit their own sovereignty (instead of being limited by the global community) by enforcing those protections through their institutions, such as the courts. He notes, "Europe . . . is the region with the highest density of inter- and supranational rights norms and regimes anywhere in the world; and still most migrant rights are grounded in domestic law" (264). Since most immigrants' rights are based in domestic law, it is then instructive to look to a specific country and its treatment of immigrants in the judicial system.

Peter Schuck argues that immigration law in the United States before the 1980s was in a classical period (1998: 22). Under this conception the state is all powerful and has the right to determine whom to let in and whom to permit to stay. Because of this approach the liberal ideology that is very much a part of the United States' framework was not being applied to immigrants.

Congress defined qualifications for legal status, and the courts enforced those requirements. Schuck argues that the Supreme Court before the 1980s took a different approach to immigration cases than to other issues. While the Court generally applied the principle of judicial review in other situations, in the majority of immigration cases prior to the 1980s "the Supreme Court reflexively confirmed the deference principle with a decision on the merits in favor of the government rather than using that principle . . . merely as a disarming prelude to judicial self-assertion" (29). Thus, the Court in most immigrant cases of that time simply interpreted and enforced the requirements set forth by the legislative and executive branches.

The Supreme Court allowed the Immigration and Naturalization Service (INS) broad discretion in its treatment of aliens and citizens. Two examples of the abuses upheld by the Court are *United States ex rel. Knauff v. Shaughnessy* (338 U.S. 537 [1950]) and *Shaughnessy v. United States ex rel. Mezei* (345 U.S. 206 [1953]). In *Knauff* the Court upheld the exclusion of a foreign-born wife (who served and was honorably discharged from the United States Army) of a citizen without a formal hearing. The attorney general denied a hearing and excluded her on the grounds of confidential information he received (never disclosed to the husband, the wife, nor the Court) and that led him to conclude that her admission posed a danger to public security. In *Shaughnessy v. Mezei*, a twenty-five-year resident of the United States was denied readmission to the country, without a hearing, after a nineteen-month trip to Hungary. Although the order actually resulted in a three-year incarceration, based on confidential information only known to the attorney general, the Court upheld an indefinite detention of Mezei. While both of these cases were decided during the Cold War era, the ideology within them has been utilized thirty years after the decisions were issued when the cases were cited as precedents in *Landon v. Plasencia* (1982) and *Fiallo v. Bell* (1977).

The very nature of INS deportation procedures, civil not criminal, ensures that many constitutional guarantees of the Sixth Amendment are not applicable because they are specific to criminal procedures. In *INS v. Jong Ha Wang* (450 U.S. 139 [1981]) the Court upheld the attorney general's refusal to suspend deportation proceedings of two alien parents and their two citizen children. In its opinion the Supreme Court criticized the court of appeals for encroaching on the right of the INS to construe statutory standards for suspension as narrowly as it pleases. The following year the Court upheld the right of the INS to deport an immigrant whose eligibility for a visa expired because it failed to act on his application for eighteen months (*INS v. Miranda*, 103 S. Ct. 281 [1982]). Further, detention procedures, which may be used during pending cases or deportation proceedings, although they are meant to be used on a limited basis as the exception rather than the rule, are often abused. A case in point would be the *Shaughnessy v. Mezei* case mentioned above.

One notable exception to the Court's deference doctrine occurred in 1971 in *Graham v. Richardson* (450 U.S. 139 [1981]). In this case the Court invalidated a state statute withholding welfare payments from noncitizens. The Court argued that this was a violation of the Fourteenth Amendment because the state could not prove that withholding tax revenue benefits (to which all residents contributed) served a special public interest. This was a landmark case for immigrants because the Court bestowed a special designation upon noncitizens. The justices stated that "strict scrutiny" would be utilized in cases concerning resident aliens because of their vulnerable status as a nonvoting minority. While *Graham* only applied to state laws (federal laws are discussed later in this section) and only a small percentage of foreigners in this country who have legal resident status, it nonetheless led the way to invalidating various statutes that were discriminatory to noncitizens.

The impact of *Graham* was somewhat reduced, however, because of the evolution of a new doctrine first exhibited by the Court in *Sugarman v. Dougall* (413 U.S. 634 [1973]) and later used in other cases. The new doctrine held that states had the right to limit participation of aliens if this was done to maintain the integrity of their political communities. Although in 1973 the Court invalidated a New York statute in *Sugarman* because of inconsistencies in the law, the doctrine that was born in that case was later applied to uphold other New York statutes prohibiting resident aliens from becoming state troopers (435 U.S. 291 [1978]), teachers (*Ambach v. Norwick*, 441 U.S. 68 [1979]), and peace officers (*Cabell v. Jose Chavez Salido*, 454 U.S. 432 [1982]). On the federal law front the Court had issued a number of decisions upholding various discriminatory practices against resident aliens. In a number of cases in the 1970s (*Espinoza v. Farah Manufacturing Company*, 414 U.S. 86 [1973]; *Matthews v. Diaz*, 426 U.S. 67 [1976]; *Hampton v. Mow Sun Wong*, 426 U.S. 88 [1976]; *Fiallo v. Bell* 430 U.S. 787 [1977]) the Court held that limiting employment only to citizens is not in violation of the Civil Rights Act. The Court deferred to the political branches' power over noncitizens, noting that Congress has the authority to regulate legal status and the executive branch holds control over foreign relations matters.

The above-mentioned cases were limited to resident aliens and did not consider the Court's treatment of illegal immigrants. Next, we look at a series of immigration cases concerning this particularly vulnerable group. In *De Canas v. Bica* (424 U.S. 351 [1976]) the Court upheld a California statute prohibiting an employer from knowingly hiring an undocumented alien and ruled that the state law did not constitute an encroachment on Congress' sole power to regulate immigration. However, six years after *De Canas*, in 1982, the Court concluded that illegal aliens are afforded Fourteenth Amendment rights protections in *Plyler v. Doe* (457 U.S. 202 [1982]). *Plyler* was a decided victory for aliens since the Court invalidated a Texas statute denying illegal alien children access to public education. The justices argued the state could not prove this measure served a compelling state interest and the statute violated the Equal Protection Clause of the Fourteenth Amendment. Just two years later, however, the Court yet again upheld an INS practice: workplace sweeps. In *INS v. Delgado* (466 U.S. 210 [1984]) the Court overruled the United States Court of Appeals for the Ninth District, which decided that INS surveys constituted a seizure of all employees and that the agents could not question individuals unless it had a suspicion that the individual was an illegal alien. The Supreme Court however, in a 6–3 majority, held that INS agents were permitted to survey factories in search of undocumented employees. Later that year the Court also held that an alien must satisfy a clear probability of persecution standard in order to reopen deportation proceedings on the basis of Section 243 (h) of the Immigration and Nationality Act of 1952 (*Immigration and Naturalization Service v. Stevic*, 467 U.S. 407 [1984]).

In a 2002 decision, *Hoffman Plastic Compounds, Inc. v. National Labor Relations Board* (NLRB) (535 U.S. 137, 00-1595 [2002]), the Court considered whether an undocumented employee who was not authorized to work in the United States could be awarded back pay at the discretion of the NLRB. Jose Castro, born in Mexico, was employed by Hoffman on the basis of a document that indicated he was authorized to work in the United States. The company laid off Castro because he had participated in union-organizing activities. The NLRB found that the layoff constituted a violation of the National Labor Relations Act and Castro was entitled to back pay. An administrative law judge found that Castro was prevented from the right to back pay by the Immigration Reform and Control Act of 1986 (IRCA), which made it unlawful for employers to knowingly hire undocumented workers. The NLRB argued, and the Court of Appeals agreed, that the most effective way to enforce the policies in the IRCA was to provide the undocumented employees the same protections and remedies that other employees received. The Supreme Court, however, ruled in a 5–4 decision that awarding back pay to undocumented aliens ran counter to the enforcement of federal immigration policies. Chief Justice Rehnquist noted that "Far from 'accommodating' IRCA, the Board's position, recognizing employer misconduct but discounting the misconduct of illegal alien employees, subverts it."

The above-discussed examples illustrate the uncertain nature of immigrant rights. While the Supreme Court until the end of the 1970s tended to defer its judgment to the other branches of government, in some cases before and after that time it recognized the vulnerability of this group and stood up for the protection of migrant rights. However, as many of the examples indicate, the courts cannot be relied on as a sole protector of these rights, for as the Court's composition changes so do the conceptions of how much protection immigrants need and what types of rights they deserve. Further, court rulings for the migrant in individual cases seeking monetary redress do not necessarily indicate compliance on the part of the offending party. Thus it is imperative to consider what other avenues migrants can take to ensure their rights are not violated. We now turn to examples of real-world efforts of migrants and those working on their behalf.

THE WORLD OUT THERE: WORK ON BEHALF OF MIGRANT RIGHTS

Most people of a progressive political persuasion would agree with us that any effort to attain rights for migrants, especially to advance the range of benefits to which migrants are entitled, is a worthy goal. And today there are many situations in which migrants are able to enjoy a range of benefits. In Germany, for example, guest workers who have established long-term residence and become self-supporting (i.e., they are not dependent on welfare from the state) are now entitled to a wide range of benefits (Morris, 2002). Moreover, most Western nations, which have clearly profited from the addition of migrant workers in recent decades, have generally followed a liberalizing trend in the benefits they provide to migrants and their families (Joppke, 2002; Morris, 2002).

However, the forces of resistance are not only substantial but from some indications actually expanding—and they have done so especially after the September 11 attacks in the United States. The murder of Dutch filmmaker Theo Van Gogh by a Muslim immigrant in November 2004 brought to light the growing animosity between Muslims and the Dutch. Van Gogh, the great-grandson of Vincent Van Gogh's brother, Theo, had made a fictional film that was critical of the Muslim community. It was the story of a woman who was routinely subjected to violence by her husband and also raped by another relative. Muslims around the world were outraged by the film. In France, there is a similar growing concern about the Muslim population, and the split between the Islamic community and the French people seems to be widening. And in the United States, the resistance to immigration, in general, has been growing as well. In Arizona, a local vigilante group formed. Its members patrol the borders with Mexico in an effort to halt the flow of undocumented workers into the United States. Since the attacks local law enforcement agencies have been asked to aid the federal government in enforcing immigration laws. This request was met with various responses from full compliance to questions of what impact these new measures will have on immigrants reporting crimes or offering help to police.

What are the prospects in the future for attaining some level of acceptance, and an ever expanding set of rights, for people who wish to migrate across borders in search of work, but also retain ties to their homeland? Obviously these are matters that are to be settled only through the exercise of power and efforts at negotiation between migrants, and their allies, on the one hand, and legal bodies, such as states, on the other. Most of the literature on migrant rights to date approaches these matters simply as one of how states make as well as change their policies, especially with regard to the issue of membership—who is a citizen, or not, and what rights they are entitled to. But where, and how, is the leverage on behalf of migrants and their families to be found?

Sociologists who study social movements have recognized that the key to a successful effort to advance the interests of particular groups of aggrieved citizens rests, in part, on the success at mobilizing people through organizations. Organization, as Lenin wrote long ago, is the key to a successful movement for change. It has worked especially well in the history of industrial democracies. Unions, which began to form in countries like the United States and Great Britain at the end of the nineteenth century, were powerful and important advocates for workers—many of them, in fact, migrants from foreign lands. The unions often used the ethnicity or nationality of migrants as a device to organize people to compete effectively in the political arena. In such cities in the United States as St. Louis and Cincinnati, workers of German and Polish origin were recruited for political ventures in their native tongue, a fact made necessary because many migrants lacked a facility in the language of their new land.

Over the long course of the twentieth century, unions became a vital fixture in the politics of industrial nations. They recruited workers from a variety of industries, but especially in industrial factories, in steel and automobile making, among others. With a larger membership, the unions became an effective vehicle for pressing employers to grant higher wages to the workers themselves. All of this worked fine—and it was an effective way to advance the interests of migrant workers—until the nature of the world economy changed. Once the managers of plants decided that work could be done more cheaply in Third World countries, like India or China, the plants moved and hired cheap labor, and their profits rose accordingly. The industrial workers, however, were left behind in countries like Great Britain. And as the shape of the economy shifted in the industrial countries, from manufacturing jobs to service jobs, there was a parallel decline in union membership. Unions, it turns out, are effective political vehicles, but they are more easily established in manufacturing plants and offices than they are in the service industry.

In light of the success of unions in the past, many observers wonder whether a similar effort could work today on behalf of migrant workers—or migrants in general. If not unions, perhaps, is there some other form of organization that could become a substitute for unions, a vehicle for pressing forward with claims to advance the rights of migrants as workers, or simply as people who deserve the same level of respect and benefits as other citizens?

We believe that such efforts can succeed, but that such success must begin first, in effect, at home in local situations with local forces. The liberal voices of political parties—those that would press for migrant rights, for example—in countries like the United States have been in retreat in recent years. Thus, much of the work must be done at the local level, in the cities, suburbs, and villages in which we live. And it must be done in an effective and strategically inventive way. We now turn to consider an example of such an effort in the United States. It is only one of perhaps as many as 150 such groups that have been working, often invisibly, to advance the cause of migrant rights.

The Workplace Project was begun by Jennifer Gordon in Long Island, New York, in 1992. She tells the story of her group in a recent book (2005). Gordon had been trained as a lawyer; was exposed to the problems immigrants faced while working for immigrant community agencies; and then, deeply troubled and concerned about the ways in which immigrant workers were being treated in the Long Island suburbs, she became an advocate for the workers by setting up a legal clinic for immigrants. Initially she began by taking on cases of individual migrants who were wronged by their employers. A migrant worker from El Salvador—and of the one hundred thousand or so immigrants in Long Island, the large majority are Salvadorans—for example, worked long hours for a landscaping firm for far below minimum wage only to be fired without cause after the employer withheld his pay for four weeks. Such a worker, potentially undocumented, would have felt like there was nothing he could do because of his status and the resulting lack of protection.

Or it might have been a migrant woman who worked for a particular household and found that her employers would not give her free time for herself, thus owing her much unpaid overtime. Since she was living in the household she was isolated from other migrants in similar situations. She might have thought that this was simply the way domestic employment worked, until she was able to learn from other migrants of similar issues of abuse at the Workplace Project. These were some of the situations that Long Island's poor immigrants faced, and Gordon made an effort to seek legal redress for their concerns and encouraged them to share their stories to see the prevalence of these types of abuses.

But the Workplace Project grew to be far more complicated and involved than a simple clinic with a lawyer working on behalf of specific cases. Eventually Gordon brought in other staff members, many of whom were immigrants she had helped previously with legal issues. Thus, the project became a vehicle through which the migrants not only shared similar stories of abuse and mistreatment with one another, but one in which they could try to formulate strategies for remedying those injustices. And its goals became diversified—one the one hand, it offered legal services to individual clients, but, on the other hand, it also became, for lack of a better word, a political movement for broadening and advancing the cause of migrant rights, in general.

Gordon writes, in unusually vivid and compelling terms, of the "rights" talk that developed among staff members and participants. In an effort to teach immigrants about their rights, the Workplace Project developed a Workers Course. The course was necessary for membership in the project and designed to enable migrants to get out of a mind-set that prevented them from even believing they had rights and were entitled to protection.

They had to create a new sense of themselves. Despite their undocumented status, they had to develop a sense that they deserved fair and equal treatment as did other workers, and that if they did not receive such treatment they could utilize both legal and political means to get it. There were certain obstacles and quandaries for the organization. They had to get funds to support their work, and they turned to such organizations as the MacArthur Foundation. They also had to consider the paradox created by their joint legal and political purposes: on the one hand, if they were successful in pressing forward with a particular individual's legal case, thus, securing proper wages, that often meant the individual would have far less interest in the political cause; on the other hand, if the advancement of a political cause was successful, with demonstrations or protests, that could come at the expense of securing unpaid wages and benefits for any single individual.

We can learn many lessons from the Workplace Project. The chief among them is that the success of securing rights and benefits for migrants is a long, hard process, one that will involve (high-minded) individuals, like Gordon, who use their expertise to work and to help migrants, as a group. It means the creation of local movements that can press forward and, in the interplay of politics and struggles, come out with victories, but also learn from their failures. As we have already noted, much of the literature on the rights of migrants speaks at the broad and abstract level of states. Jennifer Gordon's stories, however, are about real people—migrants and their allies—and what the fight is all about in reality. Unless we, ourselves, are prepared to acknowledge and to work in that realm, all the high-minded talk about rights and states will be just that—high-minded!

CONCLUSIONS

In this chapter we have discussed the impact of globalization on a select group of people: migrants. We argued that as the global economy has been successful in eroding regional boundaries and national borders, it has simultaneously had a great impact on migration. While we recognize that the sheer number of migrants in individual states can prompt the nations to enact legislation that is favorable to migrants and extends rights and freedoms to this group in exchange for assimilation, we argued that states remain central players in the control of migration to their nations as well as the promotion of rights for migrants. Thus, migrants are dependent on the whims of the nation in which they reside.

Some argue that with the growth of globalization a new set of human rights has emerged. Although we recognize the theoretical existence of transnational rights, we question the extent to which these rights actually protect migrants in the real world. With a series of United States Supreme Court cases and migrants' organizing efforts we show that national laws and local forces are still among the most influential factors in determining the extent to which the rights of migrants are protected. We note that the courts are not always a favorable venue for the promotion of migrant rights because while they can serve as the protector of rights and freedoms of minority groups they can also, by deferring their power to other government bodies, serve simply as an actor of the state. The example of the Workplace Project's organizing efforts reveals that local organizations are needed to ensure protections for those most vulnerable to abuses arising from the development of global capitalism.

We strongly believe that the rights of migrants need to be protected. Although the growing concern for migrant rights by global institutions is a good venue for organization and promotion of those efforts, the cautious response from nations to these efforts prompts more localized action. Thus, we believe that the extension and promotion of these rights can be more successful if local forces (both of migrants and their supporters) come together and fight for the advancement of these rights. With the universal acknowledgment of the humanity of migrants and the support of every one of us, the range of migrants' rights and freedoms can be expanded. Whether through individual or group action, this otherwise vulnerable group can have a political impact despite their lack of franchise.

REFERENCES

Brubaker, Rogers. 1992. *Citizenship and Nationhood in France and Germany.* Cambridge, Mass.: Harvard University Press.

Castles, Stephen, and Alastair Davidson. 2000. *Citizenship and Migration.* New York: Routledge.

———, and Mark J. Miller. 1998. *The Age of Migration.* 2nd ed. New York: Guilford.

Chen, Xiangming. 2005. *As Borders Bend: Transnational Spaces on the Pacific Rim.* Lanham, Md.: Rowman & Littlefield Publishers.

Friedman, Thomas L. 2000. *The Lexus and the Olive Tree.* New York: Anchor Books.

Gordon, Jennifer. 2005. *Suburban Sweatshops: The Fight for Immigrant Rights.* Cambridge, Mass.: Belknap.

International Organization for Migration. 2005. *World Migration, 2005: Costs and Benefits of International Migration.* Geneva, Switzerland.

Joppke, Christian. 2002. "Sovereignty and Citizenship in a World of Migration." In *Transnational Legal Processes,* ed. Michael Likosky, 259–74. London: Butterworths Tolley.

———. 1999. *Immigration and the Nation-State: The United States, Germany and Great Britain.* Oxford: Oxford University Press.

Likosky, Michael (ed.). 2002. *Transnational Legal Processes.* London: Butterworths Tolley.

Morris, Lydia. 2002. *Managing Migration: Civic Stratification and Migrants Rights.* London: Routledge.

Schuck, Peter H. 1998. *Citizens, Strangers, and In-Betweens: Essays on Immigration and Citizenship.* Boulder, Colo.: Westview.

Soysal, Yasemin Nuhoglu. 1994. *Limits of Citizenship: Migrants and Postnational Membership in Europe.* Chicago: University of Chicago Press.

Tilly, Charles. 1995. *Popular Contention in Great Britain: 1758–1834.* Cambridge, Mass.: Harvard University Press.

SUSTAINABILITY AND PEACE

11

Understanding Disasters: Vulnerability, Sustainable Development, and Resiliency

Havidán Rodríguez and Carla N. Russell

Disaster researchers study, describe, and analyze problems and issues that are at the very core of the field of sociology. Disasters are intrinsically tied to social structures and social processes. Organizational and community behavior and response are critical to our understanding of disasters; inequality, stratification, and poverty are key factors that increase a population's vulnerability to disasters. For example, as we will discuss later in this chapter, disaster research has shown that the social and economic problems that women and racial and ethnic minority groups confront in societies throughout the world have significant implications for disaster preparedness, response, and recovery. Further, disasters tend to exacerbate and bring to the forefront the social and economic problems that marginalized groups confront.

The primary goals of this chapter are to focus on disasters (primarily "natural" disasters) and their impact on human societies. We seek to explore the relationship between disasters and development and to show how low-income countries are differentially impacted by disasters and the difficulties that they confront in preparing for, responding to, and recovering from these devastating events. These issues will be further explored by focusing on the impact and consequences of Hurricane Mitch in Honduras (1998) and the 2004 Indian Ocean tsunami. This chapter highlights how variables such as development, poverty, inequality, gender, and race/ethnicity impact our vulnerability to disasters. We conclude by providing a brief discussion on the importance of developing disaster-resilient communities while emphasizing the need to develop and implement sustainable development strategies, as well as the role that local governments and nongovernmental organizations (NGOs) can play in this process.

Burawoy (2004: 1607) argues that "public sociology engages publics beyond the academy in a dialogue about matters of political and moral concerns." Fifty years of disaster research have not only made important contributions to our understanding of social systems, organizational theory, and community response and adaptation to disasters but have also allowed us to initiate a dialogue between scholars, researchers, practitioners, communities, and policy makers to better understand the causes and consequences of disasters and to develop policies and initiatives to mitigate their deleterious effects.

DISASTERS AS SOCIAL PROCESSES

Disasters are social constructions. They are highly influenced by the social and political structure, the availability of resources (or lack thereof), stratification and inequality, population pressures (i.e., population growth, density, and distribution), and environmental degradation, among other factors. Consequently, some societies are better able to prepare for, respond to, and recover from hazard events (i.e., hurricanes, tornadoes, tsunamis, terrorist attacks) while others have a limited capacity to resist and recover from the tragic effects of a hazard event thus leading to an extensive loss of life, injuries, and a significant impact on the economic well-being of the impacted population. Disasters are therefore not caused by the "natural" environment but are the result of the social, political, and economic environment and reflect a community's or society's inability to prepare for and manage the outcomes of such events.

A hazard event does not necessarily cause a disaster; these are essentially "triggering" events that interact with the social and economic environment, particularly impacting populations that are highly vulnerable. In this context, disasters cannot be seen as "acts of nature" or "acts of God" but as a consequence of the actions or inactions of a particular community or society. These actions are influenced by or can be the result of decisions made (or not made) by governments, industries, and other institutions. Disasters are intrinsically linked with the social processes and economic development of the societies that we aim to study and understand. Particularly, a country's level of economic development impacts the creation of a social environment that predisposes its population to disasters. For example, we know that disasters are most likely to occur in low-income countries, that poor communities are disproportionately impacted by disasters, and that they have greater difficulties in recovering from these devastating events. We also know that, generally, women, children, the elderly, and racial and ethnic minorities are more likely to disproportionately suffer the negative impacts of these events and to experience severe problems in the process of preparing for, responding to, and recovering from disasters. That is, given their limited resources, lack of access to power, relatively low representation in the political decision-making structures, and marginalization, these groups are more vulnerable to disasters.

It is important to note that disasters do not happen "overnight," but are "in the making," as a result of the cultural, historical, political, and economic processes that have shaped our societies. However, we should also note that communities and societies throughout the world have developed coping mechanisms, strategies, and practices that allow them to better prepare and recover from the devastating impacts of a disaster (i.e., resiliency). In this context, *resiliency* refers to the ability or capacity of individuals, communities, or countries to resist the impact of a disaster or to "respond appropriately to a moment of crisis that has not been anticipated" (Aguirre, 2004: 497). Hoffman and Oliver-Smith (2002: 10) indicate that "disasters provide a unique view of a society's capacities for resistance or resilience in the face of disruption." Moreover, Aguirre (2004: 491) argues that resiliency can have a cumulative effect, transforming itself into disaster mitigation and preparedness practices, and becomes part of a community's social capital. One of the primary questions that we should pose is, How can we develop strategies and initiatives that will reduce our vulnerability to disasters and thus contribute to generating disaster-resilient communities? In our concluding remarks, we will attempt to provide some answers to this question.

DISASTERS AND VULNERABILITY

Sociological literature dating back to the 1950s has shown that there is more to a disaster than the physical hazard associated with this event. The interpretations and definitions of what is a disaster span many of the established sociological perspectives, ranging from a functionalist perspective (Fritz, 1961) to an organizational approach (Quarantelli, 1998) to a social constructionist perspective (Kreps, 1998; for a more extensive discussion of what is a disaster, see Perry and Quarantelli, 2005). For example, Fritz defines a disaster as "an event, concentrated in time and space, in which a society, or relatively self-sufficient subdivision of a society, undergoes severe danger and incurs such losses to its members and physical appurtenances that the social structure is disrupted and the fulfillment of all or some of the essential functions of the society is prevented" (1961: 655).

Fritz does not discount the role of the hazard ("triggering") event but emphasizes the disruption of the social structure that results in some level of societal disarticulation and the interruption of the daily or "normal" functions of the impacted society. Dynes (1970) asserts that while hazards "randomly" occur, their effects are not random at all, but are arranged according to the social structure. Therefore groups that tend to be at a greater socioeconomic disadvantage are also impacted more severely by the disaster. Disasters are thus not "equal opportunity" events but they disproportionately impact some groups (e.g., the powerless, the poor, the disenfranchised; see Wisner et al., 2004) more than others. Moreover, disasters tend to reveal and exacerbate the preexisting weaknesses and inequalities in the impacted societies (Cuny, 1983).

Using a political-ecology perspective, Oliver-Smith (1998) provides a more holistic approach to disasters, defining them as "totalizing events." In this context, disasters are intrinsically connected to and dependent on social, environmental, cultural, political, economic, physical, and technological factors. According to Oliver-Smith, disasters are a combination of a "destructive agent" and a vulnerable population, resulting in societal disruption. The role and impact of development, social stratification and inequality, and environmental degradation on a population's vulnerability to disasters are central to the political-ecology perspective. Disasters exploit inherent and human-made weaknesses in a social system, possibly being advantageous to some groups while others are more adversely affected.

If a society has a relative strong economy with access to the necessary resources, a hazard event may have a relatively small impact on that community in terms of the loss of life and injuries, although given increasing modernization and the construction of new and highly sophisticated infrastructures, property damages will tend to be significantly higher in "modern" societies. However, communities in this setting may have the necessary economic and institutional resources to adequately recover from these types of events. Nevertheless, even in these types of economies, disadvantaged groups will disproportionately suffer the outcomes of a hazard event and will have significant difficulties in recovering from the same (Bolin and Stanford, 1999; Peacock, Morrow, and Gladwin, 1997).

Conversely, a low-income country that also lacks the necessary economic and organizational structure and resources will be adversely affected by the hazard event and will experience significant difficulties in the disaster response and recovery efforts. Differences in the social and political structures, economic opportunities, and demographic characteristics will lead to differential outcomes between low-income and high-income countries following a hazard event.

For the purposes of this discussion, *vulnerability* is defined as the susceptibility to experiencing negative outcomes as a consequence of a hazard event and reflects an individual's, community's, or a society's capacity (or perhaps inability) to prepare for, respond to, and recover from a disaster (Wisner et al., 2004). Vulnerability is dependent on both individual and group characteristics as well as on the social structure, development, social inequality, and stratification. A group cannot be completely impervious or completely vulnerable to a hazard event; they do not experience vulnerability absolutely, rather individuals, groups, or communities are "vulnerable to a hazard to the degree that they are susceptible to suffer damages and have difficulty in recovering from those losses" (Rodríguez, Díaz, and Aguirre, 2004: 10). Vulnerability also has an element of risk and outcome. For instance, some groups choose to live in an area of high risk (Bolin and Stanford, 1999) while others do so out of economic necessity. In the following section, we discuss intra- and intersocietal vulnerability and the determinants and consequences of these types of vulnerabilities.

INTRASOCIETAL VULNERABILITY

The disaster literature focusing on vulnerability tends to highlight individual or group characteristics that influence their capacity to anticipate, cope, resist, weather, and recover from a hazard (Cannon, 1994; Mileti, 1999; Wisner et al., 2004) or what we call intrasocietal vulnerability. Within a given society, factors such as race/ethnicity, socioeconomic status, age, and gender can influence an individual's or group's vulnerability to disasters. Groups that are vulnerable to disasters often face serious difficulties in securing their basic needs. Morrow (1999) points out that the poor often lack adequate economic reserves to effectively prepare for and respond to a hazard event. Furthermore, as a consequence of their limited economic conditions, these groups tend to be marginalized and live in poorly constructed housing and in areas of high risk (Martine and Guzman, 2002; Morrow, 1999). As indicated by Morrow, "the poor are likely to have little alternatives if their livelihoods are tied to tourism, fishing and other coastal enterprises" (1999: 3).

Although some scholars would argue that vulnerability is synonymous with poverty (Aguirre, 2004), and while vulnerability appears to be highly correlated to poverty, it is important to highlight that the two concepts are not equivalent (Cannon, 1994; Wisner et al., 2004). Vulnerability is the result of many interrelated and interacting factors. Using the two terms interchangeably severely underestimates the critical role played by race, gender, and age, among other factors (Cutter, Boruff, and Shirley, 2003). For example, Nigg and Miller indicate that "social location [i.e., race, class, gender] is central to a sociological understanding of patterns of inequality" (1994: 3). Racial and ethnic minorities lack access to resources and often experience greater social marginalization than those of the dominant race (Cutter, Boruff, and Shirley, 2003); this in turn impacts their vulnerability to disasters. Moreover, the social inequities that these groups experience as a "matter of fact" in their daily lives are exacerbated in a disaster event (Peacock and Girard, 1997: 172; Nigg and Miller, 1994).

As discussed previously, women also tend to experience higher vulnerability to disasters due to gender-based inequities inherent in our societies, particularly influencing ownership and access to resources. There is no doubt that in societies throughout the world "economic and cultural systems are generally male-dominated, and allocate power and resources in favour of men" (Wisner et al., 2004: 238). Women's experiences in disasters, as is the case with racial/ethnic minorities, are an extension of their "traditional" roles; "gender power and privilege shape the division of labor in everyday routine" (Enarson and Morrow, 1998: 3). Moreover, type of employment, low wages, poverty, marginalization, and secondary responsibilities (i.e., family/child care) experienced by women impact their ability to recover from a disaster (Enarson and Morrow, 1998) and may even put them at greater risk of being impacted by the event (e.g., given their traditional roles in fishing communities, women experienced higher rates of mortality, relative to their male counterparts, as a consequence of the 2004 Indian Ocean tsunami).

There are other important social and demographic factors that also impact intrasocietal vulnerability, including age, physical disability, immigration status, political ideologies, state practices, density of the built environment, single-sector economic dependence, housing stock and tenancy, occupation, and infrastructure dependence (Bolin and Stanford, 1999; Morrow, 1999; Cutter, Boruff, and Shirley, 2003). While these factors might influence vulnerability to a lesser extent, they do impact an individual or group's susceptibility to the negative consequences of a hazard.

INTERSOCIETAL VULNERABILITY

As documented by a number of researchers, entire nations may be disproportionately impacted by disasters and, given their socioeconomic and demographic characteristics, level of development, and disaster planning and management practices, among others, they may be highly vulnerable to these events (Wisner et al., 2004; Easterly, 2001; Jeffery, 1982; Lavell, 1994; Martine and Guzman, 2002; Pielke et al., 2003). An intersocietal vulnerability approach to disasters focuses on the inequality faced by a number of countries throughout the world as a consequence of globalization, development, poverty, rapid urbanization, high fertility rates, low levels of literacy, and environmental degradation, among other factors, that tend to erode a country's ability to prepare for, respond to, and recover from disasters. Intersocietal vulnerability examines larger social processes that impact the outcomes of a hazard event. Just as on a societal level some groups experience greater vulnerability, poor nations also experience higher levels of disaster vulnerability and are disproportionately impacted by hazard events relative to their high-income counterparts. In this context, the role of development is critical.

Development and Disasters

Research focusing on the relationship between disasters and development has been a fairly recent phenomenon (Cuny, 1983). While a causal relationship between development and disaster remains unsubstantiated, scholars have observed a general association between the level of development of a particular country and the frequency and severity of disasters (Wisner et al., 2004; Easterly, 2001). For instance, in her study of the Dominican Republic, Jeffery (1982) concluded that increased vulnerability to natural hazards and subsequent outcomes may result from many of the social and economic processes that mark a developing country (i.e., environmental degradation, economic inflation, and rapid urbanization).

Lavell (1994: 49) also notes that Central America is considered "one of the more disaster-prone areas of the world." This region is exposed to many hazards, yet the precarious social and economic status of these countries, the vast majority of which are considered low-income, creates an atmosphere ripe for disasters (Lavell, 1994). Likewise, Martine and Guzman (2002) note that many development processes have increased disaster vulnerability throughout the Central American isthmus. They argue that the disasters experienced over the last thirty years have exacerbated the already deteriorating conditions of Central America through economic devastation and high death tolls. Poor countries, such as Bangladesh, Indonesia, Haiti, and India, among others, experience hazard events that result in tens of thousands of deaths, economic displacement, the exacerbation of poverty, and social isolation. Not surprisingly, Easterly (2001) points out that the overwhelming amount of disasters and disaster-related deaths occur in the most impoverished regions of the world, as illustrated by the following example.

During the 2004 hurricane season, in a period of about six weeks, four major hurricanes impacted the southern portion of the United States, particularly Florida and neighboring states. Hurricanes Charley, Frances, Ivan, and Jeanne left a death toll of about 125 in the United States, and the combined total economic damages as a consequence of these four events exceeded the costs of Hurricane Andrew (1992), which was considered to be the costliest "natural" disaster to strike the United States. By any standard, these hurricanes had a significant impact on the United States, in terms of the loss of life and economic losses. However, prior to its arrival in the United States, one hurricane alone, Jeanne, impacted Haiti, the poorest country in the Western Hemisphere. As a consequence of widespread poverty, large-scale deforestation, political instability, and lack of adequate disaster mitigation and preparedness strategies, Jeanne left a death toll estimated at about fifteen hundred to three thousand; over twenty-six hundred injuries were reported; nine hundred people were declared "missing"; and over three hundred thousand were rendered homeless. Similarly, previous disasters in low-income countries have resulted in millions of injuries and fatalities; millions displaced; entire communities destroyed; and billions of dollars in damages to the infrastructure, industry, and personal property. Epidemics, cyclones, droughts, floods, and technological disasters have been all too common in these countries. Moreover, the victims of these disasters will continue to increase as the number of poor people also increases and they continue to build "unsafe houses on dangerous grounds" (World Commission on Environment and Development—WCED—1987: 33). (It is noteworthy that globalization has contributed to exacerbating the existing inequities among and within countries and thus has exacerbated the populations' vulnerability to disasters [Rodríguez, 2004; Oliver-Smith, 2004].)

Among Latin American countries, Rodríguez (2004) indicates that the "expected" outcome of increasing development (that is, increasing wealth and equality) has not been realized. Actually, development in many countries remains significantly stunted. Even more alarming is the fact that since the 1990s, some of these low-income countries have experienced no or negative economic growth (UNDP, 2003; Rodríguez, 2004) thus exacerbating their vulnerability to disasters.

Easterly points out that a country's initial economic condition is an important variable to predict future economic growth, particularly after it has been impacted by a disaster: "If an economy starts from a favorable position, it will take off. If a natural disaster or historical initial poverty has it below the threshold, it won't take off" (2001: 199). However, although development is influenced by economic factors, it must also be understood beyond the economic context. For example, as Sen (1999) asserts, a higher prevalence in female mortality is not simply the result of poverty, but is also related to demographic processes, access to resources and social networks, and overall gender inequality. Thus, in order to understand disasters we must also understand and acknowledge the impact of the social structure and social processes.

HURRICANE MITCH AND ITS SOCIOECONOMIC IMPACT ON HONDURAS

Honduras is considered to be one of the poorest countries in the Western Hemisphere. In 2004, Honduras had the second lowest per capita gross national income in purchasing power parity (PPP) in Central America, $2,540 compared to $7,540 for the region and $36,110 for the United States (Population Reference Bureau—PRB—2004). More than half of the Honduran population lives below the national poverty line, about 44 percent are living on two dollars a day, and 23 percent on one dollar a day (UNDP, 2004). The continued deterioration of the agricultural sector has led to higher unemployment rates in the country, reaching 27 percent in 2003. Further, about 25 to 30 percent of the population has no access to health care services. One of the most important indicators of a country's economic well-being, the infant mortality rate (IMR), is very high in Honduras at about 34 per 1,000 live births in 2004 compared to 6.7 for the United States. Honduras also has very high levels of fertility, thus contributing to its rapid population growth and youthful age structure, which in turn will contribute to further population growth. Moreover, environmental degradation in Honduras is a key factor in enhancing the country's vulnerability to disasters.

It was under these circumstances of extreme poverty, also prevalent in 1998, that Honduras suffered the devastating effects of Hurricane Mitch. By the time the storm made landfall in Honduras, Mitch was downgraded to a Category 1 storm with winds of approximately ninety-nine miles per hour. Nonetheless, this slow-moving system stalled over Honduras for several days, dumping up to a year's worth of rain; extreme flooding and landslides led to widespread devastation, particularly among the country's poor residents. Contrary to the relatively low fatalities (about fifteen deaths directly and twenty-five deaths indirectly) associated with the Category 4 Hurricane Andrew that struck southern Florida in 1992, Hurricane Mitch resulted in an estimated sixty-six hundred deaths in Honduras alone, comprising 69 percent of the total fatalities for the affected Central American region. Another eight thousand individuals were reported missing; over seventy thousand homes were destroyed or damaged, leaving approximately 1.4 million Hondurans homeless; and over 2.1 million people were impacted by the storm (United Nations, OCHA *Situation Report 14*, 1998).

In the days immediately following Hurricane Mitch, Honduran president Carlos Flores Facussé stated, "We have before us a panorama of death, destruction and ruin throughout the countryside" (Price, 1998). His words conveyed the overwhelming devastation and the sensation of despair and suffering faced by this country and its population following Mitch. As a consequence of this storm, the transportation infrastructure, communication systems, health centers, schools, and sanitation systems were severely damaged (United Nations, OCHA *Situation Report 15*, 1998). According to news media reports, Hurricane Mitch "crippled Honduras's already delicate economy" (Chacon, 1999). Economic losses in the agricultural sector alone were estimated as ranging from $200 to $500 million. Total damages and economic losses were estimated to fluctuate around six to seven billion dollars (Pielke et al., 2003). It has been reported that the storm set back development efforts in Honduras at least thirty to fifty years.

Martine and Guzman (2002) argue that the poor were disproportionately represented among the casualties resulting from Mitch. This disaster also caused a direct loss of income to the rural poor through the extensive disruption of the country's economic activities (Morris et al., 2002). Poor populations were particularly vulnerable to Mitch as a result of limited income and access to alternative employment and to external resources (e.g., disaster relief aid) to sustain them through the response and recovery period (Morris et al., 2002). It also seems that the poor rely more directly on the environment for their basic needs, thus they were more significantly impacted by Mitch's destruction of the natural environment. The groups most directly and severely affected by Mitch were those occupying the lowest income strata, with limited political power and lacking adequate economic resources, and those residing in inadequate housing and in high-risk areas (General Secretariat, 1999: 13).

Honduras's high population growth rates, high levels of poverty, limited access to education, and poor health conditions exacerbate its people's vulnerability to disasters. Further, the environment is increasingly taxed as a result of soil erosion, pollution, and settlements in hazardous locations—most of which are the result of poor environmental management practices, industrialization, and lack of government policies to protect the environment. For example, Roberts and Thanos (2003) argue that the effects of the heavy and continuous rainfalls from Mitch were intensified by the widespread deforestation practices financed by multinational companies.

Hurricane Mitch exacerbated Honduras's social and economic problems, particularly for the country's poor population. Unfortunately, one year later,

Honduras had seen little progress in restoring its infrastructure, and the long-term development initiatives needed to reduce vulnerability seemed to elude this impoverished nation. As is generally the case after the shock and impact of the disaster has disappeared from the national and international arena, disaster relief aid and other types of support from the international community begin to wither away and the impacted country is left on its own to remedy its long-term social and economic problems that were aggravated by the disaster. Not surprisingly, Honduras continues to experience difficulties in recovering from this devastating event and has experienced modest or limited improvements following Hurricane Mitch.

THE 2004 INDIAN OCEAN TSUNAMI

Describing the devastating impact of the 2004 Indian Ocean tsunami, Rodriguez, Wachtendorf, Kendra, and Trainor indicate:

> The December 26, 2004 earthquake and the tsunami that it generated across the Indian Ocean have been described as creating one of the "worst disasters" in recent history. . . . Preliminary estimates show the death toll at over 200,000. It is also estimated that there are over 141,000 "missing" persons, over two million people displaced, and an economic impact ranging in the billions of dollars. . . . entire communities were shattered and tens of thousands of families were significantly impacted as a consequence of the loss of life and of their livelihoods (2005: 1).

The majority if not all the countries impacted by this tsunami were low-income or poor nations, and the primary victims of the tsunami were impoverished fishing communities. For example, India is characterized by its low per capita income and high levels of poverty. In 2002, India's per capita gross national income in purchasing power parity was only $2,650 (PRB, 2004). A report on *Disaster Response in India* indicates that despite all the economic development experienced by India in recent decades, it still confronts severe economic problems, poverty, inequality, and high illiteracy rates (Parasuraman and Unnikrishnan, 2005: 8).

Once again, the Indian Ocean tsunami exacerbated and brought to the forefront the social and economic problems and difficulties that India confronts. Increasing population pressures in high-risk areas, combined with extreme poverty and inequality, provided the optimal conditions for the development of a disaster. In terms of the economic losses and long-term economic impacts, unfortunately and as is traditionally the case, the communities primarily impacted by the tsunami represent populations living at the margins of poverty, struggling to survive from day to day. Krishnakumar (2005), referring to the fishing communities in Chennai or Madras, India, indicates that the tsunami "exposed the systemic vulnerabilities Chennai's coastal communities face—ranging from declining incomes to an utter lack of sanitation and health care to deficiencies in literacy and alternative skills." Further, it is argued that a number of factors, such as high levels of poverty, high population density, rudimentary housing, poor sanitation, inadequate health care systems, and high levels of illiteracy (Krishnakumar, 2005: 1–2) made the coastal population of Chennai more vulnerable to this disaster and thus impacted its ability to recover from the same.

Also, an Oxfam (2005) briefing note indicates that, as a consequence of the 2004 Indian Ocean tsunami, a higher proportion of women and children died relative to men in the Aceh province in Indonesia, India, and Sri Lanka. Further, Lalasz (2005: 1) highlights the difficulties that women are confronting in India following the tsunami, such as lack of access to maternal and health care, sexual abuse in refugee camps, and their new roles as sole or primary economic providers for their families. In summary, both Hurricane Mitch and the Indian Ocean tsunami show how the effects of disasters are exacerbated in regions characterized by low levels of economic development and by populations with high levels of poverty and illiteracy and lacking access to basic necessities, such as adequate health care and education; thus making populations more vulnerable to disasters.

CONCLUSION

Rodríguez states that "the problems of impoverished nations throughout the world have been exacerbated by environmental degradation and natural hazards" (2004: 400). Disasters frequently interrupt economic and social development in poor countries, often causing a regression in the progress that has been achieved (General Secretariat, 1999; Cuny, 1983). Moreover, disasters are on the rise. Given some of the issues that we have discussed in this chapter (i.e., increasing population numbers, increasing poverty, more people living in high-risk or disaster-prone areas, and continued environmental degradation, among others), we can expect to have more frequent and severe disasters that will be more damaging than in the past (Hoffman and Oliver-Smith, 2002; Quarantelli, 1985). Local and international governments must therefore intervene to promote effective disaster mitigation and preparedness strategies through the implementation of sustainable development policies that promote equitable growth and participatory processes. As set forth by the WCED (1987: 24), "sustainable development requires meeting the basic needs of all and extending to all the opportunity to fulfill their aspirations for a better life. A world in which poverty is endemic will be prone to ecological and other catastrophes." It is through sustainable development practices, building disaster-resilient communities as well as implementing effective disaster preparedness and mitigation initiatives, that we will be able reduce communities' vulnerability to disasters, thus alleviating the social and economic impacts of hazard events. However, economic development is imperative for the reduction of the population's vulnerability to disasters.

According to the 1990 UNDP-HDR, economic development, in addition to the growth of the gross national product (GNP), should entail equitable distribution of income and other resources, well-structured social expenditures by the government, and developing intervention structures during disasters or any other circumstances that may interrupt economic growth. However, for Nobel Laureate Amartya Sen (1999), development is a much more dynamic process and requires the expansion of political freedoms, civil rights, economic facilities, social opportunities (e.g., access to social or public goods, such as health care and education), the provision of transparent processes that will enhance societal trust in its basic institutions, and the extension of security and protection to the general population. Moreover, the promotion of social justice is or should be a critical aspect of a government's sustainable development initiatives. Effective disaster planning and management begin with the implementation of policies aimed at promoting sustainable development, thus enhancing economic opportunities for the general population, reducing poverty, increasing access to adequate health care, increasing the population's level of education and, consequently, reducing vulnerability to disasters. It is also important not to forget (as discussed earlier in this chapter) that human societies and communities also have an element of resilience. Karanci and Aksit (2000) argue that resilience should begin at the local level by empowering communities to develop actions plans for mitigation and preparedness.

In the following section, we highlight three factors or strategies that, in our view, are critical in order to promote and generate disaster-resilient communities and thus reduce disaster vulnerability: (1) empower communities through participatory processes, engaging them in disaster planning and management practices and in developing self-help initiatives (in this context, social organization is indispensable); (2) enhance the role of NGOs in the disaster recovery process and in promoting sustainable recovery; and (3) encourage governments to take an active role in disaster mitigation and preparedness and in incorporating these initiatives into sustainable development programs thus building disaster-resilient communities.

Social Organization and Participatory Processes

The fishing villages that Rodriguez and colleagues (2005) visited in both India and Sri Lanka, following the 2004 Indian Ocean tsunami, appeared to be closely knitted communities, and there appeared to be a high level of social cohesion. Their preliminary findings suggest that, one month after the disaster, there was significant social organization, extensive participation of community members (at least in some communities) in the recovery process, a strong sense of camaraderie and community membership among the individuals residing in the same area, and an eagerness to help and provide support to the impacted communities. There was also an emergence of self-help groups constituted by women that took an active role in the disaster response and recovery process. (Within a month of the Sumatra earthquake and the tsunami it generated, researchers from the University of Delaware's Disaster Research Center [DRC] and the Emergency Administration and Planning Program [EADP] at the University of North Texas participated in an Earthquake Engineering Research Institute [EERI, based in California] social science reconnaissance team, which traveled to some of the most affected areas in India and Sri Lanka. The team engaged in a two-week field research expedition that yielded important and perishable data on disaster preparedness, response, and recovery from this devastating tsunami [see Rodriguez et al., 2005].)

Community engagement and participation in the response and rebuilding process is also extremely important in order to encourage and achieve sustainable recovery. However, community participation implies and requires that its members be empowered and must be actively engaged in decision-making processes, and that their participation and recommendations must be seriously taken into account by decision and policy makers. The development of strategies aimed at fostering or encouraging community resilience to catastrophic disaster events is extremely important in furthering the population's ability to protect itself. Therefore, these types of initiatives, also aimed at developing social cohesion and participatory processes, must be endorsed, encouraged, and funded by local governments and NGOs in order to promote the development of disaster-resilient communities.

The Role of NGOs

The role of NGOs, particularly local and long-established NGOs, can be critical in the promotion of sustainable development and in building disaster-resilient communities. In the case of India, our observations suggest that NGOs have played a significant role not only in the distribution of material resources but also in addressing issues related to community development and the social-psychological needs of its members. Some activities in which NGOs have been actively engaged in include the construction of temporary shelters, distribution and preparation of food, debris removal, repairing damaged boats, providing emotional support and (albeit limited) counseling to local residents, and encouraging the formation of self-help groups primarily consisting of women (Rodriguez et al., 2005). Despite some problems identified by community members with the distribution of disaster relief aid, the contributions made by NGOs seemed to be very important and contributed to meeting many of the communities' basic needs. Moreover, it appeared that local NGOs that had established long-term relationships with local communities (prior to the Indian Ocean tsunami) and that promoted the creation of self-help groups and sustainable development practices were quite effective and were well received by communities during the aftermath of the tsunami. NGOs, particularly local NGOs, have played, and can continue to play, a critical role in promoting sustainable recovery and disaster-resilient communities in countries throughout the Indian Ocean. During the past decades, they have gained significant momentum and have been quite effective in "enabling people to help themselves" (UNDP-HDR, 1990).

The Role of Local Governments

The role of the local government in disaster management and planning (including mitigation, preparedness, response, and recovery) is crucial and must be taken seriously by government officials throughout the world, but particularly in impoverished countries, which, as we have seen, disproportionately suffer the impacts of disasters. Disaster planning and management strategies will be much more effective if they are integrated into a country's agenda that promotes sustainable development programs. As such, these initiatives must address the severe problems and difficulties that these societies confront, including chronic poverty, gender inequality, low levels of education, high illiteracy rates, and lack of access to basic necessities such as adequate health care and potable water, among others. These issues are or should be an integral part of sustainable development programs.

However, as Dilley et al. (2005: 16) indicate: "it may be impossible to achieve development goals such as poverty alleviation in these areas without concerted efforts to reduce recurrent losses" from disaster events. Disasters are part of a country's social processes and they should be used to promote social change. In this context, a significant proportion of the local, national, and international disaster aid should be directed toward disaster mitigation and preparedness and to promote sustainable recovery. Unfortunately, the majority of these funds are aimed at disaster "relief" and they do not allow for the development and implementation of policies and strategies aimed at promoting disaster-resilient communities and enhancing the country's or community's ability to prepare and respond to these types of events. Actually, disaster relief organizations, particularly international organizations, have essentially failed or have avoided any attempts to link disasters to development (Cuny, 1983). Further, the emphasis of most disaster relief aid agencies, and local governments, directed at meeting the immediate needs of the population without considering long-term and sustainable recovery, may foster dependency rather than self-sufficiency.

We should also note that, in recent times, and as terrorist attacks continue to emerge, disaster planning and management practices in many countries have returned to their top-down and "command and control" approaches. They have also become increasingly "bureaucratized," thus negating the importance of the extensive knowledge and practices and the contributions that local communities can make to disaster mitigation, preparedness, response, and recovery; consequently, these processes have become less participatory. Governments can and should play an important role in promoting growth with equity and participatory processes that take into account and respond to the short- and long-term needs of their populations. They should also acknowledge that top-down, nonparticipatory processes will not be successful in enhancing disaster preparedness and response and in reducing disaster vulnerability.

In conclusion, disasters should be regarded as part of the social processes that impact human societies; they are influenced or impacted by the social and political structures and by the choices and decisions made (or not made) by individuals, organizations, communities, and societies at large. In order to mitigate the devastating impacts of disasters, there is a need to develop strategies that foster sustainable development and are clearly linked to promoting disaster-resilient communities thus reducing their vulnerability to disasters. While developing and implementing disaster mitigation, preparedness, and recovery practices and policies have contributed to alleviate (to some extent) the impact and consequences of disasters, it is safe to say that disenfranchised and marginalized groups and societies continue to confront the disproportionate impacts of disasters.

Sustainable development practices and the building of disaster-resilient communities cannot and should not only focus on disaster preparedness and recovery but also on efforts aimed at improving the economic conditions of those differentially impacted by disasters. Improving the life conditions of the poor, increasing levels of education, providing access to education and adequate health care, and addressing issues focusing on gender and racial/

ethnic inequities are critical if we aim to foster sustainable development and disaster-resilient communities. These are issues that are (or should be) at the very core of social justice and social equity programs aimed at improving the life conditions of those impacted by disasters. Certainly, these are principles that public sociology should espouse and promote as essential public goods.

ACKNOWLEDGMENTS

This work was partially supported by the Engineering Research Centers Program of the National Science Foundation (0313747). Opinions, findings, and conclusions are those of the authors.

REFERENCES

Aguirre, B. E. 2004. "Los Desastres en Latinoamérica: Vulnerabilidad y Resistencia." *Revista Mexicana de Sociología* 3: 485–510.

Bolin, R., and L. Stanford. 1999. "Constructing Vulnerability in the First World: The Northridge Earthquake in Southern California, 1994." In *The Angry Earth: Disasters in Anthropological Perspective*, ed. A. Oliver-Smith. New York: Routledge.

Burawoy, M. 2004. "Public Sociologies: Contradictions, Dilemmas, and Possibilities." *Social Forces* 82(4): 1603–18.

Cannon, T. 1994. "Vulnerability Analysis and the Explanation of 'Natural' Disasters." In *Disasters, Development and Environment*, ed. A. Varley. New York: Wiley.

Chacon, R. 1999. "Clinton Lauds Honduras Efforts; No New U.S. Aid Offered to the Country Stricken by Hurricane Mitch." *Boston Globe*, March 10, 1999. Available through LEXIS-NEXIS Academic Universe General News (accessed June 6, 2004).

Cuny, F. C. 1983. *Disasters and Development*. New York: Oxford University Press.

Cutter, S., B. J. Boruff, and W. L. Shirley. 2003. "Social Vulnerability to Environmental Hazards." *Social Science Quarterly* 84(2): 242–61.

Dilley, M., R. S. Chen, U. Deichmann, A. L. Lerner-Lam, M. Arnold, et al. 2005. *Natural Disaster Hotspots: A Global Risk Analysis*. Washington, D.C.: The World Bank, Hazard Management Unit.

Dynes, R. 1970. *Organized Behavior in Disaster*. Lexington, Mass.: Heath Lexington Books.

Easterly, W. 2001. *The Elusive Quest for Growth*. Cambridge, Mass.: MIT Press.

Enarson, E., and B. H. Morrow. 1998. "Why Gender? Why Women? An Introduction to Women and Disaster." In *The Gendered Terrain of Disaster: Through Women's Eyes*, ed. E. Enarson and B. H. Morrow. Westport, Conn.: Praeger.

Fritz, C. 1961. "Disasters." In *Social Problems*, ed. R. Merton and R. Nisbet. New York: Harcourt Brace.

General Secretariat. 1999. *Reconstruction and Transformation of Central America after Hurricane Mitch: A Regional Vision*. Unpublished Central American Integration System Report.

Hoffman, S. M., and A. Oliver-Smith (eds.). 2002. *Catastrophe and Culture: The Anthropology of Disasters*. Santa Fe, N.M.: School of American Research Press.

Jeffery, S. E. 1982. "The Creation of Vulnerability to Natural Disaster: Case Studies from the Dominican Republic." *Disasters* 6(1): 38–43.

Karanci, N., and B. Aksit. 2000. "Building Disaster-Resistant Communities: Lessons Learned from Past Earthquakes in Turkey and Suggestions for the Future." *International Journal of Mass Emergencies and Disasters* 18(3): 403–16.

Kreps, G. A. 1998. "Disasters as Systemic Event and Social Catalyst." In *What Is a Disaster? Perspectives on the Question*, ed. E. L. Quarantelli. New York: Routledge.

Krishnakumar, A. 2005. "Tsunami Exposes Chennai Fisherfolk's Poor Social Conditions." Population Reference Bureau: www.prb.org (accessed June 6, 2005).

Lalasz, R. 2005. "The Indian Ocean Tsunami: Special Challenges for Women Survivors." Population Reference Bureau: www.prb.org (accessed June 6, 2005).

Lavell, A. 1994. "Prevention and Mitigation of Disasters in Central America: Vulnerability to Disasters at the Local Level." In *Disasters, Development and Environment*, ed. A. Varley. New York: Wiley.

Martine, G., and J. M. Guzman. 2002. "Population, Poverty, and Vulnerability: Mitigating the Effects of Natural Disasters." *ECSP Report* 8: 45–68.

Mileti, D. 1999. *Disasters by Design: A Reassessment of Natural Hazards in the United States*. Washington, D.C.: Joseph Henry Press.

Morris, S. S., O. Neidecker-Gonzales, C. Carletto, M. Munguía, J. M. Medina, and Q. Wodon. 2002. "Hurricane Mitch and the Livelihoods of the Rural Poor in Honduras." *World Development* 30(1): 49–60.

Morrow, B. H. 1999. "Identifying and Mapping Community Vulnerability." *Disasters* 23(1): 1–18.

Nigg, J., and K. Miller. 1994. "Event and Consequence Vulnerability: Effects on the Disaster Recovery Process." Disaster Research Center, Preliminary Paper #217.

Oliver-Smith, A. 2004. "Theorizing Vulnerability in a Globalized World: A Political Ecological Perspective." In *Mapping Vulnerability: Disasters, Development, and People*, ed. G. Bankoff, G. Frerks, and D. Hilhorst. Sterling, Va.: Earthscan.

———. 1998. "Global Changes and the Definition of Disaster." In *What Is a Disaster? Perspective on the Question*, ed. E. L. Quarantelli. New York: Routledge.

Oxfam International. 2005. *The Tsunami's Impact on Women*. www.oxfam.org.nz/resources/The_tsunami_impact_on_women.pdf (accessed June 10, 2005).

Parasuraman, S., and P. V. Unnikrishnan. 2005. *Disaster Response in India: An Overview*. www.punjabilok.com/india_disaster_rep/introduction/overview.htm (accessed July 7, 2005).

Peacock, W. G., and C. Girard. 1997. "Ethnic and Racial Inequalities in Hurricane Damage and Insurance Settlements." In *Hurricane Andrew: Ethnicity, Gender and the Sociology of Disasters*, ed. W. G. Peacock, B. H. Morrow, and H. Gladwin. Miami: Florida International University.

———, B. H. Morrow, and H. Gladwin (eds.). 1997. *Hurricane Andrew: Ethnicity, Gender and the Sociology of Disasters*. Miami: Florida International University.

Perry, R. W., and E. L. Quarantelli (eds.). 2005. *What Is a Disaster: New Answers to Old Questions*. USA: Xlibris Corporation.

Pielke, R. A., Jr., J. Rubiera, C. Landsea, M. L. Férnández, and R. Klien. 2003. "Hurricane

Vulnerability in Latin America and the Caribbean: Normalized Damage and Loss Potentials." *Natural Hazards Review* 4: 101–14.

Population Reference Bureau (PRB). 2004. *World Population Data Sheet.* Washington, D.C.: Population Reference Bureau.

Price, N. 1998. "Officials Overwhelmed by Disaster, Estimate at Least 7,000 Dead." *Associated Press*, November 2, 1998.

Quarantelli, E. L. 1998. "Epilogue: Where We Have Been and Where We Might Go." In *What Is a Disaster? Perspective on the Question*, ed. E. L. Quarantelli. New York: Routledge.

———. 1985. "The Need for Planning, Training, and Policy on Emergency Preparedness." University of Delaware, Disaster Research Center, Preliminary Paper #101.

Roberts, J. T., and N. D. Thanos. 2003. *Trouble in Paradise: Globalization and Environmental Crises in Latin America.* New York: Routledge.

Rodríguez, H. 2004. "A 'Long Walk to Freedom' and Democracy: Human Rights, Globalization, and Social Injustice." *Social Forces* 83(1): 391–412.

———, W. Díaz, and B. Aguirre. 2004. "The Role of Science, Technology, and the Media in Communication of Risk and Warnings: An Interdisciplinary Approach." Disaster Research Center Preliminary Paper #337.

Rodriguez, H., T. Wachtendorf, J. Kendra, J. Trainor. 2005. "The Great Sumatra Earthquake and the Indian Ocean Tsunami of December 26, 2004: A Preliminary Assessment of Societal Impacts and Consequences." *Earthquake Engineering Research Institute (EERI) Newsletter* 39(5) (May 2005): 1–7.

Sen, A. 1999. *Development as Freedom.* New York: Anchor Books.

UNDP [United Nations Development Programme]. 2004. *Human Development Report 2003: Cultural Liberty in Today's Diverse World.* http://hdr.undp.org/reports/global/2004/ (accessed July 1, 2005).

———. 2003. *Human Development Report 2003: Millennium Development Goals: A Compact among Nations to End Human Poverty.* http://hdr.undp.org/reports/global/2003/ (accessed June 18, 2005).

———. 1990. *Human Development Report 1990: Concept and Measurement of Human Development.* http://gd.tuwien.ac.at/soc/undp/90.htm (accessed June 17, 2005).

United Nations Office for the Coordination of Humanitarian Affairs (OCHA). 1998–1999. *Situation Reports #1-15: Hurricane Mitch.* www.reliefweb.int/rw/dbc.nsf/doc100?OpenForm (accessed June 18, 2005).

Wisner, B., T. Cannon, I. Davis, and P. Blaikie. 2004. *At Risk: Natural Hazards, People's Vulnerability and Disasters.* 2nd ed. New York: Routledge.

World Commission on Environment and Development (WCED). 1987. Report of the World Commission on Environment and Development: Our Common Future (The Brundtland Report). www.are.admin.ch/are/en/nachhaltig/international_uno/unterseite02330/ (accessed July 24, 2005).

12

Promoting Sustainability

Kenneth A. Gould

The term *sustainable development* has come to be a deeply contested and thoroughly co-opted concept. Perhaps the reason for such contestation and co-optation stems from its initial intent as a call for a radical restructuring of the social system–ecosystem dynamic. Sustainable development implies global, national, regional, and local development trajectories that meet basic social needs while ensuring the integrity of ecosystems, and doing so in a manner that does not reduce the capacity of future generations to do the same. Attaining that seemingly reasonable goal requires calling into question all aspects of the existing relationship between human society and the natural world. Social system–ecosystem interactions are mediated through economic, political, cultural, and technological systems, all of which are dominated by the narrow interests of economic elites, and all of which are contested by grassroots demands for radical democratization. The demand for sustainable development thus fuses together many of the major points of political conflict that have become forefronted in this era of globalization and global resistance.

Sustainable development is comprised of two broad components. One component is the social dimension that requires that basic human needs for food, shelter, medicine, livelihood, and community be met. Humans can only meet those needs through some form of action on and in ecosystems. The second component of sustainability is the ecological dimension that requires that the essential life-support functions of the natural environment be preserved so that the dynamic symbiotic relationships among all interdependent species may continue. The failure to achieve ecological sustainability necessarily results in ecosystem disorganization that ultimately undermines the capacity of nature to support the living species that comprise it, including humans. The failure to achieve social sustainability results in the inability of humans to meet their basic needs, and thus leads them to act upon the environment in ways that undermine ecological sustainability (Redclift, 1987). The ultimate success of any program for achieving a sustainable development trajectory requires that both ecological and social sustainability be attained, which implies a mutually and reciprocally supportive social system–ecosystem relationship. The current global development trajectory fails to produce either social or ecological sustainability. In failing to satisfy the basic social needs of a large portion of the human population while simultaneously undermining the essential functioning of ecosystems, the existing global political economy threatens both human quality of life and the long-term integrity of the natural systems upon which humans depend.

SUSTAINABILITY AND ENVIRONMENTAL JUSTICE

Inequality and the Environment

Central to any discussion of sustainable development is the issue of socioeconomic and political inequality. Economic inequality outcomes are, in fact, an indicator of a socially unsustainable social order. The trajectory of ever increasing inequality produced by global neoliberalism underscores that such political-economic arrangements are moving the world system further away from a sustainable development paradigm. Inequality represents an engine of environmental degradation through a number of mechanisms. Economic inequality forces great portions of an impoverished human population to seek daily survival through a variety of ecologically unsustainable practices, such as farming marginal lands and extracting renewable fuel resources above rates of natural regeneration. Economic inequality also produces a much smaller privileged segment of the human population that consumes renewable and nonrenewable natural resources at ecologically unsustainable rates and generates enormous quantities of synthetic ecological contaminants in order to fulfill insatiable luxury desires. And economic inequality fuels the competitive drive for ever increasing levels of aggregate consumption as people feel relatively materially deprived in relation to those with greater levels of wealth (Schor, 1998).

Most significantly, economic and political inequality (and the fusion of the two) distances the makers of natural resource decisions from the ecological and social consequences of their decisions. In doing so, inequality severs the direct mechanisms of feedback between social system actions and ecosystem consequences that is essential to socioenvironmental learning and steward-ship. In an era of globalization, the greater the inequalities, the greater the social and ecological distance between social decisions about the natural world and nature's response to those decisions. If sustainable development implies a constant dynamic dialogue between social systems and ecosystems, inequality produces potentially deadly silence. Those who are less powerful, and prevented through antidemocratic structures from making natural resource decisions, bear the brunt of the consequences of those natural resource decisions (Gedicks, 2001). Their political incapacity to effect changes in socioenvironmental dynamics after experiencing the feedback from the natural world (in the form of ecological degradation, declining health, and reduced livelihood capacities) further severs the essential mecha-nism of the society-nature dialogue. Economic and political inequality is thus a key element in society's current inability to attain a healthful and sustain-able relationship with the natural world. The antidemocratic nature of the control of scientific and technological research and development agendas reinforces this incapacity and propels it into the future, as technology is a primary means through which humans mediate their relationship with their environment.

Because of the centrality of inequality as a driver of social and ecological unsustainability, environmental justice is a core requirement of sustainable development. Only a radical redistribution of the ecological costs and social benefits of the society-environment interaction can bring a meaningful dia-logue between social decisions and ecological consequences. Environmental justice closes the gap between those who direct the socioeconomic relation-ship with nature and those who experience the negative outcomes of that rela-tionship most directly. Only when those reaping the social benefits and those paying the ecological costs are one and the same will society be able to demo-cratically determine the appropriate and viable trade-offs between ecosystem use-values and ecosystem exchange-values that must guide sustainable devel-opment. Environmental justice implies that natural resource decisions, including technological decisions, are made democratically. And only radi-cally democratic governance can guarantee that the shifting dynamics of social system uses of nature, and nature's capacity to sustain those uses, are recognized by decision makers. Those who know and monitor environmental conditions locally must be empowered to alter political-economic systems at higher levels of social organization (Gould, Schnaiberg, and Weinberg, 1996). The sustainable development agenda is then, in essence, an environmental justice agenda.

If sustainable development requires environmental justice, and environmental justice requires the radical redistribution of social and ecological costs and benefits, then sustainable development may be the single greatest conceptual challenge to neoliberalism, corporate power, market mechanisms, and capitalism as a whole. Such systems fundamentally depend upon and exacerbate social, economic, and political inequality, and thus constantly increase the distance between decision makers and the ecological consequences of their decisions. In the era of global neoliberalism, this distance between decision makers' actions and socioenvironmental consequences is expanded both spatially and intellectually, as elites are empowered to act on more physically distant ecosystems, and remain more physically and socio-emotionally distant from more locally marginalized populations. As markets generate ever greater elite insularity and ever more brutal environmental and economic poverty, they drive us further from a socially and ecologically sustainable development path. However, in threatening both social sustainability as peoples' right to meet their basic needs for food, shelter, medicine, livelihood and community, and ecological sustainability, as peoples' right to a safe, clean, healthy, and perpetually functioning environment, global neoliberalism fuses together seemingly discreet and distinct campaigns for justice and the environment. In doing so, the market itself has made increasingly clear a single line of conflict. That conflict between the great mass of citizens and the global elite is ultimately a conflict over the sustainability (with its ecological and social components) of the global development trajectory, and the right to alter that development path.

A Redistributive Strategy for Sustainability

Although the lines of conflict are increasingly clear, and the key components of the political-economic basis for making sustainable development possible are also becoming clear (grassroots democracy, equitable distribution, prioritization of basic human and ecosystem needs, etc.), what is less clear is the mechanism by which such conflicts can be successfully won and such sweeping social goals achieved. Along a number of dimensions, the transition from a growth-oriented capitalist economy to a social and environmental justice–oriented sustainable economy appears to be less possible at this point in history than ever before. Ironically, the necessity for such a transition has never been clearer, and the consequences of failure to make such a transition have never been so ominous. Ecological resistance strategies rooted in an environmental justice agenda will be a key component in the effort to force a radical transformation of the economic structure on those who control, maintain, and benefit from that structure. The fusion of production (class), place (environmental), and identity (race, ethnicity, gender) politics manifests in calls for environmental equity represents a major ideological threat to the core logic of global capitalism.

This political fusion, manifest in the people of color environmental justice movement in the United States and indigenous peoples movements transnationally, represents a combined threat to both the logic of capitalism and the racialist forces of white privilege. The relationship of identity to place is not restricted to racial and ethnic dimensions, as identity is often partially constructed through identification with a specific location or set of local resources, sometimes fused to the local means of production (i.e., fishing communities, forest products communities, etc.). However, because this fusion of production, place, and identity politics is perhaps most evident in movements where race and ethnicity are key dimensions of political power and conflict (as in struggles in Chiapas and numerous other locations around the world), they may represent the clearest manifestation of the multifaceted dynamics of the global struggle for environmental justice, and may produce the core ideology of resistance to the logic of neoliberal globalization (Gould, 1999).

In rejecting the trade-off between ecological use-values and ecological exchange-values imposed on citizen-workers by the existing political-economy (Schnaiberg, 1980), environmental justice advocates have begun to forge a new vision of a socially just and ecologically sustainable social order (Gould, Schnaiberg, and Weinberg, 1996). That vision is a compelling one for the billions of people worldwide who find that the existing economic order leaves their basic needs unmet, while degrading the natural life-support systems upon which we all depend. However, the political task of engaging in a protracted local–global conflict to replace the current socioeconomic order has only just begun. At this stage of what will inevitably be a long and difficult struggle, it is important to focus upon what is conceivably achievable in the short run without losing sight of long-term goals (Gould, 2003).

In the immediate future, environmental justice advocates can work to empower the most vulnerable communities as a starting point from which to force ecological degradation upward in the stratification system from those at the least powerful level of social system–ecosystem decision making toward those at the highest level of social system–ecosystem decision making. This implies that the political task begins in the poorest communities in those countries where socioeconomic inequality is greatest. The process of community empowerment must begin at the bottom and work its way up toward power holders. In the short term, such a strategy implies that protection of the poor (particularly poor communities of racial and ethnic minorities whose political disenfranchisement is greatest due to the independent and synergistic impacts of the class and racial distribution of power) will initially come at the expense of the working class, and that protection of the working class will come at the expense of the middle class. In an effort to socioecologically swim upstream against the normal flow of market forces such short-term outcomes are perhaps unavoidable (Gould, 2003). The logic of such a strategy stems from the reality that in a market economy, harm flows down the stratification scale, so that protection of the working class in a wealthier nation tends to chase environmental hazards downward toward the poor in less wealthy nations. Such outcomes reduce pressure on elite decision makers rather than having the intended effect of increasing that pressure.

In the longer term, as the progressive distributional logic of environmental justice pushes back the regressive distributional logic of global markets, environmental and public health threats will become more socially visible and more politically relevant to those segments of society with greater access to the decision-making mechanisms of states, transnational corporations, and international financial institutions. As environmental harm becomes an increasing social reality for power holders and their families (or at least to those constituencies that are important to power holders), their attention to the negative ecological and health consequences of their production decisions will by necessity be increased. If siting of hazardous facilities is moved closer to transnational elites as a result of the effective ecological resistance of less wealthy communities, those elites will have to either crush ecological resistance from below or reduce the level of environmental harm generated by the production processes and facilities that they control. For most capital owners, managers, and investors, ecological disruption and public health threats have been conveniently out of sight and out of mind, made by the logic of capital into a problem of the global poor and working class (Schnaiberg and Gould, 2000). What a successful transnational environmental justice struggle can do is physically and intellectually move these threats closer to the homes and consciousness of those empowered to reduce them. The political effort of environmental justice can in that way be conceptualized as an effort to raise the consciousness of treadmill elites by raising their level of environmental risk. The strategy is to redistribute the ecological costs of global production, as a step toward inversely redistributing the global economic benefits and the levers of production decision making (Gould, 2003).

There are, of course, no guarantees that the transnational economic elites will in fact choose to reorganize production around the goal of ecological integrity simply because they and their families become increasingly vulnerable to the harms that their production goals and systems generate. After all, the trade-off between ecological integrity and economic gain is much better for them than it is for the global poor and working class. They may, in the end, choose to live with greater environmental and health risks as part of the cost of gaining the enormous wealth and power that the growth economy generates for them. And their capacity to access health care, distributed by class, will help the global ruling class to survive environmental health hazards that the poor, denied adequate health care, cannot. However, the process of moving that ecological risk up through the stratification system may effectively recruit all other classes to the environmental justice struggle, as the trade-off between ecological risk and economic gain gets progressively worse for the global consumer class. Under such conditions, the political will of the great majority of citizen-workers domestically and transnationally may become too great for elites to bear, forcing them to restructure production and severely constrain the market logic that currently makes environmental injustice and socioecological unsustainability inevitable and unavoidable. Unless the cost of unsustainable natural resource decisions can be forced upon decision makers, they will continue to have great incentive to drive the global ecosystem over the precipice, and to drive the majority of the world's citizens over the edge with it.

States, Markets, and Sustainability

What is clearly implied in such a discussion of changing the patterns of distribution of ecological costs and economic benefits is a fundamental transformation of national and transnational economic structures. The distributional logic of capitalism, now under the banner of global neoliberalism, requires a reduction or elimination of political intrusion into the functioning of market forces (Daly, 1996). Those market forces dictate that environmental injustice remain a normal feature of social life on this planet. In such an economy, environmental harm is simply added to the list of sanctions against the poor along with lack of access to health care, adequate housing, adequate nutrition, and education. Environmental justice is fundamentally incompatible with the logic of capitalism. And since environmental justice is a central feature of sustainable development, capitalist political-economic arrangements are fundamentally antithetical to the attainment of socially and ecologically sustainable development trajectories.

Environmental justice struggles can increase pressure on elites to alter production practices that degrade the environment, and can slow the growth of the global economy by restricting the access of transnational corporations to local resources. However, there will remain a need to address interlocal resource uses. Not all local social system–ecosystem interactions produce ecological disruptions that remain local. In particular, air and water can easily remove environmental hazards—contaminants—from one locality by transporting them to another locality. That is, on some level, we are all subject to the individual and aggregate impacts of the natural resource decisions made by other communities, no matter how radically democratic and locally equitable such decisions are. To address such supralocal threats to sustainability, some supralocal institutions must be utilized. This implies the need for some form of state intervention in both local decision making and larger economic interactions. The challenge is to construct supralocal governance mechanisms that can democratically place limits on the democratically determined natural resource decisions of communities to ensure that local decisions do not aggregate into extralocal ecological harm, nor increase environmental risk for other communities not included in the local decision-making process. But before we engage too much in generating blueprints for what will replace the drive toward accelerating unsustainability, it is essential that we focus on the blueprints for what will stop that drive first.

SUSTAINABILITY AND THE TECHNOLOGICAL TRAJECTORY

Science, Technology, and Socioenvironmental Dynamics

The processes of scientific research and technological innovation have always been politically charged endeavors. Behind the patina of scientific objectivity and value neutrality, scientists and engineers have used their work to pursue their own political agendas or those of others (Wright, 1992). From Galileo to Newton to Oppenheimer, the social actors engaged in scientific research and engineering have shaped the political terrain of societies. Scientific research and engineering outcomes have been, and continue to be, used by those engaged in political conflicts to validate their positions and gain wider social support. Nowhere is this more evident than in the arena of environmental conflicts.

In environmental conflicts science and scientists have been employed to resolve political disputes over the existence, causes, consequences, and appropriate solutions to dysfunctional relations between social systems and ecosystems. The fact that problems in socioenvironmental dynamics are fundamentally political rather than scientific has not prevented social institutions and their challengers from appealing to science as the ultimate arbitrator of political disputes (Schnaiberg and Gould, 2000). Nor has it prevented these social actors from appealing to engineering to generate solutions to problems that are fundamentally social structural in nature. Because technology is a primary mediator of social system–ecosystem dynamics, sustainable development efforts necessarily require a radical rethinking of the origins, impacts, goals, and control of the technological trajectory, and the entire scientific and engineering enterprise.

Technological Fixes and the Environment

All new technologies are sold by institutions to publics as utopian (Nye, 1996), with particular emphasis on medical benefits and attractive consumer goods. In addition to the usual utopian benefits, states and corporations have more recently begun to emphasize a wide array of ecological sustainability benefits potentially stemming from new technologies, capitalizing on broad public concern for the deteriorating state of the global biosphere. Here the naïve and convenient notion that ecological problems are primarily techno- logical in nature, and thus amenable to engineering solutions, rather than social structural in nature, and thus requiring political-economic solutions, is reinforced (Gould, 2005). The failure of decades of technological fixes to reverse or even to slow the pace of ecological destruction is ignored in favor of the view that the next round of growth-enhancing technological innovation will resolve ecosystem–social system discontinuities. Faith in so-called eco- logical modernization is useful to states and corporations seeking to avoid the threatening political implications of the necessity of bringing social systems in line with ecological limits. In effect, the global elite promise that social systems can escape ecological limits through technological innovation. In doing so they ignore both the realities of nature and the realities of the politi- cal economy.

Recent and ongoing conflicts over global warming clearly illustrate the extent to which conflicting science and scientists have been utilized by social actors as tools in political disputes, with various institutions and organiza- tions finding politically useful research and researchers to support their claims. Similarly, engineers have been employed by actors in global warming disputes to offer technological answers to political questions in the form of alternative, clean, or limitless energy and efficiency technologies. The politi- cization of science and engineering is synergistically internally and externally generated, as science and technology workers willingly serve political ends, bring their own political beliefs and intentions to the table, and are employed by institutions with overt and covert political agendas.

Thus far, the primary thrust of the corporate and state-sponsored techno- logical fix approach to sustainable development has been in the area of energy efficiency and expanding energy sources. The institutional goal of increased energy efficiency is generally to increase total production output per unit of energy input. Thus efficiency goals tend to be economic growth goals, not sustainability goals. Despite decades of increases in energy efficiency, total human energy demand has continued to rise. Savings in energy demand per unit of production have been used to increase production rather than limit total energy use. The problem of increasing energy demand is not technological in nature but rather social structural. The growth requirement of the market economy quickly absorbs and offsets any ecological savings from increased technological efficiency (Schnaiberg and Gould, 2000). This process applies to fossil fuels and nonfossil fuel–based energy alternatives as well.

Clearly, significant reductions in fossil fuel use will have environmental benefits in terms of atmospheric contamination reduction, reduced threat of global climate shift, and reduced ecological damage from extraction and transport. However, the promise of a technologically driven alternative energy transition assumes a replacement of fossil fuels rather than an augmentation. Adding to total available energy stocks will simply increase production capacity and thus accelerate the conversion of ecosystem elements into goods and waste. Qualitative savings in natural resource demand in energy and materials will ultimately be outstripped by quantitative increases in total production unless the political economy is reoriented (Schnaiberg and Gould, 2000). Note that oil did not replace coal, nor did nuclear energy replace oil. The notion of replacement of fossil fuels with more benign alternatives also ignores the powerful political and economic interests vested in fossil fuel production. Viable alternatives to fossil fuel use already exist in many applications, and their failure to replace fossil fuels in those sectors is a result of political-economic factors, not lack of technical capacity. The lack of state investment in renewable energy options over the past quarter century is clearly illustrative of the power of private capital resistance to technological threats to continued profitability. In a world dominated by a single superpower dominated by corporate oil interests, the political realities indicate that replacement rather than augmentation is unlikely (Gould, 2005).

Technological Trajectory and Social Institutions

The progress and direction of scientific research and engineering outcomes are largely controlled by powerful social institutions pursuing specific social goals and political agendas. Such institutions exert control over the research and development process in numerous ways including the control of educational institutions, research facilities, research and development funding, and remuneration of outcomes. At each point of the research and development process, powerful social institutions are able to influence the agendas of scientists, engineers, and the entire trajectory of technological innovation. There is no "runaway technology" (Schnaiberg, 1980). There is no "natural evolution" of technological direction or scientific research thrust. The direction of scientific and technological research and development is a result of human intentionality and decision making in the context of a distribution of power stemming from national and transnational political economies. As a result, the history and contemporary trajectory of research and development is reflective of the distribution of political power that emerges from political-economic structures.

The primary social institutions determining the research and development agendas, which dominate contemporary societies, are universities, states, and corporations. Each of these institutions has specific interests that are reflected in the agendas for scientific research and technological innovation, and thus shape the social futures that the rest of the social and ecological world inherits. Universities have historically been viewed as the institutions with the greatest dedication to the "objective" pursuit of scientific truths, and as semi-autonomous of the larger political world. Here it was often scientists and engineers who set the research and development agendas largely immune from the influence of the political and economic goals and rewards stemming from states and corporations. However, as the costs of research and development increased, and public support for autonomous universities declined, states and corporations came to increasingly control the agendas, goals, and ideologies of science and technology workers within universities (White, 2000). Thus, the agendas of states and corporations ripple through the university system and dominate the trajectory of research and development now, and into the future (Noble, 1977).

States are the primary source of funding for basic scientific research. The foundations upon which future applied science will be built are therefore determined by the ways that state decision makers prioritize paths of inquiry and distribute funding. The goals of states in funding basic science are fairly clear. First, states fund basic science and some applied research and development to enhance their military capacities. Since states represent the primary markets for weapons systems they have a vested interest in assuring that a central thrust of the human technological trajectory be the creation of ever more powerful military technology (Gould, 2003). The pursuit of ever more effective military systems thus dominates the science and technology research and development agenda of the species. That such developments tend to increase the power of states relative to citizenries is an intentional exercise of power to further increase the power imbalance between states and citizens. The pursuit of higher kill ratios at lower costs is an efficiency goal that is inherently in opposition to the goals of using technology to improve human welfare and promote sustainability. And the enormous funding offered by the state for military research and development distorts the human technological trajectory toward destructive ends while sapping funding from quality-of-life-enhancing research along other paths of human inquiry.

The other goal of states in sponsoring research and development is the pursuit of maintaining and increasing their global "economic competitiveness." By using the tax revenues generated by citizen-workers to subsidize the research and development agendas of private capital interests based within their borders, states seek to boost the gross domestic products of their nations. Increasing the economic power of the country increases the relative power of a state, allowing it greater influence over the global arenas in which it competes with other states. The increasing economic power of the state thus becomes a science and technology goal in its own right, along with the increasing military power of the state. And the two goals are inextricably intertwined in a military-industrial complex as increased tax revenues through successful international economic competition makes more funding available to support military research and development, and increasing military power affords greater access to the global natural resources, waste sinks, markets, and labor pools that facilitate economic growth (Gedicks, 2001).

The interest of corporations in scientific and engineering research and development are somewhat less complex than those of states. Private capital pursues technological innovation to enhance profitability (Schnaiberg, 1980). As the primary institutional source of funding for applied science and engineering, and the primary employers of science and technology workers, the goals of corporations dominate the human technological trajectory like no other social institution. Corporations use the state subsidy of basic research as the basis for applied research that will produce profit-enhancing products to be sold to states (military), other corporations (including labor replacing technologies), and individual consumers (consumer goods). Lines of inquiry that will generate products that may produce social or ecological benefits but may fail to generate profits are not funded and not pursued. Corporate profitability is the ultimate criterion for determining the human technological trajectory.

The goal of corporate profitability distorts the thrust of technological innovation and scientific inquiry in numerous and often antisocial ways. Corporate profitability sets the research agendas of scientists both within the firm and within the university. Through corporate sponsorship of university research and development, private capital creates the system of incentives and disincentives for the pursuit of various lines of potential scientific inquiry and engineering development. By providing the physical facilities in which research and development will be pursued, corporations control the construction and nature of the scientific and engineering infrastructure of society. By offering shared profitability incentives with educational institutions and university researchers, corporations powerfully influence the physical and intellectual thrust of higher education (White, 2000). The nature and structure of scientific and engineering education is reflective of the narrow social agendas of large corporations and their economically elite decision makers (Noble, 1977). Corporations also overtly and covertly squelch lines of scientific investigation that may threaten the goal of corporate profitability (Beder, 1997).

Research on the negative ecological and social impacts of engineering products goes largely unfunded. The lack of institutional support for such research then provides the basis for the political exploitation of the unknown and of scientific uncertainty. The term "no scientific evidence to prove" a negative ecological, health, or social impact is often indicative of the fact that no institution was willing to fund the collection and analysis of such evidence. Lines of inquiry that threaten, or fail to support, state and corporate goals are realms of science that largely lay fallow. What is not known and not produced is every bit as much a result of the political agendas of powerful institutions as the stock of that which is known and is produced. Our societal ignorance of ecosystems, the health and environmental consequences of industrial chemicals, and the impacts of our technologies on the basic functioning of natural life-support systems is the direct result of the power and interests of corporations. As corporations have come to dominate states in terms of goals, ideologies, and decision-making personnel, the goals of states and corporations have further fused, leaving no social institutions available to provide support for scientific and engineering research that serves the social and ecological sustainability goals that a technological society might otherwise pursue.

Science, Technological Innovation, and Power

The trajectory of scientific research and technological innovation is controlled by a small number of elite decision makers in states and corporations who establish research priorities, provide research facilities, and determine the distribution of funding. The result is a global technological infrastructure, system, and thrust that reflect the narrow interests of a powerful and privileged few and pursue those interests despite many obvious negative consequences for social and ecological sustainability. The fact that the bulk of technological decisions are made in corporate boardrooms and opaque government institutions shields scientific research agendas and technological innovation trajectories from democratic processes. Although the outcomes of research and development decisions often become obvious to the public at large, the decision-making processes that ultimately lead to outcomes (and non-outcomes) are unavailable for public input and public influence. Citizen-workers must live with the technological consequences in terms of products that are and are not available, technologies that do and do not exist, employment opportunities that are created and destroyed, and public health and ecological impacts that are generated, but are denied agency in the determination of those consequences.

Democratic input into research agendas is extremely limited. What passes for democratic controls of technology are largely mechanisms for "public consultation" arranged after technological capacities are generated by prior research agendas. Such public consultations are organized by the very institutions that sponsor technological research, and whose political agenda is to gain public acceptance for the new innovations. These public forums are designed primarily to assuage public fears, which are viewed by those who have a vested interest in technology as irrational outcomes of ignorance and misunderstanding. Institutional power and professional expertise are used as political tools to trump public objection to the new technological trajectory. The research on the social and ecological implications of new technology is highly politicized and specifically intended to boost the chances for public acceptance. The deck is stacked against democratic efforts on the part of citizens to determine the course of their own technological future.

The Myth of "Progress"

Further shielding the public from democratic agency in science and technology decision making is the myth of "progress," a set of ideological constructs perpetuated by the institutions and elites who control the research and development process. The public is led to believe that science is objective, that research takes a natural course determined by free inquiry and the evolution of ideas, and that technologies are routed along a linear progression where one development automatically follows from another. That is, citizen-workers are led to believe that there is in fact no institutional agency in the technological trajectory, and that what little human agency exists is vested in individual experts pursuing either public good or private gain. The ideology of capitalism argues that the pursuit of private gain naturally leads to the common good. The fusion of the myth of objective science and the ideology of capitalist ethics generates a fatalistic complacency in regard to research and development on the part of the general public (Nye, 1996). This fatalistic complacency serves the interests of the institutions and elites who do have agency in determining the societal technological path.

While it is true that democratic citizenries could demand and exert greater influence over the basic research that states primarily support, the ideological power of objective science and capitalist ethics keeps this possibility from entering the public consciousness. Science and technology decision making has simply been organized out of politics (Lukes, 1974). The result is that powerful elites are left to utilize the human technological capacity in pursuit of their own self-interest largely unchecked by the vast majority. In no other arena are the long-term consequences for human society and the environment as great and the political discussion so muted. Conflicts do emerge from time to time (on nuclear technology, genetic technology, etc.), but even then the political discourse largely revolves around a ban on the implementation of a specific technological outcome rather than a quest for democratic control over the processes that generate such outcomes.

The Radical Democratization of Innovation

If we are to seriously pursue sustainable development, scientific research and technological innovation processes must be made subject to democratic controls in which their potential social and ecological impacts can be assessed by informed publics, and under conditions in which democratic citizenries are empowered to determine the goals of research and development, the prioritization and funding of that research, and the manner in which technologies shall be implemented or prohibited (Gould, 2005). This input must occur at the earliest stages of the research and development process, determining the purpose and trajectory of the most basic lines of scientific inquiry in order to harness the human scientific and technological capacity for the maximization of democratically established social benefits. After-the-fact protests and control efforts in which citizens express opposition to antidemocratic technological decisions is certainly a less then optimal scenario for democratic governance and the creation of a technological trajectory that serves sustainability goals.

Given the context of the current global political economy (which promotes corporate profitability as a central value, economic growth as the overriding social goal, and competitive advantage over appropriate caution), and the lack of understanding of (and thus, ability to mitigate) the ecological consequences of new technological developments, the social and environmental costs of such developments are likely to outweigh the overly utopian benefits promised by the institutions involved in their production, even when such developments are promoted as enhancing sustainability. Unless democratic mechanisms for the social control of the human scientific research and technological innovation processes are constructed, the future of the technological trajectory will be one of largely authoritarian institutional efforts to persuade or coerce acceptance of the political-economic vision manifest in the technological trajectory, and perhaps violent political conflict with citizen-workers forced to use extralegal means to prevent this vision from becoming their new socioenvironmental reality (Gould, 2005).

DEMOCRACY AND SUSTAINABILITY

The goal of generating a socially and ecologically sustainable relationship between social systems and ecosystems requires a radical restructuring of the global political economy along two primary lines. No sustainable socioenvironmental dynamic is likely to be attained without the pursuit of environmental justice, which implies an equitable distribution of the social benefits and ecological costs of production. Since such an environmental justice paradigm is clearly in the interest of the great majority of global citizens, the failure to meaningfully pursue such a path is illustrative of the antidemocratic nature of the current political economy. Democratic natural resource and production decision making would necessarily tend to produce more environmental justice outcomes. Thus a radical democratization of socioecological decision making is an essential requirement of environmental justice, and sustainable development.

No meaningful democratization of natural resource and production decision making can be achieved unless it includes a radical democratization of the scientific research and technological innovation process. As humans act upon their environment through the technologies they produce and implement, technological choice is at the heart of the effort to create a sustainable social system–ecosystem relationship. If the goals and outcomes of the technological innovation system represent the interest of the privileged few at the expense of the great majority and the natural environment, that innovation system is a key engine of environmental injustice. A truly deep environmental justice paradigm must include the demand that citizens wrest control of scientific research and technological innovation agendas from elite-dominated institutions and market forces, and demand that the human technological capacity be harnessed to attain a socially just and ecologically sustainable trajectory. While the first stage of environmental justice may be to equitably distribute the costs and benefits of technologically mediated socioenvironmental outcomes, the next stage must clearly be to gain democratic control over the systems and processes that produce those outcomes in the first place.

Participatory democracy is essential to both the redistributive and technological requirements of a deep and meaningful environmental justice paradigm, which is the key to a sustainable socioecological dynamic. Empowerment of the most vulnerable communities so that they may stage effective ecological resistance, thus forcing the costs of ecological disorganization up the stratification system, is essential. Also essential to a sustainability strategy is the empowerment of those communities to demand a redistribution of the socioeconomic benefits downward to where those benefits can allow people to meet their basic social needs without being structurally coerced to make anti-ecological survival decisions. Finally, scientific and technological capacity must be distributed downward, so that the key technological mediators between social systems and ecosystems can be shaped by those who must live with the trade-offs between social benefit and ecological cost. Only through such a radically democratic political economy guided by a deep environmental justice paradigm is a truly sustainable development trajectory likely to emerge.

REFERENCES

Beder, S. 1997. *Global Spin: The Corporate Assault on Environmentalism*. White River Junction, Vt.: Chelsea Green.

Daly, H. E. 1996. *Beyond Growth: The Economics of Sustainable Development*. Boston: Beacon.

Gedicks, A. 2001. *Resource Rebels: Native Challenges to Mining and Oil Corporations*. Cambridge, Mass.: South End Press.

Gould, K. A. 2005. "Os Deuses de Coisas Pequenas: Nanotecnoloia, Poder Insitutional e o Ambiente." In *Nanotecnoloia, Sociedade e Meio Ambiente*, ed. Paulo Roberto Martins. São Paulo: Associação Editora Humanitas.

———. 2003. "Classe Social, Justiça Ambiental e Conflito Politico." In *Justiça Ambiental e Cidadania*, ed. José Augusto Pádua, Henri Acselrad, and Selene Herculano. Rio de Janeiro: Relume Dumara.

———. 1999. "Tactical Tourism: A Comparative Analysis of Rainforest Tourism in Ecuador and Belize." *Organization and Environment* 12(3): 245–62.

———, A. Schnaiberg, and A. S. Weinberg. 1996. *Local Environmental Struggles: Citizen Activism in the Treadmill of Production*. Cambridge: Cambridge University Press.

Lukes, S. 1974. *Power: A Radical View*. London: Macmillan.

Noble, D. F. 1977. *America by Design: Science, Technology, and the Rise of Corporate Capitalism*. New York: Knopf.

Nye, D. E. 1996. *American Technological Sublime*. Cambridge, Mass.: MIT Press.

Redclift, M. 1987. *Sustainable Development: Exploring the Contradictions*. London: Routledge.

Schnaiberg, A. 1980. *The Environment: From Surplus to Scarcity*. New York: Oxford University Press.

———, and K. A. Gould. 2000. *Environment and Society: The Enduring Conflict*. New Jersey: Blackburn Press.

Schor, J. B. 1998. *The Overspent American: Why We Want What We Don't Need*. New York: Harper Perennial.

White, G. (ed.). 2000. *Campus Inc.* Albany, N.Y.: Prometheus Books.

Wright, W. 1992. *Wild Knowledge: Science, Language, and Social Life in a Fragile Environment*. Minneapolis: University of Minnesota Press.

13

Promoting Peace through Global Governance

Jerry Pubantz and John Allphin Moore, Jr.

Global governance is emerging from the shadows of long-established intergovernmental diplomacy. The new governance architecture is a collective of transnational organizations, specialized agencies, institutional structures, forums, programs, nongovernmental organizations (NGOs), social movements, and individuals. The network of intergovernmental organizations (IGOs) has grown from thirty-seven entities in 1909 to over three hundred in the new millennium (Russett and Oneal, 2001: 160, 169), and now addresses both global and domestic concerns.

At the network's nexus is a "new" United Nations. The only universal IGO, the UN has the broadest mandate for the maintenance of peace and security, linking sovereign states and NGOs into an enlarged international civil society that includes subnational, private sector, and social movement components. Its current humanitarian interventions, state-building efforts, promotion of democracy, embrace of globalization, protection of minorities in peacekeeping operations, and pursuit of human rights violators situate the UN at the center of contemporary international relations.

Some UN enthusiasts see these developments as the product of "Kantian" and "Habermasian" theoretical means—at work in international civil society that philosophers Immanuel Kant and Jürgen Habermas would argue promote peace. The Kantian forecast of increasing numbers of democratic states, cooperation through international organizations, and enhanced global interdependence has opened avenues for nonstate actors to play an enlarged role in an expanding republican federation at the global level. This in turn has

231

fostered democratization and cooperation within and among states. Participatory democracy by way of civil discourse about serious issues—now possible on an integrated global/local network—leads, Habermas (Borradori, 2004) has said, to will and policy formation without resort to interstate conflict.

There is, to be sure, serious skepticism about this cheeriness. Many progressives are less enamored with the United Nations and other international organizations—such as the Bretton Woods institutions—as instruments of peace. For them, contemporary IGOs are reflections of conventional "enlightenment" liberalism. Informed by Antonio Gramsci's understanding of "hegemony" and Michel Foucault's analysis of power, postmodernists, and many feminists, prefer to subject institutional arrangements to critical sociolinguistic analysis rather than examine their putative advances. Because international organizations reflect current dominant power relations, these theorists think these entities must experience elemental structural readjustments in order to effect genuine and uncorrupted global governance.

The UN's recently detected pivotal position is particularly disconcerting to scholars and policy makers in the realist tradition of international politics who believe the United Nations and other IGOs are best used as interlocutory mechanisms among sovereign states for the diplomatic adjustment of national interests; realists suggest the United Nations and similar bodies prove either ineffective or, in fact, damaging to the pursuit of peace when they try to impose global governance on an essentially anarchic world. They find it dangerous folly, not an encouragement of peace, to promote global governance structures, or to allow the United Nations to evolve beyond a traditional Westphalian institution.

However, granting insight to these assessments does not erase the concrete record of innovative UN activities over the last two decades, as well as those of other international organizations, as they have moved from purely diplomatic arenas for government-to-government diplomacy to venues where institutional actors can mobilize the world community on behalf of peace-oriented goals often at odds with the interests of individual member-states. The United Nations has promoted the development of international civil society, encouraged nonstate actors to set global agendas, and created human rights standards that have achieved universal support despite underlying cultural differences. Furthermore, Secretary-General Annan (2005), in his most sweeping proposals for UN reform, has linked the pursuit of human rights to development (economic and social) and collective security on the premise that only the guarantee of all three elements will deter conflict in the foreseeable future.

First conceived by Franklin D. Roosevelt as an instrument of the "four policemen" (United States, China, Soviet Union, and United Kingdom), the

United Nations began as a universal collective security system, dedicated to the consensual enforcement of peace by the Security Council's great powers. There is no better evidence of the early institution's priorities than its postponement of covenants assuring basic human and economic rights. At the 1945 San Francisco Conference there were several proposals to include the "protection" of human rights in the UN's charter obligations. In fact, the charter references "human rights" seven times. However, fear that reaching a consensus would be agonizingly protracted and that momentum toward establishing the world body for its intended primary purposes would dissipate led the delegates to defer the drafting of a bill of human rights for the charter. Instead, under Eleanor Roosevelt's leadership, the UN Commission on Human Rights crafted the Universal Declaration of Human Rights, derided at the time as a meaningless and unenforceable set of Western platitudes. Mrs. Roosevelt's faith rested in global public opinion and cross-cultural discourse that ultimately would move sovereign states and the United Nations to the defense of the declaration's asserted rights.

In many ways, the "rebirth" of the United Nations in the post–Cold War era has met her expectations. For two decades, the United Nations has been preoccupied with advancing democratic principles, inserting itself into the internal affairs of disintegrating member-states, and seeking to punish individuals (not just governments) for violations of citizens' rights. These trends have been accompanied by an internal democratization of the United Nations, as nonstate actors play an escalating role in its decision-making processes. Taken together these changes have produced a new United Nations better positioned to promote peace in the twenty-first century, and to mobilize other components of international civil society to the same end.

Secretary-General Annan heralded this remolded United Nations in his Millennium Summit Report *We the Peoples*, issued in September 2000.

> Even though the United Nations is an organization of states . . . the Charter is written in the name of "We the peoples." It reaffirms the dignity and worth of the human person, respect for human rights and the equal rights of men and women, and a commitment to social progress . . . in freedom from want and fear alike. Ultimately, then, the United Nations exists for, and must serve, the needs and hopes of people everywhere. . . . No shift in the way we think or act can be more critical than this: we must put people at the center of everything we do (7).

The summit committed the world community to a set of Millennium Development Goals (MDGs) to be achieved by 2015, including: to halve the number of people living on $1 a day and the proportion of people who suffer from hunger or live without sustainable access to safe drinking water; to eliminate gender disparity in education and society as a whole; and to reduce by two-thirds the mortality rate of children under five by improving maternal health, including reducing the maternal mortality ratio by 75 percent. The MDG targets also set 2015 as the deadline for halting and then beginning to reverse the spread of HIV/AIDS, malaria, and other major diseases.

The Millennium Summit was a watershed event in UN history, marking the emergence of the world body at the center of a global policy-making process, premised on the notion that international peace requires solutions of systemic human problems by the coordinated efforts of transnational, national, and subnational actors. Five current UN priorities reflect this view: internal UN democratization, thematic diplomacy, the application of human rights law to individuals in judicial procedures, nation building, and the promotion of democracy.

INTERNAL DEMOCRATIZATION

While the UN System is surely not yet what Habermas (1997a: 126) would call a "cosmopolitan democracy," with its far-flung specialized agencies and affiliated bodies, it serves as the primary forum for global policy formation, affecting individuals at least as much as governments, particularly in the developing world. This new discursive and democratic disposition arises in part from including nonstate and private sector actors as participants in decision making that once was routinely a government-to-government obligation (Eizenstat, 2004: 17–18; Johns, 2004: 57). The United Nations has become more "legislative," or "parliamentary" in character, revealing a Kantian sense of inclusion and porous democratic proceduralism.

Article 71 of the UN Charter allows the Economic and Social Council (ECOSOC) to grant "consultative status" to nongovernmental organizations that are involved with issues addressed by the United Nations. NGOs represent the "people power" that Eleanor Roosevelt believed would ultimately make the Universal Declaration of Human Rights a meaningful and enforceable reality. In the late 1980s and 1990s NGO participation in the United Nations grew dramatically. The number of nongovernmental organizations granted consultative status by ECOSOC was forty-one in 1948. This only rose to 377 by 1968. However, NGO association with ECOSOC soared to twelve hundred in 1997, and more than twenty-six hundred in mid-2005 (UN Department of Economic and Social Affairs NGO Section).

The surge in transnational organizations encouraged by the porosity of globalization, financial flows, and Internet communication persuaded these advocacy groups to target the UN system as a critical access point to international policy making. NGOs have become "citizen organizations" within the

United Nations, advocating particular goals and mobilizing support for UN initiatives. They also represent Habermas's "nodal points" in the international communications network, advancing the salient issues, possible solutions, and constructed values of a vibrant democratic process into the public sphere, thus encouraging global consensus (1996, 373). These organizations, in the language of interest group and political party theorists, articulate and aggregate disparate group agendas into coordinated advocacy programs that mimic the activities of national private groups and parties. They have taken domestic democratic political techniques to the international level.

In 1996 ECOSOC took a seminal step, passing Resolution 31, giving NGOs expanded access to the council. Those granted "general" consultative status were allowed observers at ECOSOC meetings and permitted to submit written statements to both the council and subsidiary bodies. They could also address the council on subjects of interest. As a result, these organizations regularly circulated materials to member-state missions, providing an opportunity for enhanced interest group advocacy.

The ECOSOC process has been replicated in other bodies of the UN system, including the Security Council and specialized agencies. Since 1997 the Security Council president has regularly met with a representative NGO group to garner advice on issues before the council. NGOs provide participants for panels of experts and in substantive negotiations; serve on agencies such as the Joint United Nations Programme on HIV/AIDS (UNAIDS); and develop program proposals for disease control, poverty eradication, and other improvements for the globe's poor. NGOs bring community concerns to UN bodies, monitor global policies and international agreements, provide analysis and expertise, and serve as early warning mechanisms. They are also key actors in implementing UN programs at the subnational and local levels.

Expanding NGOs' role in UN bodies and deliberative processes is not universally lauded, nor is it seen in some quarters as particularly democratic (Fonte, 2004: 118). Critics point out that NGO representatives are unelected and often do not reflect majority opinion either internationally or in the countries of their origin. Only representatives of sovereign democratic states may make that claim. However, in cases where IGOs have failed to follow the UN lead in incorporating NGO participation, they have often faced demands for "democratization" of their institutions and procedures. The most dramatic expression of these "people's demands" has been the protests directed at the World Trade Organization (WTO) and the World Bank. Frustration at the closed methods employed by the Bretton Woods institutions has spilled over into street protests and petitions for greater inclusion.

The Panel of Eminent Persons on UN–Civil Society Relations, appointed by Kofi Annan in February 2003, endorsed the increased NGO presence at the United Nations, applauded their innovative contributions to world affairs, and advised the UN to serve as the foremost convener of multiple constituencies. The panel (2004: 25) asserted that "politically active citizens now express their concerns through civil society mechanisms rather than the traditional instruments of democracy."

The nation-state no longer serves as the sole mediator between its citizens and the world. Many national governments do not have the necessary means to address cross-boundary trends such as globalization, terrorism, refugee flows, disease, and environmental degradation. Understandably, there has been a shift in perceived legitimacy toward both subnational entities on the one hand and a cosmopolitan order on the other. In the latter case, global civil society wields real power in the name of individuals, and the United Nations and other international organizations are the targets of that power. The Cardoso Report (2004: 9) recommended that "The United Nations should accept an explicit role in strengthening global governance and tackling the democratic deficits it is prone to, emphasizing participatory democracy and deeper accountability of institutions to the global public."

The amplification of NGO and even individual participation in UN activities can be seen in world conferences and in the work of special rapporteurs. A special rapporteur receives a commission from a body of the United Nations and then provides a comprehensive report on a specific global problem or area of concern to that body. During the last two decades of the twentieth century, the UN Commission on Human Rights most often made use of special rapporteurs. The commission appointed special rapporteurs to investigate thematic issues, such as torture, summary executions, violence against women, racial discrimination, inadequate housing, trafficking in persons, migration, sexual exploitation of children, and religious discrimination. In 2005 there were forty-one special rapporteurs or independent experts covering a broad range of topics and inspecting specific countries (UN Office of the UN Commission on Human Rights).

Through world conferences and special sessions of the General Assembly, NGOs, working parallel to state representatives, set policy agendas and mold world opinion. In Habermas's view (1996: 381), the great issues of our time are first broached in the "distant arenas" of civil society, then forced by advocacy groups into the public sphere where an intersubjective process of reason formation occurs. By Habermasian insinuation, UN-sponsored world conferences thus serve as defining events in the creation of international legal regimes and policies. They create the framework, momentum, and policy outlines from which international action often originates. For example, the world environment conferences, particularly the 1992 Earth Summit, generated a diplomatic process culminating in the Kyoto Protocol of 1997, which set targeted limits on greenhouse gas emissions of carbon dioxide and several other harmful effluents. The summit also enshrined "sustainable development" as the globally accepted formula for merging the protection of the global commons with the inherent right of every people to economic development.

Beginning with the 1972 UN Conference on the Human Environment (UNCHE) in Stockholm, NGOs have been invited to participate in the preparation and activities of all UN conferences. Since then, every world gathering has included a companion people's forum, and NGO representatives have been allowed to present statements and to lobby delegations. Forty-seven thousand people attended the Earth Summit in Rio de Janeiro; fifty thousand attended the Fourth World Conference on Women in Beijing; thirty thousand were accredited to the 1996 Istanbul Second World Conference on Human Settlements (HABITAT II); and 3,744 NGOs, along with seventeen thousand individuals, were accredited to the 2001 World Conference against Racism in Durban, South Africa. The General Assembly routinely requires the participation of NGO representatives in the "PrepComms"(preparatory committees) for UN-sponsored global meetings. These private participants have been able to focus UN attention on the problems and opportunities associated with human rights, the environment, women and development, human settlements, racism, ozone depletion, natural disasters, education, disarmament, children, population policy, desertification, social issues, and sustainable development.

More controversial than the inclusion of civil society organizations in the work of the United Nations has been the engagement of traditional large enterprises and multinational corporations—the bastions of global capitalism. At the 1999 World Economic Forum in Davos, Switzerland, Annan urged corporations to join in a Global Compact and work directly with the world body, bypassing national governments. The secretary-general pressed corporations to commit to principles established in important UN conventions. In so doing they could become involved in the UN's most pressing work and, in the event, reap beneficial plaudits. Annan hoped to engage private corporations particularly in the area of development, impaired by decreases in donor-state funding.

In the Global Compact, corporations are asked to fulfill ten principles established in the Rio Declaration of the Earth Summit, the International Labour Organization's Fundamental Principles on Rights of Work, the UN Convention against Corruption, and the Universal Declaration of Human Rights. They agree to: (1) support and respect international human rights within their sphere of influence, (2) make sure their own corporations are not complicit in human rights abuses, (3) uphold freedom of association and the right to collective bargaining, (4) end all forms of forced and compulsory labor, (5) promote the abolition of child labor, (6) eliminate discrimination in employment, (7) support a "precautionary approach" to environmental challenges, (8) advance greater environmental responsibility, (9) encourage and develop environmentally friendly technologies, and (10) oppose corruption in all forms, including extortion and bribery.

By the summer of 2006 membership in the Global Compact approached three thousand. In June of that year nearly five hundred chief executive officers met at UN Headquarters and made further commitments to global social and economic responsibility. At the meeting, ten stock exchanges announced their agreement with the compact. The Global Compact's goals include identifying and stressing an international corporate citizenship, articulating corporate "good practices," and making the United Nations the acknowledged forum for international civil society organizations.

All of these efforts reflected Secretary-General Annan's "stakeholder" strategy, engaging three broad categories of nonstate participants: nongovernmental organizations, civil society members (including private individuals and subnational organizations), and the international business community (Malena, 2004; Castells, 2005). Together these three components create an advocacy group for addressing wide-ranging thematic issues, a prerequisite in Jürgen Habermas's view for accountable democratic decision making within governing bodies. By extension, other intergovernmental organizations, to the extent they wish to participate in what Judith Blau and Alberto Moncada (2005: 63) call the "recent more inclusive and participatory approach" to global governance, must achieve the UN standard and be "permeable to the free-floating values, issues, contributions, and arguments of a surrounding political communication that, as such, cannot be organized as a whole" (Habermas, 1997b: 57).

THEMATIC DIPLOMACY

Having nongovernmental organizations and individuals work within UN bodies enhances the organization's role in thematic policy formation and provides conduits beyond traditional member-state agencies for implementing that policy. The contemporary UN agenda embraces thematic diplomacy, by which is meant a focus on functional human problems that confront mankind on a global level and require for their solution not only national governments working in concert but also the cooperation of international and subnational organizations. Although the United Nations is pursuing many areas of thematic diplomacy, twelve topics predominate. They are: the environment, women, international humanitarian law, sustainable development, globalization, human rights, democratization, poverty eradication (especially in

Africa), population, human settlements, disease control, and the information revolution (Moore and Pubantz, 2005: chapter 6).

This new priority underscores an enhanced democratic character to UN debate. Habermas (1996: 359) notes that "the public sphere must . . . amplify the pressure of problems, that is, not only detect and identify problems but also convincingly and *influentially* thematize them, furnish them with possible solutions, and dramatize them in such a way that they are taken up and dealt with by parliamentary complexes." Exceeding its original purposes, the United Nations more and more addresses functional or thematic issues, often without regard to autonomous state boundaries, undercutting the traditional rights of national governments to monopolize these issues domestically.

The new thematic diplomacy accentuates issues not formerly considered central to the maintenance of international peace and security, blurring the divide between international negotiation and domestic policy making. What had been the "Other" in traditional international affairs has become a part of global agenda setting and policy formation. The present agenda includes ethnic and religious tension, race and gender inequalities, urban growth, and distortions in income distribution. Accordingly, the United Nations and many international organizations, more than ever before, are addressing sociological and organizational phenomena such as the internationalization of production and markets and the consequent changing patterns of work and conditions of labor (in both developed and developing nations).

Two examples suffice to demonstrate the UN's critical policy role. They concern the issues of the environment and HIV/AIDS. In both, the UN system monopolizes the decision-making architecture, policy initiatives, conceptual framework, and terminology used for comprehending these challenges. A UN process from 1972 to the present has closed the apparent contradiction between environmental conservation and economic development with the formulation of "sustainable development." Chaired by Gro Harlem Brundtland, the World Commission on Environment and Development, following extensive interviews and negotiations with thousands of individuals and groups, first used the term in its 1987 report, *Our Common Future*. Defined as "development that meets the needs of the present without compromising the ability of future generations to meet their own needs," *sustainable development* has served as the universal rubric for developed and developing nations, environmental and development NGOs, and other intergovernmental organizations in deliberations on a global environmental agenda. That agenda includes atmospheric challenges, climate change (ozone depletion and global warming), preservation of the seas and maritime resources, biodiversity, deforestation, and desertification. The global governance network has produced binding agreements such as the Kyoto and Montreal protocols, the

Vienna Convention for the Protection of the Ozone Layer, and the Convention on Biodiversity. It has also spawned new intergovernmental organizations, leveraged billions of dollars from Bretton Woods institutions for environmental protection, and energized a new wave of civil society organizations, while simultaneously acknowledging a right to development by least developed countries.

The UN encounter with HIV/AIDS began in the mid-1980s as a coordinated effort by the World Health Organization (WHO) and the UN Development Programme (UNDP). WHO launched the Global Programme on AIDS, which focused on both disease prevention and the mitigation of the pandemic's social and economic consequences. In 1987 the UN General Assembly held an extraordinary session on AIDS and called upon all agencies in the UN system to address the crisis. The Security Council declared HIV/AIDS a threat to international peace and security, the first disease so identified. UNAIDS, created in 1996, brought together key international and national agencies, disease experts, and NGO representatives. Secretary-General Annan pressured major pharmaceutical companies to waive their patent rights and to slash the price of antiretroviral drugs. In 2001 the United Nations created a new Global AIDS Fund to raise between $8 and $10 billion to assist poor countries hurt most by the disease. These efforts were witness to the United Nations as "mobilizer" of the world governance and civil society structure. They were premised on the assumption that the greatest threats to peace in the twenty-first century are the domestic challenges that disrupt fragile societies and create instability.

WAR CRIMES TRIBUNALS

Another area of UN thematic governance is human rights. Concern with human rights began with the drafting of the UN Charter and the Universal Declaration of Human Rights. But enforcement of delineated rights was not then in the purview of international organization. Penalizing violators of those rights was left to sovereign national governments. Despite the Nuremberg Trial principles, perpetrators of war crimes and crimes against humanity were beyond the reach of the global community. Yet, no democratic political system can exist without the rule of law and its even-handed enforcement.

A new "judicial diplomacy" emerged only in the 1990s, as the Security Council created two international war crimes tribunals: the International Criminal Tribunal for the Former Yugoslavia (ICTY, 1993) and the International Criminal Tribunal for Rwanda (ICTR, 1994). Court indictments and trials seemed reasonable ways to punish political leaders who violated the rights of their own citizens, and to dissuade others with the sure expectation of criminal prosecution. These tribunals expressed the world's horror at witnessing genocide in the Balkan and Rwandan crises, and reflected a conviction that these conflicts had triggered massive human rights violations. The consequent revulsion effectively sanctioned UN intrusion into the hallowed province of juridical state sovereignty.

While the indictment, arrest, and trial of Slobodan Milosevic may mark the high point of the ICTY's activities, as of May 2006, the tribunal had indicted 161 individuals and conducted 95 trials; 43 persons had been convicted and were serving their sentences or were awaiting transfer to prison. Of those indicted, only 6 remained at large as of 2006. Among those found guilty, Radislav Krstic (chief of staff of Bosnian Serb forces that attacked civilians and UN personnel in the safe haven of Srebrenica) received the most severe sentence: 46 years' imprisonment for genocide, crimes against humanity, and violations of the laws of war.

The UN Security Council created the International Criminal Tribunal for Rwanda on November 8, 1994. Among other precedents, the ICTR recognized rape as a "war crime" for the first time in history. It also was the first international court to convict a head of government, sentencing Rwandan prime minister Jean Kambanda to life imprisonment for committing genocide and for crimes against humanity. While genocide was outlawed by international convention in 1948, the ICTR's decision in the Kambanda case was the first ever rendered by an international tribunal for this crime.

The ICTY and ICTR responded to particular atrocities occurring in specific civil conflicts. But their ad hoc nature dismayed many governments and nonstate actors who sought a long-term response to human rights crimes. They renewed the call for a permanent court to which suspected violators could be remanded for trial. In 1998, a conference of one hundred countries approved the Rome Statute of the International Criminal Court (ICC), establishing a permanent body to investigate and decide cases involving individuals responsible for the most serious crimes of international concern: aggression, genocide, war crimes, and crimes against humanity (including widespread murder of civilians, torture, and mass rape). One hundred and sixty countries, 124 NGOs, seventeen intergovernmental organizations, and fourteen UN specialized agencies and funds participated in the UN diplomatic conference that prepared the statute.

The court began operations in the summer of 2002. Unlike the International Court of Justice, the ICC supercedes the usual limitations of sovereignty by having persons, not states, before it, and by bringing cases against involuntary parties. Its jurisdiction complements national legal systems by taking cases that states refuse or are unwilling to undertake against their own nationals.

The use of international judicial procedures to punish government officials for crimes against their own people tests the existing three-century paradigm for peace by challenging the sovereignty of the state. Sovereignty arises from the will of the state's citizens to protect and provide for their well-being through the power of their government. When governments become the perpetrators of violence against their own citizens, sovereignty in principle is relinquished. By administering justice to guilty government leaders, the international community notionally restores citizens' rights and security, undercutting the causes of internal conflict.

NATION BUILDING AND THE PROMOTION OF DEMOCRACY

What connection exists between the United Nations, founded in 1945 to maintain peace and security through the cooperation of the great powers, and the new global governance system, with the United Nations at its center? Where do these two UNs fuse to strengthen world peace? Is the new United Nations so fundamentally different that its old institutional structure is either irrelevant or counterproductive to lessening the chances of conflict? If there is no connection, would it not be better to discard the older UN purposes and structure, maintain its current humanitarian initiatives, and construct more effective interstate organizations?

Arguably, the old and new United Nations intersect in the processes of nation building and global democratization. Neither term is listed in the UN Charter, but each has been pursued under the mantle of peacekeeping. For the first forty years of UN history, peacekeeping operations separated combatants, monitored armistices and peace agreements between sovereign states, and served as neutral facilitators of arrangements already agreed to by the adversaries. Since 1988, however, the conflicts brought to the United Nations have mainly involved domestic turmoil—usually civil wars—several disputing the legitimacy of an existing government or assaulting ethnic, religious, and minority groups. In response, UN interventions have become more numerous and more robust. The United Nations authorized only thirteen peacekeeping missions prior to 1988. From 1988 through 2000, more than thirty-six operations were undertaken. In 2006 there were eighteen operations under way, involving more than sixty-six thousand troops, civilian police, and observers. Several thousand additional civil administrators were also working under the UN umbrella. Costs rose to more than $5 billion annually. Most of these interventions have been in conflict-prone sub-Saharan Africa. The United Nations has also created "peace-building" and political support offices in states and regions where there is a likely threat of violent instability. (See table 13.1.)

The new missions have been authorized by the Security Council, which has emerged as the "legitimizer" of collective security. The council's actions reflect what Elisabeth Gerber and Ken Kollman (2004) call "authority migration" from the national state, both upward toward transnational organizations and downward to subnational units. Thus, the Security Council has authorized—in Namibia, Cambodia, Somalia, Congo, Kosovo, Timor-Leste, Bosnia, and other paralyzed states—direct international administration of local life, to the virtual exclusion of the national government. For example, in 1999 the UN Interim Administration Mission in Kosovo (UNMIK) undertook the invasive governance of all aspects of Kosovar life. UN administrators sought to bring ethnic Serbs and Albanians together in a peaceful multiethnic state, still within the sovereign territory of Serbia and Montenegro, whether the inhabitants wished full independence, association with Serbia, or autonomy. For the next seven years, in every hamlet and town of Kosovo, government consisted of Serb-Albanian-UN committees determining the details of public policy, the UN representative retaining final authority. UNMIK was charged with performing basic governmental functions, providing essential services to the population, and facilitating a political process to determine Kosovo's future, while in the meantime establishing autonomy and self-government in the province, providing humanitarian aid, maintaining law and order, repatriating more than one million refugees, and promoting human rights. In May 2001, UNMIK promulgated a draft democratic constitution for Kosovo that recognized individual rights and group power sharing.

In the distant Pacific island nation of Indonesia, the world's judgment was different from what it was in the Balkan crisis. There the Security Council defended the right of the East Timorese people to break the sovereign control of the central government and to establish a new state, Timor-Leste. In 1999, with the pressured consent of the Indonesian government, the Security Council authorized military intervention to restore order and, as in Kosovo, to establish UN administration of the fledgling state. In this case, however, the goal was stable independent government, not self-governing autonomy. Under UN leadership, East Timor crafted a constitution, convened national governmental organs, elected an assembly and a president, and took control of governmental affairs in May 2002.

The UN role in the new era of peacekeeping includes disparate activities such as refugee repatriation; humanitarian assistance; elimination of weapons of mass destruction; disarmament of conflicting groups; election monitoring;

Table 13.1   New Era Nation-Building, Political, and Peace-Building Operations in Africa

Angola	UN Angola Verification Mission (UNAVEM I)	December 1988–May 1991
	UN Angola Verification Mission (UNAVEM II)	May 1991–February 1995
	UN Angola Verification Mission (UNAVEM III)	February 1995–June 1997
	UN Observer Mission in Angola (MONUA)	June 1997–February 1999
	UN Office in Angola (UNOA)	October 1999–August 2002
	UN Mission in Angola (UNMA)	August 2002–February 2003
Burundi	UN Office in Burundi (UNOB)	October 1993–May 2004
	UN Operation in Burundi (ONUB)	June 2004–
Central African Republic	UN Mission in the Central African Republic (MINURCA)	April 1998–February 2000
	UN Office in the Central African Republic (BONUCA)	February 2000–
Côte d'Ivoire	UN Mission in Côte d'Ivoire (MINUCI)	May 2003–April 2004
	UN Operation in Côte d'Ivoire (UNOCI)	April 2004–
Democratic Republic of the Congo	UN Organization Mission in the Democratic Republic of the Congo (MONUC)	December 1999–
Ethiopia/Eritrea	UN Mission in Ethiopia and Eritrea (UNMEE)	July 2000–
Great Lakes Region	Office of the Special Representative of the Secretary-General for the Great Lakes Region	January 1997–
Guinea-Bissau	UN Peace-Building Support Office in Guinea-Bissau (UNOGBIS)	March 1999–
Liberia	Observer Mission in Liberia (UNOMIL)	September 1993–September 1997
	UN Peace-Building Support Office in Liberia (UNOL)	November 1997–July 2003
	UN Mission in Liberia (UNMIL)	September 2003–
Mozambique	UN Operation in Mozambique (ONUMOZ)	December 1992–December 1994
Namibia	UN Transition Assistance Group (UNTAG)	April 1989–March 1990
Rwanda	UN Assistance Mission for Rwanda (UNAMIR)	October 1993–March 1996

Rwanda/Uganda	UN Observer Mission for Uganda-Rwanda (UNOMUR)	June 1993–September 1994
Sierra Leone	UN Observer Mission in Sierra Leone (UNOMSIL)	July 1998–October 1999
	UN Mission in Sierra Leone (UNAMSIL)	October 1999–December 2005
	UN Integrated Office in Sierra Leone (UNIOSL)	January 2006–
Somalia	UN Operations in Somalia (UNOSOM I)	April 1992–March 1993
	UN Operations in Somalia (UNOSOM II)	March 1993–March 1995
	UN Political Office for Somalia (UNPOS)	April 1995–
Sudan	UN Mission in the Sudan (UNMIS)	March 2005–
West Africa	UN Office for West Africa (UNOWA)	March 2002–
Western Sahara	UN Mission for the Referendum in Western Sahara (MINURSO)	April 1991–

reconstruction of legal systems; armistice negotiation; creation of civil society organizations; constitutional reform; civil policing and criminal investigation; provision of basic services such as transportation and utility systems; protection and political advancement of women, indigenous peoples, and minority groups; economic development; and the enhancement of social justice. The much maligned Boutros Boutros-Ghali, Secretary-General Annan's predecessor, first recommended these kinds of operations in his *Agenda for Peace*, published in 1992. He saw them as indispensable to world peace, which depended, in his view, on addressing internal conflicts, social justice problems, economic deprivation, and democratic deficits in "states at risk."

Paramount for Boutros-Ghali was the democratization of states that had long suffered under authoritarian governments. Rejecting the studied neutrality on political ideology exhibited by secretaries-general during the Cold War, Boutros-Ghali urged the world body toward peacekeeping, nation building, and the promotion of Western-style democracy, particularly in Africa and Asia.

Beginning in the late 1980s, the United Nations sought to introduce democratic practices—most particularly regular elections and popular participation—in postconflict areas (see Newman and Rich, 2004). Preoccupation with electoral democracy was driven in part by Secretary-General Annan's acceptance of the Kantian thesis that democracies do not wage war with each other. UN state-building initiatives included the protection of opposition factions, the political mobilization of marginalized groups such as women and indigenous peoples, and the restoration or creation of judicial institutions in order to assure the rule of law and the defense of individual liberties. By May 2006, 140 nations had requested UN electoral assistance, and the United Nations had provided support in ninety-one cases, including troubled places such as El Salvador, Mozambique, Cambodia, Guatemala, Palestine, Bosnia, and Angola.

The first effort to pursue democratization in a postconflict setting was in Namibia (1989). The United Nations took full administrative control of the former South African mandate region, ultimately presiding over elections and the transfer of power to an independent government. A much more difficult and precedent-setting UN initiative to implant democracy came in Somalia. In December 1992, the Security Council, using its enforcement powers under Chapter VII of the UN Charter, authorized an intervention force, led by the United States. Without the invitation of the domestic government, the council sent forces not only to provide humanitarian assistance and security, but also to restore political stability, the rule of law, a functioning democracy, and reconciliation among ethnic groups. As a result, in February 2000, the UN facilitated a peace conference in Djibouti that led to the election of a new Somali president and national assembly, and the creation of a transitional national government. The Somali model of intervention under Chapter VII was replicated with varying degrees of success over the next fourteen years in Bosnia, Rwanda, Kosovo, East Timor, Afghanistan, and Liberia.

In many nation-building operations the United Nations provides a transitional administration, overseeing the entire political process. It imposes what Simon Chesterman (Newman and Rich, 2004: 12) characterizes as a "benevolent autocracy" for the task of organizing democratic politics. UN intervention is premised on the concept of "personal sovereignty," which Secretary-General Annan has argued requires intercession in nondemocratic states that do not protect the rights of their citizens. Under Annan's guidance the UN Millennium Declaration of 2000 proclaimed on behalf of the member governments: "We shall spare no effort to promote democracy and strengthen the rule of law, as well as respect . . . all internationally recognized human rights and fundamental freedoms . . . to strengthen the capacity of all our countries to implement the principles and practices of democracy and respect for human rights, including minority rights . . . [and] to work collectively for more inclusive political processes, allowing genuine participation by all citizens in all our countries."

On the eve of the Millennium Summit, the Panel on United Nations Peace Operations published a seventy-page report calling for dramatic reform of the UN's peacekeeping missions. Named for Lahkdar Brahimi, the chairman of the panel, the Brahimi Report proposed that traditional UN impartiality between combatants in a conflict not be allowed to "amount to complicity with evil." According to the panel, the credibility of UN peacekeeping depended on being able "to distinguish victim from aggressor." Enhanced UN involvement in the internal affairs of states and ethnic enclaves has necessarily required interaction with progressive forces in those communities, moving the United Nations and its affiliated international organizations from neutral administrators to interested actors in civil society.

PEACE PROSPECTS AND THE UNITED NATIONS

The World War II generation looked to the United Nations as the last best hope for mankind to rid the world of the scourge of war. This hope was premised on a faith in collective security enforced by the world's most powerful states. In the post–Cold War world the United Nations has emerged as a crucial actor in civil society, has developed new approaches to conflict, and has evolved a new identity to address the underlying causes of war.

Philosophical speculation about peace and formulas to achieve it is a continuing preoccupation of political and sociological theory. Immanuel Kant in his seminal work *Perpetual Peace* (1939 [1795]) suggested that peace could be achieved by a "federation of democratic states" exhibiting "universal hospitality." Among other things, such hospitality must include "the spirit of commerce that sooner or later takes hold of every nation and is incompatible with war" (37). A world of democratic states joined in international organizations and economically interdependent has become the accepted interpretation of what constitutes a "Kantian" prescription for peace in the twenty-first century. As the "third wave" of democracy has swept the globe, the hope has arisen that a liberal peace might be preserved through a system of common values, economic integration, and energetic intergovernmental organizations.

However, a true international federation is more than a voluntary gathering of sovereign actors, democratic or not, free to ignore higher principles whenever autonomous state interest dictates. As Jürgen Habermas has noted, the legitimacy of majority decisions in a public body arises solely from popular sovereignty exercised within the recognized constraints of equality and freedom (1997b: 37).

The sliding measure over time of the proportionate role of governments versus people individually or organized into nonstate groups in the determination of global public policy tells us much about the level of popular sovereignty in the United Nations, and therefore about the United Nations as a legitimate law-making institution. Progress in this regard depends on the state of UN internal democratization (along participatory as opposed to purely liberal representative lines), which is particularly important when the world body challenges state sovereignty through nation building, or addresses violations of human rights. Particularly in the field of human rights, this last requirement is decisive, because only rights, even if we happily admit them to be "universal" and preliminary to the state, made by democratic procedure can carry the authority of universal legitimacy (see Habermas, 1996: 33).

The opening up of UN processes to nonstate actors, the UN's efforts to address thematic issues important to billions of human beings, and its newly found commitment to reach beyond state sovereignty in the service of democratic principles and higher moral law have given the United Nations a legitimacy beyond that bestowed by the authority and power of its most important founding members. The merit of this maturation was most recently endorsed in the reform proposals presented by the secretary-general's appointed High-Level Panel (2004) that recommended significant changes in the structure of the Security Council and in the work of other UN bodies, and then by Annan himself in his 2005 report *In Larger Freedom*, in which he asserted an unbreakable link between collective security on the one hand, and human rights and development on the other. Under these democratizing conditions, the new UN governance structures increase the possibilities for peace, at least as well as any alternative yet conceived.

REFERENCES

Annan, Kofi A. 2005. Report of the Secretary-General. *In Larger Freedom: Towards Development, Security and Human Rights for All*. March 21, A/59/2005.

———. 2002. "Democracy as an International Issue." *Global Governance* 8(2) (April–June): 135–42.

———. 2000. *We the Peoples: The Role of the United Nations in the 21st Century*. New York: United Nations Department of Public Information.

Blau, Judith R., and Alberto Moncada. 2005. *Human Rights: Beyond the Liberal Vision*. Lanham, Md.: Rowman & Littlefield.

Borradori, Giovanna. 2004. *Philosophy in a Time of Terror: Dialogues with Jürgen Habermas and Jacques Derrida*. Chicago: University of Chicago Press.

Boutros-Ghali, Boutros. 1992. *An Agenda for Peace*. New York: United Nations.

Cardoso, Fernando Henrique. 2004. Report of the Panel of Eminent Persons on United Nations-Civil Society Relations. *We the Peoples: Civil Society, the United Nations, and Global Governance*. June 11, A/58/817.

Castells, Manuel. 2005. "Global Governance and Global Politics." *PS: Political Science and Politics* XXXVIII(1) (January): 9–16.

Eizenstat, Stuart E. 2004. "Nongovernmental Organizations as the Fifth Estate." *Seton Hall Journal of Diplomacy and International Relations* V(2) (Summer/Fall): 15–28.

Fonte, John. 2004. "Democracy's Trojan Horse." *National Interest*, Summer, 117–27.

Gerber, Elisabeth R., and Ken Kollman. 2004. "Introduction—Authority Migration: Defining an Emerging Research Agenda." *PS: Political Science and Politics* XXX-VII(3) (July): 397–400.

Habermas, Jürgen. 1997a. "Kant's Idea of Perpetual Peace, with the Benefit of Two Hundred Years' Hindsight." In *Perpetual Peace: Essays on Kant's Cosmopolitan Ideal*, ed. James Bohman and Matthias Lutz-Bachmann. Cambridge, Mass.: MIT Press.

———. 1997b. "Popular Sovereignty as Procedure." In *Deliberative Democracy: Essays on Reason and Politics*, ed. James Bohman and William Rehg. Cambridge, Mass.: MIT Press.

———. 1996. *Between Facts and Norms: Contributions to a Discursive Theory of Law and Democracy*. Cambridge, Mass.: MIT Press.

High-Level Panel. 2004. *Report on Threats, Challenges and Change: A More Secure World: Our Shared Responsibility*, A/59/565, December 1, 2004, 11.

Johns, Gary. 2004. "Relations with Nongovernmental Organizations: Lessons for the UN." *Seton Hall Journal of Diplomacy and International Relations* V(2) (Summer/Fall): 51–65.

Kant, Immanuel. 1939 [1795]. *Perpetual Peace*. New York: Columbia University Press.

Malena, Carmen. 2004. *Strategic Partnership: Challenges and Best Practices in the Management and Governance of Multi-Stakeholder Partnerships Involving UN and Civil Society Actors*. Background Paper for the Multi-Stakeholder Workshop on Partnerships and UN–Civil Society Relations, February.

Moore, John Allphin, Jr., and Jerry Pubantz. 2005. *The New United Nations: International Organization in the Twenty-First Century*. Englewood Cliffs, N.J.: Prentice Hall.

Newman, Edward, and Ronald Rich. 2004. *The UN Role in Promoting Democracy: Between Ideals and Reality*. Tokyo: United Nations University Press.

Russett, Bruce, and John R. Oneal. 2001. *Triangulating Peace*. New York: Norton.

United Nations. Department of Economic and Social Affairs NGO Section: www.un.org/esa/coordination/ngo/.

———. Department of Peacekeeping Operations: www.un.org/Depts/dpko/dpko/.

———. Office of the UN Commission of Human Rights: www.ohchr.org/english/bodies/chr/special/index.htm.

We the Peoples: Civil Society, the United Nations and Global Governance. 2004. Report of the Panel of Eminent Persons on United Nations–Civil Society Relations, June 21, A/58/817.

IV

RETHINKING LIBERALISM

14

Ejidos: A Utopian Project

Judith Blau and Alberto Moncada

In this chapter we explore the possibilities for invigorating public spaces as sites of community solidarity and democratic action, posing a model of self-sufficiency and self-governance. U.S. representative, liberal democracy does not express the "will of the people," as was originally envisioned with independence from Britain, but instead is driven by antidemocratic economic elites, powerful executive appointees, and the entrenched military-industrial complex. Lobbyists and large private contributors to parties and candidates wield inordinate power and exercise influence over politicians in dark recesses out of public view. Yet, it is a chicken-and-egg problem, with Americans cynical of politicians and political processes, only marginally participating in community and political life.

Lamenting the increasing consolidation of power, political theorists pose alternatives to representative democracy along the lines of participatory, or direct, democracy (for example, Green, 1999). Direct democracy is increasingly possible because of the Internet, and the main remaining challenges are, first, ensuring that all have access to broadband, and, second, creating online decision-making structures. For example, all people within a given locale could vote on important policy issues affecting their community, with elected representatives forming committees for decision making in particular areas, and elected community representatives serving on committees at the next higher level of governance, and so forth, up through all levels of jurisdictions. In other words, participatory democracy is about people's decision making in substantive areas, and structures of participation would be nested within others.

The Global Forum on Internet Governance and the United Nations Working Group on Internet Governance have worked out some of the practical details that would make it possible to implement democratic participation locally, nationally, and internationally (for example, MacLean, 2004; United Nations, 2005). The assumption is that people have a stake in their locales and their nation, and therefore deserve to exercise voice in these spheres. Technical and practical constraints are real, of course, but not insurmountable, especially when we consider that publics are layered or nested.

Attention so far has centered on the political and informational aspects of deep, direct democracy, and less on the social and community foundations. Our concern is that American society is deplorably ill prepared for genuine, substantive democracy: its political culture is highly individualistic, and communities are racially and economically segregated. Constitutional interpretations favor property rights, and there are no formal protections for human rights, namely, the social, economic, environmental, and cultural rights of persons. Civil and political rights do protect individual freedoms vis-à-vis the state, but these are not rights that protect human welfare. Yet, when people are brought together under a democratic umbrella, they discover that many of their individual concerns about, say, schools, parks, health care, and wages are indeed broadly shared. Talk soon turns to matters of human welfare and shared collective interests, and contentious partisan divisions tend to dissipate. There is empirical evidence that this is the case (United Nations, 2005).

Our argument takes the form of comparing what Max Weber referred to as "ideal types," namely, comparing liberal, individualistic American communities with what we refer to generically as *ejidos*, communities in which democratic decision making has long been part of the social fabric. Turning Tönnies's (1957 [1887]) famous contrast between *gemeinschaft* and *gesellschaft* societies on its head, we suggest that the principles that are dominant in collectivistic and self-governing communities offer useful lessons for U.S. communities and workplaces, which otherwise lack "social glue" (Annan, 2005). In short, we argue that social democracy is important in its own right, but as people implement social democracy they help to create the social glue that is necessary for an engaged public.

As far as the workplace is concerned, firms with collectivized ownership can be found in rich and poor countries, and in those with market economies as well as in those with mostly subsistence, socialist economies (Melman, 2001). On the other hand, aside from intentional communities and communes, most communities that are thoroughly democratic and collectivist are in poor, not rich, societies. They nevertheless highlight the parameters that allow us to see how communities in rich societies might be democratic.

THE COMMONS: *EJIDOS*

To best capture the principles that underlie the diverse democratic practices in poor countries, we adopt for our purposes a Spanish term, *ejido,* meaning "commons," which refers to collective agrarian practices in Latin America. Yet, these practices, which include farming commonly held land and sharing natural resources, exemplify practices elsewhere: *jiti* (China), *op tac xa nong nghiep* (Vietnam), *rangatirtanga* (Australia), *mataqalis* (Pacific Islands), *comunidades* (some of South America), *diessa* and *shenhena* (parts of Africa). (See Digital Library of the Commons; Larmour, 1997; Payne, 2002; Snyder and Torres, 1998.) Such practices are commonplace among indigenous groups all over the world. The United Nations Educational, Scientific, and Cultural Organization (2000) estimates there are approximately 350 million indigenous peoples in the world, and most of them live in *ejidosian* type communities.

Ejidos are not necessarily single communities; they are sometimes federated for efficiencies. For example, In Chiapas, Mexico, among groups in the Caribbean, and in the Niger Delta of Nigeria, relatively autonomous villages unite to form large self-governing units for loosely coordinating development, technology, and environmental projects that are too large or complicated for any single community. These communities have lately attracted the interest of anthropologists owing to members' specialized lay knowledge of plants, sea life, marshland, and animals. They also have attracted the attention of economists who are interested in cooperative strategies regarding "common-pool resources," such as water supplies (Dolak and Ostrom, 2003). Because this is a conceptual, not an empirical, argument, we will ignore the great variation that exists in *ejidosian* communities but draw on two examples. Nevertheless, in general, *ejidos* are self-governing, self-sufficient, and embrace egalitarian principles.

Ejidos are comparable in many respects to collectively owned and managed companies. Perhaps the most famous in the West is the Mondragon Cooperative Corporation (MCC) in the Basque region of Spain. It has more than thirty thousand worker-owners and uses advanced technology for the production and assembly of machines and appliances. MCC competes in the global market and has outlets now beyond Spain (Whyte and Whyte, 1991; Gibson-Graham, 2003). The earnings ratio of highest to lowest paid workers is among the lowest in Europe, and workers and their families devote time to their communities, schools, and local governments, ensuring that their communities are themselves democratic and inclusive. Basque culture and language plays some role in the coherence of these communities, but employees come from varied backgrounds.

A TYPOLOGY

To illustrate variation in their origins and modus operandi, we distinguish three types of *ejidos*. First, there are rural communities whose members have shared a habitat for generations and because of their dependence on a common resource, such as the sea or forests, as well as their relative isolation, noncooperation is not an option (see Devereux and Maxwell, 2001). Because their survival depends on it, they develop practices for self-governance, often in spite of differences in ethnicity, traditions, and language. Examples are communities in the Niger Delta and Papua New Guinea.

Second, some *ejidosian* communities evolve because members have been thrown together as refugees or through shared poverty, and owing to government indifference and neglect, must be self-sufficient. These include many African and Latin American urban slums, where members have nothing in common other than the fact that they share a space and must make the best of it.

Third, there are those that choose *ejidosian* practices, not through necessity but rather as the natural extension of members' commitments to democratic and egalitarian values. In Western societies, the paradigmatic *ejidos* are communes and intentional communities, but with new developments in e-governance, communities in Western societies are adopting forms of democratic self-governance (MacLean, 2004). A compelling reason for democratization in U.S. communities is that developers, not residents, now wield the power at the local level, and they have little interest in promoting diverse and inclusive neighborhoods, creating public spaces (such as parks and recreational areas), and advancing sound environmental practices (for example, see Canglia, 2005).

An Example

In the arid plateaus of Eritrea, the residents of peasant communities have no choice but to engage in *ejidosian* practices (Kiflmartian, 2001). Because of the infrequency of rain and their shared dependence on an unreliable water supply, they engage in many joint projects, and if they did not, they could not survive. Each family is responsible for a given plot of state-owned land, but there are clear community norms about, for example, who helps the widow with plowing when her husband dies, the use of common lands, the sharing of the village's ox or oxen, and there are elaborate rules about the storage and use of water. Social relations are partly governed by the challenges of ethnic and religious diversity. There are often three religious faiths in a village *ejido,* each with their own structures—a mosque, an Orthodox church, and a Catholic church. Additionally, many of these communities are made up of more than one ethnicity, each with its own language, with ethnicity crossing religious affiliations to create a rich demographic and cultural mosaic.

PUBLICS

In *ejidosian* projects, publics are comprehensively human, rooted in collective solidarities, and organized in terms of human rights in their most holistic sense (see Blau and Moncada, 2005). In many *ejidosian* projects, such as Eritrean communities, cooperation is achieved easily because it is linked with interrelations involving kin, as tribe or ethnicity, and, besides, differences in status and wealth are trivial compared with the crosscutting differences on dimensions of ethnicity and religion. Public spaces are therefore energetic precisely because they provide the broad arena for working out pluralistic relations, reciprocity, and social exchange.

Yet, all people everywhere are familiar with such moments in social life when people cooperate across lines that usually divide them. Such cooperation is commonplace in catastrophes. There were abundant media accounts of New Orleans residents assisting others during and after Hurricane Katrina struck, and likewise of New Yorkers after 9/11, sharing their food and housing with strangers. These might be called, among the peoples of industrialized countries, "their *ejidosian* moments," or "moments of publicness."

Western readers probably first encountered the term *public* in Plato's *Republic*. For Plato, the public was extensively participatory—at least as far as free men were concerned—and indistinguishable from democracy. But the concept of public became narrower and narrower through the course of Western history. The Romans articulated the idea in terms of *res publica,* which made finely drawn distinctions of citizenship, thus flattening out and greatly diluting the idea of public (Pocock, 1998). The Western nation-state went even further, downgrading publicness and citizenship while elevating private ownership and property rights. Even in its ideal form, say in the work of Habermas, as a sphere of rational communication, the Western public is illusive—aspatial and without concrete and specific contents.

In contrast, in *ejidos*, publics are situated realities with common purposes. An interesting example is Kibera, similar to other urban slums in Third World countries. Until recently, Kibera, located within Nairobi, was not recognized by the city of Nairobi because recognition would have obliged the city to supply Kiberans with city services. About six hundred thousand people live in Kibera, without publicly supplied water, transportation, plumbing, sanitation, electricity, paved roads, or policing. This immense community is self-governing, with the tasks of coordination taken up by tribal elders, women's social networks, and mostly indigenous nongovernmental organizations (NGOs).

So densely crowded, each household shares three walls with each of three other households, walls (cardboard and corrugated metal) so thin that you can hear the shuffle of feet on the other side. Nevertheless, overcoming dire poverty, and great diversity in tribal membership, languages, and religions, Kiberans manage self-governance relatively well. Some economic activities are collectivized, albeit on a small scale, and women barter, trade, and donate goods and services across ethnic and language lines to create and sustain intergroup bonds. Kibera is less organized than rural *ejidos* are, partly because they have cobbled together economic activities within an urban context and adapted tribal authority to a multiethnic setting. Kibera powerfully illustrates the ways that people devise cooperative strategies in the face of harsh, cruel realities.

The two cases that we have described—Eritrean villages and Kibera—may be traditional, but they hardly resemble what Tönnies termed *gemeinschaft* communities. Whereas the rural communities and Kibera are exceedingly complex as social entities, it is the typical U.S. community that is homogeneous. And, while these African communities have worked out ways of promoting inclusive democracy (not perfect, but nevertheless, participatory), it is the residents of U.S. communities who are voiceless.

Ejidosians do not have such abstract divisions between public and private, politics and publics, markets and publics. As philosopher Roy Bhaskar (2003; also see Collier, 2003) situates realism, these communities do not have the symptomatic irresolvable dualisms, notably involving the distinction between the reality of things and the representation of things. *Ejidosians* have real markets, real governance, real families, real politics, and real experiences with famine, hunger, and joblessness. With lives infused by instrumental rationality and mediated realisms, Americans, by contrast, simply abdicate their public responsibilities. Work has little to do with the workplace as a social space and entity; residence has little to do with community; and elections have little to do with governance.

MODERNITY AS FLIMSINESS

Classic social theorists, such as Emile Durkheim and Max Weber, described the progressive path of modernity as one that would be marked by increasing differentiation within societies, markets, and institutions and by the strengthening of legitimacy for the distinctions produced through differentiation. Rationality was the hallmark of modernity for classical theorists, and by this they envisioned both that the individual actor would be rational and purposeful, and that the "means-ends rationality" would dominate the elements within modern society and the capitalist economy. Yet, this does not appear to be happening. Instead, there is increasing polarization, with, on the one hand, the financial interests of the Global North increasingly dominating the world, and, on the other hand, the growing demands made by the Global South for social and economic justice. Globalization has created a great space, and the dominant actors who fill that space are transnationals.

Some Westerners protest the symptoms of globalization, such as job insecurity, but the most powerful source of resistance comes from the Third World, and some main actors in this resistance are *ejidosian* groups who are determined to preserve their autonomy, while gaining a foothold on security. The Zapatistas are perhaps the best known, but other indigenous groups such as the Kuna Indians in Panama, the Maroon groups of Jamaica, and many, many others are similarly fighting to stave off invasion by multinationals and commodified Western culture. In other words, modernity has not evolved along the lines of increasing differentiation and the expansion of legitimacy for Western institutions, but there is growing bifurcation between the Global North and the Global South, and many *ejidos* are captured, like pawns, in the middle of this struggle.

TRUSTWORTHINESS AND RIGHTS

The Western conception of the public is a liberal one, namely an aggregate of independent individuals, even if, as mythologized as civil society, it is a space in which individuals can exercise their freedoms and express their identities. Such individualized publics do not promote trustworthiness or trust. This is inevitable in societies that stress meritocratic competition over solidarity, individual achievement over community, and individual wealth over more egalitarian distribution of resources. A dominant view in American liberal social thought, perhaps most famously advanced by John Rawls, is that individual liberties are paramount, but this is accompanied by respect for the choices of others and the unacceptability of coerced conformity. The public is, in other words, a tolerant place, committed to civility. Here we highlight four central problems.

First, given the prioritization of private and property freedoms over human rights and society, the liberal doctrine is compatible with inequalities in political power, social resources, and economic wealth. Moreover, the wealthy and powerful assert their dominance in public spaces and the public sphere, reproducing the inequalities that benefit them. Second, liberalism only allows group rights to the extent that the interests of the members of groups should be protected, but the mechanisms for protection are individualistic rather than group-based. Third, because individual freedoms and efficacy trump equality, the liberal has to place hope in the idea that there are opportunities for the poor and disadvantaged, but if opportunities are not continuously presenting themselves, society can ossify into a virtual caste system. Fourth, liberal doctrine is implicitly premised on a version of the social contract that relies on individual choice and is therefore not inherently inclusive, and lacks a prior sense of solidarity. Thus, the doctrinaire liberal does not particularly like economic inequalities, the marginalization of women and minorities, and a weak public sphere, but nevertheless, viewing individual freedoms as prior to human welfare, accepts inequalities as unavoidable outcomes.

Let's move the question in another direction, and suggest that cooperation is not the same as cohesion, thus distinguishing *ejidosian* practices from communitarianism, which is a form of reaction to liberalism and individualism in the West. The communitarian argument, following for example, Alasdair MacIntyre (1981), is that individuals' welfare ought to be bound up with the welfare of their community. By this, communitarians refer to social cohesion, namely, a sense of belonging, "social capital," and shared values. This longing for group cohesion, according to Robbins (1998) grows from a sense of estrangement from zones of political influence and economic marginality. To the extent this is the case, the communitarian strategy is not the most useful for disrupting power and privilege. Nor can the communitarian position deal in a straightforward way with pluralism and social complexity.

PLURALISM

Contrary to Western preconceptions, many traditional communities—*ejidos,* in our framework—are exceptionally pluralistic and cosmopolitan. Appadurai (1996) makes a strong case that the major source of pluralism and cosmopolitanism in the world today is the Global South. Partly this is due to greater population diversity. Just to give an example, the capital of Madagascar, Antananarivo, has about thirty ethnic groups, and approximately fifteen tribes. One might surmise the public of Antananarivo to be ever much as fluid, multilayered, and socially and economically complex as New York City, if not more so owing to the lesser reliance on government agencies and the greater reliance on informal groups and networks. Additionally, many Madagascar residents have far-flung diasporic ties with people and places elsewhere, not only in Africa, but also in Britain, Germany, France, the United States, and elsewhere.

There is no question that Africa has experienced some of the most violent and bloodiest civil conflict in the last decades, a consequence of the imposition of colonial divisions, great blunders made by the International Monetary Fund, World Bank, and WTO as well as by well-meaning Western NGOs, diminished resources, and lack of government coordination and catastrophic rates of HIV and AIDS infections. But *ejidos* communities have proven to be amazingly sturdy and resilient, and increasingly articulate, and sometimes militant, in their demands for equity.

The global market economy has penetrated virtually all communities, and though far from dominant in remote communities, its spread has been cause for alarm throughout the Third World. Over the last decade or so, the global market economy has taken on new corrosive features: the rapid destruction of ecosystems and the displacement of subsistence agriculture with unreliable and unsustainable employment, and, over large continents, global capitalism has uprooted families through migration, creating havoc with community and societal stability.

The major players in the global economy have become extremely rich, and wealth and control are highly concentrated. We can give some examples. According to recent estimates, over 70 percent of the world markets in consumer durables, about 60 percent of air travel, and over half of each aircraft manufacture and of electronics and electrical equipment were accounted for by five firms. By 1998, just three firms handled over 75 percent of the value of worldwide merger and acquisition deals, and the largest global companies have reached annual sales whose value exceeded the gross domestic product of over 120 firms. This is mirrored at the level of individuals, with a handful of persons in the world having wealth that exceeds the combined GDP of several poor countries (see, Robinson, 2004). Frederick Hayek, Milton Friedman, and Adam Smith have largely been proved wrong; free markets do not raise all boats. In fact, they raise remarkably few.

A UTOPIAN PROJECT

Few Americans would like to live with the scarcities, the reoccurring droughts, and with as few amenities as peasants do. Yet *ejidos* offer lessons to Westerners who may now be concluding that neoliberalism is capaciously devouring the planet's resources and imperiling societies. If by utopian we mean, as Mannheim (1936: 205) did, a conception that involves a comprehensive transformation of the entire historical-social order, then reordering Western societies along the lines of the ideal-typical *ejido* would be utopian.

Yet, first off, we need to redistribute resources more equitably through massive grants given without strings to the Global South aimed at reducing poverty; restoring sustainability; and meeting the Millennium Development Goals on maternal health, reducing epidemics, education, and the environment. The Marshall Plan for Europe was no less a utopian project and turned out to be remarkably successful. But one lesson of the Marshall Plan has been lost during the last decades, namely, that some countries must not impose their own ideologies on others.

Thus, let us imagine, first, a massive redistribution of the world's surplus. In keeping with our emphasis on realism, we can cite Sartre: "What we choose is always the better, and nothing can be better for us unless it is better for all. . . . Our responsibility is thus much greater than we had supposed, for it concerns mankind as a whole" (1946: 29). For Sartre, humans are always pitted against the constraints of existence, no more so than for the third-worlders, victimized by colonizers for centuries. But freedom for Sartre is always an obligation and realized when one's own freedoms are used to advantage the other, compensating for harms committed against them. Thus, generally, the initial task is to compensate the world's poor, or share with them all the tools they need for economic self-determination. This is one part of the utopian solution.

Aside from what the Global North can do to ensure advancing economic progress in the Global South, *ejidos* offer lessons in return. As we have described the ideal-typical case, they have achieved self-governance through broad participation and have invented and perfected forms of economic collectivization. Yet there are indications that such forms are being adopted, at least on a small scale, in the United States. In his recent study of U.S. communities and organizations, Alperovitz (2005; see Fraser and Gordon, 1992) reports that many communities are introducing forms of democracy that are both inclusive and substantive, and there is an increase in work organizations that are collectively owned and self-managed.

It is true that utopian projects are controversial. Because Marx was somewhat hostile to the idea, Marxists often consider utopia to be a method that simply involves the "unmasking" of realities (Webb, 2000). However, there are other views of utopia. For example, Miguel de Unamuno (1996: 95–97) described the participatory and democratic character of utopia in the terms of the nitty-gritty of people's lives and "talk-talk-talk." Taking utopia as a messy, public affair makes much sense when envisioning the blossoming of participatory democracy and self-governance.

Thus, one other part of utopia is that first-worlders learn from third-worlders how to cooperate, and the other part is that first-worlders give third-worlders back what they are due and what is equitable. But the pathways back and forth will probably not be very tidy, but instead more like experiments, sometimes tentative, and sometimes lively and rambunctious. We suspect that Unamuno was on to something—there will be lots of talk, talk and chatter, chatter, back and forth—which is what public spaces must be all about.

ACKNOWLEDGMENTS

We think Berhane Araia, Rye Barcott, Kim Korinek, and Junpeng Li for useful illustrations of *ejidos*. As self-critical Westerners, we lean in the direction of erring on the side of stressing the positive features of *ejidos*.

REFERENCES

Alperovitz, Gar. 2005. *America beyond Capitalism*. New York: Wiley.

Annan. Kofi. 2005. "Our Challenge: Voices for Peace, Partnerships and Renewal." United Nations, New York, September 7–9, 2005: www.un.org/secureworld/.

Appadurai, Arjun. 1996. *Modernity at Large: Cultural Dimensions of Globalization*. Minneapolis: University of Minnesota Press.

Bhaskar, Roy. 2003. *Reflections on Meta-Reality: Transcendence, Emancipation and Everyday Life*. London: Sage.

Blau, Judith, and Alberto Moncada. 2005. *Human Rights: Beyond the Liberal Vision*. Lanham, Md.: Rowman & Littlefield.

Canglia, Beth Schaefer. 2005. "Human Behavior and Land Use." Department of Sociology, Oklahoma State University, unpublished paper.

Collier, Andrew. 2003. *In Defense of Objectivity and Other Essays*. London: Routledge.

Devereux, Stephen, and Simon Maxwell (eds.). 2001. *Food Security in Sub-Saharan Africa*. Pietermaritzburg: University of Natal Press.

Digital Library of the Commons: http://dlc.dlib.indiana.edu/.

Dolak, Nives, and Elinor Ostrom (eds.). 2003. *The Commons in the New Millennium*. Cambridge, Mass.: MIT Press, 2003.

Fraser, Nancy, and Linda Gordon. 1992. "Contract versus Charity: Why Is There No Social Citizenship in the United States?" *Socialist Review* 22: 45–68.

Gibson-Graham, J. K. 2003. "Enabling Ethical Economies: Cooperativism and Class." *Critical Sociology* 29: 129–61.

Green, Judith M. 1999. *Deep Democracy*. Lanham, Md.: Rowman & Littlefield.

Kiflmartian, Abraham. 2001. *Governance without Government: Community Managed Irrigation in Eritrea*. Tekstopmaak: Naardi Botterweg-Jansen.

Larmour, Peter (ed.). 1997. *The Governance of Common Property in the Pacific Region.* Canberra: Australian National University.

MacIntyre, Alasdair. 1981. *After Virtue.* Notre Dame, Ind.: University of Notre Dame Press.

MacLean, Don (ed.). 2004. *Internet Governance: A Grand Collaboration.* New York: United Nations.

Mannheim, Karl. 1936. *Ideology and Utopia.* Translated by Louis Wirth and Edward Shils. New York: Harcourt, Brace & World.

Melman, Seymour. 2001. *After Capitalism: From Managerialism to Workplace Democracy.* New York: Knopf.

Payne, Geoffrey (ed.). 2002. *Land, Rights & Innovation: Improving Tenure Security for the Urban Poor.* London: ITDG Publishing.

Pocock, J. G. A. 1998. "The Ideal of Citizenship since Classical Times." In *Citizenship Debates,* ed. Gershon Shafir, 2–31. New York: New York University.

Robbins, Bruce. 1998. "Actually Existing Cosmopolitanism." In *Cosmopolitics: Thinking and Feeling beyond the Nation,* ed. Pheng Cheah and Bruce Robbins, 1–19. Minneapolis: University of Minnesota Press.

Robinson, William I. 2004. *A Theory of Global Capitalism: Production, Class and State in a Transnational World.* Baltimore, Md.: Johns Hopkins University Press.

Sartre, Jean-Paul. 1946. *Existentialism and Humanism.* London: Methuen.

Snyder, Richard, and Gabriel Torres (eds.). 1998. *The Future Role of the Ejido in Rural Mexico.* La Jolla, Calif.: Center for U.S.-Mexican Studies.

Tönnies, Ferdinand. 1957 [1887]. *Community and Society (Gemeinscahft and Gesellschaft).* Translated with introduction by Charles P. Loomis. East Lansing: Michigan State University.

Unamuno, Miguel de. 1996. *Political Speeches and Journalism, 1923–1929.* Edited by Stephen G. H. Roberts. Exeter: University of Exeter Press.

United Nations. 2005. *Internet Governance.* New York: UN.

United Nations Educational, Scientific, and Cultural Organization (UNESCO). 2000. "Action in Favor of Indigenous Groups": www.unesco.org.

Webb, Darren. 2000. *Marx, Marxism and Utopia.* London: Ashgate.

Whyte, William Foote, and Kathleen King Whyte. 1991. *Making Mondragon: The Growth and Dynamics of the Mondragon Cooperative.* Ithaca, N.Y.: Cornell University Press.

15

Teaching Public Sociologies

Angela Hattery and Earl Smith

Sociology has been a discipline, like so many, that has been embroiled in raging theoretical debates. For much of the twentieth century, these debates centered on the functionalist and conflict paradigms (see Gouldner, 1980). More recently, sociologists have begun to seriously challenge the notion of positivism. And, most recently still, a "new" debate has centered on the concept of public sociology. This new addition to sociology is so important that it is newly aired in one of the leading journals in sociology, *Social Forces* (vol. 82, June 2004). In many ways, though, this debate signals a return to the methods and approaches of activist-scholars such as W. E. B. DuBois and those in the Chicago School, especially Robert Park. Our interpretation of "public sociology" is grounded in the work of Berkeley sociologist Michael Burawoy, who provides a clear definition of public sociology as "taking sociology beyond the university." (W. E. B. DuBois and sociologists in the Chicago School were noted for doing research in partnership with communities and for trying to address serious issues in these communities, though they may not have used the term *human rights* as we in public sociology employ the term today.)

Both of us have been teaching about issues of civil and human rights for many years in our traditional on-campus courses. This chapter will be devoted mainly to the discussion of an innovative course that we co-developed in response to our own frustrations with the limitations of the classroom. (Most professors are frustrated by the time constraints of a traditional class [the discussion seems to heat up just as the hour is over], with the inability to require interactions among students outside the classroom, and with the limitations as far as "field trips" or "field research" are concerned.) Since the time that sociology was codified as an academic discipline, pedagogical debates have raged about whether or not to balance between exposing students to scholarly reports and introducing them to community members who have lived experience with a traditional, value-neutral perspective, or whether to exclusively stress a "value-neutral" perspective.

We consider the first option to have big pluses. That is, teaching from a "public sociology" perspective encourages instructors to see the importance of involving students in the communities in which they are living and/or studying. Stephen Pfohl notes the following:

> If as teachers, we are to engage our students as a public we must do far more than provide them with information about how society works. This point was made by Mills (1959), who argued, "it is not only information" that students need to become *active participants in a democratic society,* particularly in a society where "information often dominates their attention and overwhelms their capacities to assimilate it" (5). Instead, what is needed most "is a quality of mind that will help them use information and to develop reason in order to achieve lucid summations of what is going on in the world and what may be happening within themselves" (2004).

Teaching from a "public sociology" perspective also frees instructors to present data that are designed to prompt discussion and reflection from a human rights perspective rather than from a purely "neutral evaluative" perspective. Further we argue that teaching from this perspective encourages students to become good, responsible citizens, and unites the community with the academy. For example, when we teach about violence against women in fraternities we focus not only on the "numbers" and the likelihood of a college woman to be raped at a fraternity party, but rather we use the data (as presented in readings and in lecture) to focus our discussion on the "rights" of women to demand that universities provide an environment that is safe for them, and to address openly situations that harm women. (We note here that almost never are universities honest about the rates of date rape on their campuses, nor do they have a record of dealing with campus rapes in a manner that is punitive for the student aggressor and protective of the student victim.)

Core courses in the discipline of sociology are natural places in which to take a "public sociology" approach to teaching. For example, social class stratification and inequality are among the most commonly explored topics in many sociology courses, from introductory courses to courses on race, class, and gender. For many social theorists, such as Marxists and neo-Marxists, social class stratification is the single most important concept in understanding human behavior. Yet college campuses are anything but diverse (Hong, 2003) in terms of social class and thus there are some very unique challenges in teaching about social stratification and human rights to students who are primarily from privileged families. This is especially so as the issues are not limited to social class but also to the intersections of social class with race and gender.

In response to this challenge, coupled with the desire to involve students in the community and the opportunity to learn from community experts, we designed a module that can be included within an on-campus course (Hattery, 2003), and we also designed an innovative course that centered around taking students off-campus to explore issues of social stratification, human rights, and "public sociology" in the contemporary United States.

This chapter explores the rationale for teaching public sociology and the pedagogical concepts that are derived from public sociology. We will then illustrate these concepts with two examples from our own teaching, one that can be incorporated into a sociology course and an off-campus course that can be modified to different university and geographic settings.

THE AGE OF SCRUTINY: I DON'T LIKE
WHAT YOU ARE TEACHING ME!

Teaching public sociology is bringing to the classroom more and more often those events and situations that are important for understanding human social relationships, whether popular or not. Here we are thinking of issues analyzed in books such as those by Kai Erikson, Elijah Anderson, Richard Gelles, and Kristen Luker that play a key role in bringing to the wider public audience concerns about deviance, poverty, family violence, and abortion and make for some very serious reading and discussion in college classrooms. Our collective and combined experiences have been that discussions of human rights and injustice are rare for the students who enter our classrooms. Rather, they are well-versed in myths like that of Horatio Alger (that everyone can get ahead if they just work hard enough), in consumerism, and in distorted political ideologies that are commonly aired on television (such as the necessity of invading Iraq). They are not exposed to information that is critical of the United States or questions the status quo. (For example, they do not realize that the battlefield deaths of American men and women are occurring at a rate that will exceed the battlefield deaths of Vietnam depending on how long the United States remains in Iraq. And yet they would have been aware of President George W. Bush parachute landing on the USS *Abraham Lincoln* with a big sign behind him saying "Mission Accomplished." To challenge them on this is risky because of all the "hoopla" about "Shock & Awe." As we have learned, so many of our students today do not consume daily news—or critically analyze what news they do consume—nor do they read beyond assigned texts.)

Therefore, when we attempt to discuss issues of human rights and inequality, be they focused on race, class, gender, sexual orientation, or any other issue, the students, lacking any empirical data but armed with standard-fare American hegemonic ideology, claim that we are "wrong" and that we are attempting to brainwash them. Furthermore, when we present empirical data they dispute it with individual experience or the experiences of their parents. For example, one of us presented data on gender inequality in wages (the gendered wage gap), opportunities (two female CEOs in the Fortune 500), power (no women have become president in the United States), and violence (rape, battering) and several female students in the class dismissed this information and the accompanying claim (based on empirical evidence) for the need to finally pass the Equal Rights Amendment (ERA) based on the fact that she (the student) had never personally experienced any of these discriminatory behaviors!

As sociologists we are constantly working to teach our students about the differences between personal experience and patterns of behavior about which we have empirical data. Yet, we find that when discussing issues of human rights we are fighting an even more difficult battle because our students, like most Americans, have been effectively trained and socialized by the hegemonic ideology that maintains that America is the country of freedom of opportunity and equality and continue to hold this opinion even when you share with them data on, for example, health care among the top industrial nations (e.g., infant mortality, maternity benefits, life expectancy, etc.).

Exacerbating the issue (or problem, from the perspective of the professor attempting to disabuse students of this powerful ideology) are conservative "watchdog" groups, such as David Horowitz's "Students for Academic Freedom." Groups of this type are feverishly working to pass laws (currently there are court cases in both California and Florida) that prohibit the academic freedom of faculty, but only when they present information that challenges the hegemonic ideology.

Thus, the challenges to teaching about human rights are increasing. And, coupled with laws such as the Patriot Act, which may track things like what books we check out of our campus library (we assign the *Communist Manifesto* in our courses), they are real. Thus, our approaches to teaching about human rights and teaching about alternatives to various hegemonic ideologies of patriotism must be well planned and innovative. Public sociology provides a framework for doing so because it does not imply that all sides are equivalent. It allows for debate and discussion and for all sides to be "heard," but by not assuming equivalency it creates a space in which we can teach students about rights: the right of every American to access to education, the right of every American to adequate health care and nutritious food and a safe place to live. Public sociology provides the framework for teaching from scholarly texts such as Marx and Engel's *Communist Manifesto*, but also from "public sociology" texts such as Jonathan Kozol's *Savage Inequalities*. Kozol, for example, does not claim that we need to consider equally the rights of students attending both "overresourced" and underresourced schools, but rather that the purpose of examining "overresourced" schools is to highlight the inequities faced by students in underresourced schools. He argues that the focus should be on becoming aware of the situation of poor students and then moving to action by developing policies that correct this wrong and deliver what is promised in the U.S. Constitution: equal access to equivalent education!

THE LACK OF DIVERSITY

College campuses are anything but diverse in terms of race/ethnicity or social class. In terms of race, campuses vary, but most are either predominantly white or predominantly black (as noted in the terms we use to refer to them: PWI—predominantly white institutions—and HBCU—historically black colleges and universities—respectively). Neither setting provides a context in which to thoroughly discuss issues of human rights as they turn on race, for example, because in either case one side of the discussion is effectively missing or invisible. The same is true of social class. Though institutions vary in their social class diversity (our institution, for example, is skewed toward the more affluent), no campus is truly reflective of the U.S. population in terms of social class. Though student loan, scholarship, and financial aid programs seek to offer the opportunity for a college education to all American students, college campuses remain remarkably middle and upper-middle class. Few college students grew up on welfare (Hong, 2003). Again, it is difficult to have honest discussions of the rights of the poor when more often than not this segment of the population is either absent or rendered invisible. Thus, we sought both in traditional on-campus courses, as well as in our off-campus course, to provide opportunities to have these kinds of conversations. And public sociology offered a mechanism to do just that.

ON-CAMPUS ILLUSTRATIONS

As part of the social stratification course taught by one of the authors (see Hattery, 2003), the attempt is to create an innovative course on-campus that creates a more diverse learning environment. This course uses a variety of strategies, but we highlight two of them here: the social stratification project and the poverty project.

The social stratification project is a semester-long project that is designed around the framework Kozol provides in *Savage Inequalities* to allow students to see the outcomes of the growing income and wealth gap in the United States. Working in teams of six to eight students, each team is assigned a "family." They are given minimal information on each "family," only the members of the family and their social class location. Families have either one or two parents and all families have two children: one who is school aged and one who is preschool aged. Across the semester, each team must find employment (by perusing the want ads and then actually meeting with potential employers), housing (which must include a visit to houses or apartments), childcare (if they choose, and also including a visit), and once they have made a housing choice a visit to the appropriate elementary school in their neighborhood. The project concludes with a trip to the grocery store in which the group is charged with buying enough food for their "family" for one week. We note that the students spend their own money and that the food is then donated to the local homeless shelter. On the final day of the semester, students put on a poster session in which they report on their "families." Most are shocked to see that the typical affluent family spends more on family vacations each year than the typical working poor family earns in a year.

The poverty project requires students to spend the night sleeping outside in a box (replicating a night on the streets for a homeless citizen) or living for two consecutive days on the typical food-stamp allotment, $2.35 per day. These activities are conducted simultaneously (all students participate in their activity on the same days) and follow an experience they have volunteering for a night at the local homeless shelter for men, the Samaritan Inn.

Like the social stratification project, the poverty project provides in an on-campus course the opportunity for students to live a different way and gain insight into the lives of those at the other end of the social class ladder. Students are required to write an essay in which they compare their experiences with their readings from Kozol. Typically they begin to draw connections about the structural causes and consequences of poverty. They note, for example, that it must be hard for poor children to learn if they are malnourished because they realize from their two days living on $2.35 a day that they were unable to stay awake in class, write papers, or study efficiently for exams. Similarly, those who spend a night sleeping in a cardboard box gain insight into the difficulties of holding down a full-time job if you can't get adequate rest, can't stay warm (or cool), and don't have access to a bathroom, shower, and so on. (See Hattery, 2003 for a lengthy description of both the projects and the learning outcomes.)

OFF-CAMPUS STUDY:
POPULAR BUT PROBLEMATIC

On our campus, which seems to be increasingly typical of most in this regard, one of the most popular curriculum crazes is study abroad. From our "unofficial" observation what we see are excursions to other places (Australia, New Zealand, etc.) where students return boasting about how much fun they had and what a great vacation it was.

One author who served on an ad-hoc committee to look at international programs was astonished to hear from one member of the registrar staff that students who go to these overseas programs and fail their courses still get official university credit hours toward graduation per a contract that guarantees students who study abroad the same number of credit hours they would have earned had they remained on campus during that semester. This staff member also noted that in her investigation of study abroad programs, a disturbing percentage had no actual mailing address or physical location.

We also found that the university's own overseas programs are all in Western Europe, and the vast majority of programs that students participate in are in Western Europe, Australia, and New Zealand. Furthermore, when the subject of expanding programs to Latin America, Africa, and Asia comes up, it is quickly dismissed based on the fact that there are too many barriers and not enough "accredited programs" to plug into.

There is a similar trend in the rise of off-campus, international service trips. Annually our campus sends forty to fifty students to the far reaches of the world (India, Vietnam, Honduras, Costa Rica, and now South Africa) to participate in two- to three-week service projects. Though grueling and challenging in many ways, these are not academically based nor do they even incorporate the tenets of service learning. Yet, because of their exotic nature and their "feel-good" quality, they are well subscribed.

It is in this context that we set out on the process of creating a course that was rigorous, was not a vacation, and would uphold all of the academic requirements and standards typical of a traditional on-campus course but with the innovation of being held entirely off-campus, and in a location considered anything but exotic—a point to which we will return. From what we know about the curriculum that goes outside of campus, ours is the only one that offers a rigorous, credit-bearing course that takes students off-campus in a domestic (though certainly exotic) setting.

Taken together, we decided that one possibility that could take students outside the "box" would be to set up a course under the rubric of social stratification, to be held off-campus, in the Deep South.

SOCIAL STRATIFICATION IN THE DEEP SOUTH: WHY THE DEEP SOUTH?

The Deep South, defined by historians, geographers, and sociologists, is frequently understood to be the deepest subsection of the South: encompassed primarily by the states of Georgia, Alabama, and Mississippi, as well as parts of Louisiana and Arkansas. The Deep South is, in many ways, the perfect place in which to examine the issue of social stratification because of the unique history of centuries of slavery followed by a century of "Jim Crow." Second, many of the most heated civil rights battles (note, we in the United States have not fought any battles for "human" rights, so studying civil rights is as close as we get) were waged in the Deep South. Third, the Deep South is one of the most stratified as well as diverse regions of the United States. And, finally, there has been a resurgence of activity in several key civil rights murders of the 1960s. In 2005, a week after we were in Philadelphia, Mississippi, eighty-year-old Edgar Ray Killen went on trial for the 1964 murders of Michael Schwerner, Andrew Goodman, and James Chaney.

Overview

This course is designed to use sociology, as a method of inquiry and a theoretical framework, to examine contemporary issues of social stratification and civil rights in the Deep South. As a result, we required some basic readings in theories of social stratification to orient students. We also trained them in some basic uses of census data so that they could complete assignments that required them to investigate a variety of empirical data—such as racial distribution, median earnings, and educational attainment—on the states and counties we studied. Finally, we made central the expertise of community collaborators who met with our students, took us on guided tours, and invited us into their offices, churches, and homes in order to learn more from the people who live what we were merely studying (for a list of readings and census assignments, please contact the authors).

Practically Speaking

There were several important steps in putting together a course such as this. First, just as with any new course, we produced a proposal that ran through the official college curriculum committee. This ensured that our course met the rigorous standards of the college. Before we were able to propose the actual course, we had to design it. We spent a great deal of time gathering information about the areas, refamiliarizing ourselves with key civil rights events, looking at courses that had done something similar, and talking to colleagues. But, in the end, perhaps the most important aspect of designing this type of course involves getting in the car and exploring the Deep South. This turned out to be the most important step as it allowed us to see for ourselves what fit and what worked. It also allowed us to begin to "map" the course, literally fixing in our own minds how to move between point A and point B, and putting together for ourselves an estimate on how long it would take to travel. Finally, we needed to recruit the students. This was important for a variety of reasons. First and foremost we wanted to be sure that they were committed to this kind of a course, that they were adaptable (as this type of course is actually very physically rigorous), and that they had a clean record (we did not want to bother ourselves with students who would cause trouble). This part of the process is very similar to the process of selecting students for study abroad programs. Second, unlike the situation associated with study abroad programs, we needed to sell the Deep South. During the summers we have taught the course in the Deep South, there were many other off-campus programs of study: tours of Europe, study in West Africa, Cuba, and Mexico. Thus we needed to convince a group of students that they would find the Deep South not only as exotic, but more challenging than these competing experiences. Finally, because we would be examining issues of social stratification focused on issues of civil rights, it was of utmost importance that we assemble as diverse a class as possible. Though admittedly we had some trouble achieving a gender balance, each time we have taught the course it has been racially diverse, with half of the class identifying as white and the other half identifying as African American. In addition, our classes have included a good mix of students from the South and from the North; from different religious traditions; and finally, for a college course, from as many social classes as possible.

Social Class Diversity

It is important to specify the mechanisms we used to achieve this last form of diversity. We opened this chapter by noting that the greatest form of homogeneity on college campuses is social class. (We note here that though it is the most common form, it is perhaps the least often discussed.) We employed key strategies for assuring that our course would be class-diverse. First, we wrote grant applications and frankly pleaded and begged in order to raise money that would pay two key expenses: the travel expenses for the instructors and the cost of transportation. The cost of a bus to travel for fourteen days, across three thousand miles, runs more than $10,000. By raising the money to pay this expense, we are able to put together a course that costs no more "off-campus" than it does on-campus. The only expenses students pay are as follows: tuition; housing (they pay for their own hotel rooms, which run $15–$20 per night or $250 for the whole course, half of what campus housing costs); and food (which runs $15–$20 per day or $225, much less than the on-campus dining fee). How do we keep the housing and food costs so low? We keep the housing costs low by staying in reasonably priced, though clean and safe, accommodations such as Hampton Inns, Holiday Inn Express, and so on and by requiring students to sleep four to a room (we choose the roommates in order to create diverse living and learning environments). We keep the food costs low by staying in hotels that offer free breakfast and by stopping regularly at grocery stores and Wal-Mart so that they can buy snacks, drinks, and items like fruit and yogurt at a much cheaper price. Finally, we recruit heavily among students who receive scholarships that support summer school. During our last course (summer 2005) we included six student athletes whose athletic scholarships provided for summer school tuition. We have also included students in the course whose academic scholarships will pay tuition and on occasion a stipend for living expenses (this was also the case with the student athletes). This work to create an affordable course and recruit a class that is diverse in terms of social class has paid big dividends. These strategies have resulted in us teaching a class that includes students from very affluent backgrounds to those raised on welfare in inner-city housing projects. The outcomes for student learning were astounding! In addition, we felt personally pleased to be able to offer low-income students a chance to study off-campus.

Designing the Stops

Putting together a course off-campus requires a great deal of attention to detail to sort out which sites to include, what activities to do at each site, and how to travel from one site to another. The only way to do this effectively is to travel to the sites, visit, talk to local residents, and determine which sites are important and which can be left out.

When we began preparing for our first "scouting trip," we began by looking at the sites that other similar courses had included. Next we considered the sites of important civil rights events that had not been included in other courses. We began with sites that are very familiar and then considered sites that may not be, despite the fact that the event itself is well known. In the end, primarily by developing relationships with local residents (which can only be established by spending time in the areas), we created unique experiences even in familiar places. We will illustrate this point with two examples: Birmingham, Alabama, and Money, Mississippi.

Birmingham, Alabama, is one of the major southern cities associated with the civil rights movement for equality. Many key events happened in Birmingham, adding spark to the movement. For example, the 1963 jailing of Martin Luther King, Jr. resulted in his writing "A Letter from Birmingham Jail"; the Children's March took place here in spring 1963; and finally in September 1963 the Sixteenth Street Baptist Church was bombed, killing four young African American girls. No visit to Birmingham is complete without being inside the Sixteenth Street Baptist Church or touring the National Civil Rights Museum and Kelly Ingram Park. Certainly we included all of these on our itinerary. Yet, what made our time in Birmingham unique is the time we spent with local residents who shared with us their memories of marching in the Children's March, of growing up on Dynamite Hill, and of being active not only during the civil rights movement itself but even today, trying to make Birmingham a better place for all of her citizens.

Money, Mississippi, is a typical rural Mississippi whistle-stop. At its peak, there were four or five stores on the one main road in Money. Most of the "residents" of Money actually live on plantations that are nearer to Money than to any other "town." Today all that remains is the shell of Bryant's store and a post office (which is in a trailer). Money is famous for the 1955 lynching and murder of fourteen-year-old Emmett Till. During one of our trips to the Mississippi Delta we established a relationship with a professor at Delta State University. He collaborated with us by climbing on our bus and taking us on a guided tour to the key spots in the Emmett Till murder case. Naturally we stopped at Bryant's store in Money, but we also visited the courthouse in Sumner, Mississippi (Tallahatchie County), were Jim Bryant and J. W. Milam were tried and acquitted. We drove past the spot where Moses Wright (Emmett Till's great-uncle) lived and where Emmett Till was staying the night he was abducted as well as the site where locals believe he was actually murdered. Finally, our colleague arranged for a meeting with a Mississippi state senator who attended the Emmett Till trial. The impact on our students of seeing these important sites and meeting with local residents was immeasurable.

Another key to our design is that we choose places that are of continued importance. So, for example, one of the bombers, Bobby Cherry, in the Six-teenth Street Baptist Church bombing was convicted in 2003, just a year before our class arrived. This forced us to make sure that we revisited the Sixteenth Street Church to bring the class up to date on what was happening in the trial.

And, while we were in Money, Mississippi, in 2005, Emmett Till's body was exhumed as part of the reopening of the murder case that "celebrates" its fiftieth anniversary this year. To provide a close-up look at the Emmett Till case and engage the students in this upcoming event we contracted for a workshop at Delta State University in Cleveland, Mississippi, for a tour of the old Bryant store where it is alleged that Till "wolf whistled" at Bryant's wife and was murdered for this act. Our students were able to stand in front of the store (in one-hundred-degree heat) listening to the updates of the fifty-year-old case and learn that a new highway was being named for Emmett Till. What a lesson in civic justice to be gleaned in the middle of the street in front of the Bryant store.

COMMUNITY PARTNERS AS COLLABORATORS

One of the key elements to teaching from within a public sociology frame-work is seeing community partners as true collaborators in the education (and, for that matter, research) process. Recognizing the expertise of commu-nity residents who may or may not have official credentials is important for several reasons.

First, local community residents have access to information about events and processes that are often otherwise unable to be tapped. Like informants in a research project, local residents are sources of data that can help both instructors and students to unlock the "truth" about both historical and con-temporary events.

Second, treating local residents as collaborators teaches students that offi-cial credentials are only one form of expertise. In most social movements for civil and human rights, those who are actively working for liberation, those who have something to lose, and those who are engaged in the process are our best sources of information. Thus, relying on these experts is a way of modeling for students the role of local residents in research and teaching part-nerships.

In the Classroom: Mr. Darryl Hunt

In 1983 a young African American man named Darryl Hunt was tried and convicted for the rape and murder of a young white woman, Deborah Sykes, in Winston-Salem, North Carolina. After spending nearly twenty years in prison and enduring a second trial, DNA evidence finally excluded Mr. Hunt as the perpetrator in the case. In December 2003 he was released from prison, and in February 2004 he was officially exonerated by the state of North Carolina.

In the summer of 2004, just months after his exoneration, the authors were teaching different courses (one on deviance and one on social stratification) and we contacted Mr. Darryl Hunt and his attorney, Mr. Mark Rabil, and asked them to come and speak to a joint meeting of our classes. They were both eager and willing to comply. Over eighteen months Mr. Hunt and Mr. Rabil visited with our classes on several occasions. Furthermore, we designed a service learning opportunity whereby our students in a first-year seminar ran the day-to-day activities of Mr. Hunt's Project for Freedom and Justice. (Our students handled the communication and paperwork between Mr. Hunt and North Carolina inmates who are seeking exoneration.)

The impact of learning about citizens who are wrongly convicted is upsetting to students at best. Meeting a man who has been convicted, sentenced, and served nearly twenty years in prison and was finally exonerated is difficult to describe. No matter how long either of us studies inequalities in the criminal justice system, no one is more "expert" than the inmate himself.

Teaching from the public sociology perspective means that the authors are open to recognizing expertise in local residents, gaining access to otherwise inaccessible information. (Mr. Hunt was very open and discussed with the students his experiences in prison, including his observations of prison gang rape.) Finally, partnering with Mr. Hunt produced the opportunity to collaborate in social change, for us and for Mr. Hunt, as well as for our students. Finally, it means being able to let go of the need to present both sides of the issue—for example some whites in Winston-Salem believe that prison must have been good for Mr. Hunt, despite his innocence—focusing instead on this horrible miscarriage of justice.

In the Deep South: Mrs. Steele

One of the most important events in the American civil rights movement is the 1964 murder of three young civil rights workers: Michael Schwerner, Andrew Goodman, and James Chaney. The three young men were murdered after they had made a show of support at the Mount Zion Methodist Church in Philadelphia, Mississippi. In June 1964 members of the Ku Klux Klan firebombed the church to send a message that the organizing and voter registration that these young men were running out of the church had to stop. After the bombing, these three young men visited the church. As they were driving home, they were pulled over by the Neshoba County sheriff and were locked up in the county jail. Four or five hours after they were locked up the three young men were released, and on their drive home to Meridian they were pulled over by three cars of Klansmen. They were murdered execution style, their car was burned, and both the car and the bodies were dumped in different swamps in Neshoba County.

Because of the importance of this case, we immediately knew that we wanted to include Philadelphia in our course. The first summer (2002) we took a "scouting trip" we arrived in Philadelphia expecting to find signs denoting Mount Zion Methodist Church and the swamps. Unlike cities such as Birmingham and Atlanta where there is signage denoting the sites of civil rights events, such is *not* the case in Philadelphia. Despite asking many local residents for directions, we were unable to find anyone who could provide accurate ones—reflective of the desire of this town and her citizens to forget this horrible tragedy. Despite hours of driving around, that first summer, we never found the church.

The following summer, when we returned with our first group of students, we asked them to "MapQuest" the church. Despite producing directions, "MapQuest" essentially quits in rural Mississippi and did not produce viable directions. Again, we sought local residents and finally we got directions that were close enough that we found the church.

In repeated visits (scouting trips) to Philadelphia, we established a relationship with an older African American woman named Mrs. Steele who has been a lifelong member of Mount Zion Methodist Church. When we arrived back at the church with our class, Mrs. Steele met us and shared for more than an hour about her experiences at the time of the bombing and the murders. The impact for us (and the students) of listening to a local resident give the history of this community was again immeasurable. In addition, Mrs. Steele climbed on our bus and gave us a driving tour of Neshoba County. We saw the houses where local residents who were injured the night of the bombing had lived, we met their children, and we drove through the swamp where the burned car had been buried. Learning history from the people who lived it has a far greater impact than any assigned reading, classroom lecture, or DVD documentary.

Finally, we note the contemporary connection of our course. Just a week after we left Philadelphia, Edgar Ray Killen was tried and convicted for his role in the murders of these three young men. With the impending trial around the corner, we encouraged our students to talk with local residents they met to learn what they could. Two of our students spent an hour talking with a woman who was selling "rims" out of her car in the parking lot at

Wal-Mart. They learned from her the ins and outs of the case, which took a month or more to appear in media reports (for example the relationship between the judge in the case and the defendant).

We note, again, the power of working with local residents as collaborators, and also as experts. These experts not only provide access to information and data that is otherwise inaccessible, but our collaboration with them is a way of modeling this form of public sociology such that our students were empowered to engage in these discussions on their own.

CONCLUSION

Teaching from a public sociology framework has allowed us to teach in a more honest, more inclusive, more in-depth manner than teaching from other pedagogies. This strategy, as outlined in other parts of this volume, allows us to move beyond the positivist notions of objectivity and to focus on the struggle for human rights and understanding. For example, there really is no other side to the murder of Emmett Till (or the three students in Philadelphia or the four young girls in Birmingham). Being relieved of the oppression of positivism allowed us to explore fully the tragedies that permeated the struggle for civil rights. Second, recognizing the power of local residents as experts and collaborators allowed us access to otherwise inaccessible information, to see that credentials are not all that certifies an expert, and teaches us and our students about the everyday people and events that shaped the struggle for civil rights. Finally, getting students out into the community, be it in an on-campus or an off-campus course, exposes them to the realities that sociologists study and teach about and offers them opportunities to engage local residents as experts.

Without a doubt, we believe in the power of teaching from a public sociology framework. It makes the issues that sociologists study and research come alive for our students and allows them to achieve a greater insight and understanding into issues that are otherwise presented only in text and/or film. We certainly do acknowledge the power of texts, of empirical data, and of films. It is the coupling of, for example, census data that describes poverty with visiting an impoverished family in the Mississippi Delta that results in the most effective learning for students.

Public sociology in the classroom should be—and is for us—about introducing students to relevant issues, however unpopular. We strive in our classes and in particular the one described above to do just that. When there is still school segregation in the "Deep South" and when there is still no justice for all the families of lynching victims and murders unsolved we feel it is important that we bring these subjects to life by having students read about them, write about them, and reflect upon them on a regular basis—not just on some one particular day such as Martin Luther King Day.

ACKNOWLEDGMENTS

For all that we accomplish in this course none of these successes would be possible without the cooperation of groups, individuals, and an array of supporters that makes the course happen. With Cicero we agree that "there is no duty more indispensable than that of returning a kindness," so in this regard we would like to say *thank you* to all of them.

REFERENCES

Anderson, Elijah. 1981. *A Place on the Corner*. Chicago: University of Chicago Press.
Burawoy, Michael. 2005. "The Return of the Repressed: Recovering the Public Face of U.S. Sociology, One Hundred Years On." *The Annals of the American Academy of Political and Social Science* 600: 1–8.
Erikson, Kai T. 1966. *Wayward Puritans: A Study in the Sociology of Deviance*. New York: Macmillan.
Gelles, R. J. 1997. *Intimate Violence in Families*. 3rd ed. Thousand Oaks, Calif.: Sage.
Gouldner, Alvin. 1980. *The Coming Crisis of Western Sociology*. New York: Basic.
Hattery, Angela J. 2003. "Sleeping in the Box, Thinking Outside the Box." *Teaching Sociology* 31: 412–27.
Hong, Peter. 2003. "Study Links UC Entry, Social Class: High Schools That Send Many Graduates to UC Are in Affluent Areas; Low-Income Schools Send Fewer Students, Researchers Find." Equal Justice Society. November 19: www.equaljusticesociety.org/press_latimes_2003_11_19.html.
Kozol, Jonathan. 1991. *Savage Inequalities*. New York: Crown.
Luker, Kristin. 1985. *Abortion and the Politics of Motherhood*. Berkeley: University of California Press.
Pfohl, Stephen. 2004. "Blessings and Curses in the Sociology Classroom." *Social Problems* 51: 113–15.

16

Feminist Strategies for Public Sociology

Barbara J. Risman

Feminist scholarship has much to offer public sociology despite distinctly different historical trajectories. While public sociology has been, in myriad guises, around as long as sociology itself, feminist sociology was born in the second half of the twentieth century, long after suffragettes fought for the right to vote. Feminist sociologists have always been public sociologists whether they knew the term or not (Stacey, 2003) if by "public sociology" we mean sociology engaged with an audience outside the academy, with an intent to create and to use knowledge for the public good. Feminist scholarship has always included both professional scientific research published in traditional academic venues and bringing knowledge back to the community. We do feminist scholarship because we have the desire, if not always success, to improve the quality of women's lives. Feminist scholarship, after all, is a product of the protest movements for equal rights during the twentieth century and is defined by the framing of research in the interest of women and gender equality.

When women active in the civil rights, student, and antiwar movements during the 1960s noticed that they spent more time making coffee than the revolution, they conceived the second wave of the American women's movement. Young women, mostly students, joined this second wave of feminism. They quickly noticed that sexism permeated academe as fully as other sectors of society. Few women made it into history books. Psychology studies used men to represent all human beings. Sociologists studied society but only where men spent their time. Women as subjects were relegated to research on families, if they were studied at all.

Women's and gender studies was an antidote to sexism in intellectual and scientific endeavors. The goal of feminist scholarship was "both/and" (e.g., Collins, 1990) from the very beginning: to both create a new interdisciplinary intellectual activity and to transform traditional disciplines themselves. This goal, from the start, was activist. We needed to study and understand the world in order to change it. What explains the scarcity of women at the top of professional elites? Does gender socialization lead girls to opt out of that game? Do women hit glass ceilings because of overt discrimination? Or is discrimination more subtle, such as the structuring of elite jobs so that human beings with moral and pragmatic responsibility for other people cannot succeed? Only good research can understand the complexity of how privilege and disadvantage work. And without understanding the relative power of each social process, we cannot intervene successfully. The very definition of feminist scholarship is knowledge in the service of social change in the academe and society.

Public sociology has been fighting for acceptance as legitimate scholarship, with varying success, since American sociology was born a century ago. Early sociologists in the United States were women and men concerned with alleviating the social problems of the day. But some of the women, like Jane Addams, split off and founded the field of social work as (mostly male) sociologists continued to develop the theoretical and research practices of a social science. Eventually World War II brought social science to the national defense, and after the war, the federal government became more willing to invest in quantitative sociology. By this time, the "pure" science notion of sociology had so come to dominate the American Sociological Association that those with more activist bents broke off to start their own association, the Society for the Study of Social Problems (see Calhoun and Duster, 2005 for more sociological history). Soon thereafter, though, leaders in that society were being elected to prominence in the ASA, and by the beginning of the twenty-first century, the best-attended ASA meeting ever had "public sociology" as its theme. And yet, public sociology still appears quite controversial (Nielsen, 2004; Tittle, 2004). In the past, we have seen the pendulum swing to and fro concerning the legitimacy of a sociology for the people. Feminist sociology is both too young and too defined by its political commitments to face the same radical shifts in academic legitimation.

At this moment in history, as public sociology once again vies for academic legitimacy, the success of feminist scholars as activists both inside and outside the academy provides hints for doing and legitimating public sociology. In this short chapter, some strategies for success based on feminist experiences are worth considering. Perhaps most important for scholarly acceptance, public sociology must, like feminist sociology, be conceptualized as one possible way to do sociology, and not claim to be the whole. I identify four specific lessons from feminist scholarship that may apply to doing public sociology more generally. First, feminists always frame academic scholarship around a mission of social justice. We have always proclaimed our belief in the equality of the sexes unashamedly. We use our commitment to equality to shape our research questions and epistemology, and openly integrate ethical goals into our research. Second, women's and gender studies programs integrate humanities and scientific faculty around substantive questions and toward a shared goal of social change. We have not wasted energy in disruptive intellectual turf battles. Third, feminists have always taken teaching seriously as a strategy to make social change. And finally, feminists have carved out careers as activist-scholars. Each of these aspects of feminist scholarship might provide strategies for how to construct a public sociology for the public good.

SCHOLARSHIP WITH A SOCIAL JUSTICE MISSION

There has been perennial debate inside the discipline of sociology as to "whose side are we on" (Becker, 1967; Gouldner, 1970), or indeed, whether we should have a side at all (Nielson, 2004). Some argue (e.g., Tittle, 2004) that we should be a value-neutral science whose goal is simply to test hypotheses and construct theory, with little attention to and no ethical responsibility for making any contribution to society at all. No time is spent on such debate among feminists because our work is by definition about providing the intellectual scaffolding for social change. If one believes that ideas matter, feminist scholarship itself is activism. Public sociology should be more like feminist scholarship than mainstream professional sociology in this regard. Public sociology is only worth doing if it is done from a value-driven standpoint. Why bother bringing sociology beyond the academy if it is only a tool, to be offered equally to paying clients hoping to control the masses, or to politicians hoping to win elections? Public sociology is worth doing if it, like feminist scholarship, is framed by the mission to use a sociological imagination, research, and analysis to help create a more just society. Public sociology does not deserve the name if it is not in the public interest.

There is often concern, among those who believe that science must be value-free, that researchers with an openly value-driven mission will somehow bias our design, process, analysis, evidence, interpretations, or conclusions or do something to cram data into a preconceived ideological framework. They fear that people with strong ideological commitments might see what they want in data. Of course, such a fear is equally valid applied to scientists who work within a theoretical tradition to which they are quite committed, and upon which they base their hypotheses. They too have good reason to see what they want in their data, to support their hypotheses. Why anyone would presume that scientists with strong moral commitments to social justice would be less ethical than "pure" scientists has always eluded me. In either case, concern about bias comes down, at the end, to trust in the ethics of each researcher.

Indeed, I would suggest that feminists' attention to power has led to reflexive concern with ethical issues of hierarchical relationships within research teams and in our classrooms. While feminist scholars have hardly jettisoned the privileges of academic rank, there is quite serious thought and attention paid to the implications of a social justice perspective toward students, and to those we study (see especially Sprague, 2005). Collins (1998) argues that we must test our theories in dialogue with our publics. The doing of feminist sociology itself, the process of teaching and research, benefits from a social justice framework.

Feminist sociology also provides quite convincing evidence that value-based research can both reject strong hypotheses and build cumulative bodies of knowledge. When feminist sociology was young, many of us were very committed to primarily structuralist explanations for gender. Feminist sociologists often argued that to focus on how gender became internalized into personality traits, and thus, why women chose roles that were subordinate, was to blame the victim (Chavetz, Farkas, and Risman, 1989). In her classic work *Men and Women of the Corporation*, Kanter (1977) suggested that few generic sex differences actually existed, at least at work, because women and men were in different kinds of jobs, and acted accordingly. The structure created the apparent sex differences. When highly educated women entered male management positions, with the same structural conditions of work, they behaved like men. Similarly, when male supervisors were in the same dead-end kinds of positions that faced most women managers, they acted in ways that had been stereotypically considered feminine. Gerson (1985) applied the same argument to families and found that women's decisions about balancing work and caretaking responsibilities were better predicted by the immediate conditions of their adult lives (work and family structures) than the gender socialization usually turned to for explanations of women's choices. Following this argument, I proposed that men could mother, but that the parenting roles we assigned to women and men kept them from doing so (1987). Indeed, I found that men could mother, but only if they faced the dramatic and traumatic consequence of the loss of a wife, through death or desertion.

As much other data have shown since then, married men might do much more childrearing than their fathers did, but still quite a lot less than their wives.

Epstein's (1988) meta-analysis of this research suggested that most sex differences found are "Deceptive Distinctions." For feminist scholars this was very good news. Changing social structural organization takes considerably less time than it would take to raise a whole generation of children without sex-stereotyped socialization. Indeed, as social activists we are likely to be more successful arguing for changes in the social structure then we are to be effective at convincing parents, en masse, to de-gender their childrearing techniques. In fact, we have not successfully changed childrearing techniques much at all, at least for boys (Martin, 2005). A purely structuralist explanation for gender inequality is an empowering theory for an activist.

And yet, the research went on. While many gender differences surely are deceptive distinctions, more recent research complicates the picture. Indeed, much of the research following Kanter (e.g., Williams, 1992; Zimmer, 1988), and my own later research on families (1998) finds that simply putting women into men's slots, and men into women's slots does not, by itself, decrease gendered behavior or stratification. Browne and England (1997) made a convincing argument that explaining some of women's disadvantage by their own internalized oppression does not "blame the victim" but rather traces causality further back temporally. Even in organizations, simply bringing women in doesn't necessarily reduce sexism. Tokenism works differently if women are the tokens, as in upper management, or men are the tokens, as in nursing. Women hit glass ceilings, and men ride glass elevators (Williams, 1992). Children raised in families totally committed to gender equality buy into the ideology but learn from their peers that girls are nice and warm and boys are mean and competitive, even if they realize this doesn't describe themselves (Risman, 1998). Gender itself structures the social expectations (Risman, 1998, 2004). Ridgeway and her colleagues (Ridgeway, 1991, 1997; Ridgeway et al., 1998; Ridgeway and Correll, 2004) show clearly that the expectations we hold are not only attached to social positions but to gender itself. My most recent research (Risman, Davis, and Zimmer, 2005) suggests, despite my social constructionist hypotheses, parental gender socialization may be quite sticky, even thirty years later.

We have found, over time, that purely structuralist explanations for gender are not, by themselves, sufficient. Structure does not trump gender. Rather, gender is an institution (Lorber, 1994) or a structure (Risman, 1998, 2004) itself and has real implications for identity and personality. Gender structure shapes interactional expectations and the organization of rights and distributions of responsibilities and privileges. Any feminist social change strategy has to be complicated, multifaceted, with attention to selves, relationships, and organizations (Lorber, 2005; Risman, 2004). The moral here is that feminist sociologists' ethical commitment to gender equality, and even perhaps a preference for findings that lead to effective, quick strategies for social change, have not driven the empirical findings or theoretical conclusions.

Another example of evidence changing both interpretations of reality and feminist scholarship is the widespread acceptance of intersectionality theory by feminist scholars. As women of color moved at least partly from margin (e.g., hooks, 2000) to center, white feminists came to realize that their generic woman was white and middle class by presumption, if not overtly. Just as feminism has rejected the generic "man" to refer to people, so has multicultural feminism rejected the existence of "woman" without attention to intersecting categories of inequality such as her race, sexuality, and social class.

No one benefits by holding on to doctrinaire ideologies when evidence points elsewhere. The lesson here, from feminist sociology, is that good research is necessary to identify just how inequality is constructed. We must understand how gender inequality is produced in order to reduce or eliminate it. So, too, for a public sociology committed to social justice; research of all stripes into how inequality is produced is vital. A commitment to social justice in no way provides us a theoretical or empirical road map to good strategy. Effective public sociology depends upon good science (Burawoy, 2005).

INTERDISCIPLINARY CRITICAL ANALYSIS

Public sociology can also learn about the effective integration of different kinds of scholarship from feminists. Within the discipline of sociology, there are often debates between those who believe their work to be social science and those who believe sociology is more humanistic. Similar debates rage between qualitative methodologists and quantitative analysts (Sprague, 2005). Each hopes to gain the upper hand as the legitimate gatekeeper that defines the center and the margins of the field.

In women's and gender studies, this kind of debate is neither usual nor necessary. Feminist scholarship draws on interdisciplinary expertise. The more tools we bring to the table, the more we have to offer. Feminist scholarship is a shining example of how humanities scholars, social scientists, and physical scientists can work together. For example, when feminists approach the social problem of the underrepresentation of women in math and science, we bring differing knowledges together to create integrated curricular, organizational, and pedagogical efforts. The National Science Foundation awards ADVANCE grants to interdisciplinary teams of scholars (www.nsf.gov/pubs/2005/nsf05584/nsf05584htm) to transform universities—a mammoth job.

Creating universities where gender equity is the norm requires radical transformation of the academy, and must involve many perspectives. Debates as to
the "best" disciplinary perspective to advance women's statuses are simply
irrelevant because feminists from different disciplines share a commitment
to equality. So, too, public sociology should be integrative, bringing critical
theoretical analyses, quantitative skills, and qualitative nuance to public conversation. Perhaps public sociology can transcend the tendency toward competition with other sociologies by remaining mindful that each type of
sociology depends upon the other. There is no public sociology without professional sociology, and we would have little disciplinary self-examination
without critical sociology (Burawoy, 2004).

TEACHING AS ACTIVISM

Feminist scholars have spent much time and thought developing a pedagogy
that actively challenges students to use personal experience for insights, to
think critically, and to engage the world around them (Naples and Bojar,
2002). Women's and gender studies courses are usually electives, many more
"programs" exist than departments, and few programs award degrees. Even
though most students take classes as electives, the courses are popular, and
they keep multiplying. While women's movement activism may be nascent
outside the academy, feminist scholarship institutionalized inside universities
has kept the women's movement alive and lively. Research now suggests
(Schnittker, Freese, and Powell, 2003; Harnois, 2005) that the most common
route to adopt feminism as an identity, at least for a white woman, is by taking a women's studies class in college. These might be classes either in a
women's studies department or classes taught by feminist scholars inside disciplinary boundaries.

This is a lesson from feminism that public sociology should heed. Education is a powerful tool for social change, especially for sharing the ideas and
analyses that a new generation may adapt and use in their own way. Feminists
do not persuade students to adopt an ideology; we educate them about
inequality and provide evidence of ongoing sexism in institutions as varied
as religion, families, and the economy. Empirical evidence used by those
with critical thinking skills is dangerous to those who try to protect the status
quo, whether that be patriarchal families or racist organizations. I see the goal
for teaching public sociology as the same, to produce critical thinkers who
understand both the structural bases of inequality, but also understand the
social construction of reality, and the role of human agency in social change.
We cannot teach our students to adopt a social justice value system, but we

can introduce them to data that indicates social inequality, and the idea that such inequality is historically contextual and socially produced.

CAREERS AS SCHOLAR-ACTIVISTS

Who does public sociology? Is this, or should it be, a career decision, an identity, as in "I am a public sociologist"? Or is it a verb, I "do" public sociology? Or both? Or neither? Such questions are addressed throughout this volume. One last lesson from feminist scholarship is a possible answer to these questions. Women's liberation birthed feminist scholarship; it has always been an arm of a social movement. By definition, the first feminist scholars were activists. They had to be. You had to actively fight for the right to study women or gender. As an undergraduate in 1972, I was told I couldn't write a literature review paper on rape for a sociology of deviance course because no literature existed to review. When I was hired for my first position in 1983, I was hired to teach "family," not gender. No one taught gender back then. To justify the first graduate seminar I ever taught on gender I had to nest it inside the study of families, "Gender in Familial Relationships." When feminist scholarship was new, simply doing it was a form of academic activism. I would hypothesize that most of the first generation of feminist scholars were activists outside the academy as well and often used their scholarship in the service of social change. That infamous feminist "clique" was hard to segment into one aspect of life. Indeed, one of the most prestigious awards given by the national feminist organization Sociologists for Women in Society is for feminist activism. This award is given each year to a scholar who has made a significant impact outside the academy to improving the status of women's lives. Winners of this award are by definition public sociologists, who teach in prisons, bring their research on rape crises back to community organizations, and work with social movement organizations.

This melding of scholarship and activism is not simply an American phenomenon. In the mid-1990s, the first Moscow Center for Gender Studies was born, housed within the Russian Academy of Sciences in Moscow. These Russian scholars, only recently free to follow their own intellectual pursuits, were not only writing important academic papers but also spearheading the women's movement in post-Soviet Russia. They were producing first-rate research, but also drafting gender-neutral language for the new laws being written, and running a domestic violence hotline out of their office (Ferree, Sperling, and Risman, 2005). This is what an American university women's studies program looked like thirty years ago. In the early moment of any women's movement, a feminist scholar is an activist by definition, both inside and outside the academy.

But movements come of age. As feminist scholarship develops, it becomes institutionalized both in academic departments and research centers, and inside home disciplines. Women's centers become the home for direct social activism on campus. It is now quite possible to study women and/or gender with no feminist mission at all, as reading most biosociology and other journal articles with "gender" in the title quickly shows. It is even possible to find arcane gender scholarship, with little obvious connection to a feminist mission, housed in women's and gender studies programs (Risman, 2004). Does this mean that feminist scholarship has failed as activism? Surely some has. But then, the very legitimacy of research on gender relations and women is evidence of the success of feminist activism. Even the cultural legitimacy and presence of such research challenges patriarchy, as it establishes the study of gender as normative, and not only for feminists.

Most feminist scholars care deeply about reducing inequality. Many feminist scholars live a both/and academic life, by teaching, writing, and also engaging with the world outside academe. How individual scholars balance such work depends on their institutional setting and their life stage. My own experience was to focus mostly on teaching, research, and feminist activism within my own institution before tenure, such as committee work that involved helping to start a women's center and a women's studies program, and to write a parental leave policy. After tenure, my graduate students encouraged me to walk the activist walk, as well as talk the talk. I started thinking about doing more public sociology without knowing it, by writing opinion pieces for newspapers and testifying at local school board hearings on the effectiveness of sex education. After promotion to the position of full professor, I became co-chair of a national organization, the Council on Contemporary Families, dedicated to bringing research and clinical expertise about families to public conversation. And now, as an administrator, I intend to find ways to legitimate and reward public sociology as one more realm of legitimate academic work. Feminist scholars often provide good models for how to bridge intellectual pursuits, teaching, and activism in the every day, and still have time to sleep.

Public sociologists might use the strategies feminists have forged by realizing that "public sociology" is better used as an adverb then as a noun. Each of us may do public sociology one part of each week, or year, or during one stage of a long career. The benefits of integrating public sociology with other kinds of sociology are the intellectual dynamism of crossing boundaries, of both learning and teaching, inside and outside of academe. If public sociology is what many of us do, some of the time, we are not likely to marginalize it or devalue it as a subspecialty for the less elite.

CONCLUSION

Feminist scholarship provides a wealth of lessons for public sociology. Perhaps they all come down to this moral: research with an ethical commitment to social justice needs doing, and then what we learn needs to be in conversation with the public, and used for the public good. We feminist sociologists are already public sociologists and can provide good role models for the rest of you.

A question for which I have no answer is whether public sociology must have a central shared ideological mission, as does feminist scholarship. Feminists are committed to knowledge production and distribution in the interest of social justice and gender equality. Scholars who do not care about gender justice are not feminists; must a sociologist care about social justice to be considered a public sociologist or does any attempt to teach a sociological imagination to students beyond one's classroom count as public sociology? Is using network analysis to help capture Saddam Hussein public sociology (Hougham, 2005)? I do not know, but it is a question well worth asking. Do public sociologists, by definition, care about social justice, or does merely talking to an audience beyond the academy define public sociology? I vote for a definition of public sociology that includes a commitment to social justice on political and practical grounds. My experience has been that integrating one's moral beliefs with one's professional work keeps both alive and lively.

REFERENCES

Becker, H. 1967. "Whose Side Are We On?" *Social Problems* 14: 239–48.

Browne, Irene, and Paula England. 1997. "Oppression from Within and Without in Sociological Theories: An Application to Gender." *Current Perspectives in Social Theory* 17: 77–104.

Burawoy, Michael. 2005. "2004 Presidential Address: For Public Sociology." *American Sociological Review* 70: 4–28.

———. 2004. "Public Sociologies: Contradictions, Dilemmas, and Possibilities." *Social Forces* 82: 1603–18.

Calhoun, Craig, and Troy Duster. 2005. "The Visions and Divisions of Sociology." *The Chronicle of Higher Education* 51(49).

Chavetz, Janet, Georgoe Farkas, and Barbara J. Risman. 1989. "Debate: Using Other Disciplines." *American Sociologist* 20: 2.

Collins, Patricia Hill. 1998. *Fighting Words: Black Women and the Search for Justice.* Minneapolis: University of Minnesota Press.

———. 1990. *Black Feminist Thought: Knowledge, Consciousness, and the Politics of Empowerment.* Cambridge, Mass.: Unwin Hyman, Inc.

Epstein, Cynthia Fuchs. 1988. *Deceptive Distinctions: Sex, Gender, and the Social Order.* New Haven, Conn.: Yale University Press.

Ferree, Myra Marx, Valerie Sperling, and Barbara Risman. 2005. "Feminist Research and Activism: Challenges of Hierarchy in a Cross-National Context." In *Rhyming Hope and History: Activists, Academics, and Social Movements Scholarship*, ed. D. Croteau, W. Hoynes, and C. Ryan. Minneapolis: University of Minnesota Press.

Gerson, Kathleen. 1985. *Hard Choices*. Berkeley: University of California Press.

Gouldner, Alvin. 1970. *The Coming Crisis of Western Sociology*. New York: Basic.

Harnois, Catherine. 2005. "Different Paths to Different Feminisms: Bridging Multiracial Feminist Theory and Quantitative Sociological Gender Research." *Gender & Society* 19(6): 809–28.

hooks, bell. 2000. *Feminist Theory: From Margin to Center*. Cambridge, Mass.: Southend Press.

Hougham, Virginia. 2005. "Sociological Skills Used in the Capture of Saddam Hussein." *Footnotes* 33(July/August): 6.

Kanter, Rosabeth. 1977. *Men and Women of the Corporation*. New York: Harper & Row.

Lorber, Judith. 2005. *Breaking the Bowls: Degendering and Feminist Change*. New York: Norton.

———. 1994. *Paradoxes of Gender*. New Haven, Conn.: Yale University Press.

Martin, Karin A. 2005. "William Wants a Doll. Can He Have One?" *Gender & Society* 19(4): 456–79.

Naples, Nancy A., and Karen Bojar (eds.). 2002. *Teaching Feminist Activism: Strategies from the Field*. New York: Routledge.

Nielsen, Francois. 2004. "The Vacant 'We': Remarks on Public Sociology." *Social Forces* 82: 1619–28.

Ridgeway, Cecilia. 1997. "Interaction and the Conservation of Gender Inequality: Considering Employment." *American Sociological Review* 62: 218–35.

———. 1991. "The Social Construction of Status Value: Gender and Other Nominal Characteristics." *Social Forces* 70: 367–86.

———, Elizabeth Boyle, Kathy Kuipers, and Dawn Robinson. 1998. "How Do Status Beliefs Develop? The Role of Resources and Interaction." *American Sociological Review* 63: 331–50.

———, and Shelly J. Correll. 2004. "Unpacking the Gender System: A Theoretical Perspective on Cultural Beliefs and Social Relations." *Gender & Society* 18: 510–31.

Risman, Barbara J. 2004. "Gender as a Social Structure: Theory Wrestling with Social Change." *Gender & Society* 18(4): 429–50.

———. 2003. "Valuing All Flavors of Feminist Sociology." *Gender & Society* 17: 659–63.

———. 1998. *Gender Vertigo: American Families in Transition*. New Haven, Conn.: Yale University Press.

———. 1987. "Intimate Relationships from a Microstructural Perspective: Mothering Men." *Gender and Society* 1:1–12.

————, Shannon Davis, and Cathy Zimmer. 2005. "Biological Constraints on Gender? Feminists Wrestle with Testosterone." Presented at American Sociological Meetings, Philadelphia.

Schnittker, Jason, Jeremy Freese, and Brian Powell. 2003. "Who Are Feminists and What Do They Believe?: The Role of Generations." *American Sociological Review* 68: 607–22.

Sprague, Joey. 2005. *Bridging Differences: Feminist Methodologies for Critical Researchers*. Lanham, Md.: Rowman & Littlefield.

Stacey, Judith. 2003. "Taking Feminist Sociology Public Can Prove Less Progressive Than You Wish." *Network News*, May: 27–28.

Tittle, Charles. 2004. "The Arrogance of Public Sociology." *Social Forces* 82: 1639–43.

Williams, Christine. 1992. "The Glass Escalator: Hidden Advantages for the Men in 'Female' Professions." *Social Problems* 39: 253–67.

Zimmer, Lynne. 1988. "Tokenism and Women in the Workplace: The Limits of Gender-Neutral Theory." *Social Problems* 35: 64–77.

17

The Challenge to Public Sociology: Neoliberalism's Illusion of Inclusion

Charles A. Gallagher

How can sociology engage a public about growing social inequalities when most people now believe such inequalities do not exist? This is not to say that the vast majority of individuals are blind to socioeconomic divisions in the United States. What is unique to this historical moment is the widespread belief that individual agency and impersonal, nondiscriminatory market forces rather than racial, gender, or class inequalities structure life chances. As the dominant political and cultural belief, neoliberalism has created an "illusion of inclusion" where economic success reflects unconstrained choices individuals make concerning their economic placement in America's socioeconomic hierarchy. As a global economic system, neoliberalism calls for the privatization of public space and resources, limited government, a dismantling of the social safety net, and unregulated markets. As an ideology neoliberalism espouses a belief that the opportunity to be successful, rich, or both is available to all regardless of one's particular social background (black, gay, poor, female...). At the individual level neoliberalism is internalized as meaning that failure reflects individual shortcomings, not poverty or institutional discrimination. The neoliberal narrative of success is analogous to an all-you-can-eat smorgasbord at an inexpensive chain restaurant. The law requires public accommodation to the general public, a majority of the public can afford to eat at this establishment, and the choices at the steam tables are available to all, regardless of social standing. A satisfying meal or one that causes discomfort, much like life itself and social mobility, is now understood as a series of unrestrained individual choices that are, by and large, the same for everyone. Neoliberalism asserts that consuming is equated with choice, and choice becomes synonymous with both equality of opportunity and equality of results. You can choose to "be like Mike" or Oprah or Donald or Condoleezza just as you make a rational choice to live in the trailer park, barrio, reservation, or federal penitentiary. In this script where hard work is always rewarded it is not racism, sexism, or elitist barriers to higher education to blame for downward mobility or being poor. The narrative of equality that now dominates American culture informs us that the social barriers that historically excluded women, racial, ethnic, and sexual minorities from fully participating in the upper ranks of America's professional classes have been exorcised by the nondiscriminatory, rational logic of the market.

The new ethos of equality is summed up in a recent Phoenix Wealth Management print advertisement that tells readers, "Barriers to making it have fallen. Once and for all." The ad juxtaposes photographs of older, white Wall Street–type male executives in pinstripe suits with a white female, a black male, and an Asian male, each young and elegantly dressed and all radiating economic success. If the political ideology of the twentieth century used the pseudo-science of social Darwinism to rationalize social inequality, the disparities of the twenty-first century are to be found in justifications based on the neoliberal assertion that rational markets by definition do not discriminate.

As the belief that success is a direct function of individual choices in unrestricted, unfettered, nondiscriminatory markets has come to dominate American culture, sociology has been relatively absent from challenging these distortions in any meaningful public way. This lack of engagement with the public concerning the social costs and implications of neoliberalism points to three troubling trends in our discipline that I will address in this chapter. The first is the growing wall between the research we do and its connection to the general public. Second is our inability to provide empirically based competing narratives that challenge the neoliberal assertion that inequality is a perhaps unfortunate but necessary social outcome of postindustrialism. Finally we face the dilemma of disseminating research findings that challenge most individuals' belief that the United States is a meritocracy. The scholarship we produce on social inequality, discrimination, and the various barriers to upward mobility is in direct competition with the rags-to-riches story lines constantly promoted in the media.

PUBLIC SOCIOLOGY AND THE
HAIR ON THE SPIDER'S LEG

In the early 1990s two sociologists I befriended from Central America asked me why a majority of American sociologists practiced a kind of sociology that typically did very little to raise public awareness of the vast social inequalities they saw in their travels throughout the United States. Why, they asked, did a majority of sociologists north of their borders engage in research that had little, if any, practical applications for public policy? What was gained, they inquired, by the long hours of tedious academic research and the ordeal of publication only to give birth to scholarship that was most times overly abstract, immersed in the impenetrable cant of one's subfield, read by few, and had a shelf life in the academic community that was often shorter than a semester. What was the point of acquiring the intellectual and methodological skills required to solve the vexing problems of modern living if one pursued research projects that had little social relevance to the average person on the street or did nothing to debunk or demystify the social world. As they saw it our discipline had moved from one where the scientific method was used to bring about social reforms generated through research to one now dominated by Kuhnian normal science where intellectual conformity to an insular academic community had become sociology's raison d'être.

They explained what they saw as a quintessentially U.S. problem by way of analogy; U.S.-trained sociologists liked to study the hair on a spider's leg. Most sociologists in the United States, they offered, focused on a single hair because they had developed the techniques, metrics, and instruments to measure the length, width, and density of an arachnid's hair with extreme methodological precision. The narrow focus on the hair as the unit of analysis obscured the fact that the follicle had been connected to one of eight legs, and those legs had been connected to the spider's body. In the end we know a great deal about an individual hair on the spider's leg and very little about the spider itself or the relationship between the physical and social world the spider inhabits or ecosystem in which the spider resides. Given the exceptional talent pool, relative abundance of intellectual and academic capital, and the status our elite institutions hold among the professional classes (the media, local and federal governments), my South American colleagues were dumbfounded that mainstream U.S. sociology did not occupy a greater and more forceful role in framing issues of social and economic injustice or bringing these topics into America's living rooms. In addition to these problems, I was told that most Americans would not be receptive or would ignore our research findings on inequality because they ran counter to the deeply held conviction that equal opportunity in the United States was now the norm. Sociologists, I was told, had painted themselves into a corner similar to the prophet Cassandra; we were able to provide accurate prophecies about societal trends and their implications but our curse was to be ignored by the very public who would most benefit from our message.

Needless to say I felt attacked by these accusations. In a somewhat defensive manner I went on to list numerous research projects carried out by mainstream sociologists that had raised the general public's consciousness on a number of important social issues. Decades of scholarship on residential segregation, racial discrimination, and gender-wage disparities emerged out of sociology and had been instrumental in legal challenges that ultimately altered institutions' practices and public perceptions. Outside of these few examples I had a more difficult time pointing to sociological research that had a major influence on shaping public policy. Their response was, quite correctly, that my example about "professional" sociological research moving into the public realm (that is, beyond the gated academic community) then going on to influence public policy was the rare exception, not the norm. In what amounted to a degradation ceremony, my colleagues then proceeded to read aloud the titles of papers and abstracts from our premier sociological journals, pointing out what appeared to be research for research's or tenure's sake rather than research that was grounded in or even tangentially linked to the social reforms that initially guided sociological research as a discipline. My response was that sociology was eclectic and that scholars had both the right and freedom to pursue their own research projects. Scholarship was not judged on the extent publications were relevant outside of one's area of specialization or if one's research findings had public policy implications, nor was there a professional obligation that the scholarship should challenge or be focused on leveling existing social hierarchies. Any of these outcomes might be welcome, but, I argued at that time, they were not necessary motivations nor expected outcomes of the research enterprise.

The discussion about what sociology's relationship to the general public should be has resurfaced once again, as it seems to do during times of social crisis or when the legitimacy of the state is called into question. The current debate that has emerged asks us once again to consider if there needs to be, or if our discipline even desires, a "public sociology." Public sociology appears to be understood by some as a shift from chronicling how society "is" to one focused on recommendations about how society "ought" to be. To explicitly politicize sociology would compromise, some argue, the scientific objectivity of our discipline. Although the mission statement on the American Sociological Society's website claims that we are an "association dedicated to advancing sociology as a scientific discipline and profession serving the public good," there is a rather shrill and disingenuous discussion that seems to have replaced the "and" in our mission statement with an "or." Those who seem most adamantly opposed to a branch of sociology that has as its goal the communication of relevant research to the general public spends a considerable amount of energy framing this debate in Manichean terms.

There appears, however, to be very little disagreement among most sociologists about what public sociology is or should be. Most sociologists do not embrace the false dichotomy of the dispassionate, objective, value-free scientist who pursues universal truths, on one hand, and those who conduct politicized research as a vehicle for social activism, on the other. It has been my experience that sociologists are excited when one of our own has scholarship that travels from journal article or book manuscript to Congress or Health and Human Services and on to the AP wire service or the *New York Times*.

There should also be little concern that our profession will soon metamorphose from one dominated by a class of "professional sociologists" to a discipline where a significant majority become little more than political talking heads, news anchors, or the go-to Sunday morning show public policy wonks. From 2000 to 2003 no sessions on "public sociology" appeared in the index of session topics in the American Sociological Association's annual meeting program book. The "Public Sociology" theme at the 2004 American Sociological Association annual meeting had forty-five sessions addressing various aspects of public sociology. In 2005 the number of sessions devoted to "public sociology" had dropped to eight. The philistines of public sociology are not storming the gates; what has taken place has been an internally manufactured moral panic. An accurate reflection of the "professional" versus "public" sociology is nicely summed up in a recent article on this topic: "there can be neither public nor policy sociology, however, without a professional sociology that develops a body of theoretical knowledge and empirical findings, put to the test of peer review. Professional sociology provides the ammunition, the expertise, the knowledge, the insight, and the legitimacy for sociologists to present themselves to publics or to powers" (Burawoy et al., 2004: 105). It is quite unlikely that sociologists would object to a vision of our discipline that used professional sociology as the means to engage the public in meaningful discussions about important social issues.

OBSTACLES TO PUBLIC SOCIOLOGY: THE ILLUSION OF INCLUSION

Even if our discipline could agree on what an expansive and more public sociology could be, we now face obstacles that are more formidable than our current internal squabbles over what constitutes a sociology that is able to meaningfully engage itself with the public. The struggle we face as sociologists transcends the question of academic insularity, the perceived irrelevance of the type of research we do, or a discipline that is viewed by many as being increasingly out of touch with the concerns of most Americans. Sociologists must now address the very real fact that most Americans see the socioeconomic playing field as now being level. For much of America, racism, sexism, and class-based inequalities are social problems that are perceived as having been addressed and rectified by the civil and gay rights movements, feminism, and trickle-down economics.

If a majority of Americans now believe race, class, and gender no longer shape life chances, then what little critical social analysis that does trickle into the public domain is viewed with suspicion or disbelief or simply discounted as liberal whining. The 1990s accelerated, and the post 9/11 climate cemented, the "illusion of inclusion" among most Americans that social inequalities have been rectified by legislative fiat.

High-profile discrimination cases (Coke, Cracker Barrel, Denny's, Merrill Lynch, and Texaco) conveyed to America via right-wing media outlets that discriminatory behavior in corporate America is no longer tolerated. The market will no longer bear such behavior, not necessarily because it is immoral or unethical, but because it incurs an additional irrational cost of doing business.

The accounts sociologists offer concerning how social inequality is maintained, reproduced, and made invisible is at odds with the deeply held conviction that America is a meritocratic society. Worse than irrelevant, what we offer the public is a view of the United States that many individuals see as just plain wrong. Outside of televised natural disasters, the suffering that millions of Americans experience on a daily basis is not a prime-time concern of the media. Using race, sexual orientation, and class as examples I describe how various types of social inequality have been in large part erased from the public consciousness and how this erasure creates both obstacles and opportunities for sociologists who wish to raise public awareness on these topics.

CONSTRUCTING THE ILLUSION OF INCLUSION

Adults born around World War II have at their disposal a Rolodex of visual memories that defined the modern civil rights movement. The decade between 1954 and 1964 saw the landmark Supreme Court *Brown* decision, Emmett Till's disfigured body laid out in a coffin, church bombings, bus boycotts, lunch counter sit-ins, police dogs mauling children, Medgar Evers's assassination, the March on Washington, and the 1964 Civil Rights Act (Andersen, 2004). These events dominated the nation's newspapers and radios, and for the first time in U.S. history, a majority of Americans could watch these events unfold in their living rooms on the television. Between 1964 and 1971 there were over 750 race riots, 15,000 acts of arson resulting in 228 deaths, and almost 13,000 injuries (Postrel, 2004). It would be difficult to have lived through these two decades and not have concluded that race relations were a serious problem in the United States.

Twenty-five years after the riot smoke had cleared over American cities a majority of white Americans concluded that the socioeconomic playing field in the United States was now level. A stunning 71 percent of the white population believe African Americans have "more" or "about the same opportunities in life" as whites, although black and brown unemployment is almost three times that of whites. A 2003 Gallup poll found that more than eight in ten white Americans thought that there is no difference in educational opportunities between blacks and whites even though blacks graduate from high school or finish college at rates significantly below those of whites. A majority of whites in 2003 (56 percent) responded that all or most of the "goals of the Civil Rights Movement" have been achieved. A near majority (49 percent) agreed with the statement that people had a "fair and equal opportunity to succeed as long as they work hard and do their best. Most poor people do have these opportunities, but just don't do enough to take responsibility and help themselves" (Hart, 1997). Sixty percent of those between the ages of fifteen and eighteen saw the poor as responsible for their own poverty because of individual shortcomings rather than due to the existence of a "system that is stacked against these people" (Hart, 1997). A majority of whites perceive the "race problem" as having been solved at a time when every quality of life indicator shows persistent and in some cases growing racial disparities.

Most of white America has convinced itself that we now live in a color-blind society, in part because the perception of racial equality is constantly reinforced through exaggerated depictions of racial harmony in popular culture. The common ground that neoliberalism promotes is consumption across the color line, creating the illusion that through such acts race no longer matters. Images once subversive are appropriated, inverted, and used incessantly to sell products that promote a color-blind vision of America. The color-blind race icons that are part of mainstream America are ubiquitous: Muhammad Ali's iconoclastic boxing poses are marketed as universal uplift to sell sneakers; blues superstar B. B. King promotes a blood glucose-monitoring system; MC Hammer, P. Diddy, Gladys Knight, Dennis Rodman, and LeBron James each pitch products to 130 million viewers in the United States and an estimated one billion potential consumers worldwide during the Super Bowl. Given the sheer repetition of black celebrities selling products in the mass media it is no wonder only 6 percent of whites in the United States believe racism is a serious problem facing African Americans. Research on exposure to race in advertisements found that "television commercials tend to leave the impression that race does not matter, that race relations are good, and that the issues of racism, discrimination and prejudice are outdated" (Graves, 1999: 711). Not only is the message sociologists are likely to convey about inequality viewed skeptically by the public, but the message itself is typically censored by the media. Juliet Schor asks "what about those who write about subjects which are farther from middle-class American experience, such as poverty or environmental racism or the critique of imperialism?" These topics are much harder sells, and more easily dismissed by the media as stories we've already heard, throwbacks to the 1960s (Burawoy et al., 2004: 123). Sociologists are competing with an America where 98 percent of households have at least one TV, the TV is on an average of seven hours and forty minutes, and the average American watches over four hours of television every day. It is safe to surmise that the overwhelming majority is not tuning in to public or educational programming.

The representations of homosexuals in popular culture mirrors the way race has been transformed through the marketing of products to the masses. Color-blind portrayals of race and the media's packaging of queer lifestyles as urban chic reduce both to benign cultural markers stripped of all forms of institutional, discriminatory, or coercive power. It is here that sociology must take into account the public's schizophrenic relationship with the media. Communication researchers explain that parasocial interaction refers "to the phenomenon that viewers form beliefs and attitudes about people they know only through television, regardless of whether such people are fictional characters or real people" (Schiappa et al., Forthcoming: 3). Like the racial minorities whites come to know through the media, Americans come to know homosexuals through situation comedies or television dramas. In a relatively short amount of time homosexuals have gone from being a relatively invisible group in the media whose sexual orientation was defined by the American Psychiatric Association as a mental disorder (up until 1973) to one that is now a desired marketing niche. Over seventeen million viewers watched *Will & Grace* each week in 2003 (Schiappa et al., Forthcoming), and with its syndication it is possible to watch this show every day of the week. Between *Queer Eye for the Straight Guy*, *Six Feet Under*, *Queer as Folk*, *The L Word*, and the *Ellen DeGeneres Show* a majority of Americans have come to know, accept, and like, at least in a virtual or parasocial kind of way, someone who is gay.

But the same slippery slope between the onetime iconoclastic representations of "outsider groups" on television and the reduction of subversive symbols to commodities available to the general public is at play. *Queer Eye for the Straight Guy*, argues Jaap Kooijman, "appropriates the term queer, depoliticizing it by turning it into a commodity. . . . the way the program uses queer is nothing more than a fashion accessory. Queer is hip, queer is fashionable. . . . *Queer Eye* is heavily sponsored and should be considered as a major advertisement for the program's sponsors. Moreover, in this fashionable queer corporate world, there is no place for alternative lifestyles, sexualities or critical politics" (2005: 107).

While gays and lesbians may appear to be integrated into the American mainstream, national polling data and hate crime statistics tell a very different story. A poll taken while President George W. Bush was pushing for a constitutional amendment that would define marriage as a union between a man and a woman asked, "Do you think marriages between homosexuals should or should not be recognized by the law as valid, with the same rights as traditional marriage?" A majority of Americans, 56 percent (with 5 percent offering no opinion), said these marriages should not be valid. A majority of Americans (53 percent) were in favor of changing the U.S. Constitution to define marriage as being only between a man and a woman. A majority (60 percent) of the U.S. population believe that it is always or almost always wrong for two adults of the same sex to have sexual relations. A majority (55 percent) as well said in 2004 that they had "a work colleague, close friend, or relative who is gay." You may work with or consider a homosexual a "close friend" in a survey, but you are statistically not likely to approve of their sex life or want to give then the same huge package of social and economic benefits that marriage confers on heterosexuals.

In 2003 the FBI's Uniform Crime report listed over four thousand hate crimes that were motivated by race or ethnicity and 1,239 hate crimes motivated by sexual orientation. Homosexuals on situation comedies may make us laugh or define homo/metrosexual fashion. We may be persuaded to purchase fast food or desire a particular pair of sneakers because we are enamored of the black sports superstars endorsing these products. We do, however, still live in a country where Matthew Shepard was tortured and killed because he was gay and perceived as being upper middle class. We live in a nation where James Byrd, Jr. was chained and pulled behind a pickup truck to his death because he was black. It was overwhelmingly the poor, brown, and black who were trapped and left to drown when Hurricane Katrina ravaged New Orleans. In this overwhelmingly black city, 35 percent of the black population did not own cars, compared to 15 percent of whites. Evacuation plans for such an emergency were based on the ability of individuals to hop in their cars and leave the city. The disaster in New Orleans makes public two warring visions of America: the popular view, which depicts America as a place of equal opportunity, and the one held by most sociologists, who see our country as being deeply cleaved by various social inequalities.

Representations of upward mobility, intergenerational transfers of wealth, and a society now free of institutional racism and sexism are viewed by many whites as the rule rather than the exception. Ignorance isn't only bliss in the case of individuals not seeing the depths of intergroup racial inequality or homophobia; ignorance becomes a form of hegemony that serves to maintain the privileges of the dominant group. It is within this context, where neoliberalism reduces all social exchanges to an equal opportunity cash nexus, that sociologists must engage Americans about social inequality. Henry Giroux explains how neoliberalism crowds out progressive voices as he observes that "neoliberalism undermines those public spaces where noncommercial values and crucial social issues can be discussed, debated and engaged. As public space is privatized, power is disconnected from social obligations" (2003: 197). Neoliberalism has successfully decoupled the sociological link made by C. Wright Mills between personal troubles and social issues by constructing a worldview that deemphasizes the public and privileges the absolute autonomy and accountability of the individual.

THE SOCIOLOGISTS' DILEMMA: MAKING PRIVATE PROBLEMS PUBLIC AGAIN

The uphill battle sociologists face in bringing their research to the public is a challenge on several fronts. Americans like to view themselves as a fair-minded people who believe they house, to quote Gunnar Myrdal, "the entire American Creed of liberty, equality and justice, and fair opportunity for everybody" (1944). However the "everybody" in Myrdal's summation of the American Creed is understood as an egalitarianism based on the efforts of individuals, not on the relative status or harms racial and sexual minorities have and continue to experience in the United States. There remains an anxious coexistence between the almost universal belief that equal opportunity should be afforded to all Americans and the resistance to using group membership as a means to ameliorate inequalities rooted in past and present forms of discrimination.

There is also a vast chasm between the attitudes individuals hold toward racial or sexual minorities and how individuals are actually treated by the dominant group. After the surveys are completed, the interviews finished, or we leave the field, what we have to offer the public is an account of reality that is often starkly different from the world our respondents picture themselves as inhabiting. As a white researcher who has spent an extensive amount of time interviewing whites around the country about race, what I have found is that most whites are under the false impression that the socioeconomic playing field *is* now level. My own research as well as that of others who research how whites construct their understanding of race have found that many whites know very little about the relative socioeconomic standing of other racial groups.

It is a very small step from falsely believing that race no longer shapes life chances to being able to argue, as a majority of whites do, that blacks "are doing at least as well or better than most whites in income and educational attainment." These whites' accounts of racial equity are not (necessarily) a self-interested dodge or an evasive strategy to minimize their own white privilege. Color-blindness as a natural extension of neoliberalism has been able to construct a commonsense view of the world for the dominant group where "equality of opportunity" has finally, once and for all, been replaced with "equality of results." We have moved to the next level of discourse on social inequality where the social definition of reality for many whites is one where they truthfully believe women, racial minorities, gays, and lesbians are both socioeconomic equals and live in a society where discrimination is a thing of the past. With social equality as the "commonsense" starting point for the dominant group, the consequences and obstacles to social justice are clear; it can now be argued on ostensibly a neutral platform that the state need not advance any solutions to social inequality because these problems have been rectified. Any such unnecessary government involvement where race was made to be a social issue after this dilemma had been rectified would constitute, as whites have responded over and over again in numerous studies, reverse discrimination or catering to the special interests of politically connected constituencies.

Sociologists seeking to engage the public must take this new frame of perceived equity into their research. We must understand that delusions of social equality and equal opportunity coexist with new census numbers that tell us over thirty-seven million Americans are at or below the poverty line. If our aim is a professional sociology that yields findings that can inform the public about growing inequalities, we must recognize that most Americans have learned the art of providing researchers with the socially appropriate answers or reflexively mouth the all-things-are-now-equal propaganda that permeates the media.

It is now the case that the United States' "imagined community" is one where neoliberalism has created the "illusion of inclusion." What public sociologists need to do is develop better techniques that accurately gauge perceptions about social inequality. These instruments need to take into account the understanding that most Americans now believe the socioeconomic playing field is level. In order to develop competing narratives that frame social inequality as a failure of society rather than the failures of individuals, we need to reflexively engage our respondents about the root causes of social inequality. At the level of the standard survey this type of interviewing is time consuming and makes managing nonstandard responses difficult. The way, however, for our research findings to resonate with the public and have some traction with media is to tell a story that the man or woman on the street would want to hear because they see themselves in the story, and it is an account that aids them in understanding and deconstructing the neoliberal bill of goods they have been sold.

REFERENCES

Andersen, Margaret. 2004. "From Brown to Grutter: The Diverse Beneficiaries of Brown V. Board of Education." *University of Illinois Law Review*: 1073–98.

Burawoy, Michael, et al. 2004. "Public Sociologies: Symposium from Boston College." *Social Problems* 5: 103–30.

Giroux, Henry. 2003. "Spectacles of Race and Pedagogies of Denial: Anti Black Racist Pedagogy under the Reign of Neoliberalism." *Communication Education* 52(3): 191–211.

Graves, Sherryle Brown. 1999. "Television and Prejudice Reduction: When Does Television as a Vicarious Experience Make a Difference?" *Journal of Social Issues* 55: 707–25.

Hart, Peter. 1997. "Final Adult Survey Data." Study #4890B.

Kooijman, Jaap. 2005. "They're Here, They're Queer, and Straight America Loves It." *GLQ: Journal of Lesbian and Gay Studies* 11: 106–9.

Myrdal, Gunnar. 1944. *An American Dilemma: The Negro Problem and Modern Democracy*. New York: Harper & Brothers Publishers.

Postrel, Virginia. 2004. "The Consequences of the 1960s Race Riots into View." *New York Times*, December 20.

Schiappa, Edward, et al. Forthcoming. "Can One TV Show Make a Difference? *Will & Grace* and the Parasocial Contact Hypothesis." *Journal of Homosexuality*.

Appendix

Annotated Guide to Online
Resources for Public Sociologists

Kevin M. Linehan and Keri E. Iyall Smith

This appendix includes a sample of the wealth of information online that might be useful to public sociologists—for both teaching and research. The list is categorized by topic of content to make it easier to find sites that are relevant. Sites are categorized by the most salient topic of content, but there is some overlap, for example, a feminist website features information on environmental protections. Consider skimming the list in its entirety for a more exhaustive selection of websites.

We have made every effort to ensure that the sites listed below were active as of publication, but the Internet is an ephemeral place and nonprofit organizations are sometimes short-lived. Titles of the organizations or websites are provided, which will enable you to search for the site if it has simply moved to a new location.

CONSTITUTIONS, LAWS,
TREATIES, AND LEGISLATION

EUROPA: Draft Treaty Establishing a Constitution for Europe

http://europa.eu.int/constitution/futurum/constitution/index_en.htm

This website is dedicated to the adoption of a constitution for Europe. The constitution, which is pending approval, is available in html form in three languages and in PDF format in all the official languages of the European Union. There is a link inviting visitors to give their opinions on the tone, laws, and bylaws of the constitution.

International Constitutional Law

www.oefre.unibe.ch/law/icl/
   This is a site that provides links to other sites: click on a country and the engine brings you to the site where the country's constitution is available for viewing. Also, the history of constitution writing is available for several countries.

Multilateral Treaties Deposited with the Secretary-General

http://untreaty.un.org/ENGLISH/bible/englishinternationalbible/bible.asp
   This site separates the United Nations Treaties from the League of Nations Treaties and breaks them down into the specific topics each chapter (or article) focuses on. The chapters are hyperlinked, enabling visitors to click on the topic of interest and bring up all relevant information.

Treaty Body Database: Documents by Treaty

www.unhchr.ch/tbs/doc.nsf
   This site is a catalog of links to human rights treaties, documents, and committees.

United Nations Documents: Research Guide

www.un.org/Depts/dhl/resguide/spechr.htm
   The site is a research guide to human rights, breaking the documentation down into categories such as "Committee against Torture" or "Committee for the Rights of the Child." Under each topic there are links to committees, articles, databases, reports, and other information on the given topic.

The United Nations Human Rights Treaties

www.bayefsky.com/
   Bayefsky.com serves as a website for the United Nations Human Rights Treaties, which are at the core of the international system for the protection of human rights. These rights are universal, meaning they legally apply to virtually every child, woman, or man in the world. The site is a vehicle to navigate the treaties, from the body itself to the amendments that have been made to the document over the years.

University of Michigan Document Center

www.lib.umich.edu/govdocs/forcons.html
   This website offers an extensive database of international and federal legal doctrine.

There are links to constitutions, the drafting of the European Union's constitution, environmental law, foreign law, foreign legal databases, and international law.

University of Minnesota Human Rights Library

www1.umn.edu/humanrts/
This is a database that provides links to human rights documents such as treaties and links to four hundred thousand other sites as well as its own search engine that provides access to more documents and human rights websites.

DEMOCRACY

The Centre for Study of Global Governance

www.lse.ac.uk/Depts/global/
The Centre's website offers many publications on global governance and civil society for download. There are public lectures by researchers and politicians, discussion papers, global civil society yearbooks (2001–2004/5), a report on human security doctrine, essays and articles, and interviews. The site also offers a few course syllabi, a newsletter, and an events listing.

Elections around the World

www.electionworld.org/
Electionworld.org serves as an information website, providing links to countries that hold elections. The links give historical information, results of recent elections, lists of dominant political parties, and links to political parties online.

Project for the First People's Century (PFPC)

http://firstpeoplescentury.net/
The PFPC website is a database that offers access to papers and articles discussing political, economic, ideological, social, and environmental consequences of U.S. foreign policy. The homepage contains articles on current events, information on U.S. involvement globally, and links to other websites that provide further information and resources.

Public Citizen's Global Trade Watch

www.citizen.org/trade/
Global Trade Watch is an organization that promotes democracy by confronting corporate globalization. On the homepage, a picture of the globe features six organizations or trade compacts: WTO, NAFTA, CAFTA, AGOA, FTAA, and Sink or Swim. You can select the pictures or select a link on the left-hand side of the page that is a direct link to the trade doctrine. There are also links to publications, a press room, public citizen divisions, and current actions.

Rights and Democracy

http://ichrdd.ca/frame2.iphtml?langue=0

An organization created by the Canadian Parliament in 1988 to promote the universal protection of basic human rights, it currently partners with human rights, indigenous peoples', and women's rights groups. It fosters cooperation between democratic movements and governments, promoting human rights globally. The site provides links to publications, programs, and urgent actions.

Speak Out

www.speakersandartists.org/index.html

Speak Out for Democratic Education and Culture is a nonprofit organization that is committed to social, political, cultural, and economic justice. It encourages critical and imaginative thinking about both domestic and international issues through artistic and educational programs. Using music, exhibits, and movies, it strives to empower young people to participate in social change. On the site is a list of the artists and performers who contribute to the organization and links to resources and movies.

ECONOMIC DEVELOPMENT
AND ECONOMIC JUSTICE

50 Years Is Enough

www.50years.org/

This organization is a network for global economic justice. It is made up of U.S. grassroots, youth, labor, and development organizations that strive to change the World Bank and the International Monetary Fund (IMF). The site offers links to research or join the campaigns. This website also features information on the issues (e.g., debt cancellation, structural adjustment policies, the environment, privatization, free trade, health and education, and women's rights), economic justice, conferences, and institutions.

Alternative Information and Development Center (AIDC)

www.aidc.org.za/

The AIDC organization is dedicated to national, regional, and international challenges to the current global economic system. Through research and information, the site educates visitors on the subjects of Third World debt, poverty, the IMF, the WTO, gender, water privatization, globalization, mobilization, and the World Social Forum. Links to resources, events, and publications make up this website.

The Bead Game

www.oxnet.org/updir/BeadGame.htm

This website offers instructions to facilitate "The Bead Game." The Bead Game is useful for teaching about inequality locally or globally and highlighting the dual dimensions of inequality: inequality of resources and opportunity.

Community Economies

http://communityeconomies.org

This site provides a space for the theorizing, discussion, representation, and enactment of new visions of community and economy. The site grew out of J. K. Gibson-Graham's feminist critique of political economy. It contains papers, stories, training, and exercises, along with links and other reading material.

Eldis

www.eldis.org/

Eldis's website contains a plethora of international development information. Links to guides on topics are wide-ranging: conflict, climate change, debt, education, governance, health systems, children and youth, biodiversity, aging populations, and food security are a few. The website also features news articles and information available on CD-ROM.

Institute for Food and Development Policy

www.foodfirst.org/

Food First is an organization that seeks to eliminate the injustices that cause hunger. It separates its campaigns into three areas: democratizing the markets, equitable access to land and resources, and ecologically and socially just farming systems. The site features links to recent media articles and links to the campaigns that Food First sponsors and promotes.

International Forum on Globalization

www.ifg.org/

Focusing on the consequences of globalization, the IFG has produced numerous publications, organized large public events, hosted seminars, and held press conferences. Recently, the IFG has initiated a program that focuses on alternatives to globalization that are compatible with human rights and environmental protections. The site has its own Google search engine and links to publications, events, and programs produced by the IFG.

Jubilee Research: Supporting Economic Justice Campaigns Worldwide

www.jubilee2000uk.org/

This is a campaign that promotes international financial reform, environmental sustainability, and the basic rights of humankind. The website provides up-to-date research, analyses, news, and data on international debt. Topics include economic and social rights, the eradication of poverty, sustainability, equity, and self-reliance.

Multilateral Treaty Framework: Invitation to Universal Participation. Sustainable Development

http://untreaty.un.org/English/TreatyEvent2002/index.htm

The main page focuses on sustainable development, with a letter from Kofi A. Annan discussing the World Summit on Sustainable Development. The main page provides links to numerous treaties and summaries of those treaties.

National Priorities Project: Better Choices, Better Communities

www.nationalpriorities.org/

The NPP links political analysis to action by taking on the role as an intermediary between policy organizations and grassroots groups. The site translates policy information—pertaining to taxes and spending, in particular—into everyday language, enabling people to understand the consequences of the policies. The site offers graphs, current articles, publications, a database, and additional resources.

NEPAD

www.nepad.org/

The New Partnership for Africa's Development (NEPAD) is a combination of a vision and strategic framework for the renewal of Africa. It addresses the current challenges of rapidly growing poverty levels, underdevelopment, and marginalization that the African continent faces. On the site a viewer can enter into a discussion area to brainstorm ideas to put on the calendar link or read articles about current events.

NetAid

www.netaid.org/

NetAid's website has several audiences: high school students, college students, educators, volunteers, and the media. For each it provides information and volunteer opportunities aimed at minimizing global poverty. There are also news articles and spotlights of model volunteers and current projects. The site also presents research on global issues and learning games.

Peoples' Global Action (PGA)

www.nadir.org/nadir.intiativ/agp/

Peoples' Global Action asserts that capitalism is part of the destruction of humanity and the planet. PGA assembles centralized demonstrations that strive to block summits such as the G8 Summit in Scotland. The website presents news articles and a calendar of past, current, and upcoming events that call for the involvement of the masses. Also, there is a section that breaks the demonstrations into themes; therefore one can choose a specific topic to research or join.

Political Economy Research Institute (PERI)

www.umass.edu/peri/
PERI's website provides information on globalization, macroeconomics, labor markets, living wages, development, peace building, and the environment. The site presents information on current research, with profiles of new books, new research completed at PERI (papers are available for download), and an interview archive.

The Religious Working Group on the World Bank and IMF

www.sndden.org/rwg/
The Religious Working Group formed to inform, inspire, and organize activists against the rise of widespread debt. The website organizes activists, provides information on upcoming events, and features articles on current activities across the globe.

War on Want

www.waronwant.org/?lid=1
The War on Want is an organization that fights poverty in developing countries that are negatively affected by globalization. This website contains information on current campaigns around the globe, links to join the War on Want, and a list of current programs.

ECONOMICS (GENERAL)

Bretton Woods Project

http://brettonwoodsproject.org/index.shtml
The Bretton Woods Project networks and regulates, examining and influencing both the World Bank and the International Monetary Fund (IMF). Through literature (reports, briefings, and the *Bretton Woods Update*) it monitors projects, reforms, and the management of the institutions under the Bretton Woods Project with specific interest on environmental and social concerns. A calendar and a link to publications are only two resources out of many that the site provides.

IFI Watch

www.ifiwatcher.org/calendar/index.shtml
The IFI Watch website serves as a connection for organizations worldwide that are

monitoring international financial institutions (IFIs) such as the World Bank, the IMF, and regional development banks. It provides a pool of independent information from a broad range of civil society sources' information on IFIs that is easy to navigate. There is a calendar that illustrates day-by-day development and decisions recorded by the IFI watchers, and there is also a page that provides contact information for the specific watchers. A documents/resources page is accessible for those who wish to research particular developments.

The Institute for Agriculture and Trade Policy (IATP)

www.iatp.org/

The IATP focuses on promoting the use of family farms instead of factory farms. They promote sustainability through clean sources of energy, safe food, healthy ecosystems, and the elimination of pesticides and antibiotics in agriculture production. The website offers current news articles, links to the WTO Policy Report on Human Rights in numerous languages, and an extensive database. The database includes information on the campaigns supported by the IATP.

The International Monetary Fund

www.imf.org/

This is an international organization established to influence international monetary cooperation, support exchange stability, and promote orderly exchange in order to foster economic growth. The IMF has adjusted to the changing needs of its members as new situations have arisen over the years. On this site are an archive service that searches current and past events and news stories that have involved the IMF, a database by country that monitors specific activity, and links to publications.

Our World Is Not For Sale (OWINFS)

www.ourworldisnotforsale.org/

OWINFS links global campaigns to end the corporate-dominated trade agenda and encourages the support of human rights, environmental issues, and democratic principles. The site acts as a hub for a range of movements and includes articles that involve the causes they support. OWINFS seeks to organize a better communication structure for the movement leaders.

They Rule

http://www.theyrule.net/

This website allows visitors to create maps of interlocking directories of the top companies in the United States. The data used to create maps was collected from corporate websites and SEC filings as of early 2004. There is a 2001 mapping site available, too.

The World Bank

www.worldbank.org/

The World Bank formed to fight poverty and improve the standards of living for people in developing countries. It offers loans, policy advice, technical assistance, and knowledge to reduce the spread of poverty. The homepage offers links to featured articles, information on upcoming and past events, a "hot topics" area, and a newsletter subscription service. This site also features video clips of World Bank conferences and meetings that are useful in the classroom.

The World Trade Organization (WTO)

www.wto.org/

The WTO focuses on the rules of trade between states. At the heart of the organization are its agreements that are negotiated and signed by the majority of the world's trading states. The WTO assists producers of goods and services, exporters, and importers, enabling them to conduct business safely and fairly. On the main page are links to WTO news, events, meetings, and other resources.

THE ENVIRONMENT

The Blue Ridge Environmental Defense League

www.bredl.org/

The Blue Ridge Environmental Defense League is a regional environmentalist organization. Their website features news articles pertaining to environmental issues in the southeastern United States. Information is available in the following areas: clean water and air, hog farms, waste management, nuclear waste, chip mills, health care, transportation, national forests, and environmental protections.

Center for Health, Environment, and Justice (CHEJ)

www.chej.org/

The CHEJ is a national environmental organization that uses a grassroots approach to creating and sustaining a healthy environment for the future. News stories and links to the CHEJ's campaigns are the focus of the main page, with links to join email newsgroups.

Climate Action Network (CAN)

www.climatenetwork.org/

CAN is a network of over 340 NGOs that are working to limit human-induced climate change to the ecosystem. The page offers links to CAN offices across the globe and informational pages on the network's campaigns.

Envirolink

www.envirolink.org/
    This site is a database on environmental issues. There are links to websites, informational pages, maps, pictures, and resources. Also, the site has a useful search engine.

Environmental Health Organization's Border Environmental Justice Campaign

www.environmentalhealth.org/border.html
    This organization uses social change strategies to influence environmental justice movements. The main page displays the mission and goal of the organization and offers links to the newsletter and other publications. The site is available in English and Spanish.

Friends of the Earth (FOE)

www.foe.org/
    FOE, an organization based in the United States, is the voice of an international network that supports a more healthy and just world through grassroots efforts. The homepage consists of links to current news articles, resources, and campaign pages.

Global Environmental Justice Organizations

http://environment.about.com
    This website serves as a resource database for environmental organizations, providing links to articles, a glossary of terms, pictures, and a search engine to navigate the site.

Greenpeace

www.greenpeace.org/international/
    Greenpeace promotes protection of the planet's biodiversity and environment. The website consists of current events and campaigns, as well as links to information and resources that are located throughout the site.

Rainforest Action Network (RAN)

www.ran.org/
    RAN campaigns for the forests and the inhabitants, both human and animal. The organization uses a grassroots approach to transform the global marketplace, focusing on sustaining the natural systems in the rain forests. This website offers links to campaigns that the organization sponsors and educational resources. This page offers an action center where users can search through the organization's campaigns.

Sierra Club: Trade and the Environment

www.sierraclub.org/trade/

The Sierra Club is working toward trade that is not only fair but protects and respects the environment. The website includes feature articles, links to news articles, the Sierra Club magazine, and an invitation to join the campaigns.

FEMINISM AND WOMEN'S RIGHTS

Feminist.com

www.feminist.com/

The information presented by Feminist.com's website focuses on antiviolence. They offer links to other sites that provide information on violence against women, current feminist news stories, antiviolence resources, and activist links. The site also provides links to a reading room, articles, and speeches.

Feminist Majority Foundation Online

www.feminist.org/

The Feminist Majority Foundation Online hosts an extensive website, with detailed news, resources, firsthand stories, and action alerts on several issues of concern to feminists. The general topics include: global feminism, student activism, reproductive rights, breast cancer center, sports and education, women and policing, Afghan women, 911 for women, and a feminist research center. Under each of these topics there are specific issues listed also. Other features on the website include feminist news and action highlights.

Gender Gap

www.gendergap.com/

This site is focused on women's participation in government, elections, and the military. Links offer connections to women in executive, judicial, and legislative branches. It provides information on the most recent elections locally and federally, and provides a history of women's service in the military.

National Organization for Women (NOW)

www.now.org/

NOW's website contains extensive information on women's rights, with links to a pressroom, NOW Times, current campaigns that NOW is engaged in, news articles, action alerts, and links to local chapters. Key issues that the website currently offers information on include: abortion rights, reproductive issues, affirmative action, constitutional equality, disability rights, women in the military, feminism, health issues, lesbian rights, social security, Title IX, marriage equality, violence against women, welfare policy, and women-friendly workplaces.

Women's Environment and Development Organization (WEDO)

www.wedo.org/

WEDO supports programs in four areas: gender and governance, economic and social justice, sustainable development, and U.S. global policy. WEDO's website includes an extensive library on topics related to peace, economic and social justice, and human rights. Specific topics that the library offers material on include: corporate accountability, decision making, economic and social justice, gender and governance, human rights, globalization, natural resources, poverty eradication, peace and security, privatization, sustainable development, trade, and United Nations reform. There are also profiles of current projects that WEDO is pursuing.

HEALTH

Health and Human Rights

www.who.int/hhr/en/

This site is a database of NGOs that uphold human rights standards and provide health care, and focuses on strengthening the World Health Organization's role in providing leadership in the field of health and human rights. It emphasizes the importance of protecting, respecting, and fulfilling human rights by avoiding and standing up to violations of human rights in the health field. This site provides information via databases, links, news forums, and opportunities to participate in activities.

Link to the Database on Health and Human Rights Actors

www.who.int/hhr/databases/en/

This website provides information on existing expertise in the area of health and human rights and promotes collaboration and information sharing. This database, collected from a sixty-five-question survey of organizations, focuses on the organizational structures and programs of each organization.

HUMAN RIGHTS

Derechos Human Rights

www.derechos.org/

Derechos Human Rights strives to gain worldwide respect and protection of human rights. They support human rights protections by providing information and analysis, promoting the prosecutions of violators of human rights, and supporting human rights NGOs. The site provides links to "hot topics," such as the death penalty. There are also ways to find publications on specific human rights issues and links for current information.

FAHAMU

www.fahamu.org/
FAHAMU is an organization that serves the needs of social movements that strive to promote and protect human rights. The website serves as a tool to promote social justice. The site provides learning materials for human rights and civil society organizations, accessible information pages, an area for debates on social programs, and e-newsletters.

Global Exchange

www.globalexchange.org/
The Global Exchange is an international human rights organization that strives to promote social, economic, and environmental changes globally. Using the website as both an area for information and access to resources, the organization now has the capabilities to connect its international members in one arena. On the main page there are links to current developing stories as well as to areas of specific interests.

HURIDOCS International: Human Rights Information and Documentation Systems, International

www.huridocs.org/index.htm
This website is dedicated to publishing human rights–related information. It presents news, announcements, a calendar, and photos. Huridocs.org also provides tools for training, networking, and outreach. The site index is particularly useful, breaking the website into links by topic.

National Human Rights Institutions Forum

www.nhri.net/
This site, created by the Danish Institute for Human Rights and the Office of the High Commissioner for Human Rights, serves as an international forum for researchers and activists in the field of human rights. The site provides global and regional documents, information on and from human rights institutions, and access to training resource programs.

Office of the High Commissioner for Human Rights: International Human Rights Instruments

www.unhchr.ch/html/intlinst.htm
The website provides links to the Charter for Human Rights. Each human right is separated, with a selection of links pertaining to the topic.

Office of the High Commissioner for Human Rights: United Nations Human Rights Documents

www.unhchr.ch/data.htm
This website describes how to properly link documents from the charter database and the treaty database. There are also links to both of those databases.

UN: Documents of Charter Based Bodies

www.unhchr.ch/huridocda/huridoca.nsf/Documents?OpenFrameset
Links on this main page connect to the Commission of Human Rights, the General Assembly, and other offices in the United Nations.

INDIGENOUS PEOPLES

Center for World Indigenous Studies

www.cwis.org/
The center is an independent, nonprofit organization that uses research and education to spread understanding and appreciation of the ideas and knowledge of indigenous peoples as well as the social, economic, and political views of indigenous nations. The main page provides an online database that contains scanned documents, reports, publications, and images that are held in hardcopy form in the library archives. There are links to current news stories to show that it is a current struggle being fought by everyday people.

The Indigenous Environmental Network

www.ienearth.org/
The Indigenous Environmental Network is a global organization that offers programs and campaigns on environmental issues of particular interest to indigenous peoples. Members of the IEN are indigenous peoples or individuals. The website is an information clearinghouse for its members and other indigenous communities. Some of the topics that the site provides information on are: mining of oil and gas, climate justice, globalization, youth, water, toxics and environmental health, and the Precautionary Principle. There are also news articles, community profiles, and a resources page.

International Working Group for Indigenous Affairs (IWGIA)

www.iwgia.org/sw153.asp
The IWGIA's site provides extensive data on indigenous groups around the globe. There are links to publications, including its annual *Indigenous World* report and other topic-related publications. The site features recent news articles, indigenous issues, events that the organization is sponsoring, a news archive, and meeting announcements. This site is available in English and Spanish.

Inuit Circumpolar Conference

www.inuitcircumpolar.com/
By clicking on a region—Canada, Russia, Greenland, or Alaska—visitors to this site will be able to view material from each region of the Circumpolar Conference. The sites are in various languages: Greenland, Alaska, and Canada's sites are in English. The site

provides a news archive, culture and education information, and links on the conference's activities, commissions, and general assembly meetings.

NativeWeb

www.nativeweb.org/
NativeWeb is a teaching and resource site that offers news articles, a resource center, links to books and music, profiles of indigenous peoples, and announcements on upcoming events. The resources it provides are extensive, including over fifty-eight hundred listings on a range of topics related to indigenous peoples: law and legal issues, literature, U.S. tribal websites, women, museums, art, the environment, history, health, genealogy, food, elders, education, religion, organizations, news and media, and others.

The South and Meso-American Indian Rights Center (SAIIC)

http://saiic.nativeweb.org/index.html
SAIIC recognizes the rights and needs of Latin America's indigenous peoples: for example, the right to self-determination and international respect. The homepage contains links to reports, notices, and news stories.

JUSTICE

50 Communities List

www.iisd.org/50comm/map/50_list.htm
This websites provides links to fifty social movement organizations around the world. The communities are categorized by topic: peace and security, environment and sustainable development, economic and social development, human rights, human settlements, education and health, women and children, cultural development, humanitarian activities, and food, agriculture, fisheries, and forests.

A SEED Europe

www.aseed.net/index.htm
A SEED Europe focuses on the production, distribution, and consumption of food and the coordination of the World Bank Boycott in Europe. The website promotes discussions, positive action, and distributing information. There are articles from across Europe that illustrate the causes of the A SEED organization and links to other agencies.

Citizen Works

http://citizenworks.org/
Working to develop a means to the progressive citizen movement, this organization

enhances other organizations by sharing information, building coalitions, and teaching them strategies that can band activists together. Also, it recruits, trains, and organizes citizens while acting as a catalyst when needed. The main page offers a link to the newest publications as well as connection to the campaigns of Citizen Works.

Coalition on Human Needs

www.chn.org/index.html

The Coalition on Human Needs promotes policies that address the needs of low-income and vulnerable people in the United States. The organization gathers data and publishes an annual Human Needs Report (archived editions available online also). The website also features news articles, toolkits, and information about the federal budget advocacy project, "The Opportunity for All Campaign."

Council for Responsible Genetics

www.gene-watch.org/

The Council for Responsible Genetics encourages debate about the social, ethical, and environmental implications of genetic technologies. The website contains information on genetics and the law, case studies, the GeneWatch journal (current and archived issues), and program and project sites. Current programs include a genetic bill of rights, biowarfare, biotechnology and agriculture, genetic testing and discrimination, and cloning and genetic manipulation.

The Earth Charter Initiative (ECI)

http://earthcharter.org/

The goal of the ECI is to create a sustainable world by promoting respect for nature, human rights, economic justice, and a culture that encourages peace. The site provides links to local events, news, the charter, an annual report, and country-level information. Visitors to the site are encouraged to endorse the charter.

Eritrea and Eritrean News Online

http://dehai.org/

This site is dedicated to reporting the news. The main page provides links to the most recent news articles—often from an African perspective. The articles are free of charge and new articles are added daily.

Focus on the Global South

www.focusweb.org/main/html/index.php?Itmemid = 1

Focus on the Global South is a program of research, analysis, and action that reflects the goals and rights of a people's movement against the inevitable impact of globalization. It strives to promote peace building, dismantle the economic and political structures, and create structures that protect the human rights and freedoms of individuals. The site serves as a news source where a viewer has access to hundreds of articles and news stories in numerous languages and time frames.

Global Justice Movement (GJM)

www.globaljusticemovement.net/
This website is the framework for the Global Justice Movement. The site provides information on various types of justice: monetary, social, economic, environmental, and peace justice. The site features news, actions, articles, events, and a discussion page.

IBON Foundation Inc., Research Group

http://ibon.org/index.php
IBON conducts research, educates, and provides information on socioeconomic issues. The site has its own database and provides access to search its database. Also, there are links to educational areas, news, and resources.

Living Knowledge: International Science Shop Network

www.scienceshops.org/new%20web-content/index-nieuw.html
This website is a network of small scientific research organizations, many of which are linked to civil society. The term *Science Shop* refers to organizations that "provide independent, participatory research support in response to concerns expressed by civil society." The website publishes news articles, a journal, newsletter, database, and documentation.

Mobilization for Global Justice

www.globalizethis.org/
Mobilization for Global Justice is a group that acts to change the institutional violence that stems from international financial and trade institutions such as the World Bank, IMF, and WTO. The main page calls visitors to action in its campaigns and has links to upcoming events that a person can join. Also, there are articles and other resources available to research the global justice movement.

Praxis: Resources for Social and Economic Development

http://caster.ssw.upenn.edu/~restes/praxis.html
This site, created by Professor Richard J. Estes of the University of Pennsylvania, provides links to articles, documents, and resources for research. The site offers a breadth of resources on the subjects of economic, social, and political development. The site is regularly updated and categorizes links by topic, type of population, or region. This site supports social change through informed action.

Resource Center of the Americas

www.americas.org/

This website is a resource on globalization, with special attention to the ways that globalization impacts both the Global South and Minnesota. The site offers information on globalization, articles about cases or campaigns, and news items that are listed by country or subject.

Ruckus Society

www.ruckus.org/

The Ruckus Society website provides environmental, human rights, and social justice campaigns with organizational tools, training, and support to obtain their objectives. It offers links to its photo gallery of campaigns, training, resources, links to other sites like it, and news articles of Ruckus activities. The belief that "actions speak louder than words" is the motto of this group as they strive to change the relationship between the environment and each other.

School of the Americas Watch

www.soaw.org/new/

The School of the Americas Watch is a pro-peace website that chronicles attempts to shut down one of the United States' military academies, the School of the Americas at Fort Benning, Georgia. The site also profiles prisoners of conscience, related legislative action, and pro-peace event news items.

SocialAction.com

www.socialaction.com/corporateglobalization.html

SocialAction.com is an online Jewish magazine focused on social justice issues. The site contains a breadth of information on topics, with a Jewish perspective. Issues that are currently featured on the site are: environment, feminism, health activism, Israel, literacy, human rights, hunger and homelessness, tobacco, and world Jewry. The site also includes religious teachings, a listing of holidays, communities, curriculum, and additional resources.

Social Science Information Gateway

http://sosig.esrc.bris.ac.uk/

This website is an online search engine for social scientists. It also offers an extensive catalog of links available by social science discipline. The site also includes Grapevine, an opportunity to network with other social sciences by sharing conferences, CVs, events, courses, and department information. Finally, there is a training section that provides tools for learning about or teaching Internet researching skills.

Sociologists without Borders

http://sociologistswithoutborders.org/
Sociologists without Borders seeks to use the tools of the sociologist to promote social justice around the world. The website includes teaching and research links, social justice–oriented poetry and photography, and papers.

South African Indymedia

http://southafrica.indymedia.org/
A collection of independent media makers and activists who serve as a global information network make up this website. It is a noncommercial, noncorporate, anticapitalist organization whose website serves the dual role of being an information provider and propaganda spreader. The homepage consists of current news stories and links to a calendar of events.

TomDispatch: A Project of the Nation Institute

www.tomdispatch.com/
Tomdispatch.com is created, updated, written, and edited by Tom Engelhardt. The site serves to introduce the viewer to voices who might be able to convey, a little more clearly than others, how the imperial world works. The main page offers samples of "Tomgrams," articles written by Tom on events in mainstream media. There are links to past articles and topics.

Transnational Institute: A Worldwide Fellowship of Committed Scholar-Activists

www.tni.org/
The TNI website is an international database of scholarship produced by activist-scholars, analyzing the global problems of today and tomorrow. The research tends to focus on social justice topics such as democracy, equality, and environmental sustainability. The site has links to current topics and the views of activist-scholars. Members of the TNI use the website to advertise their publications and articles, which are available on the site.

UNESCO WebWorld: Communication and Information

http://portal/unesco.org (Select the Communication and Information link at the top of the page)
The United Nations Educational, Scientific, and Cultural Organization created this site to focus on its role in the media. There are links to news stories, articles, and current events as well as information about the topics addressed by the article. The site provides real-world examples, which provide illustrative links to UNESCO's activities.

World Heritage Sites

http://whc.unesco.org/pg.cfm

This site allows visitors to view World Heritage Sites, such as the Statue of Liberty or the Eiffel Tower. The sites are located on a map of the world with links to hundreds of other items, statues, and places of heritage. Then the site has links to explain the convention to protect cultural and social heritage sites around the globe.

LABOR

AFL-CIO

www.aflcio.org/

This website contains a wealth of information on labor, social security, news, union membership and organizations, a legislative action center, and factual and statistical information on topics related to the workplace and union participation. The statistical data are rich, including information on working families in the United States. The data are divided by topics, including type of work, unemployment, wages, health insurance coverage, education, poverty, and others.

Behind the Label

www.behindthelabel.org/

BehindTheLabel.org is a news website that reports the stories of people fighting for basic human rights and labor rights against the global clothing industry. The site provides multimedia coverage, providing links to movies, audio, and written reports. Members are sweatshop workers, students, and religious leaders, and there are many personal stories on the site. The site provides information on the events that take place on a daily basis.

CorpWatch

www.corpwatch.org/index.php

CorpWatch uses education, network-building, and activism to battle against corporate globalization. Their goal is to spread a movement for human rights and dignity, labor rights, and environmental justice but on a grassroots level. The site provides links to current news articles as well as links to campaigns and specific issues that they are striving to bring to corporate attention.

Global Policy Forum: Labor Rights and Trade Unions

www.globalpolicy.org/resource/weblinks/linklab.htm

The GPF monitors policy making in the United Nations, enforces the accountability of global decisions, educates citizens, and fights for global peace and justice. The Labor Rights and Trade Unions site serves as a database that provides links to other relevant websites. Also, the site has an internal search engine.

Global Unions

www.global-unions.org/
Twelve Global Union Organizations maintain the website and use it to inform their members and partners, and to illustrate the news and campaigns they run. Global Unions is focused on the international trade movement. The homepage consists of current articles that are published worldwide, and there are links to news and ongoing campaigns, including campaigns to protect workers rights (in Burma and Nepal), the prevention of sexual harassment, and opening unions to women.

International Center for Trade Union Rights

www/ictur.labournet.org/
This website serves as a forum for discussion and debate between trade unionists, academics, and people throughout the world. It seeks to defend and improve the rights of trade unions and unionists across the globe. On the homepage there are summaries of reports from different councils and countries, as well as links to publications.

International Confederation of Free Trade Unions (ICFTU)

www.icftu.org/
The ICFTU is an organization of national trade union centers and links together those same trade unions globally. On the homepage there are current news stories and a clock to illustrate what time it is in Europe. A links section connects to the other campaigns that the organization focuses on, press releases, and organizations that sponsor the site.

International Labour Organization

www.ilo.org/
The International Labour Organization is part of the UN and it seeks to promote social justice and international human and labor rights. Part of the organization's goals are to set basic labor rights, equality of opportunity and treatment, and regulations in work-related conditions. The homepage consists of featured articles, links to publications, and a newsroom. This site is available in multiple languages.

Labor Notes

www.labornotes.org/
Labor Notes publishes *The Troublemaker's Handbook* (available for ordering), hosts conferences, and provides links to news articles online. The website also contains archives of the newsletter "Labor Notes" and useful links.

LabourStart

www.labourstart.org/
LabourStart.org is a site that acts to inform trade unionists on upcoming and ongoing

stories globally. The main page has links to the most recent stories and there is a search engine that allows access to older articles.

PRISONERS' RIGHTS

Earth Liberation Prisoners Support Network

www.spiritoffreedom.org.uk/

This website is designed to support members of the Earth Liberation organization who are in prison due to protest actions in defense of the earth. The website presents information on prisoners around the world, and provides contact information enabling site visitors to write letters on behalf of prisoners. The site also collects funds for legal fees.

Missouri Prison Labor Union

www.angelfire.com/sc2/mplu/

The Missouri Prison Labor Union website presents information on one case: the Missouri prisoners who work for Palmolive and its subsidiaries. This website promotes a boycott of Palmolive for its refusal to support union organization among the prison laborers.

Prison Activist Resource Center

www.prisonactivist.org/

The Prison Activist Resource Center supports prisoners' rights, is against institutional racism, and seeks to educate the public on relevant issues. This website contains monthly alerts, pamphlets on immigration and incarceration, an extensive archive cataloged by date, a library of links, and discussion forums. It also hosts websites for other grassroots groups.

Stop Prison Rape

www.spr.org/

Stop Prison Rape is a website that seeks to end sexual violence in prisons and detention centers. There is a plethora of information available here, with academic articles, human rights reports, fact sheets, special reports, action updates, press releases, survivor support, and publications by survivors. The site also features legislation pertaining to sexual violence in prisons, and additional useful resources.

RACIAL AND ETHNIC RELATIONS

African American History, Black History, and the Civil Rights Movement

www.nyise.org/blackhistory/

This site offers links to the civil rights movement, African American history, and black history. Links connect visitors to other useful sites or information pages.

AntiRacism Net

www.antiracismnet.org/main.html

AntiRacismNet is an online resource that provides information about antiracism activities. The site offers an online directory of social justice organizations, a calendar for posting national and international events, and a portal for publishing information on issues.

The Black Commentator

www.blackcommentator.com/

The *Black Commentator* is a publication that is available on the Internet and in print. Both publications ally with African Americans in the struggle for social and economical justice, sharing African American perspectives with the rest of the world. The site provides commentary, analysis, and investigation via links to current and past publications.

Latin America Working Group

www.lawg.org/index.htm

The Latin America Working Group lobbies in the United States for improved policies to protect the rights of Latin Americans. They publish a newsletter, "The Advocate," which is available (both current and archived editions) online. The site also provides current events and news, activist tools, and publications related to recent policies (e.g., Plan Colombia).

Latino Issues Forum (LIF)

www.lif.org/

LIF formed to improve the lives of Latinos by using research, community forums, coalitions, the media, and advocacy. The information and publications are free of charge, enabling broad access. It serves as a bridge to provide relevant information to the public. The website offers links to stories, articles, events, and resources.

NAACP

www.naacp.org/

The National Association for the Advancement of Colored People (NAACP) promotes civil rights through books, articles, campaigns, pamphlets, magazines, and the Internet. Through these resources it has united people to awaken the moral and ethical consciousness of Americans. The main page offers information on active campaigns, links to news stories, and an area to join the organization.

Stop the Hate

http://stop-the-hate.org/

The site offers quotes about the importance of not hating one another. At the bottom of the page are links to other sites that wish to stop the hate.

STATISTICAL INFORMATION

International Strategic Analysis: Understanding Tomorrow's World Today

www.isa-world.com/

ISA gathers data for clients and researchers and provides global analysis and information. The site is international in scope, providing links to current issues and links to topics, country or regional reports, economic forecasts, risk forecasts, and special topic reports.

United Nations CyberSchool Bus

http://cyberschoolbus.un.org/infonation3/menu/advanced.asp

This is an interactive site that compares countries across variables. Select individual countries and a category, and the site produces a comparison chart.

United Nations Statistics Division

http://unstats.un.org/unsd/default.htm

The United Nations Statistics Division website serves as a database for information on international trade, national accounts, energy, industry, environment, transport, and social statistics gathered from around the globe. The homepage features links to the publications of the division, current statistical reports, commissions, and a search engine for navigating the site.

Index

329

About the Editors and Contributors

Judith Blau is professor of sociology at the University of North Carolina, Chapel Hill, and president of the U.S. Chapter of Sociologists without Borders. Her articles have appeared in scholarly journals, and her books include *Race in the Schools, Architects and Firms, Social Contracts and Economic Markets, The Shape of Culture*, and a trilogy on human rights coauthored with Alberto Moncada: *Human Rights: Beyond the Liberal Tradition* (2005), *Justice in the United States: Human Rights and the U.S. Constitution* (2006), and *Freedom and Solidarities* (forthcoming). She coedits the journal *Societies without Borders*.

Michael Burawoy teaches sociology at the University of California, Berkeley. For thirty years an ethnographer of industries across the world—Zambia, United States, Hungary, and the Soviet Union—he is now studying the academic workplace and the human consequences of its products.

Rodney Coates, a professor of sociology, gerontology, and black studies at Miami University of Ohio, specializes in the study of race and ethnic relations, inequality, and social justice. He takes a critical perspective with regards to race and ethnic relations, inequality, and social justice. Over the past few years Dr. Coates's theoretical orientation has shifted to encompass a social justice paradigm. He has also authored several book chapters and has edited several volumes. His most recent edited book published by Brill is entitled *Race and Ethnicity: Across Time, Space and Discipline* and is currently in its second printing. Coates is currently working on two special issues of *American Behavioral Science* dealing with micro- and macro-level social justice projects. He is under contract with Roxbury Press to produce an edited volume on *Covert Racism*.

Gerard Delanty is professor of sociology, University of Liverpool, UK, and has written on various issues in social theory and general sociology. He is editor of the *European Journal of Social Theory* and author of ten books and editor of five, including *Inventing Europe*; *Social Science* (1997; new edition 2005); *Social Theory in a Changing World*; *Modernity and Postmodernity*; *Citizenship in a Global Age*; *Challenging Knowledge: The University in the Knowledge Society*; (with Patrick O' Mahony) *Nationalism and Social Theory*; *Community*; *Rethinking Europe: Social Theory and the Implications of Europeanization*; and has edited the *Handbook of Contemporary European Social Theory* (2005) and (with Krishan Kumar) *The Handbook of Nations and Nationalism* (2006).

Charles A. Gallagher is an associate professor in the department of sociology at Georgia State University. His research focuses on racial and social inequality and the ways in which the media, the state, and popular culture shape representations of race. He has published articles on the sociological functions of color-blind political narratives, how racial categories expand and contract within the context of interracial marriages, race theory, racial innumeracy, and how one's ethnic history shapes perceptions of privilege.

Kenneth A. Gould is professor of sociology at St. Lawrence University. Gould's work in the political economy of environment, technology, and development examines the responses of communities to environmental problems, the role of socioeconomic inequality in environmental conflicts, and the impacts of economic globalization on efforts to achieve ecologically and socially sustainable development trajectories. He is coauthor of *Environment and Society: The Enduring Conflict*, St. Martin's Press, 1994 (Blackburn Press, 2000), and *Local Environmental Struggles: Citizen Activism in the Treadmill of Production*, Cambridge University Press, 1996.

Arlette Grabczynska is currently pursuing her JD at the University of Illinois College of Law. Her interests, while varied, have focused on juvenile law; her master's thesis explored children's ability to comprehend and apply *Miranda* rights. She is currently working on a project that involves mandatory juvenile DNA collection statutes and Fourth Amendment protections.

Angela Hattery holds the Zachary T. Smith Reynolds Associate Professorship in the Department of Sociology at Wake Forest University. She earned her BA from Carleton College and her MS and PhD from the University of Wisconsin–Madison. She joined the faculty at Wake Forest in 1998. Hattery has done research in the areas of gender, power, violence, family, social stratification, work, and the sociology of sport. She has published numerous articles and book chapters in these areas. She published her first book in 2001 and has two more due out in 2007, one on African American families and the other on intimate partner violence. She teaches courses on the sociology of gender, social stratification, family, violence, and methods.

Núria Homedes is a physician and an associate professor at the School of Public Health, University of Texas–Houston. Her areas of expertise include comparative health systems and pharmaceutical policies, and she has researched and published on Latin American health reforms and on U.S.-Mexico border health problems. She is the coeditor of the electronic journal *Boletín Fármacos*.

Keri E. Iyall Smith is assistant professor of sociology at Stonehill College in Easton, Massachusetts. She has published articles on hybridity and world society, human rights, and teaching sociology. She is also the author of *The State and Indigenous Movements* (forthcoming). She teaches courses on introductory sociology, globalization, indigenous peoples, and sociological theory.

Walda Katz-Fishman is a scholar-activist and popular educator who combines her research and teaching interests in class, race/ethnicity/nationality, and gender inequality and political economy with political activism in bottom-up struggles for economic equality and race and gender justice. She is a professor of sociology at Howard University—where she has taught since 1970—board chair of Project South: Institute for the Elimination of Poverty & Genocide, a steering committee member of Grassroots Global Justice, and a coordinating committee member of the U.S. Social Forum. She was corecipient with Jerome Scott of the American Sociological Association's 2004 Award for the Public Understanding of Sociology and has written numerous articles on political economy, race-class-gender inequality, today's globalization, and popular movements for justice, equality, and popular democracy. wkatzfishman@igc.org www.projectsouth.org

Turbado Marabou studied at Florida A&M University under Professor Kenneth Falana, where he received his BS degree. He received his MFA in printmaking from the University of Wisconsin–Madison, and as art director of the Memorial Union, Turbado organized the first African Continuum Project that spearheaded programs that gave recognition to groups previously ignored. He received the Porter Butts Award for outstanding talents in the Arts at the University of Wisconsin. Turbado was involved in several lead mural and mosaic projects through the Chicago Public Art Group. He worked as an artist-in-residence with Urban Gateways, which provides arts for learning programs in the inner city, rural, and urban areas of Chicago. Turbado is currently an art instructor in the public schools in Bryan, Texas.

Alberto Moncada is president of Sociologists without Borders. He has taught at the University of Madrid, Stanford, the University of Lima, Florida International, and Alcalá University. He was the cofounder and first president of the University of Piura, Peru. He has published nearly thirty books (in Spanish) on a wide range of topics, including the media, sociology of education, politics, sociology of culture and the arts, Latinos in the United States, and sociology of religion, and collaborates with Judith Blau on English-language monographs on human rights.

John Allphin Moore, Jr. is professor emeritus at California State Polytechnic University, Pomona. His tenth book, *The New United Nations*, coauthored with Jerry Pubantz, was published in late 2005. In 2004, on his second Fulbright assignment, Moore was László Országh Distinguished Chair of History in Hungary. For their first coauthored book, Moore and Pubantz received an award for "Outstanding Academic Title for 2000" from the American Library Association's *Choice* magazine.

Anthony M. Orum is professor of sociology and political science at the University of Illinois at Chicago. He has published widely on a number of topics, including the politics of African Americans, the origins of the civil rights movement in the United States, and the nature of American politics in general. Among his books on these topics are *Black Students in Protest* (1973) and *Introduction to Political Sociology* (fourth edition, 2000). He is currently the editor of *City & Community* and has just recently been awarded a Fulbright scholarship to teach in China in 2007.

Robert Pollin is professor of economics and founding codirector of the Political Economy Research Institute at UMass Amherst. His research centers on macroeconomics, conditions for low-wage workers in the United States and globally, and the analysis of financial markets. His recent books include *Contours of Descent: U.S. Economic Fractures and the Landscape of Global Austerity* (2003) and *The Living Wage: Building a Fair Economy* (1998, with Stephanie Luce).

Jerry Pubantz is professor of political science at the University of North Carolina at Greensboro. His writings include works on the United Nations, international civil society and democratization, U.S.-Russian relations, the Middle East, and American foreign policy. He is the coeditor of *The Encyclopedia of the United Nations* and the coeditor of *The New United Nations: International Organization in the 21st Century* and of *To Create a New World? American Presidents and the United Nations*. His articles have appeared in *Social Forces, Alternatives, ArabiesTrends, Politics and Policy*, and the *International Journal of the Humanities*. Dr. Pubantz may be reached at j_pubant@uncg.edu.

Jill Quadagno is professor of sociology at Florida State University, where she holds the Mildred and Claude Pepper Eminent Scholar Chair. She is past president of the American Sociological Association and the author of more than fifty articles and twelve books on social policy issues. In 2004 she received the Eliot Friedson Outstanding Publication Award for her article "Why the US Has No National Health Insurance." Her most recent book is *One Nation, Uninsured: Why the US Has No National Health Insurance* (Oxford, 2005).

Barbara J. Risman is professor and head of the Sociology Department at the University of Illinois at Chicago. She is the author of *Gender Vertigo: American Families in Transition* (Yale, 1998) and nearly two dozen articles in major sociology journals. Risman is the past editor of *Contemporary Sociology*. She is currently co-chair of the Council on Contemporary Families, and also served on the Executive Council of the American Sociological Association and the Southern Sociological Association, and is past president of Sociologists for Women in Society. In 2002 she was selected as the National Feminist Lecturer by Sociologists for Women in Society, and in 2004 she was awarded the Katherine Jocher Belle-Boone Award from the Southern Sociological Society, for lifetime contributions to the study of gender.

William I. Robinson lived for many years abroad, in Africa and Latin America, as a scholar-activist. He is currently professor of sociology, global and international studies, and Latin American and Iberian studies at the University of California–Santa Barbara. His most recent books are *A Theory of Global Capitalism* and *Transnational Conflicts: Central America, Social Change, and Globalization*. His Web page is www.soc.ucsb.edu/faculty/robinson/.

Havidán Rodríguez is the director of the Disaster Research Center (DRC) and professor in the Department of Sociology and Criminal Justice at the

University of Delaware. His areas of interest include social vulnerability, risk communication, and demographic processes and disasters. Along with his colleagues E. L. Quarantelli and R. R. Dynes, he is editing the *Handbook of Disaster Research* to be published by Springer in 2006.

Deana Rohlinger is an assistant professor in the Department of Sociology at Florida State University. She was the recipient of the Best Graduate Student Paper Award from the ASA Section on Collective Behavior and Social Movements and from the Southern Sociological Society. Her current research focuses on how activists mobilizing on both sides of the abortion issue use mass media to get their ideas to a broader audience and affect political outcomes. She has published articles in *The Sociological Quarterly* and *Sex Roles* as well as edited book chapters.

Carla N. Russell is a graduate student at University of Massachusetts–Amherst. Her main research interest is social inequality, specifically focusing on how vulnerability impacts disasters. Carla's senior thesis was a comparative case study between Hurricanes Andrew and Mitch to further understand the impact of vulnerability within and between societies. She is currently working on labor market issues tied to the displacement resulting from Hurricane Katrina.

Jerome Scott is a labor and community organizer and popular educator who brings activists and scholars together for popular economic and political education and action research to develop new leadership for building today's bottom-up movement for fundamental social change. He was a founding member of the League of Revolutionary Black Workers in the auto plants of Detroit, Michigan, in the late 1960s. He is director of Project South: Institute for the Elimination of Poverty & Genocide (Atlanta, Georgia), a Steering Committee member of Grassroots Global Justice, and a Coordinating Committee member of the U.S. Social Forum. jerome@projectsouth.org www .projectsouth.org

Earl Smith is professor of sociology and the Rubin Distinguished Professor of American Ethnic Studies at Wake Forest University. He is the director of the American Ethnic Studies Program and former chair of the Department of Sociology. Prior to his appointment at Wake Forest University in 1996, Professor Smith was chairperson (Comparative American Cultures) and professor of sociology at Washington State University. In 1994 he left Washington State University to become professor and chair of the Department of Sociology, and then dean, at Pacific Lutheran University in Tacoma, Washington.

Professor Smith has numerous publications in the areas of professions, stratification, and urban sociology; has published research on university faculty; and has published extensively in the area of the sociology of sport.

Jackie Smith is associate professor of sociology and peace studies at the University of Notre Dame. Her most recent book, *Coalitions Across Borders: Transnational Protest in a Neoliberal Era* (coedited with Joe Bandy), explores how people have developed organizations and techniques to help build transnational alliances among people of widely varying cultural, political, and economic backgrounds. Her forthcoming book, *Changing the World: Struggles for Global Democracy*, explores the strategies groups have used to promote a more democratic global order, and it considers how their struggles can be strengthened.

Antonio Ugalde is a professor emeritus (Department of Sociology, University of Texas–Austin). His research interests include the study of international health policies and of the pharmaceutical industry. Professor Ugalde has done extensive field work in Mexico, Central America, and Colombia. He is the coeditor of the electronic journal *Boletín Fármacos* (www.boletinfarmacos .org).